Power and Need in Africa

POWER AND NEED IN AFRICA

Ben Wisner

Earthscan Publications Ltd
London

First published 1988 by
Earthscan Publications Limited
3 Endsleigh Street, London WC1H 0DD

British Library Cataloguing in Publication Data

Wisner, Ben
    Power and need in Africa: basic human needs
    and development policies.
    1. Africa. Economic development. Politics.
    Influence of mass media
    I. Title
    330.96′0328

    ISBN 1–85538–300–1

Set in Great Britain by DP Photosetting, Aylesbury, Bucks
Printed by Richard Clay

Contents

There came a time when the common people, both men and women, raised a great outcry against their fellow Jews. Some complained that they were giving their sons and daughters as pledges for food to keep themselves alive; others that they were mortgaging their fields, vineyards and houses to buy corn in the famine; others again that they were borrowing money on their fields and vineyards to pay the king's tax. "But," they said, "our bodily needs are the same as other people's, our children are as good as theirs; yet here we are, forcing our sons and daughters to become slaves.

Nehemiah 5:1

Preface

This book is the indirect result of more than twenty years of work in Eastern and Southern Africa. That work began with the half-baked construction of a small dam, a village grain store that fell down a few years later and many nights of enthusiastic discussion of the Arusha Declaration in a Tanzanian *ujamaa* village. I have to thank those patient, cheerful, moody, generous and greedy friends and foes of so long ago. I was fascinated by their lives, learned a bit about their lands and how they cared for them, and shared their dreams.

Some might think that a book on the need and possibility of radical grassroots participation in Africa in the 1990s is a middle-aged, former Tanzanophile hippie's attempt to hold on to the dream of Nyerere's village-based socialism and self-reliance. That could be. I'll let the arguments and evidence in this book answer that question.

My thanks are due to many people: to Anthony Paulo, the little stonemason from Songea for one, and to Bernardo Kilonzo, the most memorable chairman Mbambara *ujamaa* village ever had. Kilonzo tried being Trotsky and then Robin Hood before he finally gave up, took the village's money and ran away to Machakos. From Kenya he wrote the village a self-righteous letter justifying his theft and berating the villagers for not being good socialists. He was extradited and served time near Morogoro.

I must thank Germano Mwabu, a quiet boy from the dry lower portion of Meru District in Kenya called Tharaka, for his generosity with his family and with his knowledge of how people survive droughts in already dry regions. He told me that the old people spoke of deserving reparations from the upland area of Meru. Germano has a Ph.D. now but has not forgotten Tharaka.

9

Aquino de Braganca died in 1986 in the plane crash that killed Samora Machel. He taught me more than anyone about the way in which culture, ecology, economics and politics fit together and make sense of one another. Mozambique lost both a president and a great scholar and strategist.

The notion of writing a book on basic needs came to me slowly. I was teaching and researching drought and family nutrition in Kenya when the idea first occurred to me, and it grew while I was teaching health care at the medical faculty of Dar es Salaam University and during later work on resettlement in Mozambique and in refugee camps in Somalia. Its outlines hardened during a stint in Botswana, where I was working for SADCC on energy sources. I saw that people were trying to meet their basic needs in ingenious and varied ways: in Botswana, people built oxcarts, called "Toyotas", from cannibalized truck parts. It was clear, too, that people were tremendously knowledgeable about their environments. In the mountains of Lesotho I met herdboys killing time before it became their turn to go to the South African mines. They are experts on animals and the land, but they are shunned as pugilistic and vulgar by urban Basotho. What was more important, from my point of view, was that the herdboys' knowledge was in no way being tapped by the multilateral aid programmes from which they were meant to benefit and of which I was a part. Were these integrated rural development projects, I wondered, meeting basic needs? Were they even responding to what people themselves perceived as basic needs? Certainly the aid projects, as I could see with my own eyes, were neglecting their most important potential ally: the resourcefulness and expertise of the local people. Two years in Mozambique had shown me just how resilient people could be. Africa was not, as the US media liked to call it, a "basket case". The problem was that despite aid agencies' talk of "basic needs", no one had begun to use this approach to its fullest – in other words, to allow African people the power to determine and meet their own basic needs.

In the early 1980s I went to Kenya to work with a Beijer Institute team doing energy planning, and it was there that I decided that I would have to write this book. I have Gordon Goodman, Phil O'Keefe and Lars Kristofersen of the Beijer

Institute to thank for early financial support (received from SIDA) and encouragement.

Since then the work has been enriched in numerous ways by Ignacy Sachs and his colleagues involved in the United Nations University Food-Energy Nexus and by debates with friends at the ETH Zurich such as Dieter Steiner, Carlo Jaeger and Urs Geiser. Calestous Juma and Joseph Ssennyonga visited Zurich from Kenya to teach with me and tell me where my thinking had gone astray. The Social Science Research Council in New York provided support for a lengthy study of the political economy of health and disease in Africa and Latin America and through this my seemingly never-ending book was greatly enhanced by my meeting Randy Packard, a marvellous historian. My ideas about health and food were refined in seminars taught at the New School for Social Research, where Rayna Rapp, Bill Roseberry and Shirley Lindenbaum made that a stimulating and rewarding time.

My home port through this period, 1981-7, was the Department of Human Ecology at Rutgers University. I thank colleagues and friends there for hospitality and stimulating confusion across a dozen disciplines.

Interviews with people and the collection of materials in many international organizations were an important part of the work. I have a very long list of people to thank, too long to put down here. I thank them all, but single out Nora McKeon, Dharam Ghai, Mike Hopkins, Pat Rosenfield, Duane Smith, David Pitt, Solon Barraclough, Pierre Spitz and Philip Alston. This book is also the fruit of many intersecting networks – the World Food Assembly, International Council for Adult Education's Participatory Research Network, Food First, International Peace Research Association's Food and Nutrition Group, the Africa Peace Committee, Association of Concerned African Scholars, Antipode and the staff of the *Review of African Political Economy*. It is, therefore, in itself a form of thanks and a testimony to the efficacy of organizations striving towards a just and sustainable future.

Final revisions took place while I was beginning work at Hampshire College. I thank the Luce Foundation for supporting the programme in Food, Resources and International Policy which I established there and Hampshire students and colleagues, especially Frank Holmquist, for causing me to rethink many of these arguments. Finally, I have to thank generous, tireless and very critical readers of drafts, especially Phil Raikes, Gavin Williams, Paul Richards, Kassahun Checole, Harold Miller, Joe Kreisler and Sonia Kruks.

Introduction

Disappointing Decades

In an intuitive way everyone can attach a meaning to "basic human needs". The term seems self-evident: people need food, water, shelter, a minimum level of health care. Surely, one might think, there can be no dispute over the meaning of "basic human needs" when they are so obvious and so pressing in the countries of the Third World.

This apparent but misleading assumption is, in part, the cause of the problem for the Basic Needs Approach (BNA) to development. Should poor people themselves define their needs or should the "experts" of the international development and aid agencies? Do needs imply a positive right to the satisfaction of those needs? Is it enough simply to "deliver" packages of "need-meeting" services (water pumps, health care, emergency bags of grain) as aid agencies so often do, or must poor people control the resources required to meet their needs? What difference does it make in the pace, character and future of development in the Third World?

We are living through the disturbing end of several International Decades. There has been a Decade for solving environmental problems (1972–82), a Decade for world hunger (1974–84) and a Decade for women (1975–85); in 1991 we will see the conclusion of the International Water Supply and Sanitation Decade (1980–91). It has also been ten years since many of the aid and development agencies decided to focus their efforts on a Basic Human Needs approach.

These overlapping Decades and the thinking that underlay them were born out of the failure of growth-oriented modernization. They were controversial from the start and became more so as various forms of alternative development strategy took shape

13

under the headings "eco-development", "feminism", "self-reliance" and "basic needs". Today they are under fire from both the political Left and Right. These critics argue that the new strategies are, in turn, utopian, romantic, populist, anarchic, inefficient and slow, and that they obscure the fundamental international problems that frequently cause poverty (the lack of freer trade, for example, or of fairer prices, depending on the political viewpoint). Frequently these criticisms overlap, but they have the common effect of resurrecting growth-oriented development. In the course of this debate, a number of babies are in danger of being thrown out with the bathwater.

Few would dispute the fact that the development-as-growth strategies of the 1950s and 1960s brought scant benefit to the poorest forty per cent of people in the Third World. The poorest twenty per cent, which included Africa's pastoralists, households headed by women, and others who had fallen through traditional safety nets, were virtually ignored by development efforts. Even today such people are often considered to be an irreducible residual, the biblical poor who are "always with you" – a view which is shared by the former president of the World Bank (Clausen, 1985). Where the critics diverge is over what should be done.

In the 1970s, radical critics of growth theory advocated a new style of development which was radically participatory and in which land reform, asset redistribution and other necessary preconditions set the stage for the poor to take control of their own development, usually through grassroots organizations. This school of thought now underpins what we can call the "strong" interpretation of the basic needs approach (BNA).

On the other side was the "weak" interpretation of participatory development, promoted mostly by the bilateral and multilateral aid agencies. Where the first approach implied popular political action, the weaker version saw participation as a limited, formalized process, stripped of the political volatility of direct popular involvement. The concept of "basic needs" was similarly watered down, and in the end the approach bore an uncanny resemblance to the old modernization model of development. But it was this weakened view of participatory development which prevailed, and which has provided the underpinning for

14

most of today's development projects. The strong interpretation of BNA has come to share the criticisms levelled at its weaker counterpart without ever being attempted.

This book is about the strong interpretation of the basic needs approach. Rooted in people's own analysis of their situation and needs and the obstacles to meeting them, the strong BNA logically moves towards group action. Conflict with vested interests, where the obstacles are social or socio-environmental, often ensues. The poor learn from these conflicts; if the group can stay together, or – as often happens – dissolves only to regroup around another concrete basic need, it and its members will grow in consciousness and political power. It has been undermined by the failure of other departures from orthodox theories of growth-as-development to which it is connected such as eco-development and feminism. Like them it has been distorted, applied half-heartedly and often subjected to criticism for projects which are but an echo of the original development strategy.

Basic needs is an approach that deserves to be tried – and tried properly – in its strong rather than weak version before being abandoned. But as the history of three UN decades – on environment, food and women – show, we have come very close indeed to discarding the basic needs approach altogether.

DISAPPOINTING DECADES: THE CONTEXT

Eco-development: From Stockholm to Bhopal?

Ten years after the 1972 world conference in Stockholm on the human environment, little had changed in the pace and scope of environmental destruction. In fact, official UN Environment Programme (UNEP) and unofficial panels of non-governmental organizations (NGOs) found that some of these problems were more rather than less severe after ten years' international action (Clarke and Timberlake, 1982). Africa, for example, was in the grip of an increasingly serious environmental crisis. A conference organized by the Swedish Academy of Sciences identified the danger signs (*Ambio*, 12,2, 1983: 63): desertification; depletion of

15

tropical forests; river basin mismanagement; population growth and urbanization; species loss; and a fuelwood crisis.

Another summary highlighted the deterioration of semi-arid lands and irrigated soils in the post-Stockholm years and singled out destruction of moist tropical forests for special concern (White, 1982). Indeed, a review of six such studies conducted by agencies of the French and US governments and other independent bodies shows continued and even accelerated deterioration of Third World environments as a significant feature of the decade 1972–82.

In May 1984, well into a decade of action against desertification, to take but one instance, the United Nations Environment Programme reported that only two of the hundred nations affected by desert encroachment had prepared the agreed plans. None of the recommendations of the original 1977 world meeting had been carried out, and four-fifths of the money that had been spent had gone on "support" and other bureaucratic expenses. Only a fifth had been spent at the desert front line (ICIHI, 1985: 84–8).

Whatever happened to ecologically sustainable development? Is one to conclude that eco-development was tried for ten years, and has failed? Or was it never attempted? The cruel and vivid proof of the lack of progress on environment since Stockholm came in the form of the Bhopal gas leak from a Union Carbide pesticide factory in India in 1984, followed by a leak from a fertilizer plant in Delhi a year later, and by the largest famine Africa has ever known.

Criticism of efforts to stem the deterioration of the human environment in the Third World has come from the Left and the Right. The Left says that the programmes were cosmetic and never addressed the underlying economic forces that drive poor people to expand their farms into forested lands, to overgraze pastures, to cut trees for sale of charcoal or to squat in unsanitary slums near dangerous factories. The Right has revived a Malthusian interpretation which has never really been silent since the eighteenth century: environmental programmes are bound to fail if they do not face up to the challenge of unchecked population growth. Somewhere in the crossfire, eco-development as a strongly participatory – hence political – approach to

16

environment has been ignored. It will become clear in subsequent chapters that a strong interpretation of basic needs must embrace much of the eco-development perspective and its emphasis on the sustainable use of local human and natural resources for meeting locally-defined needs (Sachs, 1974, 1981; Glaeser, ed., 1984).

No Child Shall Go to Bed Hungry: Food Self-Reliance

In 1974 the UN's World Food Conference announced its ambitious Declaration on the Eradication of Hunger and Malnutrition. A decade on, the World Food Council was forced to admit that while the locus of urgent concern had shifted from Asia to Africa, absolute numbers of the chronically hungry and those at risk from famine had increased (WFC, 1984). A meeting of 120 NGOs working on hunger met in November 1984 in Rome and went even further, stating that (WFA, 1984):

> Governments and the aid establishment have had their chance. More people today are hungry, more rural families continue to be forced off their land, more and more land is being destroyed. For nearly all of us, rich and poor, the prescriptions of aid and agribusiness have made things worse not better.

Per capita food production in Africa fell throughout the 1970s despite a $10 billion programme for rehabilitating the lands and people who suffered the Great Sahelian Drought of 1968–73. In the midst of a major turn toward agricultural project lending by the World Bank and a good deal of talk about self-reliance and food security, twenty African countries required emergency food aid in 1984 (ICIHI, 1985).

Are we to conclude that radically new approaches to food self-reliance and security were actually tried over those ten years and can now be said to have failed? Or should we instead look at their inability – or unwillingness – to push the development process far enough? Faced with programmes with fancy titles such as "integrated rural development", the ordinary small farmer had little or no opportunity to exert control over the aims and directions of development efforts. Nor did millions of women farmers, pastoralists or fishermen. Indeed, the issue of popular control was rarely even raised by the development planners of the 1970s.

Sisterhood is Drudgery? Feminism's Decade

After the Nairobi conference officially ended a decade's special effort to fight women's oppression, Kate Young, a researcher at the Institute of Development Studies at Sussex University, asked the pertinent question: "What have we learned about development or about women during the UN Decade for Women?" One thing that surely has been learned is how little impact this Decade has had on the day-to-day situation of women. Women are still among the worst-off in the Third World; in Africa, the gap between legislated equality and daily inequality is enormous, and the burdens of the double-day – long hours of domestic labour on top of work in the field or for a wage – are increased by growing economic and environmental crises. A recent UNICEF-commissioned study of the effect of world recession on women and children demonstrates that poor women are probably worse off than they were at the beginning of "their" decade (Jolly and Cornia, 1984).

This book argues that the failure of women's programmes is not only linked with the massive external problems that faced Africa in the period 1975–85 but is closely related to the failure to support women's struggle for economic power. The converse will also become evident: the strong basic needs approach requires a central emphasis on women.

The poorest rural households in Africa are those headed by women. In many countries the proportion of female-headed households is as high as twenty to thirty per cent. These women know at first-hand what the failure of the UN Decades means. Even where they have not faced famine, they have had to work harder and harder with shrinking resources for their families and declining productivity on their small plots of agricultural land. For women farmers the problem is acute, usually they lack the organization and solidarity to negotiate higher prices for their export crops and lower, seasonally stable prices for food, when they turn to the market. They have lost old forms of social organization that previously maintained the fertility of the soil,

18

checked erosion and provided access to fuelwood, water and mutual aid in times of labour shortage. Necessities such as fuelwood, which was once free and readily available, must now be purchased. Poor rural households are therefore forced to damage local ecosystems in their struggle to make ends meet. They overgraze the land, cut trees to make charcoal and cultivate fields before the fallow regrowth that would have restored fertility is mature. Caught in this vicious spiral, these women find their limited land, labour and money must stretch among competing needs: for food, school fees, house repairs, journeys to the health post with a sick child, fuelwood that used to be free. Where these women have entered the workforce – as plantation workers, for instance – their wages are low and buy little in unstable rural markets, especially in failing national economies suffering high inflation. Access to waged work has not meant emancipation for these women of the UN Decade for Women, but increased exploitation.

These rural poor have been by-passed in most of the so-called "integrated" programmes and projects discussed in this book. Before we abandon the basic needs approach, we have to find out why such women were left out and whether a true implementation of basic needs would enable them to gain power.

THE UNTAPPED POTENTIAL OF THE BASIC NEEDS APPROACH

The critiques of growth implicit in the UN Decades share the vision of a just, sustainable and participatory world order, whether they emphasize the environment, women, self-reliance or basic needs. The common problem of these critiques, however, is that the development strategies inspired by them have been piecemeal and contradictory, and implemented through aid and development agencies of a world order that is anything but just, sustainable and participatory. Both the political Left and Right have been ready to seize on the inevitable failures as evidence of the worthlessness of the entire endeavour.

As early as 1976, when basic needs was distilled out of several years' debate and experimentation by the World Employment

Conference, the Left expressed concern that the BNA would draw attention away from the fundamental injustices of the international order. In other words, the BNA was an ineffectual palliative. The Right was worried that the BNA would require an array of special programmes, including controls over market forces and state intervention. In its weakened form, the BNA did what both sides feared.

Were the 1970s really such a development fool's paradise? Was the BNA ever really tried? The answer to both questions is no. The counter-strategies of the 1970s were indeed about supporting poor people's attempts to control their lives, but they failed to put this aim into practice. In the 1980s and beyond, this failure must not be allowed to continue: if development is to take place, ordinary people in Africa must have control over their own lives. Africans are already beginning to win that control against great odds. Examples can be found in Senegal, where producers have joined together to demand a higher price for groundnuts; in Kenya, where some women's groups now employ young female lawyers to help them compete with the "big men" who monopolize trade; and in Mozambique, where, in the Fourth Congress of the party, the small farmer won support for the family sector's competition with state farms and co-operatives for scarce state resources. Returning again to the opinion of the 120 NGOs gathered in Rome for the World Food Assembly "the ingredients do exist for a more hopeful, sustainable future. Tested by people in thousands of small-scale schemes around the world though scattered far and wide, this is the new frontier" (WFA, 1984).

The rural poor are up against established structures and strong interests. The strong BNA is a weapon with which they can protect themselves. As they grow in organizational and political strength, the BNA becomes a means of creating new social and economic structures and of asserting popular interests over those of the élite. In its weakened, technocratic form, the BNA could appear to be – and indeed was – a product of planning and of detached or neutral science. There can be no confusing the value-orientation of the strong BNA. It is not a "scientific", externally imposed plan but is, instead, using the language of the World Council of Churches, "putting the last first" (Chambers, 1983).

A parallel situation is that of the Third World Catholic
20

Church, where a dynamic, participatory struggle for development is underway. Commenting on liberation theology, Kovel (1985: 26) notes that critics of the structures that preserve Third World underdevelopment should recognize a "friend" in liberation theology. He writes: "What is startling here is the degree to which an organic unity has been created out of spiritual and revolutionary appeals. For centuries the church has pre-empted the dimension of spirit in the cause of reaction. Now, suddenly, these limits have been shattered. No wonder the Vatican is alarmed."

The basic needs approach, in its strong form, is just as alarming to established economic and political interests. The purpose of this book is to reveal the strong potential of the BNA and to make a case for its recognition as a "friend" by those in search of alternatives to the disappointing strategies of the recent UN Decades.

A Kenyan Focus

I have chosen to focus on Africa for two reasons: first because an analysis of the strong versus weak interpretations of the BNA helps us to understand the crisis in Africa; and, secondly, because the resilience and creativity of ordinary Africans in the face of crisis shows us what can be lost if empowerment, justice and sustainability are abandoned as development goals.

Each of the following chapters draws on the African experience with various forms of the BNA. Wherever possible I have discussed the BNA in Kenya, again for two reasons. I know it well, having worked there in the early 1970s as both a scholar and as an activist supporting the National Christian Council of Kenya's efforts to develop creative, participatory alternatives to famine relief. I worked there again in the 1980s, when I revisited many of my old haunts and travelled widely in parts of Kenya that were new to me; the changes in ten years were striking. More recent visits up to 1986 give fifteen years' perspective on the struggles of ordinary Kenyans to taste what was once called "the fruit of *Uhuru* [freedom]". The second, less personal reason for choosing Kenya is that it, together with Côte d'Ivoire, has often been considered a miracle of economic development on the

21

continent. If basic human needs are in danger there, the problem elsewhere is likely to be very grim indeed. If the weak version of the BNA can work anywhere on the continent, it must be Kenya.

Kenya is neither as poor nor as war-torn as other African countries such as Ethiopia, Chad, Sudan, Mozambique. It does not bear the burden of hosting hundreds of thousands of refugees as do Somalia, Sudan, Uganda, Tanzania, Burundi, Cameroon and Zaire. It is known for its political stability and, until recently, for its democratic government, and for its rapid economic growth of the 1960s and early 1970s. By the mid-1970s, Kenya had achieved a higher degree of "need satisfaction" than other countries in East Africa and was above the African average for life expectancy, low infant mortality and percentage of children in school, as we can see from the following table.

Kenya is none the less a good case for assessing the ways in which the potentially strong BNA has been defeated. The Kenya government has given basic needs considerable rhetorical support, and there have been various government programmes conceived as implementing the basic needs approach in various forms. The Kenyan state has been quick to reformulate its rhetoric and to some extent the style of its development projects as fashions in the development world have come and gone. Contrary to most expectations, Kenya even jumped aboard the African socialism bandwagon in 1965 (GOK, 1965). Kenya is also important to us because of the vitality and breadth of its grassroots organizations, which include women's self-help organizations, church-based development groups, environmental groups, legal reform organizations and human rights groups.

Finally, Kenya presents an excellent opportunity to seek the logic of a strong BNA in the survival strategies of ordinary people. As we will see in the chapters on health, water, housing and food, African people are not mere victims but historical agents. As the economic situation has worsened Kenya's poor smallholders have responded by developing complex and ingenious strategies to ensure their survival. Up to 70 per cent of their income now comes from non-farm sources made up of wage labour, rural industry, trade, gifts and clientage.

In some of the poorest parts of Kenya, where much of our attention will focus, as many as 30 per cent of the households are

BASIC NEEDS INDICATORS: WORLD, AFRICA, KENYA

Basic Need Indicator	Kenya	East Africa	Africa	Less Developed Countries	More Developed Countries
	(Figures given for males and females)				
Life Expectancy at birth (years)	54/58	46/49	47/50	54/56	68/76
Infant Mortality (1970s) (deaths/year/1000 live births of those aged under one year)	90/76	142/121	151/129	116/104	24/18
% in school of population aged 6–11 (1975)	98/91	52/41	59/43	70/53	94/94
% in school of population aged 12–17 (1975)	58/40	33/20	39/24	42/28	84/85
% of adult population literate	30/10	29/14	33/15	52/32	98/97

Source: Haub *et al.*, 1980

headed by women. While they are perhaps not as famous for their economic *savoir faire* as Ghana's market women or the "shebeen queens" of southern Africa, they do manage to survive under very stressful and rapidly deteriorating conditions. Their creativity and strength in the face of crisis must be supported. This book argues that the strong BNA – far from being ready for the historical dustbin of failed development strategies – can provide that support.

Chapter 1

Background and Debate: Need as a Verb, not a Noun

THEORY, PRACTICE AND MORE THEORY

Interest in defining "basic human needs" is not new. As early as the eighteenth century, Carr-Hill (1978: 8) reminds us, "the French school of hygienists spent a great deal of effort working out norms of nutrition, housing and comfort in order to produce an effective race of miners". In sub-Saharan Africa some of the first nutrition studies were the work of the South African gold mines, intent on improving the productivity of their black labour force. Today's interest in basic needs is somewhat different. The satisfaction of needs – however they are defined – is taken to be a universal priority. "A basic needs approach," writes Stewart (1985: 1) "is one which gives priority to meeting the basic needs of *all* the people."

Universal Rights, Specific Struggles

Such universalism is expressed in the UN's Universal Declaration of Human Rights. Article 25 (1), adopted with the Declaration in 1948, is quite explicit:

> Everyone has the right to a standard of living adequate for the health and well-being of himself and his family, including food, clothing, housing and medical care and necessary social services, and the right to security in the event of unemployment, sickness, disability, widowhood, old age or lack of livelihood in circumstances beyond his control.

Forty years and many failed development projects later, these aims may arouse some scepticism. How far have we actually moved beyond the rhetoric of equality and entitlement? Fortunately we have seen some intermittent attempts, the strong BNA among them, to make the rhetoric a reality. Despite arguments that human rights are not transcultural (Alston, 1984) or that human need does not imply the right to fulfilment of that need (Streeten, 1981, 1984), a substantial group of development planners has sought to support poor people in their struggle to safeguard their rights.

The key to achieving this aim is popular participation. Thus Dias and Paul (1984: 203), writing about the concept of a human right to food, stress that:

> it is vital that groups of the rural poor presently confronted with hunger and malnutrition (and other support and action groups working with them) articulate *their* concerns and needs in regard to deteriorating food situations and formulate *their* strategies to develop and enforce a body of law to secure *their* right to food.

In this process, the poor themselves define and control their own struggle. The development project becomes, in other words, radically participatory. This was the central feature of the counter-strategies (such as feminism and eco-development) and wider social movements of the 1970s. In liberation theology, for instance, a fundamental idea is that the poor themselves can do theology, which is defined as a set of theological reflections by the poor on their own struggle to liberate themselves. Similarly, across virtually all domains of human activity that had been thought to be the terrain of rural development "experts", it has been recognized that ordinary people are themselves already quite expert, and could do more to further development if obstacles were removed. In Africa, for example, farmers have done their own agricultural research (Richards, 1985), created food storage systems (Wisner *et al.*, 1979), developed new types of stoves (Carr, 1984: 70–3) and implemented health care systems (Edwards and Lyons, 1983: 109ff), while blacksmiths have produced their own appropriate tools (Müller, 1980).

A Participatory Definition of Needs

The radical version of the BNA shares this insistence on participation. The strong BNA *begins* when the poor themselves reflect collectively on their own needs. "To need" is a verb,* an experience of deprivation that has been created socially. The strong BNA encourages poor people to understand the social origins of their poverty and to struggle to change them.

By contrast, the weak BNA either imposes a set of needs on the poor from the outside and/or limits the radical potential of participation. Most commonly, the weak BNA involves the delivery of a bundle of goods and services (e.g. school lunches, clean water, housing sites, health care) thought to correspond to needs. Another typical weak BNA approach is to provide skills and technology that are supposed to allow a family to produce or earn a basic needs income – what Stewart (1985: 2–3) refers to as the "three acres and a cow" or the "chicken in every pot" approach. Whatever the particular strategy, the essence of the weak BNA is that the poor are recipients, not activists.

One small step up from this is the "full life" view, according to which a "minimum decent bundle" of goods and services is defined in relation to its contribution to actual improvements in the quality of life. Here at least one is measuring "outputs" (e.g. lifespan) rather than "delivered inputs" (e.g. the number of vaccinations, water wells, etc.). However, this view of basic needs still assumes that quality of life can be defined solely by experts. Planners are assumed to be able to "count" the corresponding goods and services required, to "cost" the social effort required to meet need, and to "carry" these goods and services to "target groups". In this "count–cost–carry" formulation, target groups are passive or at most participate by volunteering their labour. The scope for popular participation is narrow indeed, even the sale of labour in food-for-work programmes is thought to be participatory. Ominously, recent statements on aid to Africa put

* John Turner, one of the first systematic students of self-built housing, is quoted by Bawtree (1982): "To need, in English anyway, is a *verb*. It is a personal *act*. When needs become *nouns*, they are *things* used to control and oppress people by corporate commercial producers, by corporate state bureaucrats or by the professional mystifiers who serve them both."

heavy emphasis on food-for-work (Council on Foreign Relations, 1985). From the viewpoint of the radical BNA, even such "full life" definitions of basic needs block or truncate the process of self-organization and struggle by the poor themselves.

Need Typologies

The foregoing does not imply that all attempts by outsiders to think about needs are useless. Typologies of need can provide a sounding board for groups engaged in clarifying their own situations (for example, typologies of Galtung, 1980a; Mallman, 1980; McHale and McHale, 1978). A core list of needs can, for instance, provide popular organizations with a starting point for discussion focusing on whether or not such needs pertain to the local situation (for example, the core lists of Lee, 1976; Ghai and Alfthan, 1977). One experiment with radically participatory rural development, to which we will return in some detail later, begins the process of self-help group formation by defining one dominant, clearly perceived need (e.g. clean water or fair marketing). From that point onwards, however, all outside aid is subordinated to the group's judgement of the next logical step or of the next need to be addressed.

For groups just beginning to discuss their priorities, Galtung proposes a useful typology of human needs (1980a: 66):

- *Security needs:* avoidance of violence such as war, assault, torture;

- *Welfare needs:* avoidance of misery because of lack of food, water, protection from the climate, etc.;

- *Identity needs:* avoidance of alienation through self-expression, affection, understanding of the world around one, sense of purpose; and

- *Freedom needs:* avoidance of repression through choice in receiving and expressing information, choice of occupation, choice of confrontations, choice of spouse, choice of place to live, etc.

Another useful catalogue is the product of a long, multina-

28

tional dialogue concerning the elements of "quality of life" (OECD, 1976 summarized by Carr-Hill, 1978: 7–8):

- Without a minimal level of health one cannot biologically survive, hence *health* is basic;
- The essence of humanity is knowledge so that without learning there is no real human existence, hence *education* is basic;
- (Wo)man is defined by what s/he does, hence the essential nature of a person depends upon the characteristics of their *employment and the quality of (their) working life*;
- (Wo)man is defined by her/his creativity so that the way in which s/he spends time and the types of leisure available are basic to the definition of existence;
- An income and economic security are the prerequisite of satisfying material needs so that livelihood depends on one's *personal economic situation*;
- A physical shelter and hospitable environment are essential for warmth, food and water, hence the *physical environment* is basic;
- The social relationships within which our daily life is enmeshed defines our personality, hence the nature of the personality depends on the *social environment*;
- (Wo)men's life is nasty, brutish and short without mutual protection (both from each other and from the state) so that *personal safety* and the (correct) *administration of justice* is fundamental;
- The prevailing social organization permits all other forms of activity (or even existence, socially defined) and so the type of *inequality and social participation* is basic.

On their own, these typologies can help foment local debate and discussion, at worst they are irrelevant. Where they become harmful is when intervention inspired by such ideas is imposed from outside. Indeed, Sopher (1981) shows that the language of "need" is very often used by political authorities to justify policies imposed from above on people. Stewart regards the political commitment to basic needs as leaving open the question concerning the means by which this objective is achieved (1985: 2). This is the crux of the matter, not whether needs are absolute or subjective (Fitzgerald, 1977; Heller, 1986), whether there is a "natural" hierarchy of needs (Maslow, 1970), or whether needs imply "rights".

The difference between strong and weak versions of BNA lies precisely in this question of means and ends. It has caused a good deal of confusion; in a general way, of course, everyone who uses the language of the BNA sees the meeting of basic needs as desirable. Proponents of the strong BNA believe that this goal can only be attained if the *means* of meeting basic needs so empowers poor people that they become agents in creating a more just society. Advocates of the weak BNA, by contrast, assume uncritically (or argue assertively) that needs can be met through existing structures of society (delivery systems, markets, courts of law, etc.). In other words, poverty can be solved without recourse to the massive restructuring implied by notions of social justice and people's power.

A Brief History of Basic Needs*

According to Stewart, the BNA "evolved logically from earlier views on development" (1985: 8). We can take this a step further and say that the views of aid donors and agencies evolved in response to changes in world events, and to two developments in particular: the resounding failure of capitalist development in its "growth-only" phase in the 1950s and 1960s; and the extraordinary successes of socialist countries such as China and Cuba in raising welfare levels. At the same time, a key part of the world development apparatus, not least the UN system, had been drawing attention to the need for social as well as economic development indicators throughout the period when growth maximization and industrialization were uncritically accepted in

---

* Two bibliographic studies, Gaudier (1980) and Rutges (1979), cover the huge literature that grew up around basic needs in the late 1970s.

most quarters. UNICEF, the specialized agency for children, began to suggest the explicit integration of children's needs into development planning from the late 1960s onwards (Singer, 1972). Thus both the practical evidence of the value of, and a lobby for, the basic needs approach was in place before the BNA became fashionable.

It was in the generally turbulent intellectual and political climate of the late 1960s that criticism of growth-orthodoxy rose to a crescendo. Growth *per se* in such economic "miracles" as Brazil, Kenya and Côte d'Ivoire was not "trickling down"; the result of economic growth, in fact, was appalling impoverishment. Adelman and Moris (1973) looked at a series of such cases and concluded that development-as-growth was associated with an absolute and relative decline in average income of the poor (Stewart, 1985: 10). In the face of this failure was the obvious ability of the new socialist republics to improve the nutrition, health and education of enormous numbers of people. China in particular was held up as a model of development (Aziz, 1978), especially its spatial organization of development (Buchanan, 1970), health care system (Horn, 1969), and use of appropriate technology (Science for the People, 1974).

Revolutionary socialism in Asia, Latin America and Africa provided urgent encouragement for the established development theorists to get back to the drawing board. The failure of trickle-down and the success of a kind of basic needs approach in China and the liberated zones of a number of countries undergoing revolutionary change (Vietnam and Mozambique, for instance) meant that great masses of unemployed and impoverished people in the Third World might take to revolution unless something was done.

Meanwhile, national élites in a number of countries, especially in Latin America, began to voice their disappointment and anger that "development" had actually increased their economies' dependence on European and North American technology, markets and capital. The interests of these élites and of their ideologies were clearly not identical to those of the poor people in their countries, but their criticism of growth-orthodoxy – expressed as dependency theory and the political demand for renegotiation of trade relations – reinforced the message from the

31

revolutionary and potentially revolutionary poor.

The response was a series of theoretical initiatives in many sections of the development establishment. Robert McNamara, then president of the World Bank, began to shift the Bank's lending dramatically into small farmer credit, health and education infrastructure, and to increase agricultural lending in general (van de Laar, 1980; Williams, 1981; Payer, 1982; Ayres, 1983; Hayter and Watson, 1985). Elsewhere within the Bank, theoreticians worked overtime to preserve growth as a high development priority despite these new commitments. This theoretical *tour de force* was called "redistribution with growth" (Chenery *et al.*, 1974). One admittedly simplistic, but interesting, perspective on the Bank "poverty reaction" initiative is given by McNamara himself, who had been in charge of the US war in Vietnam until he came to the Bank (McNamara, 1968, quoted by Allain, 1980: 232): "the rich countries will realize that one Dollar more in military equipment buys them less security than a Dollar of development aid."

The International Labour Office (ILO) created a World Employment Programme in 1969 and continued to heap up evidence from country after country visited by its employment missions (e.g. the mission to Kenya: ILO, 1972) that great social restructuring (e.g. land reform) and economic redistribution were necessary if jobs (and even poverty-line incomes) were to be provided for the majority of people. This field work by ILO missions has continued in Africa up to the present, resulting in a series of very useful and revealing studies (1977; 1981a, b; 1982) by the Jobs and Skills Programme for Africa (JASPA), based in Addis Ababa.

Radicals from the Third World, however, felt that most of these efforts fell far short of the profound changes in the global order that were required if the poorest were to have a chance. This radical Third World perspective on the need for a New International Economic Order (NIEO) merged with an early post-Stockholm perspective on environment and development in a meeting in Cocoyoc, Mexico in 1974 (Cocoyoc Declaration, 1975). Others (e.g. Tinbergen *et al.*, 1977) were worried about the slow start of the newly-formed United Nations Environment Programme (UNEP).

The fusion of socially and ecologically radical thinking in the Third World reached a high point in the attempt by a team of Latin American scholars at the Barilloche Foundation to refute the pessimistic, Malthusian world model of the Club of Rome. The Club of Rome dissented from growth-orthodoxy, but it critically failed to question the dominant relations and structures of production. The Barilloche team demonstrated that basic food, education and housing needs could be met within existing so-called resource/population constraints if economies were restructured (Herrera *et al.*, 1976). It did not, however, discuss the means of doing so.

Simultaneously, a parallel and influential set of analyses was being produced by the project on development and international cooperation sponsored by the Dag Hammarskjöld Foundation (Dag Hammarskjöld Foundation, 1975; Matthews, ed., 1976; Nerfin, ed., 1977). The emerging notion of "another development" juxtaposed "maldevelopment" in the dominant industrial societies to "underdevelopment" in the Third World. The project questioned the global order while taking up a number of the themes now identified with need-oriented development. Alternatives to growth-development were sought under such terms as eco-development (Sachs, 1974; Sachs *et al.*, 1981) and self-reliance (Galtung *et al.*, eds., 1980; IUED, ed., 1980).

THE WORLD EMPLOYMENT CONFERENCE AND THE STRONG VERSION OF THE BNA

All of this was in the air when the ILO convened its World Employment Conference in 1976. The conference pulled together the diverse critiques of growth-orthodoxy and, as its Programme of Action shows, crystallized a BNA which supported the radical demands of the poor. The Programme of Action defined needs but was, in essence, a statement of the strong BNA (ILO, 1976: 182):

(1) Strategies and national development plans and policies should include explicitly as a priority objective the promo-

33

tion of employment and the satisfaction of the basic needs of each country's population.

(2) Basic needs, as understood in this Programme of Action, include two elements. First, they include certain minimum requirements of a family for private consumption: adequate food, shelter and clothing, as well as certain household equipment and furniture. Second, they include essential services provided by and for the community at large, such as safe drinking water, sanitation, public transport and health, educational and cultural facilities.

(3) A basic-needs-oriented policy implies the participation of the people in making the decisions which effect them through organizations of their own choice.

(4) In all countries freely chosen employment enters into a basic-needs policy both as a means and as an end. Employment yields an output. It provides an income to the employed, and gives the individual a feeling of self-respect, dignity and of being a worthy member of society.

Despite its forceful words, however, the Programme of Action was sufficiently vague to be seen as supporting either the strong or weak school of thought on the BNA. It adopted a working definition of need and a core list of needs, which became an excuse for technocratic donors to limit their commitment to basic needs while continuing to promote export-led growth. Those same interests are today supporting "debt-adjustment with a human face", a strategy discussed in later chapters. On the other hand, the Programme of Action championed popular participation and the right of poor people to organize. Side by side with the core list of needs and the ILO's typical concern with employment, the emphasis on participation and self-organization opened the door to the more radical interpretations of the BNA. Indeed, the ILO's own post-conference discussion on the BNA tended to strengthen the case for the radical or strong interpretation.

The conference was not unique in its concern with basic needs. As Ghai (1977: 4–14) notes, the Programme of Action was one of a series of international statements on development made between 1974 and 1977. These statements had in common their assertion of the urgency of meeting the basic needs of all people

34

in the shortest time possible and a recognition that self-reliant or endogenous solutions would be required. They also acknowledge the necessity of changes in the power structures within societies as well as in the international order.

This approach to basic needs lays a heavy and repeated emphasis on participation at all stages of programme and project creation, and further argues that "the main thrust of a basic-needs strategy must be to ensure that there is effective mass participation of the rural population in the political process in order to safeguard their interests" (ILO, 1979a: 59). There is clear endorsement of people's participation in deciding "the scope, content and priority of their own basic needs"; a participation which should be direct where possible, and through representative institutions where it is not feasible (Ghai and Alfthan, 1977: 20). Emphasis is therefore laid on strengthening a wide range of representative institutions, especially those representing the rural poor (ILO, 1979a: 59–64).

As discussed earlier, this version of the basic needs approach is consistent with other strategies calling for structural change and redistribution at national and international levels. It is compatible with economic growth, although it questions the pattern of growth in most countries to date (Hopkins and Van Der Hoeven, 1981: 4–5; Ghai, 1978). Its emphasis on self-reliance and participation align it closely with strategies that have become identified with the goal of eco-development (Sachs, 1974; Sachs *et al.*, 1981). We can see the similarities in Sachs's description of eco-development (1974: 17–19):

> In each ecoregion, an effort is made to develop specific resources for the satisfaction of the fundamental needs of the population as regards food, housing, health and education, these needs being defined realistically and autonomously so as to avoid the harmful "demonstration effects" of the consumption style of rich countries.
>
> Since man is the most valuable resource, ecodevelopment should contribute primarily to his self-realization. Employment, security, quality of human relationships, respect for cultural diversity ... form part of the concept.
>
> Ecodevelopment requires setting up a horizontal author-

35

ity who can transcend sectoral particularism, who is concerned with all the facets of development and makes continual use of the complementarity of the different actions undertaken.... Such an authority could not be efficient without the effective participation of the populations concerned in the implementation of ecodevelopment strategies. *This participation is essential for the definition and harmonization of the concrete needs*, the identification of the productive potentials of the ecosystem and the organization of collective efforts for its exploitation [emphasis added].

Green, another scholar responsible for crystallizing this perspective in the mid-1970s, sees the difference between the strong and weak BNA as that of "basic human needs" versus "basic needs". The advocates of basic human needs (or the strong BNA) are characterized by their emphasis on "participation and productive employment as vital means as well as integral ends" (Green, 1978: 10); the second group tends to emphasize minimum income and survival needs only. Green also differentiates between "conservative" and "progressive/radical" advocates of need-oriented strategies. Extreme conservatives (following Milton Friedman) argue that *laissez faire* capitalism plus minimum income guarantees suffice to satisfy the minimum needs of the poor. Participation has no role here, nor does government generation of productive employment or provision of social services. At the other extreme, "progressive/radical" (social democratic) analyses normally include participation and the political aspects of productive employment (op. cit.: 11).

Our strong/weak distinction has other parallels, too. Galtung, for instance, distinguishes "shallow" from "deep" need approaches (1980d); Sandbrook (1982) juxtaposes "conservative" to "radical" basic needs; Gish (1983) writes of the difference between the "common" or "vulgar" view of the basic needs approach and a "richer" interpretation. Still others have distinguished between basic need strategies in which "human need" is synonymous with "human right" (Alston, 1979; Galtung and Wirak, 1977; Alston, 1984) and those for whom "need" does not have the normative force of "right" (for instance Streeten, 1981: 184–92).

36

Blaikie *et al.* (1979) distinguish between a "liberal BNS" (Basic Needs Strategy) and a "radical BNS". The liberal version is characterized by an emphasis on identifying target groups of poor in such a way that they are "divorced from social relationships as a stratum". One of its central concerns is the difficulty of measuring poverty. The radical BNS, by contrast, argues that it is the relations among classes and among strata of society (e.g. between rich landowners and poor labourers) that define poverty, not technical measurements of deficiency, and that what needs to be developed is a "theory of the reproduction of poverty" (pp. 109–12).

But the main conflict between the two is over participation. For the liberal BNS, participation is a "kind of luxury once consumption minima have been met" (p. 110) – an idea which is now gaining increasing support in agencies such as UNICEF. Under liberal BNS conceptions, the state intervenes to make up for the deficiencies of trickle-down by directly providing subsidized food, housing, etc. The radical BNS focuses on the causes of poverty, recognizes the on-going struggle of the poor themselves to provide their basic needs, and emphasizes participation and employment. As Blaikie writes (p. 114):

> The poor, as a passive (but deserving) recipient of aid from above, is both a misleading and counter-productive image. The existing struggles by the deprived to secure their own basic needs through direct action and local organization (local self-help groups, trade unions, etc.) are themselves an important part of a BNS which needs no official opening ceremony, and which already has a long history.

This emphasis on organized efforts to secure basic needs echoes the pro-participation sentiment of the ILO/World Employment Conference. But the strong BNA has been best summarized by church development workers: "betting on the weak", they call it – a position implying solidarity and partnership in common struggle (World Council of Churches, 1976).

THE WORLD BANK AND THE WEAK VERSION

Major aid donors and lenders, including the World Bank system, had been trying to grapple with the problems of absolute poverty for some time before basic needs came into the international debate. McNamara's speech to World Bank directors in Nairobi in 1973 was supposed to have launched a period of new-style projects in human resources development and poverty alleviation (World Bank, 1980a; Isenman *et al.*, 1982), in education, health, nutrition and family planning. In addition, McNamara's war on poverty was to include a new approach to rural development that included a reassessment of the Bank's earlier disparaging attitude towards land reform and the small farmer (McNamara, 1973: 16–17, cited in van der Laar, 1980: 143; World Bank, 1975; Lele, 1975).

At the same time, some parts of the Bank began to flirt with notions of redistribution with growth (Chenery *et al.*, 1974; Ul Haq, 1976). Despite their differences, however, both approaches were a reaction to the failure of earlier growth strategies (primary export and import-substitution industrialization) and the inability of urban employment-generation strategies to absorb the increasing numbers of urban and rural poor (Streeten, 1981: 8–23). USAID, began similarly to shift its rhetoric at the same time (Ayre, 1983: 9).

One of the most striking features of the Bank's version of the BNA is its specific rejection of questions of distributive justice. In fact, Streeten (1981: 17), writing for the Bank, seems to conceive of the BNA as a clever way of circumventing such issues:

> In societies with very low levels of living ... meeting basic needs is more important than reducing inequality for three reasons. First, equality as such is probably not an objective of great importance to most people.... Second, this lack of concern is justified, because meeting basic human needs is morally a more important objective than reducing inequality. Third, reducing inequality is a highly complex, abstract objective, open to many different interpretations and, therefore, operationally ambiguous.

Likewise Uphoff, also writing for the Bank, makes it clear that basic needs have nothing to do with the redistribution of wealth (1980: 7):

> On the credit side, human development programs are essentially more distributive than redistributive compared to some other poverty reducing programs. The increments gained in knowledge, health and vitality are not attained at the cost of comparable reductions for someone else. Thus the politics surrounding them should involve less conflict, though this does not mean that there are no issues of allocation....
>
> Even if they are not able to avoid some zero-sum competition, human development programs remain attractive politically for a number of additional reasons. There are substantial externalities for richer sectors even from poverty-oriented programs. Human development expenditures often have the double impact of being both consumption *and* investment, making them more popular than some other kinds....
>
> They are generally regarded as quite legitimate programs and can enhance the legitimacy of the government. Because they are so divisible, they can be allocated in ways that enhance political support.

This is not to say that the Bank's BNA is simply the old concept of economic growth in new form. The language of "investment", "cost" and "productivity" is the same (World Bank, 1980a: 63; Horton and King, 1981), but while the degree of opposition may have been exaggerated, the Bank's BNA does pose basic needs against growth theory (World Bank, 1980a: 52). None the less, popular participation for the Bank is clearly secondary (Streeten and Burki, 1978: 413, quoted by Blaikie *et al.*, 1979: 110). Usually it reduces the scope of that ambiguous term by defining it in its narrowest sense, as voluntary enrolment or as taking part in Bank projects and services – road building, attendance at health clinics, the use of credit and marketing facilities and the like. Such participation is, to say the least, rather passive, and is structured in such a way that it will never challenge the participant's role as a consumer of commodities and alienated worker (Roberts, 1979). It contrasts with the active participation of people politically mobilized, for whom employment is an end as well as a means. Occasionally Bank documents refer to the ideal of participation in project design and evaluation, but it is a goal which has seldom been put into practice (Williams, 1981; Payer, 1982; Hayter and Watson, 1985).

One must contrast the Bank's limited notion and practice of participation – which has as its aim the ultimate cost-effectiveness of projects through local financing and volunteer labour (White, 1982: 20–34) – with a more ambitious one. The latter has been called "transformative" (Kruks, 1983), "empowering" (Oakley and Marsden, 1984) and "self-reliant and self-governing" (FAO/DSE, 1984). "Radical" might also serve as a way of distinguishing the more ambitious variant, as it nearly always challenges fundamental economic and political interests. Thus Bugnicourt (1982: 73) concludes:

> There is a choice to be made not only by government, but at every level where authority is exercised. If popular participation is to be limited solely to the execution of tasks, it will have little chance of obtaining real and lasting support. If it is accepted that participation should start at the stage of conception and still be in evidence at the stage of supervision, then it is necessary to agree to share certain elements of power.

The Bank's understanding of participation never included society-wide political involvement. In fact, in his account of work in the Bank on basic needs from 1978, Streeten finds such an interpretation of participation an aberration:

> A fourth interpretation emphasizes the non-economic, non-material aspects of human autonomy and embraces individual and group participation in the formulation and implementation of projects, and in some cases political mobilization. This widely ranging sociological interpretation sometimes verges on the notion that the satisfaction of basic needs is a human right: freedom from want is like the right not to be tortured. In its more general formulation it

40

comes near the view that "all good things go together" (1981: 26).

And again:

> According to one interpretation, the basic needs approach is revolutionary because it calls for the radical redistribution not only of income and assets but also of power, and for the political mobilization of the poor themselves.... At the other extreme, the approach has been interpreted as a minimum welfare sop to keep the poor quiet.... An intermediate interpretation is that basic needs have been met by a variety of political regimes ... and that a revolution is neither a necessary nor a sufficient condition ... (op cit.: 26–7).

Streeten and the World Bank clearly approve of the "middle" way despite (or because of) its failure to challenge the structures that reproduce poverty.

Reflecting this failure is the fact that the weak BNA is not an integrative approach, but a simple planning scheme for external provision of goods and services that may or may not alleviate the very poverty that conventional development funding often provokes. Ul Haq (1976: 68–9) describes this "count-cost-carry" process:

> There are at least three steps which are essential to formulating a need-oriented development strategy. First, the target groups ... must be defined with a good deal of precision, after collecting the necessary data on the profile of poverty within these countries. Second, quantitative studies must be undertaken to estimate the population which is below the minimum human needs (as defined by that society), and an estimate made regarding the production and investment targets which should be set to meet these consumption targets over a defined period of time. Third, the necessary instruments of implementation should be defined to indicate how these consumption targets are to be realized in a market where the demand signals may all be leading in a different direction.

While the weak BNA often seems similar to older concepts of economic growth and justifies investment in "human resource development", for example, in terms of additional productivity, changes in income and the eventual decline in fertility, the two concepts of development are still distinct. The degree and frequency of opposition between them may have been exaggerated (World Bank, 1980a: 51), but the friction is there: "Even at the margin, the key question is not whether the returns to human development are high, but whether they are *higher* than returns to alternative uses of the resources concerned." (p. 52.)

Despite talk of a "seamless web" of interrelations among basic needs (World Bank, 1980a: 36), programmes funded under this concept have tended to be either piecemeal sectoral reforms (Sandbrook, 1982: 7) or mere afterthoughts associated with growth-oriented projects such as agro-industry (van der Laar, 1980; Hayter and Watson, 1985). In both cases the result has been a "shopping-list" approach to development planning. It became *de rigeur* for projects to be seen to address certain basic needs (health, nutrition, education) and certain target groups (e.g. women), regardless of the economic justification. Other shopping-list approaches had appeared earlier when environmental and then social impact analyses became formal requirements for project planning (Derman and Whitford, 1985).

Some social benefits, of course, have come from the shopping-list approach to basic needs. Fundamentally, however, the weak BNA is out of touch with efforts by the people themselves to satisfy their basic needs. It does not deal with such underlying factors as the distribution of income, assets and power in society. In the long run, therefore, the ability of the weak BNA to reverse the accelerating spiral of poverty and environmental degradation is very limited.

Yet even this rather limited approach to basic needs has begun to disappear in recent Bank documents. As Freeman (1984: 100) observes:

> Now the emphasis is almost exclusively on economic growth, efficiency and a much greater reliance on the private sector. Gone are the 1970s' themes of basic needs and participation. Equity is out. Back are the preoccupations of

orthodox Western neoclassical economics – building on the best, creating an open economy and, above all, the "magic of the marketplace".

A recent World Development Report (World Bank, 1982) continues to use increased productivity to justify investment in human development. However, the balance between productivity-enhancing inputs and the direct intervention described in an earlier World Development Report (1978: 3) seems to be moving rapidly in the direction of "improving the productivity of the poor" (1982: 80–86). This shift indicates the Bank's increasing abandonment of the weak version of basic needs; in some cases, such as the Bank's strategy for African agriculture, this abandonment is quite explicit. "Improving the productivity of the poor" in this context means something entirely different from the economic and social restructuring implied by the strong BNA.

The Bank's most recent idea is to decrease direct need-provision while improving productivity entirely within existing social relations of production. This is clear in the Bank's 1982 report, which advocates the development of "human resources" through education for labour mobility within the existing structure of employment (together with a curious little aside suggesting that perhaps the vast flood of the unemployed to Third World cities is not such a bad thing after all). Both small-farmer programmes and rural public works are conceived entirely within the existing class and spatial division of labour. Agrarian reform, the fourth and final set of the 1982 programmes designed to boost the productivity of the poor, is seen in economistic, apolitical terms and implemented in small, non-threatening pilot programmes (1982: 84).

THE STRONG–WEAK DISTINCTION IN PRACTICE: EXAMPLES FROM EDUCATION

Education is almost always included in basic need strategies. The World Bank stresses that a better educated population – in particular, a literate and numerate one – is capable of responding

43

to opportunities for improving the techniques of production. It further notes the statistical correlation between mothers' level of education and the health of their children, suggesting that the more women are educated, the greater the social benefits (Streeten, 1981: 134–49, 152–61; World Bank, 1980a: 14–21; Haddad, 1980: 36–8; World Bank, 1982: 81). The response, according to this view, should be to increase the "inputs" (measured as literacy teachers per thousand of the population and classrooms), encourage "participation" (defined as attendance at and exam scores in literacy and other programmes) and evaluate the "results" (measured as the percentage of adult literacy, female literacy and female children in school).

There is no denying the importance of education, especially given the evidence of the value of women's schooling. For the strong BNA, however, these principles are simply the starting point.

The weak BNA accepts the existing arrangement of productive and power relations. Education, in this perspective, is "education for employment" – as opposed to "education for self-reliance" (Chinapah and Fägerland, 1979: 45–58). Thus many of the non-formal as well as formal "delivery systems" for education discussed approvingly by the World Bank (1975; Coombs and Ahmed, 1974) have tended to teach skills that are applicable only in the formal labour market. This has been one of the severe problems of Botswana's "youth brigades" and Kenya's "village polytechnics" (Ahmed and Coombs, 1975), for example.

Education for self-reliance bases all educational activities (literacy, primary and vocational) on the daily realities and needs of the local people (Freire, 1970). It reflects as far as possible the local culture, and minimizes the distinctions between school and community and between study and production (World Bank, 1974: Colclough, 1976, 1978).

While education for self-reliance is linked in practical ways to production and to daily life, its implications go further. Participation here begins with the study of the local social and physical environment – the first step in an ongoing process of people defining their own needs. Indeed, continuing dialogue about needs, rooted in the study of local social and physical reality, could be the only way out of the philosophical confusion

44

concerning "true" and "false" needs (Soper, 1981).

Applied in this way, adult education can become liberatory. This process is in fact central to the strong BNA strategy. It is not a "luxury" in the World Bank's sense. Group discussions do require time and energy, but while the Bank sees this as an indulgence more properly deferred until other basic needs are met (Davies, 1963, 1977), the BNA sees dialogue in the educational process as a necessity (Galtung, 1980a). Green (1977: 15) quotes the Guidelines of the Tanzania African National Union approvingly on this point: "Development means liberation. Any action that gives the people more control of their *own* affairs is an action for development, even if it does not offer them better health and more bread."

In practice such a broadly conceived education process is hard to separate from the struggle for bread and health. (The gap between Tanzanian rhetoric and reality in this regard will be discussed below.) Education gives people the skills necessary for their effective political participation, and hence for their ability to fight for a better standard of living and social services. These skills include literacy (Udaipur Literacy Declaration, 1981), knowledge of how to organize (Green, 1977: 21) and the development of a critical understanding of social change (UNESCO, 1982: 12; Vio Grossi, 1982). Education in this sense might be called "education for civic participation" (UNICEF, 1973, quoted by Chinapah and Fägerlind, 1979: 45). It also builds the self-esteem and self-confidence of the poor (Vio Grossi, 1982: 19). Most importantly, new locally-based knowledge becomes the foundation of self-reliance (de Oliveira and de Oliveira, 1980: 213–20).

THE STRONG BNA IN ACTION: NINE HALLMARKS

The rest of this book reviews a number of strong and weak basic need-inspired projects in Africa. It is here that we can see what the ideal characteristics of the strong BNA ought to be. Most strong BNA projects tend to be geographically scattered and are supported by small NGOs; on the basis of these projects alone it would be difficult to form firm and lasting conclusions about the

45

nature of the strong BNA. When set in the context of other cases in which the state has embraced a strong BNA (as in Nicaragua and the state of Kerala in India) or where the NGOs involved are strong, indigenous and widespread (as with the Sarvodaya movement in Sri Lanka), however, these unique African projects offer us important guidelines for participatory, effective development.

1. Need Discourse Has No *A Priori* Limit

There are many reasons for collecting social indicators (Carr-Hill, 1984). What data are collected, and what questions are asked, are determined by the interests of those doing the collecting and asking. Is information gathered to predict and control social conflict? Is its purpose the assessment of government bureaux performance, to vindicate or pressure them?

Similar questions must be asked of the social activity surrounding the BNA. For what reason are needs defined, and for whom does the process take place? In the strong BNA, the answer is clear: a local group's definition of its needs helps strengthen its position in negotiations with, perhaps, landlords, employers or state bureaucrats. The "indicators" chosen by the group, the "needs" they choose to define and pursue, are defined in the context of a struggle for power to satisfy their needs. There is, therefore, no *a priori* limit on the scope of such discussions to strictly material needs such as food, water and shelter. Indeed, a Latin American priest noted in the early 1970s (about the time when basic needs were entering the vocabulary of development theory) that for peasants struggling against unjust land distribution and indebtedness, "'liberation' from these fatal trends is often felt more strongly as a 'basic need' ... than the material gains accruing from well-intentioned agricultural development schemes ..." (Gutierrez, quoted in Huizer, 1984: 15).

Similarly, some women in Asia, Latin America and Africa feel strongly that they have a need and a right to control their own sexuality (Mies, 1976; Omvedt, 1980; Cutrufelli, 1983). Although the view of Third World women may have been overstated by western feminists (Roberts, 1984: 175–84), it is clear that many Third World women tacitly define control of their bodies and

46

reproduction as a basic human need. "Sexuality" is nowhere to be found on the shopping-list of basic needs produced by the World Bank!

The weak form of basic needs is essentially quantitative: development is measured by Kcal per day, litres of water, square metres of window space, etc. Such a numbers game has several social and political functions, but these are not the same purposes served by need-definition by local people themselves. On the contrary, the shopping-list approach pre-empts this process by assuming a hierarchy of pre-defined needs (McHale and McHale, 1978). Some experts base their definitions on physiological and psychological data, while others, principally administrators and planners, take the pragmatic view that any response to absolute poverty requires prepackaged "need satisfiers" selected by the planners according to the urgency, nature and extent of the problem. This is the World Bank's justification for its "count-cost-carry" approach (Ul Haq, 1976). The top-down assessment of needs is now being questioned even in such seemingly straightforward situations as natural disasters. As recent authors have shown, a large amount of disaster aid is unwanted, inappropriate and unnecessary (Cuny, 1983).

2. Need Discourse is Continuous

The strong form of need definition does not end once a "wish list" has been drawn up. The group then takes action, typically encounters some obstacles, and analyses these obstacles. In this way needs may be redefined, links among needs may become evident, alliances and tactics in dealing with obstacles may be identified and refined. As the group pursues its analysis of obstacles – perhaps a landowner, perhaps the entire land tenure system – it can move in almost any direction. Herein lies the potential challenge to powerful interests (and some reassurance to critics who worry that a focus on basic needs will distract attention from injustices in the international and national political economy).

What makes this approach particularly politically volatile is that it crosses the boundaries between production and reproduction, between the workplace and the home. In the African context one is dealing essentially with the distinction between production of a surplus for trade or sale and activities (particularly of women) that ensure a level of production necessary to reproduce the next generation. This distinction is blurred where families cultivate their own land. It becomes clearer where workers have been separated from the means of production, such as land, or "proletarianized".

In Africa the process of proletarianization is not complete. Many families – still the majority in most of the continent – have not been separated from the means of subsistence, the land. Exploitation occurs therefore not through the sale of labour in a factory, but through the market relations into which the family is forced to enter. These forms of exploitation are complex and varied. They will be discussed in some detail in later chapters, where so-called "rural development" is placed in critical perspective (Williams, 1981).

At this early stage of the argument, however, it is enough to recognize that basic needs involve both the sphere of production and the sphere of reproduction, especially where the household is the basis of rural livelihoods. In its strong form, discussion of obstacles to need satisfaction by groups facing common obstacles will sooner or later focus on issues of relations with the market, with urban areas, with sellers or providers of technology (including the most recent advocates of an African Green Revolution) as well as with buyers of their cash crops and food surplus.

3. Internal As Well As External Contradictions Will Emerge

Situated at the point of interaction of production and reproduction, strong need analysis is also quite likely to highlight internal contradictions. Is the local environment being stripped of trees? Is the pasture being degraded by overuse? Such internal limitations on sustainability (hence need satisfaction) will emerge from a continuous discussion of obstacles to actions taken by the group as well as those contradictions located where the local people interact with the market and other groups. The so-called "tragedy of the commons" – the alleged conflict between individual and social good leading to the overuse and destruction

48

of common resources such as fish, pasture, forests – has been repeatedly revealed to be a comedy of misapplied social science. Detailed anthropological descriptions now exist of the social control over resource use and its breakdown in such cases (McKay and Atkinson, 1988). The form of social unity developed in the course of radical needs analysis and action by local groups is usually adequate to control self-destructive behaviour of this kind.

4. The Process Is Conflictual, Not Harmonizing

Radical need discourse necessarily revolves around the identification and confrontation of external and internal contradictions at the point where production and reproduction meet. Less technically, the oppression of women, exploitation by landlords or money-lenders and harmful technical packages proposed by bureaucrats will come to light. The development philosophy underlying the strong needs approach is one which views conflicts of interest as the motor force in human history. These conflicts need not be violent. On the contrary, the suppression of "silent" conflicts of interest is itself a form of violence. This is what the World Council of Churches and peace studies scholars mean by "structural violence" – the silent violence of children's deaths from malnutrition, or of the daily toll of South African apartheid.

5. The Process of Need Definition Is Political

The process described so far is political. Politics is about conflicts of interest. The organizational expression of women's, rural landless people's and urban squatters' interests are at the heart of the strong needs approach. This approach is about confrontation, not harmony. It is about the day-to-day definition of needs and the next steps people take in demanding the conditions so that they can fulfill these needs. While these daily struggles are seldom couched in terms of the demand for a just, participatory and sustainable society, the BNA is grounded in an interpretation of human history that believes the sum total of such daily

49

struggles is movement in that direction. In particular, three kinds of conflicts are likely to emerge: regional, gender and class.

6. Need Discourse Will Identify Regional Conflict

The uneven development of capitalism, especially in countries with a recent colonial past, has left a legacy of a spatially unjust distribution of services and opportunities. Inequity is complicated in many cases by regional differences in culture and ethnicity – the farmer versus the nomad in the Sahel (Franke, 1984) or in East Africa (Rigby, 1985), for instance. Exacerbated by colonial capitalism, it is not surprising that these differences are often expressed in regional or ethnic terms at an early stage of the strong needs discussion. With time, the divisiveness of regional or ethnic loyalties can be overcome; common obstacles and common enemies eventually create cohesive local communities if for no other reason than to gain a specific aim – a wage increase, the right to use pasture land, a better price for cash crops.

The importance of these divisions, however, should not be underestimated. Conventional modernizers and radicals will recoil from what sounds like an argument for "tribalism" and "petty-bourgeois consciousness", but just as the implicit hierarchy of needs contained in the expert shopping-list must be rejected by a strong interpretation, there is no reason to assume that a radical local dialogue about basic needs will immediately identify common interests. Workers, peasants and members of ethnic and regional groups are as tied to their culture and past as any of us; and although this view may dismay professors, planners, church leaders and party functionaries, regional and ethnic conflict is a reality which must be addressed.

7. Need Discourse Will Identify Gender Conflict

Situated where production meets reproduction, needs dialogue quite naturally reveals conflicts of interest between men and women. As with the identification of regional and cultural differences that sometimes set the needs of one group against those of another, gender conflict is likely to slip to a secondary – though real – position as the analysis of needs and contradictions continues. The particular forms that colonial history have given to women's "double oppression" (Urdang, 1979) in much of Africa are likely to raise the woman question at a certain stage of local dialogue, although the way the question gets articulated will vary considerably since part of the colonial inheritance is often a "culture of silence" on the part of women.

8. Need Discourse Will Reveal Class Interests

The household is still the major unit of production and of reproduction in Africa. This is true in urban squatter areas as well as in the countryside, although the demographic form of the household is complex, as is the mixture of employment and activities (Gerry, ed., 1979; Guyer, 1981; Vaughan and Hirschman, 1983). Despite the centrality of the household, confrontations, analysis of obstacles to common effort, definitions and redefinitions of need in the light of these struggles will produce a growing consciousness of economic exploitation. In these circumstances "class consciousness" will never be quite as tidy as the dogmatic left would wish. But the reality none the less is a rich class content – a mixture of gender, ethnic, regional, generational and class consciousness.

9. Struggle Based on Need Is Not "Modern"

Neither enthusiasts of capitalist nor of socialist modernization will have much favourable to say about the strong BNA. Modernization theory defines development as the erection of a modern state and market structure. (The state socialist variant modifies the form of the state and market, but is identical in spirit.) In the view of the modernizers, proper states and markets should not (and normally do not) allow hunger, disease, illiteracy or hopelessness (Sen, 1981; Streeten, 1981). Modern social life is supposed to be about the sublimation of regional, cultural, gender and class differences to a greater, harmonizing whole, not their free expression. The purpose of the state is to unify disparate interests, while the market impersonally levels out differences and democratic institutions channel and institutionalize the atavistic energy inherent in regionalism, tribalism, class struggle and

51

sexual politics. A strategy that would turn loose such "pre-modern" forces, then, would appear to be in danger of defeating itself. But as our examples from Africa show, the emergence of these conflicts in the BNA dialogue can be liberating. Far from being a step backwards, they are both true to people's experiences and a key first step in the move towards popular control over the development process.

Conclusion

The radical BNA seems to open a veritable Pandora's Box. Impatient with state and market structures that have not addressed the poverty of the poorest forty per cent, it threatens to unleash seemingly uncontrollable regional, ethnic and class conflict. Reform and evolution, say the proponents of the weak BNA, is the better path; governments and markets will eventually solve the problems (e.g. Bates, 1983; Eicher, 1984). The strong BNA is simply an over-reaction to temporary deficiencies in the welfare system.

Yet as the history of welfare shows (Fox Piven and Cloward, 1971), the weak needs position is nothing more than a justification for social control of political upheaval during periods of economic crisis and a mechanism for regulating the labour force during "normal" times. It is absurd to think that the employment and welfare system in Africa could develop to even the tattered and crumbling state of the present-day British or US "safety net", although this remains the dream of many modernization reformers. For them, the construction of a safety net in Africa has simply been temporarily slowed by, in the words of James Grant, the head of UNICEF, the "head winds of recession" (1983: 2).

In the next three chapters we examine both strong and weak basic needs approaches in African health care. In no other area of development efforts is the emptiness of the modernization vision clearer.

Chapter 2

Health For All Means Power For All:
Primary Health Care, Basic Services and
the Legitimacy of the African State

Primary Health Care (PHC) is the major form in which the BNA in health has been articulated. PHC requires considerable political and financial commitment. In a period of profound political and economic crisis in Africa, it is not surprising that many governments have begun to adopt weakened versions of the BNA in their health care systems. It is here that we can see the glaring disparities between the language of basic needs and the reality of the inadequate health care of the weak BNA.

PRIMARY HEALTH CARE AND "HEALTH FOR ALL"

In the early 1950s, the World Health Organization voiced concern that mass campaigns, such as those against smallpox and malaria, needed the backing of a comprehensive health care system which could reach the most remote rural areas (Djukanovic and Mach, 1975: 108ff). Awareness increased through the 1960s of the urban and clinical bias of health services in the Third World and of their inability to address the health needs of the majority of the population of these countries (Bryant, 1969).

Clearly the capital-intensive, biomedical approach of many governments was inappropriate. Gish (1973: 35) gives three reasons why the Third World needed another approach to health:

• Scarcity of monetary and human resources;

- Differences in spatial organization, the highly dispersed rural populations and growing urban slums;

- Differences in the patterns of disease, where the majority of deaths in the Third World are due to preventable conditions of childhood lived in poverty and malnutrition. These include immunization-preventable diseases such as measles, neo-natal tetanus, tuberculosis, polio, and whooping-cough as well as diarrhoeas, pneumonia and malaria – all closely related to the management of the physical environment.

The notion of economically feasible, appropriately staffed, accessible basic health services emerged in response, along with the idea of comprehensive health care. Meanwhile, UNICEF had widened its interests and had begun to seek ways of planning for the needs of children in a comprehensive manner (UNICEF, 1965). Its mother and child health (MCH) initiatives were an important stage in developing a BNA in health. In this way UNICEF's experience converged with WHO's. Both laid emphasis on basic health services, including monitoring, surveillance and health care delivery, as a prerequisite for successful MCH (King, ed., 1966).

New decentralized, simplified health care systems in China, Cuba, Tanzania and Venezuela attracted WHO and UNICEF attention in the early 1970s (Newell, ed., 1975; Djukanovic and Mach, 1975). Panels, symposia and conferences gathered to assess the significance of these attempts to tailor health services to the needs of rural people. A central figure in the effort to reconcile limited budgets and tremendous need was the medical auxiliary, variously known as the barefoot doctor, village medical helper or traditional birth attendant, depending on the country and health care systems (Gish, 1971).

In 1977, WHO's World Health Assembly endorsed the goal of "Health for All by the Year 2000". Its goals, summarized in Table 2.1 (WHO, 1981a: 74–7), included locally accessible health programmes which should offer (Pitt, 1982):

Education concerning the prevailing health problems and the methods of preventing and controlling them; promotion of food supply and proper nutrition; an adequate supply of safe water and basic sanitation; maternal and child health care, including family planning; immunization against the major infectious diseases; prevention and control of locally endemic diseases; appropriate treatment of common diseases and injuries; provision of essential drugs.

WHO's goals were to be met through a combination of a decentralized, hierarchical basic health system plus two further ingredients: community participation and increased inter-sectoral emphasis on basic preconditions of health such as adequate food and water supply. This strategy was called primary health care (PHC) and was endorsed at another world conference a year later in Alma Ata. Here PHC was defined (WHO, 1981a: 32) as:

> essential health care based on practical, scientifically sound and socially acceptable methods and technology made universally accessible to individuals and families in the community through their full participation and at a cost that the community and the country can afford.... It forms an integral part both of the country's health system, of which it is the central function and main focus, and of the overall social and economic development of the community. It is the first level of contact of individuals, the family and the community with the national health system bringing health care as close as possible to where people live and work, and constitutes the first element of a continuing health care process.

Like every other aspect of the BNA, this definition of a basic needs approach in health is open to both weak and strong interpretations.

STRONG AND WEAK INTERPRETATIONS OF PHC

Despite explicit commitments to health for all (as WHO put it, "Health is a fundamental human right and a worldwide social goal" – WHO, 1981a: 34), weakened versions of primary health care soon appeared. Based on a "human capital" concept of human worth, agencies such as the World Bank supported primary health care investments that would increase the productivity of labour (World Bank, 1980a). The count–cost–carry formula was once again brought into play with its concomitant minimization of popular participation and reliance on experts. Some commentators have gone as far as to suggest that this weak BNA approach is actually about the needs of capital, not of people (Makhoul, 1984: 380ff):

> "Basic needs" is a formula for the optimal targetting of public health and nutritional programs at restoring the legitimacy that capitalism is losing owing to its failure to alleviate in any other way the underdevelopment of health it had created at the periphery – a last resort strategy to prove the social feasibility of underdeveloped capitalism: its compatibility with health as an objective of development.

Table 2.1

"HEALTH FOR ALL" GOALS

By Year 2000 in All Countries ...

(1) Health for all will have received endorsement as policy at the highest official level;

(2) Mechanisms for involving people in the implementation of strategies have been formed or strengthened, and are actually functioning;

(3) At least five per cent of the gross national product is spent on health;

(4) A reasonable percentage of the national health expenditure is devoted to local health care, i.e. the first level contact;

(5) Resources are equitably distributed;

(6) Well-defined strategies for health for all, accompanied by explicit resource allocation, are receiving sustained support from more affluent countries where necessary;

(7) Primary health care is available to the whole population, with at least the following:

- safe water in the home within 15 minutes' walking distance and adequate sanitary facilities in the home or immediate vicinity;
- immunization against diphtheria, tetanus, whooping-cough, measles, poliomyelitis and tuberculosis;
- local health care, including availability of at least 20 essential drugs, within one hour's walk or travel;
- trained personnel for attending pregnancy and childbirth, and caring for children up to at least one year of age;

(8) The nutritional status is adequate;

(9) The infant mortality rate for all identifiable subgroups is below 50 per 1000 live-births;

(10) Life expectancy at birth is over 60 years;

(11) The adult literacy rate for both men and women exceeds 70 per cent;

(12) The gross national product per head exceeds $500.

In the hands of weak BNA planners, PHC becomes merely a technical "package of preventive and curative services that can be delivered by auxiliary personnel" (Turshen and Thebaud, 1981: 39), which "stops short of what would be necessary to change the conditions that produce malnutrition and an unhealthy environment" (op. cit.: 40). There is a power relation at work in this version of the BNA, and it works only one way, from the top down, involving "the provision of some basic sets of commodities to those not having control over any resources, by those with such control" (Gish, 1983).

The weak conception traces ill health to its origin in poverty without seeking the cause of poverty. It focuses on the effects of poverty such as bad housing and sanitation (World Bank, 1975: 341–425; Golladay, 1980: 23–7), rather than dealing with its root. In fact, the eradication of poverty and malnutrition "is *unrealistic* to aspire for in the development framework it comes to defend" (Makhoul, 1984: 380). Such a view does not question the relations of production and reproduction within a society, but typically sets minimum income goals deemed necessary for adequate nutrition, housing and health within them. In this, the proponents of the weak BNA are following in a long tradition of poverty studies that go back to the attempts of the nineteenth-century capitalists, Rowntree and Cadbury, to determine the needs of a contented workforce.

In what other way could PHC be implemented? A strong needs perspective would encourage local groups to discuss and define their own health needs. More importantly, such groups would be encouraged to seek the causes of their problems and to organize themselves to prevent them (ICAE, 1982). In the years since the Alma Ata primary health care conference, for instance, many nutritionists and health educators have grown impatient with the role of experts and have encouraged others to stop dispensing advice about what to eat and instead to mobilize people to demand the ability to grow or to purchase the food they need (Barth-Eide, 1978).

While debate continues about how to tap the full potential of such radical participation in health care (Rifkin, 1980; Morley *et al.*, 1983), WHO's *Global Strategy for Health for All by the Year 2000* helps to move us in this direction. As we will see, however, we are a long way from achieving the goal of a strong primary health care system.

SHIFTING INTERPRETATIONS OF NEED

One might ask why language so explicitly non-technocratic, comprehensive and participatory is implemented as its opposite. One obvious but not very helpful answer is that inertia in health care systems is as great as, or even greater than, it is in other institutions. In Africa, urban-based, hospital-oriented systems were established by the colonial powers, and the pattern was set. Interestingly, where the colonial system promoted more decentralized financing, as under the French in Niger on Mali, experiments in decentralized rural health care emerged after

58

independence more readily that in some former British territories (Fourier and Djermakoye, 1975; UNICEF/WHO, 1981). Church-owned health facilities did penetrate the more peripheral areas to some degree during the colonial period, but they were also essentially hospital-based and reinforced the colonial health system (Hartwig, 1979). On the whole, however, institutional inertia must be considered a constant. While minor differences in the colonial experience made expansion of the number of auxiliary workers more acceptable at independence in the Sudan, for instance, than in Tanganyika (Bryant, 1969: 66–71; Titmus *et al.*, 1964), at independence all the ex-colonies in Africa inherited essentially the same system, committed to what WHO then called "internationally acceptable minimum standards of medical education" (WHO, 1962). Given their similar start, we must look beyond institutional inertia to the BNA to understand the differences in the quality of African health care and the different interpretations of BNA.

For instance, Tanganyika (present Tanzania minus Zanzibar) was actually advised at independence to reduce the number of paramedics (Titmus *et al.*, 1964: 180). Ten years later, however, there were 4,386 workers trained in similar auxiliary categories (69 per cent of all health personnel) and 48 per cent of the health development budget was going for training, with less than ten per cent of that spent in the capital city (Chagula and Tarimo, 1975: 161, 163). In the same year (1973), Kenya had a total of 3,120 health workers in the same staff categories, making up 65 per cent of the health care establishment (GOK, 1974: 455). Both countries had reacted to the racial segregation of services and training under British colonial rule (Mburu, 1981; Doyal, 1979). Both former British colonies had begun independence with a commitment to producing highly trained doctors. Both had been forced by popular political demand for health care to decentralize and to use less highly trained staff. With virtually the same size population and similar medical needs, one would have expected parallel health systems to emerge.

Yet ten years after independence the differences were clear. Kenya had kept to the old style of health service: a large auxiliary staff worked in conventional nursing categories and under conventional supervision, and health care was centred in hospi-

59

tals (although there were also 131 health centres and 572 dispensaries) (GOK, 1974: 454). In Tanzania in 1973, nearly 1,700 of the auxiliary staff were rural- and village-based MCH aides, village midwives or rural medical aides, staffing 108 health centres and 1,515 dispensaries (Chagula and Tarimo, 1975: 149). This meant that 73 per cent of the Tanzanian population was within ten kilometres of a health service centre of some kind.

Class Interests

Of more help in understanding distortions of the strong BN approach in health is a class analysis of bureaucracy (Turshen, 1984: 198) that takes us beyond notions of institutional inertia. Doyal (1981: 258–9) captures one aspect of the class interest involved. She follows Fanon in noting that:

> the bourgeoisie of underdeveloped countries shares with the metropolitan class which it emulates, a "spirit of indulgence", and this is particularly significant in any attempt to understand third world medical policies.... [W]estern scientific medicine – with its associated apparatus – represents yet another item of luxury consumption for the few who can afford it.

In much of Africa, however, the post-colonial élite's lack of solid economic base has exacerbated the state's legitimation crisis. As a colonial doctor remarked in Kenya, it was necessary to give "the Native tangible evidence that government is something more than a mere tax collector" (Beck, 1974, quoted by Mburu, 1981: 525). Given the high expectations of a politicized working class and peasantry, this populist demand had to be weighed against the élitist imperative urged by the urban middle class.

Kenya's élite inherited a more thoroughly developed apparatus of administration and repression than their counterparts in Tanzania. The new ruling class also had a firm economic base in large-scale land ownership due to the internationally-financed sale of white settler farms to this new élite. (We return to Kenya's land question in Chapters 5 and 6.) Ironically, it was the

60

propaganda value of the simultaneous division of about 14 per cent of this formerly alienated land among some 40,000 landless families (the Million-Acre Scheme) that probably blunted, for a time, the political demands for other tangible "fruits of *uhuru* [freedom]" such as rural health services (Leys, 1975). In addition, the Kenyan peasant was largely semi-proletarianized at the time of independence, and the rural, family-based producer was more dependent on the casual and migrant sale of labour and on the sale of cash crops than in Tanzania. This gave the Kenyan élite both more control over a greater number of ordinary citizens and more sophisticated ways of dividing them and buying them off through the manipulation of pricing and marketing.

Tanganyika's different role in the British colonial political economy meant that there was less economic and administrative infrastructure through which the new élite could control the population. There had been neither a large white settler farm sector nor a large plantation sector. Shivji (1976) suggests that an emergent bureaucratic bourgeoisie was forced to use its managerial control of the government bureaucracy as the principal means of controlling and exploiting the dispersed peasantry, a state of affairs that was not without its contradictions. Rapidly expanded access to health care and to education were about the only immediate benefits of *uhuru* this bureaucratic élite could offer – hence Tanzania's well-known pioneering role in the use of auxiliaries and its development of village-based facilities in contrast with the much slower development of even pilot programmes in Kenya. Such a populist imperative in Tanzania was, however, not only balanced by the urban-clinical élitist imperative mentioned earlier, but by what could be called a bureaucratic imperative. The expansion of access to health services could only take place in such a way that the villagers remained dependent on the state despite the evolution of village-based abilities and consciousness. We will return to these contradictions below in looking more closely at the crisis of Primary Health Care.

CRISIS HERE, CRISIS THERE

Class interests are not the only factors in understanding the evolution of basic health care and the interpretation of health needs. The interaction of these interests in changing international and regional environments has provoked more than one major crisis. Is it not significant that PHC grew and blossomed briefly in the ten years between two of the most severe famines in Africa in this century?

The early 1970s in Africa were years of famine in the Sahel and the Horn. They were years of food shortage and doubt about the stability of food systems in Kenya, Tanzania, Ghana and a number of other countries. National reliance on food imports in an unstable international grain market was already worrying bureaucrats having trouble enough keeping pace with rising expectations in the years leading up to the UN World Food Conference in 1974. Significantly, this was the year that Tanzania created a national Food and Nutrition Commission to monitor the nutritional status of the population, but, as Turshen comments (1984: 201), "without a productive agricultural base in the country, it cannot succeed in correcting poor diets, which are ultimately determined by food availability and purchasing power." If concern on the part of the élite for social peace was insufficient, there was the economic calculus of development benefits and the costs of underdevelopment. The cost of the 1970–71 drought in Kenya, for example, is reckoned to have been around K£ 75.6 million, or ten per cent of the country's GNP for 1971 (Wisner, 1978: 74–92). Since the early 1970s, Third World planners have had these kinds of figures set before them and have been shown studies demonstrating "a return of 150 dollars for every dollar spent" on tuberculosis control, "benefit-cost ratio of 280 to 1" in programmes treating anemic workers with iron, etc. (Golladay *et al.*, 1980: 30–31). Such calculations and the resulting arguments for preventive and promotive health care focused on reducing worker absenteeism and increasing worker productivity.

There were, therefore, many reasons why African governments turned toward PHC. The general combined with the specific, populist with utilitarian. Ten years of "development" had not brought the fruits of *uhuru* to the poor. Rates of death from tuberculosis were actually increasing in Botswana (Colclough and McCarthy, 1980: 223). Malaria, measles and neonatal tetnus killed a million African children each year (World Bank, 1980a: 22). Cholera had swept through many African nations (Stock, 1976). Sleeping sickness and river blindness remained forbiddingly endemic in the isolated hinterlands of a dozen African nations (Wisner, 1976a). Early warnings were being sounded about the "diseases of development" that accompanied irrigation development, resettlement and urbanization (Hughes and Hunter, 1970).

The result was a severe legitimation crisis provoked by the "disappointing decade of development". In the early 1970s, food crises further fuelled the combined efforts of populist and utilitarian elements among the new ruling classes. If more crises were needed to push these governments to find new, low-cost ways of satisfying the health and food security demands of their people, the energy crisis and deepening world economic recession were soon added.

Africa had urbanized rapidly between 1960 and 1970. Not only did this process create and aggravate a series of serious health problems related to poor housing, poor sanitation, changing diets and social conditions (Ebrahim, 1984), but it gave rise to a politically articulate proletariat. Food riots, strikes and demonstrations by doctors, students and workers toppled the Numeiry regime in Sudan; other governments, fearing the same possibility, shaped their health and food policies accordingly.

Refugees added to these strains on the health care systems of Africa's newly independent nations. Although the numbers were not as great as they were to become in the late 1970s and 1980s, already in 1964 the refugee population in Africa was estimated to be 400,000 (Kibreab, 1985: 21). By 1968, the number had grown to 800,000 – a hundred per cent increase. By 1972, when other crises were beginning to bite, there were more than a million refugees, and this number swelled to well over five million in 1980. For some African countries the burden was extraordinary. For instance, in 1980, Somalia hosted 443 refugees for each thousand Somalis; Djibouti played host to 131 refugees for each

63

thousand citizens; in Burundi, Cameroon and Sudan the ratios were 52, 32 and 28 respectively (ibid., p. 26).

How could urban demands be met and rural expectations be fulfilled in the face of inflation and declining crop prices? How could the specific health problems of development schemes and underdeveloped regions be alleviated in the face of declining government revenue in a period of economic crisis? A cheap solution was needed, and this turned out to be the weak form of PHC.

Cheap is Beautiful?

The bureaucratic response to this series of crises was generally two-staged. First, governments made considerable effort to extend basic needs services to rural areas. Second, as the economic and food crises of African countries continued to deepen, elements of the PHC strategy were incorporated into the overall health programmes as part of an effort to extend access and effectiveness at the lowest possible cost. Usually PHC was weakened despite rhetorical commitment to the words of the Alma Ata Declaration; its implementation amounted to little more than continuing with long-delayed and faltering basic service projects in the villages. The contextual concerns of Alma Ata seldom surfaced. In particular, land and labour issues surrounding the local food system, control of other productive resources such as water and marketing, and the work load of women were missing in weak BNA-inspired forms of Primary Health Care. Participation often remained instrumental, not transformative: popular involvement began and ended with the election of a resident to be trained and possibly how he or she would be compensated, or the construction of a local health post or work on a sanitation project.

Botswana, for instance, increased access dramatically (Colclough and McCarthy, 1980: 223–4). In 1973, half the population lived more than ten miles from any staffed health facility. By 1976, three-quarters of the population lived within ten miles of some unit of the expanded health system. Village health posts increased in number from 20 to 280; clinics grew from 45 to 64;

the number of health centres rose from five to seven and the country had seven hospitals. In the course of this push some 63 per cent of the national health development budget was allocated to rural services. About the same time Tanzania began to allocate a third of its health budget to rural services (Turshen, 1984: 200ff), dramatically reversing the hospital bias of its first ten years of independence. Niger, Ghana and the Sudan, among others, committed resources to pilot experiments in rural service enhancement. Kenya's Ministry of Health developed an elaborate and ambitious plan for rural service expansion and training (GOK/MOH, 1972). These plans were reflected in the next Five-Year Plan, but, as we shall see below, they were never fully implemented.

Despite this flurry of activity, UNICEF reported in its 1985 *State of the World's Children* that 75 per cent of Africa's health expenditure and roughly the same proportion of health-related foreign aid was still going to high-technology health care for the privileged urban élite. Citing World Bank and UNICEF sources, Timberlake (1985: 50–51) summarizes a reality that falls considerably short of PHC and Health for All rhetoric:

> Health care of all types gets little government money. Sudan devotes 1.4% of GNP to this purpose; Nigeria, 1.8%. Because GNP in most African countries is so small, the absolute figures are absurdly low. Thus Ethiopia, Burkina Faso, Chad, Rwanda, Mozambique and Zaire spend just $1 per capita on health care. The corresponding figures for Sweden, Canada, France, and Japan are $550, $457, $370, and $171.
>
> But even in those countries where a higher proportion of the nation's money is spent on health (Ghana, 7%; Tanzania, 5.5%; Zambia, 6.1%), spending is likely to be directed at cities rather than rural areas. In Ghana, 40% of the national health expenditure is devoted to specialist hospital care for less than 1% of the population, with a further 45% going to another 9% of the population. Only 15% of the budget goes to the remaining 90%.

Such statistics led a recent UNICEF/WHO panel (1981: 48) to comment that "words abound, but concrete results are frequently thin on the ground". Painting a picture of this weak basic needs approach, the panel added:

> What progress there is seems often to be along conventional basic health service lines, *sometimes extended in a cheaper version in the form of village-based health workers. The scope and depth of community involvement are often doubtful.* The coordination of health and development planning is often poor and intersectoral health-related activities are frequently rudimentary [emphasis added].

Some may justifiably question the commitment to rural health care in the first place. Turshen (1984: 204) notes that Tanzania invited considerable foreign aid in expanding its rural services so that it could leave its urban hospital programme intact. Certainly it became clear as the trade balance, energy and food crises bit harder in the 1970s that "prevention" was quite a bit more expensive than some had thought (Klouda, 1983). In Zambia, for instance, it was calculated that implementation of PHC would cost 15 per cent more than the entire health budget during the 1980s (JASPA, 1981, Vol. 1: 105).

In Nigeria, it seemed unlikely that a strong urban hospital bias and conservative resistance to the political implications of PHC could be overcome despite its oil wealth. Even though money had been set aside for PHC, "in some States, as little as 10 per cent of the total budgeted had been spent by the end of the fourth year of the Plan" (Cole-King, 1981: 144). Wali and Ong Bie (1985: 121) report that no improvement is apparent since the early 1970s in measles, malaria and dysentery in Nigeria's Sokoto State. They describe an ambitious programme in rural health which saw 3,482 first-aid centres established to serve Sokoto's population of seven million (about one centre for every 2,000 people). Lack of back-up funding for drugs and training meant that the attempt was short-lived, however, and it ended in a flourishing black market for drugs and increased control by village heads. Cole-King (1981: 145ff) found that Nigeria's half-hearted PHC plan meant that maternal and child services were even less accessible than dispensaries, although much African experience shows that MCH delivery points need "to be much closer to home than primary medical care if it is to be effectively utilized". Partly as a

66

result, immunization results were poor: the rate of measles vaccinations ranged from only six per cent of the population at risk in Rivers State in 1975 to nearly 41 per cent in Kwara state, with an average coverage of a mere 20 per cent across the 13 states despite the fact that the immunization programme had begun in 1966 (1981: 146–7). Cole-King's conclusion rings true for many African countries: "If the current resource allocation patterns continue, it is difficult to see how the targets for meeting the basic health service needs of Nigeria's population can be met within this century, or indeed the next" (ibid.: 145).

The problem, of course, is not just financial. A strong PHC poses a political challenge. Wali and Ong Bie conclude that PHC has encountered resistance because of "its far-reaching political consequences" since "the fundamental idea underlying PHC is the alleviation of poverty and underdevelopment" and that elements of a "coherent policy to attack the roots of rural poverty" necessarily "attack the foundations of the power system" (1985: 121).

The World Bank voiced a more general sentiment that the cost of social and inter-regional justice in redistributive programmes are "luxuries" until requisite economic growth has been attained (World Bank, 1981b). The Bank's "agenda for action" paralleled that of health ministries, which began to reconsider their ambitious PHC programmes and to seek means of "local financing".

As Fox Piven and Cloward (1971) have demonstrated in a series of historical studies of welfare systems, the health system had been expanded at a time of crisis for the sake of social peace, only to contract when the considerably expanded participation of the labour force in the production of export crops and the sale of labour power made private acquisition of health care theoretically possible. Thus, the World Bank's rhetorical promotion of basic needs since 1973 in no way contradicts its "production first" strategy for the 1980s. The fact that the Bank's BNA consistently took the weak form of minimum income targeting is fully consistent with a long-run plan to draw poor farmers throughout Africa's peripheries into export crop production (Feder, 1976; Payer, 1979; Williams, 1981). The tragic irony of this way of thinking is that about the time these new cash-crop farmers should have been happily buying their "basic needs", including drugs and health care, they faced unprecedented food insecurity due precisely to their incorporation in a system of production for the world market.

The former president of the World Bank readily admits that the process of "economic adjustment" is painful, but pledges the intellectual resources of the Bank to detecting those groups in poor countries most vulnerable to the cuts in health, education and other services that are the bitter medicine these countries must swallow (Clausen, 1985). One cannot imagine a greater distortion of the potential meaning of "basic human needs". The Bank skilfully steps outside of a crisis it has helped to create and adopts the posture of a compassionate bystander. UNICEF echoes the Bank when it proposes "economic adjustment with a human face" (UNICEF, 1985). We return to the Bank's new safety-net approach – the weakest of weak BNAs to date – in Chapter 4.

THE CRISIS OF HEALTH IN KENYA

The story of African health services is mirrored in the Kenyan experience. The government's 1984–8 Development Plan calls attention to its health achievements since independence. Infant mortality is said to have dropped from 120 per thousand in 1963 to 86 per thousand in 1982. The number of health centres in rural areas are said to have increased from 160 to 274 in the same period. A somewhat closer look at these numbers, however, reveals a cycle of recurring crisis and a failure of the state to assure the preconditions for health.

Disaggregating these "achievements" temporally, we find that by the early 1970s infant mortality had improved little since independence. The decade of the 1960s was one of rapid accumulation on the part of Kenya's new élite. Farm after farm in the former Highland reserves fell into the hands of the wealthy, a process which drew a few individuals into a growing rural petty bourgeoisie, but also created many landless families. These now-landless families moved both to the burgeoning squatter settlements in the city and to the margins of arable land to the north

68

and east of the Highlands, where crop failure was highly likely one year in five (Mbithi and Barnes, 1975; Wisner, 1978; Porter, 1979). Rates of moderate malnutrition among children under five in these new refugees were commonly 25 to 30 per cent (Blankhart, 1974). The 1969 census revealed the movement of "marginal people" to such "marginal places" to be the most significant rural-to-rural movement in the inter-censal period (Wisner, 1978), involving around two million of the country's eleven million inhabitants.

Thus a brutal process or rural and urban marginalization was the opposite side of the new coin struck by the newly independent nation. Thirty thousand families (one per cent of the population) were enriched and earned, by the early 1970s, more than K£ 1,000 a year, while nearly 1.5 million households (63 per cent) made less than K£ 60 (ILO, 1972; Wisner, 1978: 268). The lack of progress in bringing down infant mortality, then, can hardly be a surprise.

Similarly, the early period of independence actually witnessed a deterioration in the access rural people had to health services. While 56,000 people were (in theory) served by each of the 160 health centres in 1963, more than 94,000 people were using each of the 131 that remained in service in 1973.

Despite the Kenyan élite's control over its workers and peasants and its consequent ability to delay its response to the "populist imperative", the crisis in health and health service created during the period of Africanization and expansion of the capitalist core of Kenya's colonial economy was ultimately too great to ignore. In 1972, therefore, the Ministry of Health published plans for a significantly expanded rural service and for the training of auxiliary health workers (GOK/MOH, 1972). It is no coincidence that in the same year an ILO employment mission to Kenya published its findings. "Africanization and expansion" – as the land-grabbing and use of the state apparatus for accumulation was politely called – was bound to cause chaos and defeat long-term growth. "Redistribution with growth" was therefore advisable. Prudent counsel for the new ruling class to temper its avarice with a touch of populism was presented in the language of a new development decade striving to distance itself from the failure of the 1960s.

The government of Kenya accepted little of the redistribution

69

package (GOK, 1973), but it did take on board some of the more easily implemented technical recommendations such as the creation of a basic health service network and more integrated rural development activities. Thus by 1978 the population per health centre had dropped to 72,000, and by 1982 there were 274 health centres, or one for each 64,000 inhabitants (Ghai *et al.*, 1979: 35; GOK, 1983: 35).

No doubt the Kenyan state had been rendered more sympathetic to such reforms by the serious food shortages requiring famine relief during 1970–1. Yet though the "populist imperative" became compelling during these years, the expansion of rural health services did not signify the erosion of urban privilege. Rural dispensary and health centre capital investment (much of it in the form of upgrading poorly constructed and maintained facilities from earlier plan periods and the products of "self-help" labour) increased from 14 per cent of the health capital budget (in 1974) to 26 per cent in the period 1979–83 and to 41 per cent in 1984–8. This left 74 per cent and 59 per cent, respectively, for specialist urban facilities (which were substantially in place by 1984). Overall health spending, in any event, had increased from about $3 per capita in 1963 to $8 in 1982, so the total pie was bigger.

Since the mid-1970s there has been a happy coincidence of national and local élite political interests in the "populist" health service. Somewhat alarmed by arguments that accumulation in the early period had taken place too quickly, the national and local élites began to use "self-help" as a form of patronage and as a substitute for meaningful redistribution. In the health sector, Members of Parliament could build on the growing demand for health services by encouraging self-help contributions while dispensing contracts to favoured construction firms and suppliers; central government would be seen as committed to people's welfare at relatively little cost. It is worth recalling Uphoff's advice to the World Bank that since basic needs expenditures are "divisible", "they can be allocated in ways that enhance political support" for the ruling political group (Uphoff, 1980: 7).

Self-help programmes in Kenya have a complex and regionally-varied history (Mbithi and Rasmussen, 1977; Thomas, 1985). Certain smallholders and the rural petty bourgeoisie have

70

been able to win concessions from the urban élite through the mechanisms of "self-help" (Holmquist, 1979 and 1982a). However, as the 1970s progressed – with no real advance in economic redistribution (Livingstone, 1981; Collier and Lal, 1980; Ghai *et al.*, 1979) – local enthusiasm for "self-help" waned. Some Kenyans expressed strong criticism of top-down, officially sponsored *Harambee* (self-help) in a document circulated shortly before the recent unsuccessful airforce coup (anon., 1982: 73; cf. GOK, 1974b, "Ten Great Years for Self-Help in Kenya"):

> Traditionally, all Kenyan ethnic groups had evolved communal organizations for mutual self-help and communal improvement. These were strengthened during the colonial period, and some of them turned into important instruments of resistance. Significantly, none of these democratic institutions were given new life after 1963. Instead, they were replaced by large, centralized bureaucratic bodies which were unresponsive to the people they "served". *Harambee* projects and cooperatives became mere vehicles of exploitation, under the control of an oppressive ruling class.

While less vehement in her criticism, the director of a major PHC pilot project complained of competition with *Harambee* efforts in the project area (Were, n.d.: 78–9).

> As has been observed elsewhere, the way these funds are obtained from the people is not always "freely and voluntarily", thus introducing an element of forced contribution.... On any one day in most rural areas funds are being collected for one Harambee function or another ... it is evident that the burden can become unbearable to rural families who even though outside the cash economy have to contribute to this frequent "voluntary" fund raising.... A certain state of dismay appears to be felt in the society since no public accounting *to the people* is undertaken to explain how funds have been spent in large Harambee fund raising.

The Recent Kenyan Crisis

A second series of crises preceded the adoption, in the 1979–83

71

Development Plan, of a health strategy that sounds very much like PHC and led to a series of ongoing pilot experiments in community-based health care. In brief, these crises – discussed more fully in Chapters 5–7 – reflected the country's economic disintegration. Smaller farmers who had originally benefited from the "Africanization and expansion" of the settler economy, principally those who grew coffee and tea, began to fall behind in real terms as inflation, crop price fluctuation and corrupt cooperative marketing cut away their margin for risk in the late 1970s. What the World Bank refers to as "external shocks" such as energy price increases and falling terms of trade for export crops had been hitting Kenya since 1974. Mismanagement of the economy and staggering corruption made the situation of an increasing proportion of the population more and more difficult. The landless, poor smallholders, pastoral peoples and the urban poor – groups totalling 37 per cent of all Kenyans according to the government's own reckoning (Ghai et al., 1979: 32) – faced severe nutritional problems. Weaning practices were taking a nutritionally dangerous turn, childhood malnutrition remained high and even increased in areas associated with certain export crops and contract farming and diarrhoea as well as malaria remained the chief killers of children (GOK, 1977; USAID, 1982).

Above all, the "achievement" of infant mortality decline (from 120 per thousand in 1963 to 86 per thousand in 1982) was clouded by class and regional differences. Rates as high as 166 to 222 per thousand can be calculated from the 1979 census for such densely-populated, impoverished labour reserves as the western districts of Kisumu, Siaya, South Nyanza and Busia as well as in four coastal districts and two districts in the northern portion of the Rift Valley. Eleven districts of the western part of the country, the arid north-east and the semi-arid eastern Foreland Plateau have 1979 rates in the range of 121 to 165 per thousand. Against this are results for all districts in the Central Province and five others with rates less than 90 per thousand.

The Kenyan élite faced, therefore, an even more serious crisis on the eve of the end of its second decade of independent rule than it had at the end of its first. Health and nutritional status is bad. Food shortages are chronic, making the import of grain a

72

necessity despite good harvests in 1977 and 1978. Inflation is making it difficult for urban families and an increasing proportion of rural families to purchase food, clothing and essential services. The extended network of area and family health services lacks adequately trained staff, sufficient drugs, transport, referral and supervision and is failing to make a serious dent in the morbidity and mortality associated with the main poverty-related causes: lack of food, poor sanitation and lack of vector control. A regression analysis of factors associated with infant mortality convincingly demonstrates that malaria, mother's literacy and access to fertile agricultural land were most closely associated with the immediate survival chances of infants (Kibet, 1981).

In these circumstances the Kenyan government is understandably attracted to the PHC approach. But, as in the case of "self-help" in the earlier phase of expansion of the health care system, it is interested in PHC only on its own terms. First, due to the extreme rigours of the Kenyan economy during the ten years since the first oil price shock, the new "integrated rural health" strategy has got to be inexpensive, especially in running costs. Thus despite the increased capital outlays on rural health infrastructure discussed earlier, the share of *recurrent* health budget has fluctuated around ten per cent since 1974, and the most recent 1984–8 Development Plan keeps it that way.

Lack of sufficient ongoing funding had been one of the reasons why the earlier expanded area and family health approach had not been effective despite reasonable levels of "coverage" in some cases (65–70 per cent of pregnant women and 55–60 per cent of newborns, for instance) (USAID, 1982: 216). A survey in 1973–4 found 25 per cent of health centres, 37 per cent of health sub-centres and 60 per cent of dispensaries had no piped water; 82 per cent, 78 per cent and 89 per cent respectively, had no electricity; two-thirds of these rural facilities had "no specific method" of disposing of waste water and sewage (Ghai *et al.*, 1976: 36). Much of the increased health spending went into upgrading health facilities. However, funding constraints continue to hamper the functioning of some rural units, especially those built with self-help efforts. Commenting on a self-help dispensary in one of the most central and highly developed parts of the country, one study team (Göricke and Spiegel, 1976: 42–4) note in 1976:

> The almost completed buildings are often in very bad condition, already showing the first signs of serious deterioration. This is mainly due to the lack of financial support from the Government which was supposed to complete the work started by Harambee. It seems to be especially difficult for Harambee to provide a stable financial source for the needed equipment and the payment of staff. ...

The 1979–83 Plan envisioned improving 91 health centres against constructing five new ones – further evidence that the problem of health care quality persists (Ghai *et al.*, 1979: 131). In 1980, Were (n.d.: 10) observed that "many such potential Harambee health centres remain incomplete or unoccupied". She also noted that because of the irregular supply of drugs and vaccines to local health centres, visits with children for immunization became "a hit or miss gamble".

One view of the "new" adherence to such PHC ideas as "community participation" is that the burden of compensating the primary health worker is transferred to the people themselves. This well may be seen as a continuation of what one Kenyan observer has called the "rhetoric-implementation gap" (Mburu, 1979).

Pilot Community-Based Health Care in Kenya

Community-based care (CBHC) in Kenya is part of a two-pronged approach that depends on a continuation of conventional clinic-based curative service (plus some increases in mobile immunization and health education from health centres) and the newer community-based activities focused on a village health committee, village health fund and a locally-chosen primary worker trained and supported by a team of professionals (Ghai *et al.*, 1979: 131; Were, n.d.: 8–10; GOK, 1979b). This "community health care team" is supposed to consist of the public health officer, an enrolled community nurse, the community development assistant and the family field education officer. The spatial-administrative organization of this sytem, known in the 1984–8 Development Plan as the "integrated rural health and family

74

planning programme" (IRH/FP) was to have been the "rural health unit" (RHU) from 1978–9 onwards. The country was divided up into 258 RHUs with populations ranging from 10,000 to over 100,000. The target was 50,000 per RHU (Were, n.d.: 23), which was supposed to focus on a health centre and a series of satellite sub-centres and dispensaries.

Whatever else this reorganization and incorporation of "community participation" signified at the time, the moves are consistent with the picture of interplay among populist, élite and bureaucratic imperatives in response to the series of interlinked crises described above. The government speaks clearly of the need to "increase alternative financing mechanisms" (GOK, 1983: 153–4) through "maintenance of health facilities through harambee efforts", "community-based health care", "establishment and improvement of amenity wards", and "selective charges for hospital out-patient and in-patient medical services". While the class content of the last two clearly refers to the relative power of the urban élite and "working poor" in the rapidly growing primary and secondary towns, reference to Harambee and CBHC reflects urban-rural and intra-rural struggle over available resources.

This new organization was also supposed to expand family planning dramatically. The 1970s reinforced a Malthusian view on the part of Kenya's élite and their state planners. Kenya's high population growth rate became a frequently mentioned "brake" on growth even before it was known to be considerably higher than the estimates used in preparing the 1979–84 Development Plan (GOK, 1979b: 15; cf. GOK, 1979c: 8):

> Much of our increased national output since Independence has gone to provide necessities for our larger population, limiting the goods and services available for improving the quality of life. Increased pressure on scarce supplies of good land, higher risks of environment destruction, and the social problems that accompany large scale rural–urban migration, are all affected by our high rate of population growth.

Kenyan women have an average of 8.1 live births as they pass through their child-bearing years, according to the World Fertility Survey (GOK, 1980b). This so-called "total fertility

75

rate" and an annual population growth rate of over four per cent are quite high by world averages. What role has population growth actually had in undermining basic needs in Kenya and what role has it had attributed to it by a government facing a number of crises? This is not the place for a full discussion of the role of Malthusianism, but we can note that the new initiatives in CBHC are a sub-programme within a major ministry programme (IRH/FP), the three aims of which are reducing rates of mortality, morbidity *and fertility* (GOK, 1983: 154, emphasis added). To be sure, family planning (in the context of maternal and child health care) appears as one of the elements of PHC approved at Alma Ata, and rightly so. However, family planning can be integrated into community health in either coercive or liberatory ways (Gutto, 1980; Raikes, 1985). Family planning can increase women's control over their fertility or can subject them to outside control. In Kenya birth control has become a highly charged political issue among rural people already deeply suspicious of the élite who, for two decades have diverted the fruits of *uhuru* (this diversion is another reason for the scarcity of resources in a growing population).

A Recent Kenyan Case Study

The National Pilot Project on Community-based Health Care, sponsored by the Ministry of Health with UNICEF assistance, reveals many of the contradictions arising from a weak interpretation of the BNA. This case also reveals certain potentials of a strong interpretation. The programme was located in Kakamega District in Western Province and ran between 1977 and 1980. As noted earlier, Kakamega has one of the highest infant mortality rates in the country.

Poverty is also endemic in Kakamega, where outright landlessness is less a problem than the fact that farms are too small to support peasant families, also called in international circles "the land poor" (Ghai *et al.*, 1979: 26; Lenton and Silliman, 1985). In one of the pilot areas crop land per household was 0.28 acres (Were, n.d.: 32). For the district as a whole, the average holding was 1.4 hectares in 1979, which contrasts with the three hectares calculated to be necessary for a family to live above the poverty line (GOK, 1980c). Historically Kakamega has functioned as a labour reserve, and many men still migrate to towns and other rural areas in search of a living. In 1976, remittance wages were estimated to be more than K£ six million (GOK, 1980c: 15). In other words, the district's income from wage remittance almost equalled the value of its total agricultural production (K£ 7 million), came to twice the value of the first-ranking crop, sugarcane (K£ 3.3m) and was greater than the income from sugar, maize and beans (K£ 5.8m). Roughly one-third of the district's households are headed by women.

The pilot project established some 92 health committees in villages ranging in size from 70 to 376 households. Most committees took from four to twelve weeks to be formed and were preceded by a long series of preparatory studies beginning in 1973 and by considerable discussion which started with Provincial and District administrations and worked its way down to the level of local chiefs.

The committees chose community health workers (CHW), who were trained, given drugs and dressings and were paid a small amount from the proceeds of a small community health fund and income from health services. Working in the villages, these women functioned as a clinical resource in cases of malaria, scabies (a skin disease), intestinal worms, discharging eyes, and diarrhoea and vomiting with mild dehydration (Were, n.d.: 81). For more serious ailments – pneumonia, neck stiffness, bloody diarrhoeas, persistent coughs and convulsions – patients were referred to the nearest health centre. The health workers seemed to be very well accepted. They also had considerable success in referring high-risk pregnancies (using a checklist) to the antenatal services. Less successful were CHW efforts to encourage visits to the nearest child welfare clinic, probably because of the irregular availability of drugs and vaccines (Were, n.d.: 97). The percentage of women using contraceptives in the communities rose from eight per cent to 34 per cent between 1979 and 1980 (Were, n.d.: 96).

The aspect of this pilot experience that comes closest to the contextual and participatory core of strong PHC is the discussion and prioritization of community health problems by the 92 committees and community-wide meetings as well as local

77

fundraising, self-help and individual actions taken on these priorities. A definitive list of health problems, ranked one to ten, was developed by the communities, which then listed possible solutions corresponding to each of the ten problems. The communities decided that their most serious ailments were (Were, n.d.: 88):

(1) malaria
(2) diarrhoea
(3) measles and whooping-cough
(4) intestinal worms
(5) pregnancy-related diseases
(6) childbirth problems
(7) general body/joint pains
(8) homestead/environmental/water-related
(9) short birth-interval problems
(10) special needs of school-age children

A total of 52 proposals, as shown in Table 2.2 (at the end of this chapter) arose from discussions at the village level. These included diverse actions such as filling in potholes to eliminate mosquito breeding, and encouraging of breastfeeding. The critical question from the point of view of a strong BNA is whether this community action developed to the point of focusing on the roots of poverty.

There are, of course, a number of fairly obvious constraints on the ability of poor women in Kakamega to carry out most of these actions. Again, looking at Table 2.2, we can see what these constraints are: time, money and the accessibility of resources such as water or fuelwood. Chapter 7 will look in detail at the way in which such constraints interact to produce a situation of "basic need conflict" symptomatic of the underlying problems of powerlessness and lack of access to resources. Did the community health pilot project generate discussion and action concerning such constraints? Did it address the fundamental problems such as women's status in their families and the community and poor women's lack of power? The decision "to get all children immunized against measles and whooping cough in the first year of life" (Item 3a, Table 2.2) provides us with a good example. It is also a good case in point since it belongs to the major campaign launched recently by UNICEF, to be discussed at length in Chapter 4.

We are told of one obstacle: "Availability of vaccines seem variable from one year to another" (Were, n.d.: 97). As a result, the immunization results for the 92 communities (with a total of 5,393 children) were not as impressive as some of the other achievements. Attendance at child welfare clinics actually fell from a baseline 26 per cent to 12 per cent between 1977 and 1979, but rose again to 41 per cent in 1980. Did the communities discuss the vaccine problem? Did this become an issue of ministry mismanagement, or local corruption, or of regional neglect in the eyes of the people? Did they demand better service? Did they take the issue to their MP? We are not told anything about such "second order" community action, that is, action following reflection on the unsatisfactory outcome of a prior action.

In other cases, there is evidence of secondary action. Of the immediate actions listed as a result of community brain-storming about "special needs of school-age children" (Item 10, Table 2.2), we find two concerning diet and nutrition: "parents to ensure children had porridge rather than the current preference of tea for breakfast" and "parents to provide or organize some midday meal programme". We are not told the outcome of these two resolutions, but the report does say that the frequency of ownership of kitchen gardens in the 92 communities rose from 27 to 63 per cent (1980), frequency of mixed cropping from 25 to 68 per cent, and poultry-keeping from 27 to 82 per cent (Were, n.d.: 98). It seems that early collective action in organizing a school feeding programme collapsed, and that the response was to attack the unresolved issue of nutritional improvement from a more individualistic perspective. That may have been a reasonable tactical decision; the immediate nutritional results are still impressive: the prevalence of severe malnutrition (weight/age less than 60 per cent of standard) fell from 11 per cent to zero between October 1977 and March 1979 (Were, n.d.: 102). One must ask, what more could have been achieved if the community had continued collectively to demand an adequate school feeding programme?

A Zimbabwean case is suggestive. There, mothers had been

directly involved in screening children and in administering emergency food supplements in the rural areas that had suffered during the last year of the liberation struggle. When emergency feeding was stopped, they decided to continue with a food supplement programme. In their study of their own limited means and the available community resources, the mothers decided to request land from the local chief where together they could grow peanuts for enriching the maize porridge provided at midday in the school. This action led to unity and continuity in the group of mothers, who went on to define and address other health and nutrition problems (Sanders, 1985a). In another example in rural Lesotho, parents reacted to perceived misman-agement of school feeding supplies by primary school teachers by demanding more direct community control of the school as well as systematic democratization of the notional village develop-ment committees (Inqui, 1984).

Collective action can be difficult and lead to uncomfortable confrontations. Whether this feature of collective endeavour will cause groups to forgo major breakthroughs in the future, repeated reports from such rural projects tell us that without dramatic results, collective action is the first component to wither away. The typical danger is that the village health worker becomes a low-level clinical practitioner while committee and community action comes to a halt. It would seem, therefore, that the issue is not choosing between strong or weak BN approaches in health, but choosing either a strong approach that manages to maintain group commitment or having no programme in the end because the weak approach has led to the degeneration of health initiatives into the individualistic *status quo ante*.

The Kakamega pilot project seems to have suffered that fate, according to one account (Willms, 1983: 6): "Since its inception in September 1977, this CBHC has also witnessed the demise of community participation and involvement and a shift in CHW orientations from disease prevention to curative and clinical concerns." The Provincial Commissioner of Western Province, meanwhile, regretfully noted that "The people started out with much enthusiasm but in some places are slowing down. This leads to: (a) irregular, sometimes poorly attended community health committees; and (b) poor community efforts in things like carrying stones for protection of springs" (ibid.). Likewise, the project directors have voiced their concern that they have not yet found the key to what they term "a self-sustaining mechanism" (Wan'gombe, 1980: 34, cited by Willms, 1983: 6).

Another, more recent, Kenyan experiment in CBHC shows a similar problem with continuity. The project, located in Siaya District of Nyanza Province (Kaseje, 1980), confronted the highest infant mortality rate in all Kenya and a history of extreme economic and political marginalization within the national system.

In emphasizing the "marginalization" of these western regions of Kenya into migrant labour reserves, the heterodox, non-modernizing spirit of the strong BNA is clear. "Modern" African societies are not supposed to emphasize their regional and ethnic disparities. That is "tribalism" and is a taboo subject. But can the poor in Kakamega and Siaya Districts of Kenya effectively organize themselves for health unless the process of community health mobilization addresses the fact of ethnic and regional disparities, if only as an initial stage of local health struggle? One also has to ask why it is that radically participatory initiatives often decline when official bureaucracies do extend into former peripheries. Speaking of a scheme of PHC controlled by local people in southern Zimbabwe, Sanders (1985b: 212) notes that "with this extension of the central State to local level, and through the resources available to District Councils, the popular committees have become in many instances marginalized."

A former director of WHO's Division of Strengthening Health Services seems to support this view, although he is quick to recognize that "to some people, in the health field, such ideas may be strange, objectionable, or absurd" (Newall, 1975: 192). In characterizing such a "contextual" view of health improvements, he points out that:

> expressions of community action will inevitably follow if you proceed in a reasonable way and take the wider issues into account. The wider issues ... include productivity and sufficient resources to enable people to eat and be educated; a sense of community responsibility and involvement; a functioning community organization; self-sufficiency in all

81

important matters and a reliance on outside resources only for emergencies; an understanding of the uniqueness of each community coupled with the individual and group pride and dignity associated with it; and, lastly, the feeling that people have a true unity between their land, their work, and their household.

CONCLUSION

Primary Health Care has had the seeds of both strong and weak BNAs within it from the start. Health is a popular demand by Africans still waiting for the "fruits of freedom". As implemented, however, PHC in Africa has seldom allowed health to become the arena for increasing community consciousness of the roots of poverty and the contextual pre-conditions for health. The potential for a strong BNA in health remains, although economic and political crises in Africa combined with the ambivalent position of the ruling élites – pushed by contending élite, populist and bureaucratic imperatives – have resulted in a big question mark over the PHC in Africa.

Partly in response to the uncertain future of PHC, a series of short-cuts to health improvement have been put forward. The next two chapters study these short-cuts as examples of a variety of weak BN strategy one might call the "campaign" approach. First we look at single issue campaigns for improved water provision and campaigns focused on housing standards. Later we look at UNICEF's major new campaign, the Child Survival Revolution that focuses on a small number of technical innovations including increased immunization coverage, growth monitoring and administration by parents of liquids to children suffering diarrhoea.

Table 2.2

VILLAGERS' LIST OF ACTIVITIES TO SOLVE IDENTIFIED HEALTH PROBLEMS

(*Indicates practice included in UNICEF's GOBI package discussed in Chapter 4)

(**Letter codes refer to time, money, fuel, water and housing constraints on adoption discussed below and in Chapter 7)

1. MALARIA
   a) To reduce mosquito breeding by filling up potholes that hold stagnant water near the homestead and in the neighbourhood. (t = time constraint)
   b) To have a CHW in the community to give advice on treatment of malaria illness in children. (t, m = money constraint)

2. DIARRHOEAL DISEASES
   a) Practise personal hygiene, especially washing hands. (m)
   b) To keep cooked food clean and well covered when not eaten right away. (t, h = housing space constraints)
   c) To keep flies from residences by removing things which may attract them, such as dirty dishes, which should be washed and kept in a dishrack. (t, m, h)
   d) To build and use latrines that have covers, so that flies do not come from faeces to food. (t, m, h)
   e) To protect drinking water sources and encourage people to defecate only in latrines so that water is not contaminated. (t, m)
   f) To keep cattle from drinking water sources and people from bathing at the drinking water sources by constructing places for these functions downstream. (t, m)
   g) To encourage breastfeeding and cup or bowl and spoon or clean fingers feeding and discourage the use of a bottle.* (t)

83

    h) To feed weaning infants a well-cooked soft food made up of various food types. (t)

    i) To have a CHW in the community to teach mothers about prevention and treatment of diarrhoea.* (t, m, w = water constraint)

3. MEASLES AND WHOOPING-COUGH

    a) To get all children immunized against measles and whooping-cough in the first year of life.* (t)

    b) To keep children in good health.

    c) To have a CHW to advise if the disease occurs. (t)

4. INTESTINAL WORMS

    a) Everybody to defecate in latrines.

    b) To wash anything raw before eating it. (w, t)

    c) To cook meats for long periods. (f = woodfuel constraint)

    d) To wash hands before putting anything into the mouth.

    e) To use shoes whenever they can be afforded. (m) [This protects feet from contact with some parasites.]

    f) To have a CHW to advise on treatment of worms in those who have them. (t, m)

5. PREGNANCY-RELATED PROBLEMS

    a) To have CHW who can screen those who may have problems during pregnancy and delivery according to the high-risk checklist.

    b) Husbands are to encourage [wives'] attending antenatal screening by the CHW or Health Centre Clinics. (t)

    c) All mothers are to be made aware of those things that tend to lead to trouble in pregnancy and delivery so as to recognize them and seek help.

    d) To encourage proper diet during pregnancy. (m, l = land)

    e) To encourage proper attendance at a clinic or health centre in case of illness during pregnancy. (m – if only for transport, t)

6. CHILDBIRTH PROBLEMS
   a) To encourage those with any problems during antenatal screening to deliver in a health centre or hospital. (m, t)
   b) To encourage the practice of clean birth procedures including washing hands before assisting in delivery and good care of the umbilical cord.
   c) Recognition of obstructed labour and the need for immediate transfer to a hospital. (m)
   d) Importance of recognition of and immediate transfer to hospital of cases of retained products of conception and any excessive bleeding or unusual observation after birth. (m)
   e) The immediate care of the newborn.
   f) The importance of breastfeeding.*

7. GENERAL BODY/JOINT PAINS
   a) Observation by CHW for any evidence of swelling or pain and referral to hospital in those cases. (m)
   b) Reassurance and dispensing of aspirin by CHW.
   c) Referral to health centre or hospital if complaints continue. (m)

8. HOMESTEAD, ENVIRONMENTAL AND WATER RELATED PROBLEMS
   See Chapter 3.

9. SHORT BIRTH-INTERVAL PROBLEMS
   a) Problems resulting from short birth intervals to be presented and discussed as understood by the people.
   b) Health consequences to mother and child to be discussed.
   c) Other consequences, e.g. land availability related to family size, to be discussed.
   d) Traditional patterns for regulating birth intervals to be discussed.
   e) Outline of types of modern contraceptives to be discussed and encouragement to attend family planning clinic for instruction and service. (t, m)
   f) To investigate possibilities of "bringing some family planning methods to the village".

85

10. SPECIAL NEEDS OF SCHOOL-AGE CHILDREN
   a) Parents to ensure children had porridge rather than the current preference of tea for breakfast. (t, m)
   b) Parents to provide or organize some midday meal programme. (m)
   c) Parents to look out for evidence of poor growth* and poor health such as scabies, and refer child to CHW or health centre.

Chapter 3

Short-cuts Can Be Hazardous To Your Health: Campaign Approaches to Water Supply, Sanitation and Housing

We have seen that primary health care was a reaction to non-comprehensive, fragmented approaches to the health problems of poor people. Chief among these approaches was the tradition of hospital-based curative medicine inherited from colonial Africa. Chapter 2 traced the interaction of contradictory political imperatives that have shaped the reform and preservation of these élite urban systems of health care in many African countries, certainly in Kenya.

The damaging effects of technocratic "know-how" are most obvious in the history of curative care. But the same story is true elsewhere. Public health has a double history, too, which demonstrates a parallel set of strong and weak possibilities. As a system of class control over the rapidly urbanizing mass of European workers, the "health police" (*Gesundheitspolizei*) have been active in Europe from the nineteenth century. Foucault's notion of "bio-power" of the state over our bodies is developed in his accounts of the evolution of European hospitals (1975) and prisons (1977) and controls over sexuality (1979). As with the other previously mentioned more philosophical issues surrounding basic needs, there is no room in this book to do more than signal the importance of extending such analysis to the colonies of Europe.

Such a top-down approach to public health was carried over to the colonies in Africa, where the purpose of the earliest campaigns against smallpox and cholera was to prevent white supervisors from being infected by African mine and railroad workers. During the First World War, Africans in the Carrier Corps suffered appalling mortality rates from water-borne disease, influenza and malnutrition (Ferguson, 1980). The colonial response was to launch single-issue campaigns against malaria, smallpox, etc., which became common from the end of the Second World War onwards. As mentioned above, early attempts to put such campaigns into the context of comprehensive, basic services later led to the understanding that community-based PHC was required.

Yet campaign approaches remain. Today these campaigns focus on water supply, sanitation and housing, three issues that have interacted with the emerging philosophy and implementation of PHC in complex ways. In some cases, struggles over water and housing have mobilized African communities; certainly the housing question arose early as a focus of trade union militancy. But in other instances, investments in water supply and site-and-service self-help housing have been used as a "quick fix" to defuse demands for broader economic reforms.

Making matters even muddier is the fact that during the Basic Needs Decade water supply and housing provided two key foci for international meetings and initiatives that resulted in programmes, secretariats and even agencies. The UN Conference on the Human Habitat and the UN Conference on Water were but two more expressions of this Decade and of the same mild-to-moderate critique of growth modernization that gave rise to the PHC conference in Alma Ata, the World Food Conference, the World Employment Conference, The Cocoyoc Declaration and the Decade of Women.

The polarization of interpretations of water and housing into strong (politicizing, mobilizing) or weak (top-down, technocratic, mystifying) basic needs approaches was never far away. The implementation of projects inspired by these international meetings took place both within basic service and PHC programmes and in parallel efforts. As it has become more and more apparent that PHC in its most comprehensive sense has been thwarted (for the internal and external reasons discussed in Chapter 2), it has become clear that, at least in some African countries, it is really only in these parallel water supply and housing projects that the forward movement of popular participation has been maintained. Thus it is possible, and probably necessary, to see water and housing projects in two ways: as points of social conflict which are now taking up some of the popular support that weak PHC programmes have lost; and simultaneously as potentially state-organized diversions of that same popular energy.

A HOLE IN THE BUCKET? REFLECTIONS ON THE WATER DECADE

The strong BNA has very seldom been implemented because of its politically challenging nature. In every sectoral need-approach (health, water, food, etc.), there are potentially two strong demands: local production for local need, and local definition of "need". The first leads logically to the demand for a New International Economic Order (NIEO). The second soon leads people who are engaged in defining their own needs to a perception of the obstacles to satisfying those needs. They become clearer about gender, ethnic and eventually class contradictions. Since the industrially powerful nations (the donors) are very little interested in the NIEO and since the élite regimes in Africa are very little interested in popular demands, there has been a tacit agreement between the internationally-powerful donors and the locally-powerful state aparatniks that the BNA should only be implemented as a series of unrelated programmes for the provision (a word which strongly suggests the familiar top-down orientation) of water, food, shelter, health care, etc., sector by sector, population group by population group. In the form of a de-politicized shopping-list, this basic needs strategy amounts to little more than new accounting and budgeting techniques for state planners. There is little chance that the "sectors" would come together in the more troubling form of "self-reliance"; nor is it likely that the population groups being provided for would begin to see common interests among themselves (e.g. among the rural and the urban poor).

By the early 1980s the shopping-list approach had succeeded in defusing the BNA. In its watered-down version it has been vulnerable to mounting criticism from the World Bank and the

IMF of public expenditure and unproductive investment. Some evidence of the Bank's retrenchment from even a weak basic needs approach is presented later in this chapter and in the next.

The crowning achievement of the shopping-list approach was the late 1970s' "mega-lists": "Food for All", "Rural Energy for All", and "Health for All" are typical of the slogans created in a number of UN agencies. This chapter seeks to show that the mega-shopping-list consistently overlooks the fundamental political dimensions of development and underdevelopment. This is true no matter what sector is concerned: whether they are in shelter, education or food security, projects suffer the same tendency toward political sterility. Our focus here is the International Drinking Water Supply and Sanitation Decade, but much that is said could be easily applied to other recent visions of a better fed, sheltered, educated or healthier humanity.

Slogans such as "health for all by the year 2000" or "1981–1990, drinking water and sanitation decade" serve a variety of useful functions in mobilizing popular political support for donor activity, focusing national planning activity, clarifying anew the disastrous state of the world and by their sheer wishfulness highlighting the enormity of the task. It is pointless to criticize these slogans, or to explain why their goals will not be achieved. A more useful exercise is to consider current water supply projects and the international guidelines that seek to move such activities "beyond palliative measures, seeking long-term solutions that focus on ways of releasing under-utilized resources" (WHO, 1981b: 5). The problem of community water supply has been systematically misconceived. Water Decade authorities such as WHO diagnose the problem as one of ineffectiveness in the provision of water. They describe an administrative problem, the difficulty of "extending coverage", when "there seems always to be a shortage of trained manpower", and "systems are not maintained", and when "institutions and agencies ... become overstretched", "financing ... is inadequate", and "there is little coordination of water-supply development, sanitation and public hygiene" (ibid.). Against this view we can argue that a more basic problem is one of the control of water, not merely the ineffectiveness in provision. The problem, in brief, is political not simply administrative.

90

Internal Policy Contradictions

Water Decade goals must have as their context the pattern of day-to-day water use as well as a whole series of governmental intrusions into these patterns. Chief among these are pre-existing domestic water supply programmes, livestock watering schemes, large-scale hydro-engineering works, irrigation initiatives and resettlement programmes. Although water is obviously a vital, though "silent", nutrient as well as an essential means of production (Oyebande, 1975), it is not at all clear that the treatment water has received as a basic need in Africa is consistent with human welfare or with a radical BNA.

"Normal" Domestic Water Use

In rural Africa, women and children are for the most part responsible for collecting water for domestic purposes. Although average per capita daily consumption of water is low by urban European standards – about 10 litres versus 100–200 (White *et al.*, 1972) – patterns of water-use are quite complex. Even in quite dry environments, women know of multiple sources of water which they rank according to various criteria: quality, taste, distance and physical as well as social accessibility. The last concerns social relations between the user and other users, between user and people whose land must be traversed to reach the water, and, in some cases such as Botswana, the relations between the user and the owner of a water source.

There is evidence that the management of domestic water and the decisions women make surrounding it are just as rational and complex as the management of water in rural production, of soil or of vegetation (Beyer, 1980; Roundy, 1985; Richards, 1985). In fact, viewed from the perspective of rural women, such management of multiple needs for water, shelter and food form an interdependent, interacting system, a point we take up in Chapter 7.

African water use is virtually always "multiple use". It can be used simultaneously for food processing, washing, drinking, stock-watering and small-scale irrigation. Where this is the case, systems of social regulations control, for instance, access by livestock, ensure culturally-agreed standards of maintenance and cleanliness and mobilize community labour for maintenance and extension of the systems. Ruthenberg (1971) identifies thirteen indigenous African systems of irrigation without even mentioning the dozens of indigenous irrigation systems based on the retreat of flood waters (Harrison-Church, 1974; Bradley *et al.*, 1977). Outside interventions seeking to "improve" water management for single purposes – be it domestic water supply, livestock watering or irrigation – have generally tended to destroy the control of local communities over their formerly integrated water resource systems.

Pre-Decade Water Schemes

These patterns, and the history of colonial and post-colonial state water supply, form the context of the Water Decade's campaigns. Reviews of pre-Decade programmes emphasize their high cost, poor maintenance and resulting short lifespan (Saunders and Warford, 1976). It has also been suggested that a large number of such water schemes were thrust upon communities whose priorities may have been elsewhere (Tschannerl, 1975). What Chauhan and Gopalakrishnan (1983) conclude from their careful village study in India could be said for many villages in Africa. They call attention to a profound difference in perceptions and consequent priorities: water planners perceive clean water and adequate sanitation as a basic human need and believe that the technology for delivering these is cheap and simple and that the benefits are obvious. The village poor, however (1983: 55):

> have their own equally clear perceptions of basic human needs, and of the benefits of improved water supply and sanitation. Earning enough, from employment or land, to buy more and better food for the family and to build a more durable house, are considered fundamental. Sanitation and even health are not.

Since it is the weakest of the weak approaches to basic needs, a single-issue campaign has no way of adapting to community priorities when they differ from those of the campaign planners. This problem is not just one of differing world views or perceptions (e.g. a "modern" versus a "traditional" outlook). The campaign does not address whole functioning systems. It addresses symptoms and not causes. Thus Chauhan and Gopalakrishnan ask whether, with such campaign approaches, the poor can ever be healthy. In the same spirit a recent review of water programmes in Kenya concluded (Agarwal *et al.*, 1981: 117) that "[e]ven in the most inaccessible areas of Kenya, water supply is unlikely to improve the livelihood of people without attention also being paid to such issues as cattle diseases, minor roads, health centres and sewerage facilities at the same time."

Livestock Watering Schemes

Though water is essential for human life and for productive activities, great damage has been done to Africa's environment and therefore to the long-run ability to meet basic needs through single-purpose water schemes. The history of stock-watering wells and boreholes in Africa is bleak, and (Timberlake, 1985: 94) the maintenance record is even worse. Moreover, unplanned concentrations of stock caused by drilling new supplies has often led to overgrazing and desertification (Galaty, ed., 1981; Sandford, 1983).

Often the distribution of new stock-watering points is determined by and superimposed on a highly unequal pattern of livestock ownership. This can make it even more difficult for the poor to satisfy their basic needs since access to productive resources becomes even further skewed. Such is the case in Botswana, for instance.

Fifteen per cent of Botswana's population own three-quarters of the nation's cattle (Colclough and McCarthy, 1980: 112), and this fifteen per cent has actively lobbied for the extention of water supplies into potential pasture lands. Over the past two decades it has, on the whole, received encouragement from the state. Expansion of boreholes into drier areas has unleashed a cycle of exploitation and degradation in one area after another. Botswana has been left overstocked with cattle, overextended into marginal sandveld pastures, with little hardier pastureland in reserve than when (in the mid-1960s, early 1970s and again in 1979–80) severe drought conditions prevailed (Cliffe and Moorsom, 1979).

The direct negative economic and environmental effects of such water and pasture mismanagement are obvious enough, but they are not the focus of this chapter. The *indirect* effect of the livestock bias in water development activity has been to *politicize all water supply questions* in Botswana.

Ownership of boreholes, wells, hafirs and other water sources has become privatized outside towns and villages, and efforts to improve access of the poor to domestic supplies has involved complicated negotiations with owners. Fortunately Botswana is better set up for such decentralized project work than others thanks to the relative strength of its District administrations and remaining traditional councils (*kgotla*). In fact, despite these complex problems of water rights, the government had been able by the end of March 1982 to include 33 per cent of the rural population in water schemes.

The situation is eased by the fact that 20 per cent of the people of Botswana live in 17 large villages (all covered by government schemes), 13 per cent live in another 337 rural villages (of which 128 were already included and the rest scheduled for government schemes by 1989) and 16 per cent live in towns. Some 225,000 people (24 per cent) live on cattle posts and freehold farms, where the problems of water rights is most acute and where the government assumes that "the totality of this population is served either through private boreholes or through boreholes provided by private associations such as syndicates, religious groups and welfare organizations" (Government of Botswana, 1982: 20).

Whatever Botswana's degree of success in meeting Water Decade goals, two things are clear: first, success comes despite complications created by capitalist penetration; secondly, the interaction of local political economic organization and the global beef market has produced conditions within which a simple administrative approach to achieving the goals of the Water Decade is impossible. Water issues have been politicized once and for all.

Large-scale Hydro-Engineering Works

Many of the astounding human welfare failures of water resource management in Africa are due to the lack of a comprehensive approach to water. This is not the result of a technical error. The fragmentation of water planning mirrors the fragmented, indeed quite conflicting, patterns of class interest in water. Large-scale

94

hydro-electric dams in Africa have caused the forced resettlement of at least half a million people during the last twenty years. On the whole, these uprooted people have not benefited from the impoundment of Africa's rivers, but have suffered disease, famine and profound social disorganization (Scudder, 1980). Women have suffered particularly (Rogers, 1980). The beneficiaries have been urban middle-class consumers of electricity, contractors and investors.

In a class society, the needs of the rich and powerful are more important than the needs of the poor. Thus planners have not dealt with the various uses of water – for drinking, stock-watering, power-generating and irrigating – in accordance with the numbers of people dependent upon each use. Sanitation and health components are added on to major hydro-engineering and irrigation projects in Africa (Lee, 1985). When ordinary people – tenants on an irrigation scheme, for instance – vote with their feet and meet their own needs by drinking pesticide-laden water from irrigation canals, scholars suddenly discover "non-agricultural uses of irrigation systems" (Yoder, 1981; Jones, 1981).

The contrast between water provision (the Water Decade perspective) and water control (the radical needs perspective) in irrigation schemes is profound. The relationship between large-scale irrigation and the spread of water-borne disease has been well-documented in Africa for some time (Hughes and Hunter, 1970), and recent studies confirm that these disease problems are increasing (Bradley, 1977; Hunter *et al.*, 1982). As in India and Central America, Africa is experiencing a resurgence of malaria, a major killer of children (Chapin and Wasserstrom, 1981; Grant, 1985b: 114).

But isn't the Water Decade supposed to be about the positive connections between water and health? Can the provision of water, as in Decade schemes, balance the negative health consequences of those situations where irrigation water is not controlled by workers for health and profit, but by state bureaucrats who attempt only to maximize profit?

Ethiopia provides a striking example of the damage irrigation projects can do. In the early 1970s, Afar pastoralists began to lose large amounts of their dry season riverine pasture to newly irrigated cotton fields. A few years later, their drought reserves

95

taken from them in this way, 25 to 30 per cent of the Afar population in the Awash valley died in a terrible famine (Bondestam, 1974). Today, some of the survivors – grown tired of trampling the cotton with their herds and, fighting the authorities, and resigned to the changes – work as casual labourers on the irrigation schemes. A recent UN study of disease transmission and environmental vector control at one of these sites found that the irrigation system was designed and managed in such a way that excess water was simply diverted into an open field around which the Afar labourers lived, and which became a major site of disease transmission (PEEM, 1984: 3).

What list of basic needs would emerge from a dialogue among tenants of such schemes? Or among wives of tenants (Hanger and Moris, 1973)? Or among groups of casual labourers such as the *fellatta*, who work for tenants on Sudan's Gezira scheme (Barnett, 1981)? There have already been reports of tenants' strikes (Conti, 1979) over conditions and prices and of "passive resistance" by tenants trying to adapt the new systems to their needs (Wallace, 1981; Sorbö, 1977; Ali and O'Brien, 1984). Some farmers have gone so far as to refuse to join such schemes (Adams, 1981). The chances are that a radical needs dialogue would produce a water-control plan significantly different than that of both the irrigation authorities and Water Decade officials.

Resettlement Schemes

By now there are few who doubt that Tanzania's original idea of the *ujamaa* village as the core of a strategy of rural self-reliance has become something quite different. Numerous studies have documented how the bureaucratic élite have used the creation of villages as a means of controlling rural producers and extracting surplus through marketing channels (Raikes, 1978 and 1982; Boesen *et al.*, 1977; Freyhold, 1979; de Gennaro, 1981; Coulson, 1982). Simultaneously, participation in the form of popular control and initiative has been systematically undermined. This is the case, for example, in the Ruvuma Development Association, where locally initiated actions were emerging from radical needs discourse in 14 villages (de Gennaro, 1981: 129–38). Other examples are the Lushoto Integrated Rural Development Project (Matango, 1979), and, again, the Mbambara village, one of the earliest *ujamaa* experiments. In all three cases attempts at investment and farm planning were crushed by regional "experts" (Wisner *et al.*, 1975: 384–8).

While resettlement of 80 per cent of the rural population into something over 6,000 villages by 1976 moved some people closer to water, others were moved away from their preferred sources (Raikes, 1983). In the new villages, water provision projects were top-down and plagued with mechanical breakdowns even before Tanzania was hit by external financial shocks (Tschannerl, 1979).

The issue of context and control becomes very clear from one extreme and well-documented case. Following the flooding of the Rufiji river in 1969, the whole population living in the floodplain was resettled (with considerable coercion) to a series of fourteen new villages on the northern riverine terrace. These people's livelihood had depended on a complex soil, crop and water management strategy adapted to the seasonal river flood, a system known as "recessional" or "flood retreat" irrigation that is common to many parts of Africa. Malnutrition of children, dietary changes and social adjustment problems all compounded each other as the resettled farmers tried to learn to work in their totally new environment with only the crudest, mechanistic advice from extension agents (Angwazi and Ndulu, 1973; Sandberg, 1974; Turok, 1975). It is the reality of such enforced lack of control over their own lives and environments by ordinary African farmers that challenges the narrow "guidelines" of the Water Decade.

Resettlement is not necessarily harmful, of course. One recent study in Mozambique, for instance, found that of 40 new villages in the dry northern Cabo Delgado province, 33 had been sited in such a way that women had better access to water points than before resettlement (Swain, 1982).

EXTERNAL SHOCKS

The Water Decade does, in all fairness, call for an integrated approach to water as a basic need. In addition to the internally inconsistent national policies that form the context of Water Decade planning, considered above, external shocks such as war and foreign financial pressure play havoc with the ability to respond to that call.

War and Militarization

War in Africa and the preparation for war divert scarce resources, primarily foreign exchange and skilled people, away from development activities. Many African governments spend a high proportion of their budgets on weapons (e.g. Mozambique and Chad, 30 per cent; Ethiopia, 40 per cent) and an even higher percentage of total imports are weapon purchases (30 to 60 per cent of all imports in Cape Verde, Somalia and Uganda). Government expenditure on weapons exceeds that on agriculture in Nigeria, Mali, Niger, Ethiopia, Senegal and Burkina Faso. Imported weapon systems are becoming more and more expensive, and the heavy deforming influence of such imports on these economies is increasing rapidly (Shindo, 1985; cf. Tinbergen, 1977: 26–8, 387–92; Kaldor, 1978).

War also destroys infrastructure from hydro-engineering works at one extreme to village wells at the other. War-time refugees make up much of Africa's refugee population, estimated to number four million in 1979 (Adepoju, 1982: 21) and five million in 1981 (UNHCR, 1981). These people place urgent demands on the water and sanitation facilities of their host countries, which in turn can distort development plans in those countries by, for example, compelling investment in urban rather than rural water sources.

The reader may object that war, like environmental hazards, cannot be considered part of the "normal" context of development planning. Hurricanes, droughts and floods disrupt development projects, create refugee populations and create their own subsequent health hazards (Cuny, 1983). They share many of these characteristics with the effects of military activity, but neither war nor natural disaster, the argument runs, can be included in a rational framework for basic needs provision.

In fact, war has become lamentably frequent in Africa. It is no longer an anomaly; like environmental hazards and national budgetary crises, the effects of war are felt increasingly and must be dealt with. As one school of thought concerning environmen-

98

tal disasters argues, the suffering of the very poor during droughts or floods is merely an intensification of their normal state of vulnerability. In Africa it is striking that the marginal populations at greatest risk to drought and desertification are often to be found in precisely those geopolitical border zones most vulnerable to cross-border attack (e.g. Mozambique's dry south-western frontier with South Africa, southern Angola and the Ogaden) or the destructive "search and destroy" activity associated with state response to separatist or other armed movements in or retreating to a country's peripheral zones (e.g. Eritrea, western Sahara, northern Namibia and the Karamojong area of Uganda). If such disruptive forces affect water supplies, calls for their serious consideration cannot be dismissed as "special pleading".

Somalia

Somalia is a case in point, although one could as well discuss Ethiopia, Uganda, Chad, Angola, the Sudan or Mozambique. This country's recent Five Year Plan (1974–8) gave little attention to the provision of reliable water supplies to its rural, mostly nomadic population. An ILO report to the Somalia government criticized the plan's strong urban bias, uneven regional distribution of rural projects and poor implementation record (JASPA, 1977: 399–401). The following Three Year Development Plan (1979–81) was also highly skewed: roughly three-quarters of water sector expenditure was to go to the cities (Somali Democratic Republic, 1979). At first glance this situation of limited government ability to implement, poor maintenance and urban bias seems precisely the type criticized by leaders of the Water Decade. Was the problem, then, as Decade critiques would have us believe, simply administrative?

During the years of the first plan Somalia was dealing with a serious drought that displaced thousands of nomads in the north-central zones. Considerable government effort was directed at integrating some 200,000 of these drought victims into irrigation schemes in the valleys of the Shebelli and Juba rivers and into coastal fishing activities at five sites on the southern coast (World Food Programme, 1980). No one knows how many drought victims swelled Somalia's towns and cities, but given the well-

known family links between Somalia's urban and rural populations (Lewis, 1978), the number must have been large, adding
pressure for urban water supplies. The second plan period
suffered from an even more traumatic event: the Ogaden war and
its aftermath.

The war between Ethiopia and Somalia in the Ogaden
produced two great waves of refugees, one in 1977–8 and another
in 1979–80. With continued hostilities and disruption in other
eastern and southern parts of Ethiopia outside the war zone, the
refugee population increased to 1.3 million in the spring of 1981.
The refugees were accommodated in some 32 camps in four parts
of Somalia and supported by massive international aid shipments. The wider significance of this influx for Somali planning
is only partly captured by the numbers. Nearly one resident in
every three is a refugee, if government figures are accurate, but
more to the point, possibly half of these – certainly several
hundred thousand – have not settled in the camps, but are living
with relatives in the towns, placing both urban and rural water
supply systems under profound stress.

Urban refugees reinforce the pre-existing urban bias in water
planning. On the other hand, rural camps, many of which are in
the flood plains of the Shebelli and Juba river systems, raise a
series of interrelated environmental management problems
among which domestic water use and sanitation find their places.
These problems include the risk of flood (some camps on the
upper Shebelli were flooded in 1981) and devegetation for fuel in
the areas surrounding the camps, which in turn adds to run-off,
drainage problems and turbidity of surface water. Added to this
was the sometimes ill-advised desire to irrigate land near the
camps in efforts to supplement refugee food supply. By March
1981, emergency camp water supplies were being provided by
international organizations, but no one was taking an overall
"water control" or a broader environmental management view
of the problem.

The presence of the rural (or officially recognized) refugees
created local environmental pressure that also affected the host
population. As in many refugee situations, the reluctance of the
host government to view the refugees as long-term residents has
hampered an integrated approach to their health and sanitation

100

needs as well as their ability to produce some of their own food. Meanwhile, camp populations near regional towns make use of markets, schools and other facilities, adding further strain. That strain can only be reduced by planning in an integrated way for both host and refugee populations (Kibreab, 1985), but this would require a political decision by the Somali authorities to accept the likelihood that the refugees cannot soon be repatriated.

The political nature of the kind of basic need provision envisioned by the Water Decade is starkly revealed in such an extreme situation. The increasing frequency with which African governments must face one sort of crisis or another means that guidelines and frameworks couched in purely administrative language are in many cases irrelevant.

The "extreme" or "exceptional" disaster has become the norm in Africa. The chances are great that a nation attempting to work toward the goal of universal access to safe, adequate and reliable water by 1990 will, during this decade, confront a war, environmental disaster, an influx of refugees or catastrophic drop in the world price of one of its principle exports. Such situations immediately throw administrative-seeming water programmes onto the political agenda.

Foreign Financial Pressure and Investment

One does not have to agree with dependency theories of underdevelopment to recognize that large foreign concentrations of capital and capitalist markets for African products and labour disrupt, distort and otherwise help to define "development" in Africa. Water programmes seeking to achieve the goals of the Water Decade take place in this economic environment.

In Tanzania, for instance, international finance capital has compounded the internal policy contradictions already described. Lesotho's water system is shaped by its total dependence on the export of male labour to South Africa. In Kenya, multinational corporations and the state continue to invest in irrigation schemes prejudicial to health.

Tanzania

The major agent of international finance capital is the International Monetary Fund (IMF). Besides channelling loans itself, the IMF has a large role in defining the credit-worthiness of Third World countries seeking commercial loans. Over the last few years credit-worthiness has increasingly depended on a country's adherence to a package of fiscal policies laid down by the IMF – the IMF's policy of "conditionality". These conditions usually include a wage freeze, the devaluation of the national currency, the elimination of subsidies on basic goods and food and a reduction in public sector spending.

Doubts have been raised concerning the IMF's use of conditionality to dictate economic policy in the Third World. (Daniel, 1981; Castro, 1984: 77–94; Manley and Brandt, 1985). President Nyerere of Tanzania, rejecting what he saw as "IMF meddling", said (Nyerere, 1980: 5): "My government is not prepared to give up our national endeavour to provide primary education for every child, basic medicines and some clean water for all our people." In fact, by the late 1970s Tanzania was doing better than many countries in providing the clean water to which the President referred, despite the problems in its development programme.

In 1971, well in advance of the Water Decade, Tanzania adopted two specific and ambitious goals (Van Der Hoeven, 1979: 26):

- to provide a source of clean and potable water within a reasonable distance of every village by 1981 as a free basic service; and

- to provide a piped water supply to the rural area by 1991 so that all people will have ease of access (a distance of 500 metres) to a public domestic water point.

Although the first goal was not met, one study thought it possible that the 1981 targets could be met by 1990, on schedule from the point of view of the Water Decade (Van Der Hoeven, op. cit.).

In the five years between 1971 and 1976, the percentage of the rural population served by government water schemes increased

102

from 13 to 25 (Van Der Hoeven, op. cit.: 27). The World Bank commended Tanzania in its World Development Review for 1980 for managing to provide basic water access, education and health care to a large proportion of its people (World Bank, 1981a).

Since then, however, foreign debt and trade imbalances have forced Tanzania to cut water programmes. Between early 1981 and mid-1986, Tanzania and the IMF were locked in negotiations over a loan package with conditions that would not cause the Tanzanian people to suffer (Biermann and Wagao, 1986). Ironically, however, Tanzania itself had to introduce an austerity budget during this difficult period that began to bite into its water supply programme. With the current IMF agreement, public expenditure will be even more tightly constrained and the goal of "water for all" by the year 1990 will recede even further. According to Green and Singer (1984: 115):

> In many cases deferred maintenance from 1974–5 was never fully made good and arrears increased rapidly after 1979. As a result many infrastructural and directly productive assets cannot be utilized at capacity or are available only intermittently (e.g. in Tanzania up to 50% of rural water systems have been out of operation for significant periods each year since 1980).

The official basic needs-oriented development strategy for Tanzania (JASPA, 1982) is appropriately called *Basic Needs in Danger*. The section on water correctly points out significant improvements in access between 1968–9, when the *Household Budget Surveys* found 68 per cent of its sample using "lake, river, riverbed, spring" for water and only 28 per cent using "shallow wells", and 1976–7, when only 34 per cent reported using "lake, etc." and some 34 per cent had access to "shallow wells". The increase in access to "pipeline and tap outside" was from seven to 18 per cent. Yet the same report says that water programmes are faltering and that there is an "urgent need to rehabilitate water supply schemes which are in poor condition".

Lesotho

This small, mountainous country is completely surrounded by South Africa. Income earned by Basotho working in South Africa totals more than the country's entire GDP (Feachem *et al.*, 1978: 199). Over half of rural households have a member in paid employment at any one time and half report receiving remittance income (ibid.: 18). In one village sample in 1976, the majority of households produced fewer than five bags of grain from their own fields. The resulting market dependency for food is mirrored on the national level by a dramatic decline in grain production, from three million to only 1.6 million bags between 1950 and 1970 (ibid.: 19; cf. Murray, 1981: 1–36).

The remaining agricultural activity, such as it is, is concentrated in relatively few large holdings where livestock ownership and grain production appear correlated. The majority of households, many of them female-headed, depend on income from beer brewing and from wages sent by spouses in South Africa (ibid.: 20–1).

Lesotho is well supplied with springs. It is estimated that most villages have one or more perennial sources of spring water within a few hundred metres (ibid.: 25). Government programmes have attempted to protect these sources from fecal pollution. Indeed, Lesotho has been cited as one of the African countries where Water Decade activities have been most successful (UNDP, 1984: 3). None the less, water-related diseases are on the rise, as the results of one study show (Feachem *et al.*, 1978: 175):

(1) Water-related disease is a significant component of reported disease in Lesotho, especially in under-fives.
(2) Diarrhoeal disease and infectious skin disease are the main types of reported water-related disease.
(3) There is a very marked degree of wet season peaking of diarrhoeal disease and typhoid.
(4) Villages with improved water supplies are similar in their water-related disease picture to other villages.

The researchers concluded that "water supplies as presently constructed and used in Lesotho have little impact on health".

104

Moreover, they found that village self-help activity in water supply improvement did not result in any "spin-off" of economic or social activity (ibid.: 199). In their words, "the Lesotho village economy ... is not one in which any kind of development 'take-off' can be induced by measures such as the installation of water supplies" (ibid.: 24).

Why such a bleak picture? The researchers attribute it to the complete domination of the local economy by neighbouring South Africa. They point out that studies of diarrhoeal disease in South Africa have also shown that the improvement of water supply alone does little to reduce the prevalence of infection (ibid.: 174).

The reasons for this are evident. Both black communities in apartheid South Africa and village areas of majority-ruled Lesotho have low, externally-dependent incomes, female-headed households, considerable beer brewing under unsanitary conditions and reliance on purchased food. Mothers on both sides of the border tend to bottle feed their infants with widely advertised commercial preparations (WHO, 1983). Under these conditions, children are chronically malnourished and have less resistance to infection. Furthermore, the children come into contact with organisms producing diarrhoea through unsanitary preparation of breast milk substitute.

In both cases the agricultural, industrial and mining sectors of South Africa's capitalist economy rely on black migrant labour. The cumulative effect of such labour recruitment has not been the "trickle-down" of prosperity, but the creation of conditions in which basic needs goals such as those of the Water Decade are made nonsensical. Here again one sees how a set of narrowly administrative guidelines for the Water Decade leaves the real problem untouched.

In addition, the extreme dependency created by the migrant labour system seems to provoke social fragmentation that makes cumulative self-help activities based on a radical BN dialogue in homogeneous interest groups all the more difficult. This is borne out by both Feachem's conclusion that social and economic "spin off" from water activities were not forthcoming and a recent FAO study questioning the development role of Lesotho's Village Development Committees (FAO, 1985).

Kenya

In planning and administrative terms, Kenya's approach to domestic and livestock water needs falls well within the Decade guidelines. Kenya is one of the 25 African countries that had produced such plans by the middle of 1984 (UNDP, 1984: 3). A Water Master Plan and provisions in the 1979–83 Development Plan included the aims of improving sources of water to roughly four million urban and four million rural dwellers by 1983 (Ghai *et al.*, 1979: 128; Masakhalia, 1979: 216–17), covering slightly less than 30 per cent of the rural population.

The corresponding rural coverage in Tanzania in 1982, at least on paper, was 40–42 per cent (JASPA, 1982: 102). It is important to note, however, that the UNDP has criticized excessive reliance on figures as a measure of achievements (UNDP, 1984: 4–5), and that such numbers are obtained by drawing circles on population maps and aerial photographs. In Tanzania, for instance, it was found that only 25 to 75 per cent of the "covered" population was actually using a particular water source (JASPA, 1982: 102).

The capital costs of installation have been reduced by providing only primary water systems, leaving secondary and tertiary distribution up to local initiatives organized by the District Development Committees. In contrast to earlier water programmes, emphasis is on communal water points rather than on individual house connections and metered provision. The earlier system did not benefit the poor (Agarwal *et al.*, 1981: 117), but the present system lacks ongoing funding (Ghai *et al.*, 1979: 129).

To meet its national goal of water for all by the year 2000, Kenya must find at least $500 million of foreign funding – about a third of the total sum required during the period 1980–99 (Ghai *et al.*, 1979: 128). Thousands of semi-skilled and skilled workers would have to be trained for water service installation, inspection, maintenance and planning (Ghai *et al.*, 1979: 129–30).

By the end of 1979, under phase one of the rural water supply programme, 72 projects had been completed and were now serving 395,000 people. This modest progress has caused Kenyan planners to rely even more heavily on "participatory" modes of implementation. Self-help projects organized around existing

Table 3.1
STAFF REQUIRED FOR KENYAN DOMESTIC WATER PROGRAMME

Staff category	Requirements 1977	1999
Inspectors and assistants	120	1,878
Operators	350	4,550
Artisans (repair)	n/a	5,690
Planning, design and construction	258	2,000
Technical, foremen and artisans (construction)	131	1,040

Source: Ghai *et al.*, 1979: 129–30

women's groups began in the wake of initiatives by UNICEF and twenty-five NGOs after International Women's Year (Gachukia, 1979). This social focus for efforts was taken up by Water Decade coordinators (UNDP, n.d.) and by Kenya's Ministry of Health, at least in an experimental way. What one has to ask is whether "participation" is simply a way of getting cheap labour during the world economic crisis. Such "instrumental" participation will not produce the spin-offs Feachem was hoping for in Lesotho. "Transformative" participation (Kruks, 1983; cf. Oakley and Marsden, 1984; who contrast "instrumental" and "empowering" participation) on the other hand would lead beyond water schemes. Water Decade administrators have reported a good deal of "community participation" in African water projects since 1981, much of it focused on women's participation. Has this "participation" led people to uproot the causes of poverty?

In answer to this question, and in fairness to the Kenyan state, UNICEF and rural development workers, let us consider one of the best documented cases, Kakamega District's pilot community-based health care experiment.

This pilot project took care to establish highly decentralized structures for participation. Women were unusually prominent in these discussions; planning groups established their own view of local health priorities and the steps they could take to deal with them (Were, n.d.). In this way ten homestead, environmental and water-related interventions were identified locally, including three directly related to water sources (Were, n.d.: 91–2):

(1) To get a latrine constructed in every household and used by everyone to stop the spread of worms, and pollution of water sources;
(2) To get a dishrack constructed and used in every household so as to keep dishes off the ground;
(3) To keep grass cut and drain stagnant water places, clear homestead of containers in order to get at the place where malaria-carrying mosquitos hide;
(4) Keep house roofs repaired to keep out rain, have all new houses built with windows and maintained in good repair;
(5) To get rid of domestic insects, e.g. bedbugs, through improved home cleanliness and health service;
(6) To keep the corral of domestic animals away from the living houses in order to cut down on mud, dung, and flies close to the people;
(7) Protection/repair/improvement of water sources and the paths that lead to them;
(8) People to be discouraged from bathing at water source, but if they do, to bathe downstream and keep the source free of human waste;
(9) To protect at least one permanent spring per community;
(10) To encourage boiling of drinking water.

Preliminary results suggested that developing such a programme with local people was highly rewarding: in October 1977 only twelve per cent of communities had cleaned-up water sources; by April 1979 the figure had reached 77 per cent and by January 1980 it had grown to 81 per cent (Were, n.d.: 95). During the period 1977–9, moreover, health in the experimental area (population over 17,000) improved as measured by reduced infant mortality, reduced clinical malnutrition, and reduced numbers of helminth ova in people's stools (Were, n.d.: 99–104).

Were these improvements due only to better water supply? We can see that the answer is "no"; the changes, based on community action, had been far-reaching, involving increased access to and use of antenatal and vaccination facilities, poultry-keeping and vegetable gardening, and use of latrines, to mention a few. This, of course, highlights the point made in the case of Lesotho – that water provision in isolation is seldom able to change the health situation.

And for how long did the benefits last? Clearly in the short term peoples' health improved. In the long term, however, as we mentioned earlier, the Kakamega pilot project deteriorated into a project set on service "provision". Community involvement all but vanished, as did the project's associated preventive and health-promotive features. Armed with merely an instrumental view of participation, the project lost its dynamism and effectiveness. Once again, the weak BNA degenerated into a sectoral shopping-list.

One must also weigh the short-term health benefits of the stronger BNA against the damaging and rapidly increasing role of large-scale irrigation in Kenya.

The relationships between foreign companies, international finance and the state are diverse and complex in Kenya (Swainson, 1981). Their interests alternately conflict and complement each other, involved as they are in varying ways in the production of sugar, tea, tobacco, pineapples, beef, cotton and rice. The last two commodities are produced under the National Irrigation Board (NIB) on large, capital-intensive irrigation schemes in several places in Nyanza and Eastern provinces. Labour is provided by male tenants (who have a contract with the NIB) and their wives and dependants.

These NIB irrigation schemes raise once more the point that comprehensive water *control* must be the focus of the Water Decade if the health benefits of improved provision are not to be taken away by disease hazards produced by mismanagement. Particularly worrying is the increase of malaria endemicity associated with some of these schemes (Abok, 1982) and the possibility of explosions of schistosomiasis (bilharzia) in others (Dalton, 1982).

Kenya ambitiously plans to expand large-scale irrigation under the Tana and Athi River Development Authorities Lake Basin Development Authority and the Kerio Valley Development Authority (see Chapter 5), yet it lacks legislation that would oblige these authorities to undertake health impact assessments (PEEM, 1984b: 64–5). The NIB is supposed to provide anti-malarial drugs to all women and children on the Mwea Tebere scheme, the largest in the country, but this remedial approach is suspiciously like closing the stable door after the horse has bolted. Moreover, there is no clear evidence that women and children are getting the pills. In any event, data on the health and nutritional status of children on the Mwea scheme, presented in Chapter 5, suggest that the problems at Mwea are far too severe to be cured by a pill. One recent survey reported that the population of Mwea has to attend clinics outside the scheme area in order to enjoy health care (PEEM, 1984b: 65).

Conclusions about Water

The campaign approach to health improvement through the provision of water supplies doesn't wash. It has been shown to be deficient in several ways. First, single-issue concentration on domestic water provision and sanitation does not take into account the integrated nature of water resource use in Africa. Second, since issues of control over resources and conflicting interests among groups in society do not enter Water Decade campaign thinking (built, as it must be, on "consensus", "harmony" and the illusion that development is not conflictual), its water projects do not challenge the roots of poverty or, therefore, the roots of ill health. Third, even when the campaign approach has managed to tap popular enthusiasm – as have the women-focused water campaigns in Ethiopia, Kenya, Lesotho, Mali, Nigeria, Tanzania and the more general community-based, participatory programmes in Sudan, Uganda, Rwanda, Gambia, Burundi, Burkina Faso and the Central African Republic – participation is usually "instrumental" (UNDP, 1984; Yansheng and Elmendorf, 1985). It is short-lived, not transformative. It seldom gives groups the insight, skill and self-confidence to take their energies – and their political demands – on to other needs and issues.

What the Water Decade has accomplished is to open the way for the strong BNA both politically and technically. In political terms, water has now been the explicit focus of attention long enough to enable advocates of the radical BNA to assert people's right to decent water supplies. Scientists and technicians working under the sponsorship of the Decade have produced a number of useful and efficient low-cost pumps, latrines and drilling techniques. Like the simple technologies advocated by UNICEF in its GOBI package (see Chapter 4), these technologies do not, in themselves, constitute a strong BNA. On the contrary, they can be used as the instruments of both strong and weak approaches. Nonetheless, water does not flow uphill, and the most insightful and committed dialogue about needs and obstacles at village level will not make it do so. The technology is therefore a necessary, though not sufficient, condition for a self-sustaining BNA.

WHAT CAN SELF-HELP HOUSING ACCOMPLISH? A ROOF OVER AN EMPTY POT? A FLOOR UNDER POVERTY?

The Record So Far

Another single-issue campaign was launched in 1976 by the World Conference on Housing and Habitat. That spawned a UN Center for Human Settlements and a campaign for 1987, "the year of shelter for the homeless".

Five years after the Habitat conference, researchers at the International Institute for Environment and Development published an evaluation of the degree to which Habitat's recommendations, widely accepted by delegations to the conference, had been implemented (Hardoy and Satterthwaite, 1981). Their overall assessment was that while there was evidence of increased attention to urban development problems in the seventeen countries chosen for review, implementation of Habitat recommendations was piecemeal, some being "virtually ignored". Table 3.2 summarizes their judgement of the implementation of six major Habitat recommendations. The four sub-Saharan African cases in the sample are underlined.

111

Table 3.2

POST HABITAT IMPLEMENTATION: SELECTED COUNTRIES

	Priority to improving living conditions, especially for poorest	Encourage and support self-help	Clean water and sanitation for all	Realistic standards for housing and services	Control land speculation	Development plans to include a realistic settlement policy
Bolivia	0	0	–	0	1	2
Brazil	0	1	3	–	1	2
Colombia	2	3	2	3	3	0
Egypt	1	2	1	0	0	2
India	2	3	4	–	1	0
Indonesia	1	3	2	3	0	1
Iraq	–	0	2	0	–	–
Jordan	1	0	–	0	0	2
Kenya	2	3	3	1	1	2
Mexico	2	–	3	–	3	3
Nepal	2	1	2	–	–	2
Nigeria	2	0	2	0	2	0
Philippines	2	3	2	1	0	2
Singapore	4	0	4	–	4	4
Sudan	2	4	–	4	4	1
Tanzania	4	4	3	3	4	3
Tunisia	4	1	3	2	4	3

KEY

5 = fully implemented

4 = strongly implemented

3 = partially implemented

2 = in national plans but little or no implementation

1 = under consideration, or minor policies in force

0 = no evidence of action or of proposed policy changes

– = data not available

Source: Earthscan, 1981: 6

The main reasons given in the report for the failure of governments to take a comprehensive approach to housing are, first, the technocratic belief that improvements in habitat can be made without major changes in economic structure, and, secondly, that governments have not aggressively entered the political struggle over urban space on behalf of weaker political agents. In example after example, the report showed that governments failed to take into consideration the spatial consequences of their economic policies (pp. 212–16). Where planners *had* tried to reverse the concentration of population in older centres of industrial growth (in Mexico, Brazil, India and Tanzania, for instance), ambitious settlement plans had not been linked to effective control of industrial concentration. With few exceptions there was little evidence that structural changes in the economy were seen as a pre-condition for solving urban problems.

In a similar way Hardoy and Satterthwaite document widespread continued urban bias in housing programmes (1981: 218–20). They found this bias in country programmes as well as in the pattern of international aid in housing. This not only means that rural housing improvement is very seldom included in post-Habitat programmes, but also that the smaller urban places have seldom been recipients of housing improvement aid.

Continued industrial concentration and urban bias seem to have spanned the period of most intensive emphasis on "basic needs" in a wide range of specialized UN agencies, not just Habitat. Now, in the 1980s, at a time when the World Bank is explicitly disavowing spatial equity as a development goal in Africa, the truth seems to be that the approach of radical spatial and social redistribution has actually not yet been widely attempted where human settlement policy is concerned.

But can we afford to wait for total political and economic change before we tackle poverty? Cannot a pragmatic approach to development work effectively within the major structural limitations? The answer is "yes", but only where development is understood as continuous political struggle. Hardoy and Satterthwaite describe such struggle in the urban context (1981: 232):

All growing urban areas have conflicts of interest between the various groups seeking land for specific uses – from the

113

lowest-income groups seeking accommodation close to possible sources of income, to a multi-national seeking a site for a new factory, to an individual seeking to invest in urban land (and leave it undeveloped) since this gives a non-depreciating investment which rapidly grows in market value (in real terms). The major conflict in most urban centres was found to be between the private landowners and the housing needs of a large portion of the population. Another major conflict is between the public authorities in their efforts to control and guide the settlement's growth and those who operated contrary to public regulations: by squatting; by selling illegally subdivided land; by setting up commercial or industrial operations contrary to an area's zoning regulations; by individuals or enterprises construct-ing buildings contrary to official standards.

Hardoy and Satterthwaite also found that since the Habitat conference few countries had aggressively entered into this political struggle over urban space to shift the advantage from higher to lower income groups through increased state control of land, regulation of land markets, increased taxation to control speculation, etc. Some countries had increased state control of urban land (e.g. Tanzania, Nigeria and the Sudan), but on the whole private interests continued to avoid urban property taxes and to distort urban land prices through speculation in such a way that forced the poor to squat illegally. The authors further argue that in this context many of the recent site-and-service settlements in Third World cities are precisely a way of avoiding the need to challenge private landowners' right to the continually rising value of urban land (McAuslan, 1985). As a result, 30 per cent or more of the populations of Nairobi, Mombasa, Ibadan, Port Sudan, Tunis and Dar es Salaam still live in slums and squatter settlements, much as they did in the pre-Habitat 1960s and early 1970s (Hardoy and Satterthwaite, 1981: 232–3).

In addition, public housing remains priced out of the reach of lowest-income groups. Also the numbers of units built lag greatly behind announced targets. Under the 1974–8 Development Plan, the Kenyan government was to provide 60,000 serviced sites or core houses and the National Housing Corporation was to build

40,000 two-room units, four-fifths of them for lower income groups. The 1979–83 Plan, however, commented calmly that only eight per cent of these low-cost units had been completed and these had been built at an average cost of five times the original estimate. Of the 160,000 units said to be required during 1974–8, no more than five per cent had been built by the government (Hardoy and Satterthwaite, 1981: 176–7).

Although Hardoy and Satterthwaite note a growing acceptance of the need to improve squatter conditions and approaches to site and service projects, standards – often dating from colonial times – remain unrealistically high, and the cost of building material, much of it imported, is high. With the era of "cheap" energy gone, even locally-produced cement is increasing in price (Agarwal, 1981).

Little has been done to stimulate the "informal" construction industry in these cities (Hardoy and Satterthwaite, 1981: 257–8), although these groups of artisans (the Kenyan *fundi*, for instance) and school-leavers could provide the basis for a great expansion of house construction if standards were adjusted, low-cost material industries encouraged, and the domination of the larger construction companies broken.

Self-Help Housing: Limits to its Potential?

Although self-help housing remains experimental in contrast to more conventional public housing in the Third World, Hardoy and Satterthwaite and other commentators note that the self-help approach is on the rise. In both Tanzania and Algeria, local people have been encouraged to help design improved low-cost housing through a variety of techniques which translate perceived needs into professionally-drawn plans (Magobeko, 1976; Noui-Mehidi, 1976). There have also been attempts to mobilize urban-dwellers to improve their homes and neighbourhoods in Mali (Deyoko, 1976), Zambia (American Friends Service Committee, 1976), Tanzania (Hardoy and Satterthwaite, 1981: 182–5) and Kenya (Hardoy and Satterthwaite, 1981: 176–8). A few programmes have tackled the housing problem by giving support to the smaller, less organized construction firms of the "informal" sector, as in the Sudan (Hardoy and Satterthwaite, 1981: 45–7), or by financing housing in novel ways. Tanzania's Workers and Farmers' Fund, for example, channels a tax of two per cent on the wage bill of all employers with more than ten employees into housing improvement (Hardoy and Satterthwaite, 1981: 183).

The most socially complex experiments in self-help have involved the participation of urban-dwellers in neighbourhood groups that have a say in planning decisions. In Zambia (American Friends Service Committee, 1982) and Mozambique (Pinsky, 1980) such groups have had a role in deciding which local structures had to be demolished to make road and water main improvements possible. A similar approach has been taken in Ouagadougou, Burkina Faso, where people evicted by the opening of new roads were allocated plots on the basis of community group decisions.

As encouraging as some of these reports are, there have been equally important worries often voiced by the same workers who report partial success. Despite the high level of initial participation in a squatter improvement project in Lusaka, Zambia, for example, there has been little success in mobilizing former participants to maintain earlier self-help works (such as water systems) or to pay service fees (American Friends Service Committee, 1982). Moreover the demand for wages for construction work has grown with time as the percentage of home-owners has dropped and the percentage of tenants has risen (114–15).

In other instances, projects can exacerbate the inequalities within the poor. As Wolfe puts it, there are "seeds of exclusion in all forms of organization" (Wolfe, 1982: 102). Participatory home and neighbourhood improvement in Nairobi or Lusaka may end up shifting rent exploitation down the socio-economic ladder, giving poor home-owners the chance to exploit even poorer lodgers, or by increasing the existing urban bias in state investment to the further exclusion of poor rural groups (Nelson, 1979: 289–90; Sandbrook, 1982: 241–2).

Still others recognize "dilemmas of participation" in the very fact that individuals are asked to undertake costs (in, for instance, most infrastructure projects) while *groups* (including some "free riders") enjoy the benefits (Bryant and White, 1980: 16–20). In urban upgrading, for instance, certain houses usually have to be destroyed in order to align roads (Mozambique: Pinsky, 1980; Zambia: Martin, 1983). Many benefit, but some suffer.

Some observers of the self-help process go as far as to argue that the danger exists that such programmes give authorities a way of forestalling more fundamental demands for the reform of economic and political systems (Coutsinas, 1976: 180; Sandbrook, 1982) or even that self-help movements are in fact often controlled by élite elements (Ng'ethe, 1980).

None of this criticism is particularly new, of course. Colonial powers were wary of the potential political power of urban Africans (Hake, 1977; Worger, 1983; White, 1983). Stren (1970: 64–6) recounts how unrest among railway workers as early as 1939 in Mombasa was explicitly linked to the cost of accommodation. The resulting report to the Labour Commissioner spoke of a "state of emergency" sparked by high rents pushed up by the demand for housing. As Africa's colonial cities matured, wariness, physical segregation and physical control evolved into more sophisticated strategies of control (Hake, 1977). Thought was given to the minimum needs of the urban working class, although most official concern centred on "law and order" and the need to contain the influx from the countryside (White, 1983). Is the weak BNA, as represented by Habitat's self-help housing campaign, simply a yet more sophisticated stage in the evolution of social control of the energies of the poor majority by the élite minority?

Critics of self-building (Turner and Fichter, 1972) argue that self-help housing not only fails to treat the causes of urban poverty (Coutsinas, 1976) but reinforces them (Burgess, 1977). Self-built housing extends private ownership of urban land and valorizes the exploitation of labour in the production of housing not only as use-value, but as a potentially saleable or rentable commodity. Within this context of private land ownership and labour exploitation, self-help housing cannot help deepening the fundamental inequalities of the economic system.

How does this process work? First, self-help labour is usually moulded and determined along the lines of the "formal" sector. "It is many times not realized," observed one expert in "informal" construction (Niilus, 1973: 9), "that the owner's role in building his original house was not that of skilled or unskilled

117

labourer, but that of *general contractor*; he begged, bought or scrounged materials, engaged workers and supervised the building work – usually very closely indeed." Secondly, these houses are often illegally subdivided and rooms rented out to lodgers even less well-off than the home owner.

Self-built housing creates potential commodities and in no way challenges the ability of a system based on commodity production and exchange for profit to house the poor majority. Langley (1976) demonstrates the way in which self-built housing in West African cities is embedded in a single web of relations with "modern" building if considered from the point of view of the flow of ideas, money, goods and work.

The interpenetration of "formal" and "informal" sectors in the African city, and the exploitation of the latter by the former, has been well documented (Gerry, 1979; Davies, 1979; Bugnicourt, 1976). This is nicely exemplified by the history of a low-cost, self-help housing scheme in an area of Nairobi called Dandora. Recent migrants from rural areas were assisted in building houses there over a period of years. They then sold them, quite against the spirit if not the letter of the aided scheme, to middle-class urbanites who in turn subdivided the houses and rented rooms to impoverished job-seekers from the countryside. A study showed that in many cases the original owners sent the money from the sale of their homes back to their rural home areas, where it was an important part of the survival strategy at certain phases of the reproductive cycle of a family (Soni, 1981, 1984). This case is not an uncommon one and provides some justification for Agarwal's observation that (1981: 94) "where large housing programmes were launched with government subsidies, benefits went largely to the rich."

Conclusion on Housing

Housing programmes, therefore, can as easily incorporate an élite stratum of the poor into dependent capitalist systems of production and reproduction as they can help Africa's poor challenge those systems. Housing projects, especially self-help housing of the site-and-service variety, can reinforce the contextual, comprehensive and participatory thrust of strong PHC and

118

can even serve as a stop gap for these broader concerns at a time when PHC is corrupted from within and buffeted by world recession from without. Alternatively, if guided by the weak BNA, housing projects can further divide the poor from one another, exacerbate inequalities in wealth, and, ultimately, undermine people's health by fragmenting the concept of and the struggle for health.

Chapter 4

A Child Survival and Development Revolution? UNICEF's Answer to the "Head Wind of Recession"

TWO VIEWS OF UNICEF'S "GOBI"

In its 1982–3 report *The State of the World's Children*, UNICEF outlined its Child Survival Revolution. This "revolution" amounts to four simple, straightforward actions to improve children's health: growth monitoring, oral rehydration therapy in cases of diarrhoea, breast feeding (as opposed to early weaning and/or bottle feeding) and immunization. The acronym "GOBI" is made up of the first letters of each of these four elements. As with water and housing improvements, there seems to be little in them to which one could object. At another level, however, this seemingly innocent package raises a whole series of issues which plunge us back into the debates surrounding the BNA – strong vs weak interpretations – as well as into broader discussions of debt, dependency and Africa's situation in the 1980s.

GOBI can be interpreted as an attempt to hasten the process of establishing Primary Health Care. We saw in Chapter 2 how long it is taking in Kenya, where, because of political demands on the élite in the face of a series of crises, there is actually a degree of state support. The slow and uneven progress of PHC in Kenya is typical. One way of interpreting UNICEF's initiative, therefore, is that implementation of GOBI on a large scale can save lives while PHC is being more painstakingly put into place. In this light, GOBI is complementary to PHC, and even, perhaps, provides it with socially appropriate technology – a point which was made in Chapter 3 in regard to Water Decade technology. In

120

social terms, GOBI's success in saving lives could provide, moreover, the satisfaction and commitment to wider change that could make it easier for communities to support, financially and otherwise, the grassroots structures of PHC. Thus GOBI could be seen as the leading edge of PHC (Grant, 1983b).

Another view of GOBI sees it as the triumph of the weak BNA, the top-down interpretation of basic needs. The GOBI package is, according to this view, the ultimate form of health care delivery. In theory, groups of parents can monitor the growth of their children, produce oral rehydration mixtures (salt, sugar, water) in their homes and raise one another's consciousness of the importance of breast feeding. In fact, the national GOBI campaigns launched to date actually pre-empt these local initiatives. Television and other coordinated media blitzes extol prepackaged oral rehydration salts; breast feeding is "sold" in precisely the same way that bottles were previously sold by the babyfood industry (probably with some of the same marketing and social science experts advising both). Immunization is still dependent on a "cold chain" that keeps vaccines cool (often without reliable electricity) and on considerable logistical prep-aration. As a result, immunization continues to come from the top down but now in massive and possibly unrepeatable campaigns. It is a matter of debate whether such campaigns will actually achieve the same order of coverage in the long run as mobile teams working from health centres and forming an integral part of the PHC-basic service structure.

The more critical view of GOBI notes that in all of this *the political momentum is to and from the centre*. In fact, it legitimizes the institutions of the *status quo*; members of the Air Force and police are drafted for the big immunization campaigns and national television carries the message that the breast is best. Where PHC brings communities together around health issues, GOBI reinforces individualist behaviour and depends for its epistemology and model of social life underlying its notion of "social marketing" (Grant, 1984, 1985a; Smith *et al.*, 1984) on *a model of individual behavioural change*. According to this view of the human condition, women *decide* to breast feed, *choose* to give oral rehydration, and *accept*, *adopt* and *cooperate* with the authorities. There is little appreciation of the fact that none of these cheerfully active verbs are possible within the sharply constrained routines of basic needs conflict – in which women run perpetually short of time, money, strength and endurance in the course of arranging adequate food, water and fuel, and in cooking, cleaning and caring for children and the sick.

Where such constraints on women are recognized (Grant, 1985a: 64–7, 1985b: 37–47), the emphasis is still informed by the naive social science assumptions carried over from the controversial Green Revolution in Asia and Latin America. On the one hand, while acknowledging constraints on women, especially limitations on their time, individual solutions are offered in the form of time-saving technologies. Social solutions of the sort that UNICEF and other agencies used to emphasize when PHC was the dominant paradigm have been all but abandoned. Running parallel to these individualistic solutions is an analysis of poor women's problems as an individual matter. Much use is made of statistical correlations linking mothers' educational achievement and family size to the life chances of children. There is no suggestion that the African crisis of child survival is rooted in fundamental changes in the way women have been forced to relate to land, commodity and labour markets (Guyer, 1981). (The contrast between the "individualizing" and "socializing" analyses of women's crisis is developed more fully in Chapter 7.)

There is, in short, a more critical view of GOBI that is suspicious of its underlying social theory. These critics see in it no more than the warmed-over "diffusionist" approaches to social change which were seriously questioned – some would say discredited – in the 1960s and 1970s for their role in underpinning the US "hearts and minds" and pacification campaigns in Vietnam and elsewhere. For such critics GOBI looks like a Trojan Horse filled with the same modernization theory that underlay the "development decades", the introduction of "miracle" rice and wheat seeds in the Green Revolution and top-down encouragement of population control.

Even less ardent critics are skeptical. Growth monitoring means little, they note, if there is no improvement in the food situation; oral rehydration for diarrhoea does nothing about the cause of diarrhoea. Improved food security, sanitation and housing require comprehensive attacks on poverty (hence some

122

form of PHC) and probably the sort of struggle for concessions from the élite which benefits from the reproduction of poverty (hence some form of the strong BNA). These critics say that the implementation of GOBI on a massive scale can divert resources that would have gone into the slower, but arguably more effective, PHC. A child may be helped by GOBI to survive a bout of diarrhoea only to die from the next bout, or the one after that, or from one of the other five common causes that, together with diarrhoea, account for 80 per cent of child deaths (acute respiratory infections, malaria, measles, malnutrition and accidents) (Cole-King, 1983: 6, 13).

What sense can one make out of such strikingly different interpretations of GOBI? Which view is correct? Or is it the case that both are correct because GOBI, like all other forms of the basic needs approach, evolved out of the contradictory pushes and pulls of different interests and contains elements of both the strong and weak BNA?

GOBI: BREAKTHROUGH OR COMPROMISE?

Since the establishment of GOBI, UNICEF's reports on PHC have changed dramatically. As we saw in Chapter 2, UNICEF made an early switch from sectoral concerns to a comprehensive approach to meeting children's needs (UNICEF 1965, 1974). Singer (1972), for instance, developed a framework for integrating children's health, education, and food needs into national economic planning by taking an intersectoral and time series perspective based on the development of needs at different points in the life cycle from before birth through adolescence. Likewise, UNICEF's "basic services strategy" shares the elaborate, comprehensive foci that GOBI and other "back to basics" approaches now seem to criticize as over-ambitious. This strategy (Hollnsteiner, 1982a: 57) included the:

> expansion of basic services in the interrelated fields of maternal and child care, family planning, production and consumption of more and better-quality foods, nutritional rehabilitation of the most vulnerable, safe water supply and

waste disposal, measures to meet the basic educational needs of the community, and the introduction of simple technologies to lighten the daily tasks of women and girls, along with special educational and social programmes designed to create greater opportunities and their participation in community affairs.

Throughout the 1970s, as the BNA was crystallized, UNICEF emphasized the central importance of participation (Mandl, 1977). In the early 1980s it published a study identifying what were essentially strong and weak forms of PHC (Hollnsteiner, 1982b). Hollnsteiner distinguishes a "general strategy of approach" (strong version) from the "narrow definition" (weak version) of PHC by its "avowal of certain values and principles as requisites of good health care". These values, she said, were (1982b: 37):

- *Equity and justice.* The basic right of every individual to health implies the reduction of gaps between those who have access and those who do not to health and other resources necessary for maintaining health – such as income, food, employment, education....

- *An overall development strategy that gives high priority to social goals in addition to economic ones.*

- *People imbued with a strong sense of self-reliance and control over their own lives exercising responsibility over their own health.* The role of governments and agencies is not to act in the people's behalf to "deliver" health, but rather to support their efforts and take joint responsibility for health.

- *The emergence of a new international economic order coupled with a new international development strategy.*

These principles seek to embed the technical content of PHC in a set of social and political relations at local, national and international levels. Timberlake (1985: 50) calls this the "hardware of health – piped water, protected wells, sanitation systems, safe food storage – rather than the hardware of disease".

Ultimately, such participation becomes a matter of power, as

Bugnicourt (1982: 74–5) remarked in another UNICEF publication:

> In the end, the stumbling block in the way of generalized participation is political: there is a social choice to be made not only by government, but at every level where authority is exercised. If popular participation is to be limited solely to the execution of tasks, it will have little chance of obtaining real and lasting support.

As recently as 1981 both WHO and UNICEF were anxious to dispel suspicions on the part of some Third World critics that "basic needs" was introduced as a substitute for a more just international system. These critics had insisted that "initiatives seeking piecemeal solutions or fragmentary measures would not be substitutes for the urgent need to rewrite, in the light of current world realities, the rules and principles governing international trade" (Gish, 1983, quoting statement by the 1979 Ministerial Meeting of the Group of 77 in Tanzania). WHO explicitly sets its Global Strategy for Health for All in the context of a New International Economic Order (WHO, 1981a: 37–8). Likewise, UNICEF's report on the state of the world's children for 1980–1 begins by linking child health to the continuing deterioration in the terms of trade for bananas in a striking case study from the village of Coolshare, Jamaica (Grant, 1982: 4–5).

Then came GOBI: a technical "fix" which could have been, but was not, part of the social and political struggles over power at local, national and global level – power of rich over poor, landed over landless, men over women, one ethnic group over another, multinational corporations over trade and local industry. It would be too simple to suggest that GOBI was a victim of the events of 1981. But the coincidence between GOBI's decline into a technical formula and the new political environment is striking. The year 1981 saw a change of administration in the United States, a not unrelated change of leadership at the World Bank and the emergence of repeated and forceful representations of "supply side", *laissez faire* economics by powerful interests at every opportunity from the economic summit at Cancun, Mexico, to negotiations over Law of the Sea. That same year the USA sabotaged the Energy Fund proposed by the UN Confer-

125

ence on New and Renewable Energy, (Spilker, 1981: 268) and the World Bank unveiled its "back to basics" approach to African development; in the WHO council vote on a Code of Practice for the infant food industry there was but one "nay" vote – the USA's.

In a world askew since the first monetarist shocks in 1979, however, one does not need to resort to conspiracy theory. Responding to the same crisis, institutions with similar ideological starting-points tend to come up with solutions. We are now seeing this pattern in the major development agencies (UNICEF, the World Bank and USAID) where the signs are of a further weakening of the BNA.

CHILDREN IN DARK TIMES

The title of UNICEF's 1981–2 report on the world's children was ominous: *Children in Dark Times*, it was called. The previous year, UNICEF had proclaimed that a concensus had been reached during the 1970s that significant progress on basic needs could be made by the year 2000 (Grant, 1981: 5ff). It was said that these goals were realizable: life expectancy over 60 years, infant mortality under 50 per 1000, literacy rates of 75 per cent and primary school enrolment for all children. China, Sri Lanka, Kerala state in India (with a population the size of Argentina, Colombia, or Zaire's), Costa Rica, Cuba, Barbados and Jamaica were cited as cases suggesting that such targets were realistic even where per capita income was low (Grant, 1981; cf. Streeten, 1981).

On the basis of its country studies, UNICEF had concluded that (Grant, 1981: 5):

- Economic growth is a necessary but not sufficient condition for the elimination of poverty;

- Policies aimed at directly meeting the needs of the poor are a more promising way forward than reliance on the trickle-down of growth;

- The redistribution of resources and incomes implied by such

126

policies need not detract from, and may even enhance, the prospects for economic growth itself.

By the time of the next report, doubts were being expressed about the targets for the year 2000 and UNICEF's conclusions about redistribution and needs seemed to have fallen by the wayside.

Children in Dark Times catalogues a "slowing down of progress" (Grant, 1982: 2). The targets proclaimed the year before had been incorporated into its new International Development Strategy for the 1980s, but to reach them "progress ... would in fact have to be two or three times as fast over the next 20 years as it has been over the last 20". Whereas infant mortality had been falling steadily,

> for the past five years, it has barely flickered. Average life expectancy, which increased by seven or eight months a year in the 1960s and early 1970s, is now increasing by only two or three months a year. School enrollment rates, which again rose by a regular four or five per cent a year up to the mid-1970s, now seems to have reached a plateau.

"In short," Grant summarizes, "the optimism of the 1960s which gave ground to the realism of the 1970s has now receded even further to make room for the doubt and pessimism which seems to be settling into the 1980s." Africa is singled out as a prime example. The litany of woes is recited: a tenth successive year of declining per capita food production, food shortages, staggering numbers of refugees.

This was the year before GOBI emerged, the year after UNICEF had reiterated its hopes for what had become the minimal or weak basic needs shopping-list. In this transitional report on children, it is interesting to note early signs of three major lines of thought that had gained currency by the mid-1980s: the idea that poverty is somehow "natural", an inescapable fact of life; an acceptance that parents are powerless to help their children; and a growing notion that technological innovations in health care can take the place of social change.

The "Naturalization" of Poverty

The report treats the world economic crisis pragmatically, as though it were something that simply "happens to" poor nations and to poor people. As Grant writes (1982: 2):

> the world economy is experiencing greater instability and a more severe disruption of steady growth than at any time since the end of the Second World War ... unless specific steps are taken, the consequences of this adverse external environment will be to increase the numbers of the absolute poor to one billion before the end of the Third Development Decade.

For some time critics of the World Bank had remarked on the way in which it "*naturalizes* poverty. [Poverty] is simply there and tends to grow in relative and absolute terms, putting the rest of the world in danger" (Alain, 1980: 234, emphasis in original). The Bank seldom seeks the roots of poverty or the forces and interests that perpetuate it. While other development agencies, in particular UNICEF, made some attempts in the 1970s to explore the causes of poverty, increasingly agencies are falling into line with the return to the "just-there-ness", as the philosophical quiddity of poverty.

By 1983, four years after FAO's World Conference on Agrarian Reform and Rural Development, only 13 of the 140 nations which had approved its Programme of Action had asked for follow-up missions, and only one had taken the next step toward implementation. Meanwhile, 1984 saw a publication by FAO that gave increasingly heavy emphasis to the natural constraints on development, particularly to the "carrying capacity" of African land (Higgins *et al.*, 1984).

The World Bank's *World Development Report* for 1984 took up the other side of the "natural" poverty equation, "people vs land". Population growth was blamed for poverty, and family planning was offered as the solution.

About this time (Grant, 1983c: 49–64), UNICEF added an "FFF" to its GOBI shorthand. This stands for "food supplements", "family spacing" and "female education". The new programme would be GOBI-FFF.

A case can be made for food supplements, especially during pregnancy. Low birth weight is highly correlated with early mortality of children. Forty to fifty per cent of infant deaths (under one year) occur in low birth-weight babies (Cole-King, 1983: 7; Kelman and McCord, 1978). Emphasis on this "F" would lead away from the "naturalization" of poverty since recent events and reflections on them are forcing most people to accept that issues of food distribution (a social, non-natural process) are more important in explaining hunger than absolute scarcity (e.g. Sen, 1981).

On the other hand, family spacing and female education are additions to the GOBI package that contribute to the ideology of "natural" poverty. To be sure, control of fertility is a woman's right, and educated women tend to lobby and struggle more effectively than do uneducated women for these and other rights (such as the right to food, health care, etc.). However, these two "F's" in the ideological package can have another use: to call attention to *population growth as a cause of poverty*, rather than a symptom. They also can be used to justify intrusive and even coercive attacks on women's control of their fertility since they seem to imply that poor women are ignorant and in a "state of nature" from which it is the duty of experts to rescue them. Many women are justifiably suspicious of these new "F's" in GOBI since white men have long experimented on them with birth control drugs such as the injection Depoprovera (used despite women's protests in Tanzania in the 1970s, for instance) and conspired, in the view of some, to sterilize as many poor women as possible (Mass, 1977; Petchesky, 1981; Davis, 1983: 202–21).

The "naturalization" of poverty continues: economic crisis strikes from somewhere "out there" much as natural disasters (e.g. droughts, floods, earthquakes) occur. The only concession to a dialectic or complex interaction between society and nature seems to be the commonly projected image of too many poor people pressing nature too hard. Similarly, the only hint that nations or even classes like peasants or workers might interact with the world economy is the assertion that poor nations have "mismanaged" industrialization, debt, marketing, etc. and that somehow workers and peasants in Africa have ceased to "produce" the way they used to.

129

A Safety Net or "A Floor Under Poverty"

The UNICEF report also foreshadows later discussions of a "safety net" for the world's poor. If parents are deprived of the power to protect their children, then the community has to do it, we are told (Grant, 1982: 2–3). Significantly, it goes on to allude to twentieth century recognition "that if a local community is unable to meet the needs of its children then the responsibility extends to the national and international community." This is an increasingly common refrain. Taken together with the interpretation of world economic crisis as an external event and as a product of fate, it implies an acceptance of the fact of the increasing powerlessness of the poor parent in the national scheme of things and of the poor nation state in the global order.

In the 1970s, the emphasis had shifted to at least a rhetorical acceptance of "empowerment" of the poor as the way forward. Parents, peasant farmers, workers and women were encouraged (usually only rhetorically, but sometimes meaningfully at the grassroots) to organize themselves and to demand the power they needed to achieve a decent standard of living. Various international meetings such as the ILO's World Employment Conference in 1976 and FAO's World Conference on Agrarian Reform and Rural Development in 1979 had clearly asserted the right of poor people to organize. At this point, the historical initiative was on the side of the strong BNA. Ten years later, discussion of a minimal safety net leaves little doubt that the initiative has been lost to resurgent technocracy and the weakest possible interpretation of the BNA. It is accepted that the "local community is unable to meet the needs of its children". One no longer seeks to aid the process of empowerment of that local community but merely to put "a floor under poverty" (UNICEF, 1985: 39–51).

Technological Substitutes for Even a Minimal Safety Net

Finally, in a brief discussion of the role of science in protecting children in dark times – specifically concerning control of mortality from diarrhoea – there is a foreshadowing of GOBI *as the substitute for even a minimal safety net*, although, for another

130

year at least, UNICEF was to remain committed to its "basic services strategy" (UNICEF, 1977; Grant, 1982: 12).

Over the last few years, however, it has become clear that technologies of many kinds have become a substitute for any kind of a safety net. The IMF has continued to insist that African governments remove wage and price controls and slash public expenditure. Meanwhile, clever, innovative, "progressive" farmers will still be able to feed their families (it is argued) since they will seize on the new African Green Revolution. They will "respond to incentives" and "price signals" individually just as the African nations "adjust" themselves to paying off their mountainous debts through a rational acceptance of their "comparative advantage" as primary product exporters.

Is it also hoped that innovative, "progressive" mothers will seize on oral rehydration therapy as a substitute for clean water and on growth monitoring as a substitute for food? Is this the reason for "female education" as the most important non-health intervention? We can ask the same question about fuel-efficient charcoal and wood-burning stoves, solar-cookers, improved mud construction techniques, agro-forestry, and a hundred more appropriate technologies that have become substitutes for social transformation rather than its content. The means of change have become the new ends.

Even as GOBI-FFF was being consolidated as a substitute for PHC, new technologies were unveiled. The *State of the World's Children 1986* added home treatment for acute respiratory infections and malaria. In this, it was implicitly accepting the failure of PHC to support village health workers who, alongside parents, were supposed to treat respiratory ailments and the resurgence of malaria, and doing so without comment on the style of development that had provoked that resurgence (Grant, 1985b).

BUILDING ON "SOCIAL BREAKTHROUGHS" OR BLOCKING THEM?

The 1982–3 report, *New Hope in Dark Times*, begins by asserting the necessity of "streamlining" UNICEF practice "against the headwind" of world recession (Grant, 1983: 2). This refers not only to the necessity of reorganizing UNICEF and rationalizing the basic services strategy in order to bring "more benefits to children for every available dollar" (Grant, 1982: 12). The application of the lessons learned from inefficient and failed projects was discussed in the prior report and was presumably underway.

The year GOBI was announced, ideology as well as UNICEF seemed to have been streamlined. The Children's Revolution became a minimum package in the face of the failure of parents to reverse the power relations determining health and the failure of poor nations to achieve a New International Economic Order.

This development can be interpreted in two ways. Possibly UNICEF recognized a quantum leap in the level of organization in the urban slums and rural areas of the Third World. It saw as a set of "social breakthroughs" the growth of "community organizations, paraprofessional development workers, primary schools and the primary health networks, the peoples' movements ..." (Grant, 1983: 6–7). Indeed, "these social breakthroughs are the missing link between the know-how of science and the needs of people." One interpretation, therefore, is that factions in UNICEF favouring social revolution and the NIEO recognized not only the slowing of progress in health indicators but a more ominous slowing of momentum in these grassroots movements. GOBI would then be seen as top-down encouragement to "re-accelerate" not only "the world's flagging progress against child malnutrition and child deaths", but also organization for demands and struggle by the poor.

New Hope supports such a view of GOBI to the extent that a long section is devoted to issues of land reform, although such struggles are explicitly set aside from the central thrust of the GOBI approach (p. 11):

> the pressure needs to be kept up on the longer-term and more fundamental solution of increasing the productivity of the poor through greater social justice – including, above all, access to land and the means to make it grow more.... This wedge of different activities – *operating on different time scales and against different degrees of financial constraint and*

political resistance – could break into the cycle of hunger which has trapped so many for so long (Emphasis added).... In the meantime, UNICEF itself is committed to that part of this same task which would most directly help individual mothers and children to improve their levels of health and nutrition *now* (Emphasis in original).

Another interpretation is possible, however. What if, fully conscious of the remarkable advances in organization among the poor, a more conservative faction in UNICEF and similar organizations created GOBI because they were frightened by the prospect of social revolution from below? Conservatives do expect increasing pressure from debtor countries for an NIEO. Debtor countries will resist IMF-imposed economic adjustments (including cuts in social service and health budgets) which are without some minimal alleviation of child deaths and malnutrition. But the evidence for this interpretation in *New Hope* and later reports is found not in their statements but in their silences.

One topic of silence is the contradiction between top-down GOBI implementation and the growth of bottom-up group action, which is acknowledged to be important for that "wedge of different activities". The sophisticated and experienced creators of GOBI cannot have failed to realize that in many places GOBI very likely will undermine local self-reliance, reinforce urban bias and legitimize the central government.

In Honduras, we are told (Grant, 1985a: 54), "mothers were very strongly predisposed towards treatments with a sophisticated urban image", and that therefore the Oral Rehydration Therapy (ORT) campaign was designed around "foil-wrapped sachets of oral rehydration salts rather then the use of home-made salt and sugar solutions". Is this consistent with long-term alternatives to an urban-élite image of development? Such an urban cultural bias is part of the problem, not the solution (Lipton, 1977). It is partly responsible for disastrous changes in diet and child-care such as the shift from locally-produced staple grains to imported wheat for bread (Andrae and Beckman, 1985), greatly increased cigarette consumption (Muller, 1978), and the popularity of bottle feeding (Jelliffe and Jelliffe, 1978).

In much of the Third World and in Africa especially,

133

dependency on internal markets has grown dramatically in the last twenty years. The reasons are several and include the drop in per capita local food production discussed in Chapter 5. Now, at a time when the World Bank and the IMF are insisting that African governments remove subsidies on consumption and cut back on public expenditure, the poor are highly vulnerable because of their recently-acquired dependency on the market. UNICEF itself has documented the fact that these "economic adjustments" fall heaviest on women and children (Jolly and Cornia, 1984; UNICEF, 1985; Cornia *et al.* 1987). Is it not contradictory for UNICEF to reinforce urban-élite images of development, urban bias and market relations with ORT programmes that depend on the centralized packaging of the rehydration salt/sugar mix?

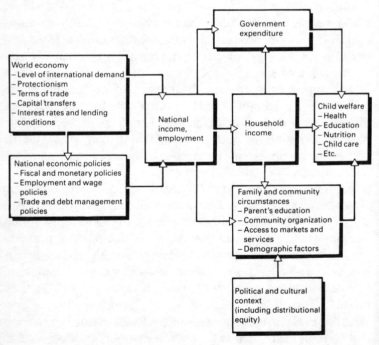

Source: Cornia, 1984: 212

Figure 4.1: Linkages between World Economic Recession and Child Welfare

By 1985, only six UNICEF-sponsored national ORT programmes used the cottage industry approach to decentralized
packaging and distribution. Another 33 were urban-based,
including programmes in Burundi, Ethiopia, Kenya, Lesotho,
Mozambique and Zaire (Grant, 1985a: 3). In Africa, only
Gambia and Burkina Faso were producing ORT salt/sugar mix
on a cottage industry basis in 1985.

UNICEF estimates that in 1985 alone ORT prevented 500,000
child deaths from diarrhoeal dehydration. No one would deny
the significance of this achievement. But one must ask what
future for these rescued children is being constructed at the same
time. The strong BNA would, for instance, encourage cottage
industry production of the ORT mix. In an extraordinary review
of rural non-farm employment of women in the Third World
called *Blacksmith, Baker, Roofing-sheet maker...* Carr (1984)
exhaustively demonstrates the little-tapped, little-encouraged
organizational ability and creativity of rural women in processing
and manufacturing. Surely UNICEF is also aware of this
potential when its president, James Grant, writes of the "social
breakthroughs" that are making the application of "science"
possible in the GOBI package.

The tragic and striking difference between the strong and weak
BN approaches is clear at precisely this point. The weak BNA
does not question the social relations that produce and reproduce
poverty. Nor does GOBI explore relations among poor people
that might overturn poverty. It is technology and the manipula-
tive social psychology developed while "selling" the Green
Revolution that receive most attention from UNICEF as "social
breakthroughs" rather than the self-organization of the poor.
"[I]n a world where information technology has become the new
wonder of our age," writes Grant (1984: 3), "shamefully little is
known about how to communicate information whose principal
value is to the poor." Such a statement makes a series of
assumptions that would require justification, but do not receive it
in UNICEF texts.

First, it is assumed that the most useful thing to communicate
is information. Others, for instance most contributors to the
recent volume *Practicing Health for All* (Morley *et al.*, eds., 1983),
seem to believe that it is communication about relationships

135

among people rather than communication of technical information that is crucial.

Second, there is the assumption that communication *to* ignorant people *from* people with know-how is what is required. This overlooks the cardinal importance of groups of people sharing knowledge and of discovering the usefulness of knowledge that had been denigrated under colonialism (Goonatilake, 1984; Richards, 1985).

Third, it is assumed that "information technology" is the missing key to communication. However, it has become a commonplace of pedagogy that the best communication takes place between two people of similar backgrounds, status, etc., in face-to-face contact (Rogers and Shoemaker, 1971). One of the lessons that could be drawn from the Green Revolution, but apparently not one recognized by the proponents of GOBI, is that useful information spreads with extraordinary speed by word of mouth. Peasants resisted a "rice revolution" offered by the Sengalese government and USAID on the shores of the river Senegal not because of ignorance, but precisely because these peasants learned from others that the rice programme was not to their advantage (Adams, 1981).

The weak BNA does not contribute to social movements. It does not, for example, create small groups with similar material interests which will stick together despite failures and disappointments. Women joined together to produce and sell ORT mix to neighbouring women could become the core of such an interest group, but this opportunity is lost under the weak approach.

Strong BN approaches could easily incorporate the technological content of GOBI. Why, therefore, despite all the rhetoric about self-health and participation, does GOBI turn out to be only a shopping-list for delivery like all the other forms of the weak BNA? The answer lies in UNICEF's reluctance to challenge the roots of Africa's crisis or to support efforts by parents to attack the sources of their "normally" low incomes and miserable environments.

When UNICEF defines parents as the new frontline health workers and coins the play on words "self-health" (Grant, 1985b), it is conceivable that it is endorsing political action by *groups* of parents. This would be in line with the radical

136

interpretation of BNA. Such parents' groups could produce and administer ORT solutions, monitor the growth of their children, encourage breastfeeding and *struggle politically* for a just and sustainable future. The cost of this type of political action, of course, can be high. Kenyan playright Ngũgĩ wa Thiongo was jailed for advocating collective action in the community-based performances of his *I Will Marry When I Want* (Ngũgĩ and Ngũgĩ, 1982). Would UN agencies take this risk?

I Will Marry, itself a reflection of the strong BNA in education (Boal, 1979; Kidd, 1979, 1982), closes with language not at all alien to UNICEF's world (Ngũgĩ and Ngũgĩ, 1982: 114 ff.):

> Come my friend
> Let's reason together.
> Our hearts are heavy with worry
> Because of the future of our children.
> Let's drive away the darkness
> From our land.

The climax may be a little more disturbing to an agency committed not only to welfare of children but to "economic adjustment with a human face" (UNICEF, 1985). One character begins to sing:

> Two hands can carry a beehive,
> One man's ability is not enough,
> One finger cannot kill a louse,
> Many hands make light work.

And everybody on stage responds:

> The trumpet –

> Of the workers has been blown
> To wake all the slaves
> To wake all the peasants
> To wake all the poor.
> To wake the masses....

These were not actors but ordinary parents and children who performed night after night in their local market towns and in their local language until the government of Kenya banned this entire genre.

UNICEF *could* be supporting parents as front-line health workers in this sense, providing the "technical support" of its GOBI package and financial and ideological support for such non-violent political protest. There is no doubt that UNICEF understands better than most large agencies who the victims of "economic adjustment" are and where the roots of poverty lie. The 1985 UNICEF report shows that "recession strikes progressively harder at those with the least to fall back on – the developing countries, the poorest population groups in those countries, and finally the most vulnerable group of all – the poorest mothers and their young children." At fault, it says, are the fall in family incomes and cutbacks in government expenditure on social services.

But then there are the silences. Nothing is said about the systems of production and reproduction that have made these poorest women and children vulnerable. Why must family income have been so close to the edge even under normal conditions? Why should social services have been the fragile thread on which hung the survival of children who should have been nurtured in their homes, before the current crisis? The 1984 and 1985 reports, like *New Hope*, are silent on these points.

Those inclined toward a more critical view of GOBI receive encouragement in the 1985 report, *A Revolution Beginning*. We are told of very impressive gain in ORT, use of growth charts to detect growth failure, and in immunization, achievements certainly not to be belittled. We also are told, again, that although "the front line in the long war on poverty and underdevelopment is and remains the struggle for economic justice and growth," these are, in a nut shell, hard times. Justice will just have to wait. "Large areas of the developing world are suffering from the backlash of the world's longest economic recession since the 1930s" (Grant, 1985a: 16). In Africa more people were unable to satisfy their basic needs in 1982 than in 1974 (258 million or 69 per cent of Africans as opposed to 205 or 68 per cent). Incomes are falling, and "the poorer a family is, the higher the percentage of

138

its income [is] spent on necessities – food, water, fuel, and health care." To make matters worse, "the social services have often been the first to suffer from cut-backs in government spending which recession, debts, or international monetary policy may enforce."

UNICEF seems to have no doubt that this "making things worse" by enforced "economic adjustment" is inevitable. In this UNICEF closely follows the analysis of the World Bank. We will therefore have to turn briefly to the Bank's current thinking on basic needs in order to unravel UNICEF's mixed messages concerning strong and weak BN strategies.

LOAVES, FISHES AND BANKERS

UNICEF is clearly uncomfortable with the Bank's plans for economic adjustment in its starkest form. Former World Bank president Clausen seems prepared to write off about half of that famous "poorest 40 per cent" that was central in the 1970s to the concern with basic needs and justice (Clausen, 1985: 6):

> We have not found very effective ways to raise the productivity of the poorest 10 to 20 per cent of the population – landless labourers, for example. Some of the very poorest people in any society are sick or handicapped and will always need help from relatives or from society as a whole.

This is no more than a subtle expression of "triage" mentality. Some people simply cannot be helped. "Anyway there's something wrong with them" is the clever effect of using the word "handicapped", although the physically and mentally disabled in the Third World make up a minute percentage of the ten to twenty per cent to which Clausen refers. We can be grateful that the next logical step doesn't bring us to Jonathan Swift's "Modest Proposal".

Instead, reflecting the twentieth century's slow but sure recognition that the responsibility for children belongs to the community, banker Clausen appropriately passes the buck. "I am not, by nature, a dreamer. I am a banker," he tells Martin

Luther King's widow (Clausen, 1985: 9). He clearly is incapable of dreaming that there is a connection between the systems of production and reproduction shored up and reinforced, moulded and restructured by the Bank and international donor agencies and the increasing vulnerability of children. On the contrary, he believes that "on the whole, the developing countries have adjusted to recession and the debt crisis remarkably well." He continues (1985: 7):

> They were forced to cut back drastically on imports and incomes, but many countries have managed to cut back in an orderly way and, therefore, reduce the destructive impact of the crisis.... Some countries have, simultaneously, eliminated long-standing inefficiencies in their economies and shifted resources into export products. *Such adjustments in economic structures may add to the short-term hurt*, but they do help to rekindle growth in the long term (Emphasis added).

UNICEF has recently commissioned studies that give it a reasonable idea that "short-term hurt" means increasing misery for the poor, despair for parents already hard-pressed to feed their children, and, above all, increasing numbers of sick, blind, stunted and dead children. Green and Singer (1984) document the effects so far on women and children in Africa of recession and enforced adjustment to recession and debt. Summarizing a series of such studies, Cornia depicts the "production of child welfare" in a diagram reproduced here as Figure 4.1.

It is clear from the diagram that national economic policies are only one factor affecting income and employment, government expenditure, family income and access to services. None the less, economic adjustment of the sort required by the Bank and IMF is underway in a large number of African countries. USAID has used considerable muscle to enforce what it calls "policy reform" during Africa's drought crisis. In the spring of 1985, it could report (Edelman, 1985: 29) that "32 African countries [are] involved in policy reform discussions with AID", and that:

- 14 have substantially increased prices paid to farmers for their crops;

- 11 are in the process of reforming or divesting inefficient state-owned business;
- 10 are attempting to stabilize their economies by reducing government spending;
- 10 have devalued their currencies to stimulate external trade;
- 9 are restricting public sector hiring, public sector wage increases, or both;
- 8 have liberalized trade or foreign exchange policies;
- 7 have decontrolled some or all consumer prices;
- 6 have increased energy or utility prices;
- 6 have reduced subsidies on agricultural tools, seeds, or fertilizers.

The impact of policy reforms such as the decontrol of prices, removal of subsidies, currency devaluation and wage and hiring freezes have hit the poor hard. Cornia (1984: 214–17) summarizes the effects from a number of countries, including a number in Africa:

- Unemployment has been rising;
- Real household incomes have been reduced;
- The fall in real incomes has been more severe for the poorer social groups;
- Absolute poverty is increasing;
- The share of social expenditure out of the total is shrinking;
- The expansion of new services has stopped;
- There has been a drop in the quality of existing services;
- Cuts in education and in food subsidies seem to precede those in health.

The impact on child survival and welfare has been disastrous. "There are clear indications that where the fall in earnings and/

or government cuts has been particularly severe infant mortality rate has shown a clear upward trend," writes Cornia (1984: 216). He continues, "Even in countries where the infant mortality rate has continued to decline, there has been a deterioration in nutrition indicators. Stagnant or deteriorating health conditions are also found in a number of countries despite sometimes notable declines in mortality" (pp. 216–17). Following up these studies with several years' additional study, including careful monitoring of the impact of economic adjustment on child welfare in sixteen sub-Saharan African countries, Cornia reports clear worsening of nutritional status. (Cornia 1987a: 34 and 1987b: 68). Therefore, he comments (1987b: 68):

> Alternatives [to the IMF adjustment packages] must be found. The urgency of finding new solutions is especially pressing when considering the poverty-inducing effects that the current approach tends to have, and the direct negative effects that some macro-economic policies have on the health and nutritional status of the poorest, and of children in particular....

Millions of children in Africa are living on a thin edge. They lack the physiological reserves to see them through bouts of illness. Their families cannot maintain food supplies when prices are decontrolled, when the harvest fails or when a breadwinner loses her or his job.

For this reason, and to their credit, authors of a recent UNICEF report argue for "economic adjustment with a human face" (UNICEF, 1985: 64). As noted above, they are uneasy with the Bank's straightforward "bottom line". They argue that the issue should be to choose the type of adjustment that protects vulnerable groups. They believe that such options exist. For instance, they propose tax increases in African countries rather than public expenditure cuts and cuts in military spending where cuts have to be made.

These authors still seem to see GOBI initiatives as an integral part of Primary Health Care in Africa, not as a substitute for it. They welcome continued training of community health workers, especially traditional birth attendants. They seem to believe that health budgets presently skewed by austerity and by the drought and refugee emergencies toward limited GOBI-type packages or "selective PHC" are only temporary distortions. They are clear that the PHC orientation should be strengthened and that the basic service network should be expanded to reach unserved people and the training and employment of community health workers. Child survival measures such as GOBI are seen as the "leading edge of PHC", but are none the less integrated within PHC.

Unfortunately this recent divergence with the Bank and with the increasing tendency in UNICEF to substitute know-how for empowerment is a minority opinion, although one strongly supported by Africans, led by Cheikh Hamidou Kane, Minister for Planning and Cooperation of Senegal. More typical of the convergence between UNICEF and the Bank is recent nostalgic prose about the safety net that emerged in response to the economic crisis of the 1930s, which, in the words of Grant (1985a: 17–19), "however imperfect it may be ... protects the majority of the vulnerable from falling into destitution". He continues, "The time has come to fashion the first strands of such a safety net for the poorest and most vulnerable families of the developing world."

Is UNICEF (Grant, 1985a: 21) here referring to "safety net woven from the strands of minimum wages, unemployment pay, sickness benefit, and family allowances"? No. That is precisely the system now being demolished in England and the United States. Perhaps, then, UNICEF is looking towards

> a more elementary safety net of minimum food entitlements, primary health care, elementary education, safe sanitation, and clean water ... put in place by most developing nations – if they can suspend one corner of that net on fair and stable policies of international trade and aid.

Again the answer is no. The safety net proposal would take us back to the consensus of the 1970s with which UNICEF began the 1980s. These notions have now been abandoned; its GOBI report, for example, is tentative and a little frail compared to the vigour of earlier years: "The subject of this report ... is an even more basic, more modest, and more immediate goal...."

The situation is politically explosive. GOBI, which has

emerged as the cheapest of the weak options, can cut the rate of child deaths produced by economic adjustment. But it does so individualistically and in a way which does not encourage the formation of local groups in the way that a strong BNA would. Because, in the long run, the costs to the ruling élites and the foreign firms exporting profits from the Third World are highest where strong forms of BNA are created, they have opted for GOBI. Hence the World Bank cannot pass the buck forever.

Will the cost of even "a few selected interventions" (such as GOBI) soon be judged too great? Cole-King (1983: 14) puts it this way:

> While it costs nothing to breastfeed and very little to give home-made fluids to a diarrhetic child, to get this implemented in the right way *does* cost money. Support in the form of information and communication and particularly through personal contacts and demonstrations by village health workers (particularly for the use of ORS), distribution of supplies, logistics for supplies and supervision, ensuring an effective cold chain for vaccines from manufacturer to child, transport costs, etc., all do cost more money than is currently being allocated to PHC.

The potential in the 1980s and 1990s for growing numbers of grassroots social groups and effective, low-cost technology is indeed great, as UNICEF points out. The issue is whether the technology will be used to divert the energies of these groups from social transformation or whether it will be used to encourage and to stimulate the development of local groups that will move on to uproot the causes of hunger and disease. The latter necessarily involves conflict, though not necessarily violence. Economic and social polarization is increasing, not deceasing. Neither science, technology nor scientists are neutral in this process.

CONCLUSION: A "SOCIAL" GOBI AND A "STRONG" PHC

Chapter 1 emphasized that a radical needs discourse is highly concrete and localized. The kinds of low-cost technologies used

144

in the GOBI campaign, in the course of the Water Decade or in self-help housing programmes (reliable, low-cost pumps, improved techniques of mud construction, etc.) have a natural role to play as the initial content of the cumulative, transformative process described as the strong BNA.

However, careful note should be taken of the word "initial". Even critics of the way GOBI seems to be developing and of "vertical" or "selective" PHC agree that *phasing* is essential to the long-term construction of popular support for the original, more comprehensive, empowering forms of PHC. Appropriate starting-points are those that give quick and dramatic results, such as GOBI actions, which undoubtedly save children's lives (Cole-King, 1983). If GOBI-like starting points were chosen flexibly, with groups of parents to whom the results of regionally-specific epidemiological surveys were presented for discussion, one would be building long-term foundations for PHC while also moving dramatically against the five or six causes of 80 per cent of child death in the Third World.

This would not require extraordinary efforts or very detailed research. In some places, for instance, malaria is a greater killer than diarrhoea. In others, diarrhoea in the wet season may be replaced by eye infections in the dry season, leading to blindness and life-long disability. There are simple, low-cost treatments for all of the regional variations of a list of the top three or four killing and disabling conditions. UNICEF has, in fact, begun to publish summaries of the technologies that would expand GOBI in just this way (Grant, 1985a: 106–66).

Care would also have to be taken that whatever the form of the initial GOBI-like interventions, they reinforce the social character of the struggle for child survival. Earlier in this chapter we discussed the tendency for GOBI, as implemented presently, to emphasize individualistic behaviour and dependency on the state. GOBI-like interventions could, on the other hand, encourage the activities of groups of parents, and reinforce the status and role of Community Health Workers (CHW) and Traditional Birth Attendants (TBA). Handled in this way, GOBI-like technology would, indeed, be an integral part of PHC, not a cheap substitute for it.

One should make no mistake about the current lack of political support for this interpretation of GOBI and PHC. Much of the past few chapters has emphasized the ruling élite's political resistance to further demands and their ways of reducing the political risk of "economic adjustment". GOBI seems tailor-made for the job, and, indeed, the inter-agency consultations that produced GOBI included the World Bank. GOBI is a set of "low-cost, low-risk, low-resistance, people's health actions which do not depend on the economic and political changes which are necessary in the longer term if poverty is to be eradicated" (Grant, 1983a: 6).

Since GOBI as it now stands does nothing by way of encouraging social transformations that would work toward eradication of poverty, and since it actually seems to block transformative participation and the strong version of PHC, it can really be seen as nothing more than a handy way of mopping up the excess mortality created by economic adjustment. No doubt hundreds of thousands of lives were saved in 1985 by ORT. But what of the hundreds of thousands who died because of "economic adjustment"? At best economic adjustment would recreate the *status quo ante*, which was simply grinding poverty.

What, then, of the future? The best that can be said is that the pharmaceutical industry can look forward to growing demand for ORT since poor environmental conditions and malnutrition, both associated strongly with diarrhoea, are unlikely to decrease. Is it, indeed, too far-fetched to imagine a Brave New World where the same corporate giants produce tranquillizers for the middle- and working-classes of the North and ORT and specially-formulated weaning foods for the peasants and workers of the South? The US government presently buys processed and blended products for its food aid programme from some fifty US companies, including grain giants such as Cargill which supplies soy-fortified wheat flour, wheat-soy-milk blends and other USAID specialities. AID frankly admits that "[c]ompanies seeking new markets play a key role in product development" (Forman and Fellers, 1985: 46).

Is it unrealistic to suggest that ORT and fortified food aid are the "down market" end of a corporate marketing strategy that has as its "up market" end multivitamin-mineral stress pills and frozen gourmet convenience food for the busy yuppy? Already work is underway to develop "Super Oral Rehydration Solutions" that cut dramatically the volume and duration of diarrhoea. Some formulas, for instance those containing popped-rice flour, could possibly be produced on a cottage industry basis. But what of the ones containing the amino acid glycine? The pharmaceutical companies producing birth control drugs may have another captive market here. And wouldn't it be interesting if the very corporations who lose out on infant formula sales due to the WHO/UNICEF Code of Practice and GOBI's emphasis on breast-feeding actually make up the difference by moving into these new growth areas: fortified food aid, weaning foods, ORS, birth control and vaccines?

UNICEF has much more to offer. Africa deserves more.

Chapter 5

An African Food Dilemma? National Self-reliance Versus Family Food Security

Who would deny that food is a basic need? On the surface, at least, all positions on the continuum from weak to the strong BNA centre on food regardless of the immediate sectoral concern. For instance, it would be hard to find a water supply or health programme so little "integrated" that the intimate connections between nutrition and infection are not taken into account. Malnourished children suffer more frequent and more severe bouts of diarrhoea and children suffering from diarrhoea (and other infections such as measles) are often pushed over the edge from chronic undernutrition into clinical malnutrition. In a similar way, even narrowly sectoral programmes designed from the top down for the delivery of site-and-service urban shelter are well aware that the poorest urban groups spend up to 80 per cent of their income on food, limiting the degree to which they can save for or invest in housing. In fact, the "double 80s" have become something of a rule of thumb in measuring poverty: a family is said to be poor when it cannot satisfy 80 per cent of its nutritional requirements even when 80 per cent of family income goes for food (Lipton, 1983). Another indication is that three of the seven elements in GOBI–FFF focus directly or indirectly on food and feeding: "growth monitoring", "breastfeeding" and one of the controversial "F's", "supplementary feeding".

So much, however, for cosy consensus. Beneath this superficial acknowledgement of an interconnected web of basic needs, great differences flow from strong and weak approaches to human needs. True to its consistent adherence to participation, empowerment and control, the strong position emphasizes control over resources for the production of food or other productive

148

resources and skills that provide the basis of exchange for food ("exchange entitlements" in the current terminology of Sen, 1981). It also asserts a "right to adequate food as well as the right to be free from hunger", as embodied in the International Covenant on Economic, Social and Cultural Rights (Alston, 1984a: 29–31).

The weak BNA stops short of accepting a right to food (Streeten, 1981: 107–11). Because it does not question existing international structures (e.g. the state) or economic allocation (e.g. capitalist markets), the weak position on food reduces the BNA to maintaining food stocks through production or import and supplementing the diet of certain target groups (Timmer *et al.*, 1983). Food policy becomes a matter of monitoring – and sometimes manipulating – prices, incomes, production and the flow of food through marketing channels. Special cases are usually recognized: the destitute, who require direct feeding or indirect income support through food-for-work programmes, are included, as are various categories of high-risk persons from a medical nutritional point of view such as weanlings, pregnant and lactating mothers, or tuberculosis patients (Mason *et al.*, 1984). Droughts and other large-scale disruptions of the food system are dealt with by the weak BNA under the headings of "emergency food management" and "timely warning". National food stocks or the "food balance sheet" is the central concern of the weak BNA in both normal and extreme conditions. Having sufficient food in stock through commercial imports and food aid, or transportation from surplus to deficit regions is the hub around which the weak BNA defines national food security.

To take an extreme but revealing example, Botswana, an arid, sparcely populated territory bordering South Africa, was, in early 1986, in its fifth year of serious drought. Livestock mortality had been high, sorghum crops had failed for several years, and even domestic water supplies in some parts were under pressure. Yet very few lives had been lost. Botswana can, in some respects with justification, be held up as a success story where timely warnings, nutritional surveillance through a network of rural clinics, expansion of school feeding and other special feeding programmes, purchase of dying livestock, public works employment, and – above all – timely commercial import of grain combined to avoid the tragic loss of life seen elsewhere in Africa since 1982–3 (Borton, 1984).

Is this a model of emergency action? Or was Botswana only able to manage the food emergency in this exemplary fashion because of its overwhelming dependency on South Africa? Grain imports were possible because of the foreign exchange earned from Botswana's export of diamonds, which are mined by the South African-based transnational De Beers. Local purchasing power is also largely dependent on the economy of South Africa. One-third of Botswana's male workforce is employed as migrants in South Africa, and roughly a third of all rural households has at least one such migrant worker. Remittances from such foreign employment averaged one-fifth of median rural income in 1974, and since then "average wages paid by the [South African] mines have more than doubled, and this has probably had an even greater proportional impact upon transfers. Incomes from agriculture, in comparison, barely increased in real terms" (Colclough and McCarthy, 1980: 171–4). Botswana's food security is illusory. Diamond earnings bought its grain (Fig. 5.1), and wages from South African mines (supplemented, of course, by some income from public works, livestock sales etc.) give its people purchasing power. From the point of view of control over the food system – the central issue of the strong BNA – all sorts of alarm bells must be sounded. Is it possible to speak meaningfully of food security in such a situation? Migrant labourers can be expelled from South Africa at any time and, as the diamond marketing crisis of 1981–2 showed, Botswana does not control the rate at which this resource is extracted and sold.

Is Botswana, together with Lesotho and Swaziland, unique in this external dependency? Or do we not see in these extremes the future of all African countries trapped in production for export markets in order to service debts incurred by importing food, industrial products and petroleum?

AFRICAN FOOD CRISIS

Burton, travelling in central Tanganyika in the 1850s, described a land of "barbarous comfort and plenty" (Kjekshus, 1977: 62).

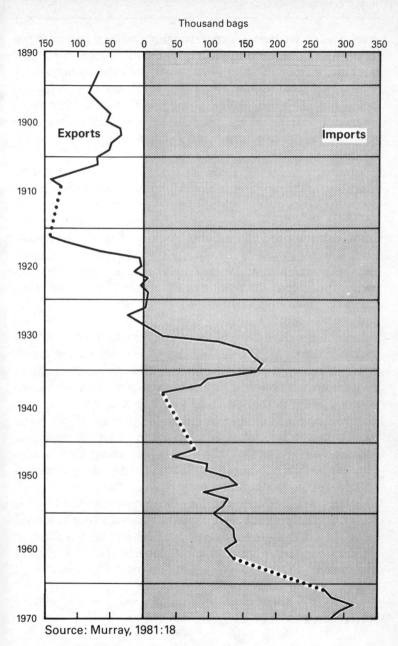

Source: Murray, 1981:18

Figure 5.1: Net Exports/Imports of Maize based on a 5 year rolling average

151

A few years after Independence, roughly a century later, Brooke reported that this central steppe region could expect a severe food shortage one out of six or seven years, that the economy was "virtually at the subsistence level" and that "serious soil erosion, including widespread active gullying, [had] resulted from over-grazing" (1967: Table 1). This contrast is repeated in much of sub-Saharan Africa (Palmer and Parsons, eds, 1977; Rotberg, ed., 1983).

The roots of chronic hunger and famine are deep and intertwined. The number of severely malnourished children in Botswana varies greatly with the season even in the best of years (Haaga *et al.*, 1983: 4). Mali's cotton exports to France increased fourfold during the Great Sahel Famine of 1967–72 (Twose, 1984: 4). The seeds of famine had been sown long before Dumont's well-known exposé (1966) of the "false start" in Africa, and, indeed, the "stranglehold on Africa" described in his sequel (Dumont and Mottin, 1983) was well-established by the time most countries were independent.

Lesotho is a classic case of transition from "granary to labour reserve" (Murray, 1981: 10–21). Figure 5.1 shows that territory's inexorable slide from food surplus to deficit as more and more male labour was drawn off into mine employment, as cereals and livestock suffered the vicissitudes of drought, epizootics and economic depression and as regional markets were closed because of the Boer War and legislative action on behalf of Afrikaner farmers across the border in the Orange Free State.

Such historical experience weakened Africa's rural production systems, and the weakening continues. Oddly, the "conjuncture" affecting food production in Lesotho between 1890 and 1940 contained many of the elements encountered in today's food crisis. External factors feature prominently in these recent analyses: the energy crisis and foreign debt that have caused governments to expand exports at the cost of domestic food production; regional conflict and destabilization that have destroyed infrastructure and provoked the movement of millions of refugees; and, of course, serious droughts.

Since the 1960s, per capita food production in Africa has fallen at an average of two per cent per year (Fig. 5.2), leading some observers to draw the conclusion that "drought, in terms of the

152

amount of locally grown food available per person, just brought forward a moment which would have been reached anyway in 1988" (ICIHI, 1985: 65). During this same period, imports of gran increased by nine per cent per year (World Bank, 1981b: 3, 45–9), meaning that the share of imported grain in total supplies was nearly a fifth in 1980–2 even before the massive expansion due to famine relief (Tabatabai, 1985).

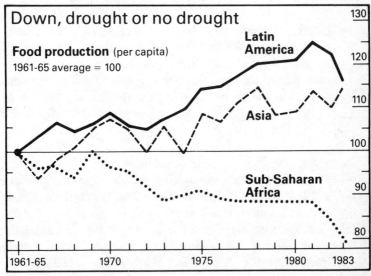

Source: ICIHI, 1985:65

Figure 5.2: Food Production per Capita

Blaming Governments and Victims

A series of internal factors are often invoked to explain this decline in combination with the exogenous forces mentioned above. These generally blame the African state for neglecting women farmers, small producers and the landless, for mismanagement of production incentives and marketing, for failure to extend basic infrastructure and services to rural areas and failure to maintain infrastructure, for encouraging agricultural research

153

of little or no relevance to the needs of the majority of farmers, for investing scarce resources in grandiose and inefficient large-scale irrigation schemes and state farms, for waste, and – as often as not – for corruption. In more sweeping condemnations the "anatomy of the personal state" is dissected and the legitimacy of the African state is called into question (Sandbrook, 1985). In milder critiques phrases such as "neglect of the peasant sector" tend to recur. Tabatabai (1985: 53) concludes, for instance:

> Starved of resources and offered few incentives, food producers have not had the opportunity, or perhaps even the reason, to improve their productivity. Except in the event of natural and man-made calamities, subsistence production could be and apparently was by and large maintained but production for market, of both food and export crops, suffered.

Such arguments about the legitimacy and efficacy of the African state are common, though probably overgeneralized (Hyden, 1983; Bates, 1981).. The "state" in Zaire, Mozambique and Mali, for instance, is not at all the same thing. Much of the blame for inappropriate research, investment in large-scale farming, unpopular top-down cooperative societies, coercive resettlement and the "cost-price squeeze" on small farmers would have to be shared with thousands of foreign advisers, experts and consultants who, as agents of donor-country and investing-agency interest, speak for the international "ad-hocracy" (ICIHI, 1985: 101–16).

Population growth, urbanization and environmental degradation in the form of erosion and deforestation usually top off a list of internal factors. Writing on these issues often comes danger-ously close to blaming the victim: people have large families, over-use the land and vegetation, and, in the end, abandon their homes and seek refuge in or around centres of food and possible employment because of the pressures of instability and the deterioration of their rural lives. But population growth, migra-tion and environmental degradation are the results of instability and deterioration of food systems, not the causes. What confuses this fundamental point is the fact that once the vicious spiral of

154

rural decline begins, the effects of poverty, such as deforestation and erosion, also become secondary causes.

Whatever else might be said of the food situation in Africa, the burden of chronic malnutrition even in the "good" years between the two great famines was very great. Figure 5.3 gives 1980 estimates of the numbers and proportions of under-fives with low weight-for-age. It is hard to find a country with fewer than a fifth of the under-fives suffering moderate protein-energy malnutrition. The absolute numbers are even more troubling: those countries with more than half a million children in this risky and marginal state during normal times are Burkina Faso, Mozambique, Uganda, Tanzania, Kenya and the Sudan; those with more than a million at risk are Zaire, Ethiopia and Nigeria. The list suggests that neither oil wealth, export diversity, nor foreign debt nor ideology is much of a predictor of malnourishment.

When disaggregated to the level of regions and social groups or considered in relation to the effects of particular food production strategies within individual countries, the complexities emerge. For instance, Kenya's 820,000 malnourished children are not at all evenly distributed socially or spatially. In eight of Kenya's 41 districts, more than 30 per cent of the children are nutritionally stunted, while the national average is nearer 20 per cent (Borton and Stephenson, 1984: 22-3). Children in poor female-headed households and children of sugar-producers are at high risk. Why? What conclusions about food as a basic need does such uneven distribution of hunger suggest? We return to the specific example of Kenya below.

Famine

This book began by noting the apparent shipwreck of the radical need-oriented and participatory alternatives of the 1970s on the crises of the 1980s. Hunger in Africa since 1981-2, building to a crescendo in 1983-4 when the UN listed 22 countries affected, diminishes the meaning of the word crisis in any other context (energy crisis, debt crisis, woodfuel crisis, a government's legitimation crisis). Even as the official list of critically affected countries was reduced to four midway through 1986, 136 million Africans were still affected by the emergency (UNOEOA, 1986a:

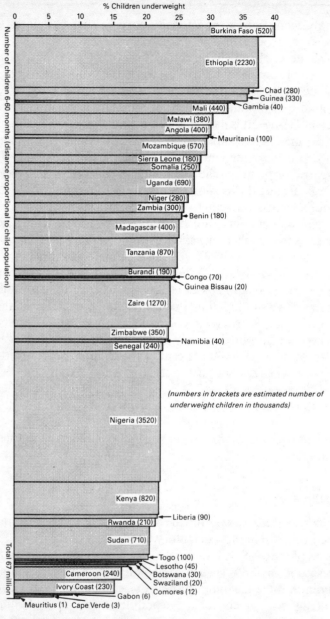

% Children underweight

Source: Haaga *et al*, 1984

Figure 5.3: Estimated Percentages of Malnourished Children, by country

19). Another seven countries were considered "in transition" but in need of close monitoring; three others were "on way to recovery".

In 1987 the cycle seemed to be starting all over again. A year after the UN General Assembly's Special Session on Africa, Perez de Cuellar noted that "Africa's margins for manoeuvre are being reduced in every respect". The same report noted that in 1986 total financial flows into Africa were $18 billion ($16 billion in aid and $2 billion private lending) while total outflows were $34 billion. The latter was composed of $15 billion of debt service and $19 billion due to the declining prices of Africa's export commodities on world markets (Lone, 1987: 1). As of November 1987 the World Food Programme (WFP) had decided that 25 African countries still faced food emergencies in 1988 and that the WFP's 1987–8 projections for African food aid requirements were grossly underestimated (Rule, 1987).

If one looks at the list of African countries said to be affected at the end of the 1986 famine cycle, it is clear that drought alone cannot explain the disaster. Ten of these thirteen critically affected and transitional countries had suffered from war, civil strife, destabilization and/or a massive influx of refugees. Compounding the problem is the rapidly accelerating import of expensive weapons by many of these affected countries. Arms purchases increase foreign debt, which in turn requires the growing of more export crops, distorts public expenditure and further undermines the economic position of the rural poor when recovery should be the highest priority (Shindo, 1985). Elsewhere in the UN list, local features of the crisis emerge under the magnifying pressure of exceptional hunger. In Lesotho the UN is seeking aid to combat an epidemic of tuberculosis in children – an endemic health problem fathers have been bringing home with them from the South African mines since the 1880s, to which is now added the deadly complication of hunger at a time of stress (de Beer, 1986). In Mali and Mauritania the UN reports a lack of emergency response to outbreaks of cholera, a relic of the world pandemic that reached the Sahel in the early 1970s with pilgrims returning from Mecca at a time when the population was weakened and concentrated around the few remaining water sources and market centres (Stock, 1976).

157

If the strong BNA is to carry weight in the period of recovery after the vast dislocation of people and time of suffering, it will have to embrace such causes and complications of hunger and show how this knowledge can be put to work and how it can empower people to reconstruct their lives.

"PRODUCTION FIRST" AND THE WEAK BNA

African leaders and intellectuals have long been aware of the growing crisis. There have been numerous discussions, plans and programmes drafted at national and regional levels responding to growing debt, rural malaise and industrial decline. Three regional associations have been founded in the past ten years to focus scientific, managerial and financial resources on the common requirements for recovery and economic independence in the Sahel, southern Africa and the Horn. Although their histories and mandates are different, they demonstrate the ability of the African leadership to conceive of radically different futures (cf. Hadjor, 1987; Kodjo, 1985). These regional associations are CILSS (Interstate Committee for the Fight Against Drought), which has grouped eight Sahelian states since 1975; SADCC (Southern African Development Coordination Conference), which since 1980 has united the efforts of nine southern African countries to break the infrastructural and economic dependency on South Africa; and IGADD (Inter-Governmental Agency for Drought and Development), involving eight countries of the Horn of Africa.

Can yet another level of urban-based technocracy help people at the grassroots? It could be argued that some of the common projects, for instance, in transportation and energy, are necessary preconditions for the restructuring of regional economies and the lessening of rural dependence on migrant labour and export crops. Yet individually, the commitment of the constituent post-colonial states to such restructuring has been weak for twenty years or more. The disappointing record of CILSS, oldest of the three regional efforts, does not augur well for the others.

Some $14 billion was channelled into the eight Sahelian countries after the drought in the late 1960s and early 1970s.

158

Estimates of what happened to this aid money vary, but as little as five per cent is said to have gone for rainfed agriculture according to one source (ICIHI, 1985: 87), although 95 per cent of Sahelian grain production is said to come from dryland farms. Another source believes that as much as 16 per cent went to rainfed food crops (Twose, 1984: 4). The sources do agree, however, that the great bulk of aid has gone for "infrastructure" and "urban support projects" and that nearly a third has gone to extend the same export crops – peanuts and cotton – that some argue have been instrumental in pushing small-scale food farmers and livestock keepers off fertile land, so gradually increasing the vulnerability of these societies to drought over the last hundred years (Franke and Chasin, 1980). According to one accounting, only 24 per cent of post-disaster aid in the Sahel between 1977 and 1984 went to any of the agricultural, pastoral or forestry sub-sectors, and of this amount, more than half (63 per cent) was spent on massive irrigation schemes (ICIHI, 1985: 85–8). The economic efficiency, environmental sustainability and social impact of these grandiose attempts to "roll back the desert" have been frequently questioned (Conti, 1979; Franke and Chasin, 1980; Reboul, 1982; Twose, 1984).

Even given these debacles, there is still the issue of whether Africans' analyses of, and solutions to, their food problems will receive more than a polite footnote if they do not coincide with the views of powerful interests such as the World Bank and the IMF. The Lagos Plan, for instance, agreed upon in 1981 by fifty African nations and the OAU's more recent Priority Programme for Economic Recovery 1986–9 lay heavy emphasis on reviving the smallholder farm sector. They also emphasize food self-sufficiency even at the (temporary) cost of export crop production (Organization of African Unity, 1981; UNOEOA, 1986b: 1 and 4). Agricultural recovery is placed in the context of industrial revitalization, production of basic production and wage goods, considerably accelerated intra-African economic cooperation, debt rescheduling and increased access to European and North American markets for African exports. These are not terribly radical proposals, but are the product of an African élite consensus. Not surprisingly, the areas of overlap with the World Bank's view of African recovery are wide; they emphasize the

159

delivery of inputs for increased productivity, not redistribution (hence control) of resources by the landless, women and smallest producers and are all, broadly speaking, "productionist" approaches. A shopping-list of reforms exhausts the social imagination of both élite African and foreign bankers' versions of the future. The shopping-list usually mentions reform of research and outreach to farmers with new technologies, improved economic incentives, changes in marketing and growth in basic infrastructure (roads, crop storage facilities, rural bank branches, etc.).

On the other hand, the subtler shades of emphasis given by the Africans could mean a good deal in containing the damage such plans will do the poorest and most vulnerable people in rural areas. Such differences have been politely ignored while the World Bank's exaggerated version of "production first" has gone through several sets of minor revisions (World Bank, 1981b, 1983, 1984). These differences centre on the balance between very small farmers and the middle-to-rich producers as priority beneficiaries of the programmes and on the balance between encouragement of food versus export crop production. Despite the vociferous debate that has centred on these issues (Green, 1984) and some evidence of dialogue and revision on the part of the Bank, its position in *Accelerated Development in Sub-Saharan Africa* (1981b) remains a very influential vision of Africa's agrarian future.

Accelerating What? For Whom?

The élite African vision and the view of foreign finance capital have a common technical origin in FAO's *Regional Food Plan for Africa*, which looks at both nutritional and economic aspects of the food problem. African leaders discussed the document in OAU meetings over a three-year period, so influencing thoughts about the necessary incentives, inputs and institutional arrangements. The World Bank bases much of its analysis on this prior policy discussion, but in its version the balance between smallholders versus larger, more successful farmers and very large commercial ventures is tipped in favour of the latter.

What is left of the smallholder emphasis resembles colonial

160

programmes to stimulate a class of progressive and yeoman farmers in the 1940s and 1950s. In the words of the World Bank (1981b: 52):

> [P]riority attention to smallholders must be selective – targeting those areas where the physical resource base and existing human and physical infrastructure provide the preconditions for repaid payoff from additional investment....

Herewith the Bank "drops distributional issues, and therefore the actual hunger of real people from the *Agenda*" (Green, 1984: 18). It particularly disavows attempts to overcome spatial inequities inherited from colonialism (World Bank, loc. cit.):

> In the 1970s, agricultural programs were often aimed at marginal regions, since the post-independence governments wanted to respond to the needs and aspirations of people in remote or disfavored regions of their countries.... But the marginal areas are only studied for food production and, even then not well suited; many are located in zones of low and unreliable rainfall, where knowledge about technical and social conditions of production is limited....

Furthermore, unworried by evidence that large farmers exploit their smaller neighbours, often holding them in debt bondage and buying out small farms and their assets, the Bank sees large farmers as a "spearhead" of progressive agriculture (loc. cit.):

> In a smallholder-based strategy which places production first, larger farmers can be used to spearhead the introduction of new methods. (This has been done in many cases in the past, but the approach has been frowned upon in recent years, as it has conflicted with the equity concerns, not so much of governments as of foreign sources of finance.)

The Bank's "production first" smallholder strategy is aimed, in the first instance, at boosting the commercial sector. Pricing, provision of inputs such as fertilizer, credit, marketing, research and extension are to be devoted to this aim. Institutional reforms are to take the form of reducing direct state involvement. Inputs and marketing can and should be privatized (at this point in the

161

argument the "comparative advantage" of transnational agri-business as provider of technology is said to join neatly with the "comparative advantage" of African countries as export crop producers).

Côte d'Ivoire and Kenya are supposed to exemplify such privatization, where transnationals have directed the expansion of palm oil, rubber, pineapple, tea and sugar production by using smallholder land and labour. The World Bank holds up the Kenya Seed Company, a government-private capital joint venture, as a model of institutional reform (World Bank, 1981b: 66; cf.: Buch-Hansen and Marcussen, 1982: 17–21).

The smallholder approach is supposed to generate foreign exchange income. Through demonstration effects and the spill-over of improved farming techniques from the export to the domestic food crop sector of the more progressive farmers, an increase in food production is also foreseen.

Food is also to be produced in large-scale irrigation schemes and state farms. Many of these were started in the years after the Sahelian famine. Existing irrigation schemes are to be rehabili-tated (another job for specialized foreign firms) and their management improved. One of the examples of "good manage-ment" cited by the Bank is the Mwea rice irrigation scheme in Kenya, a case we discuss below (World Bank, 1981b: 76–9, esp. 78).

The need for quick results that inspired the Bank's approach also lies behind its advocacy of large-scale farms. Many of these are to be joint ventures. For instance, Zambia hopes to be self-reliant in food by 1991 thanks to a $500 million, ten-year investment programme intended to set up eighteen large-scale mechanized farms. Firms from the UK, France, Japan, Bulgaria and East Germany are involved in setting up these farms (Dinham and Hines, 1982: 146–7). Nigeria's crash programme is expected to cost $8.24 billion and involves a large number of joint ventures with firms as diverse as Coca-Cola, Ford, Texaco and Fiat (*ibid.*: 152). In one form or another, agro-industrial strategies are being planned in Kenya, the Sudan, Ghana, Ethiopia, Tanzania, Mozambique, Togo and Benin as well as in Zambia and Nigeria (*ibid.*: 143).

Accelerating Dependency and Hunger

The quick fix philosophy underlying other forms of the weak BNA is apparent in the Bank's *Agenda* for African agriculture. Productivity is the cornerstone of this approach. Inputs in packaged form are to be delivered. In the US version – an extreme view of production-first that surpasses even the World Bank in its narrowness of vision – an African Green Revolution is invoked as the way "to give Africa the tools to meet her food needs", a task that will "require the best that science can offer worldwide" including biotechnology techniques such as cell and tissue culture for production of drought-tolerant and disease-resistant varieties (Brady, 1985: 1159).

The production-first approach to food security reflects the weak BNA in other ways too. In this view, neither radical participation nor control of resources and technology are important. The technical package is simply "delivered". National research and scientific establishments will not be adequate in many of the recipient countries to develop, monitor and control some of the proposed biotechnologies, let alone small farmers or groups of farmers themselves. As Green points out, "peasant participation in decision-taking and policy design is cited *en passant* as a key goal in the context of privitization, but there is little evidence of, or orientation toward, surveying or learning from peasant opinion. The dominant vehicle for participation by peasants seems to be the free market" (1984: 19).

Like other weak BN approaches, it also assumes that rising income will automatically ensure that poor smallholders will eat better. Just as issues of equity in the spatial and class or gender distribution of incentives and inputs are ruled as irrelevant in the Bank passages cited earlier, distribution of food, once the production-first strategy works its magic, is not considered to be a problem. Yet studies agree that chronic hunger and famine are seldom a result of absolute scarcity of food, but a problem of distribution (Sen, 1981). In Africa, this is often a seasonal phenomena. One study in the well-watered highlands of Kenya showed that during the "hungry" or pre-harvest season 48 per cent of the sample achieved only 59 per cent or less of standard nutritional requirements while, in the same village, 33 per cent of

163

the sample exceeded 100 per cent of requirements (Bohdal *et al.*, 1968: 111). In 1982, in Upper Volta (now Burkina Faso), traders were able to buy up the harvest for 30 francs per kilo and sell it back at the height of the dry season seven months later at 120 francs, at which time poorer villagers reported that they did not have the money to buy the grain at the traders' high price (Twose, 1984: 12). Again, in Kenya, preliminary data suggests that the children of poor smallholders who have adopted the new hybrid maize as a cash crop are at higher risk of malnutrition than the children of neighbours who have not "benefited" from the new Green Revolution. The reason seems to be that farmers do not earn enough from maize sales to enable them to buy other kinds of food such as proteins or vegetables.

"FOOD FIRST" AND THE STRONG BNA

It is not enough to criticize the World Bank's views. Are there workable alternatives? Given the deeply-rooted nature of the food crisis in Africa and the many vicious circles, no single clear-cut alternative model is likely to emerge from anyone's hat. But there are hopeful initiatives in many countries. These are found in the form of small-scale, community-based projects, usually assisted by indigenous or foreign NGOs. Several of these will be discussed more fully in the next chapter, but to give a sense of their diversity and scope, one might mention the following endeavours:

- Rehabilitation and multiplication of indigenous legume varieties in dryland, eastern Kenya (Miller, 1986);

- Community-based production credit and grain storage for resale to cooperative members at locally-controlled prices in Burkina Faso (Twose and Goldwater, 1985: 38; Twose, 1986);

- Locally-initiated and sustained women's gardening cooperatives in Senegal (Yoon, 1983) and Zimbabwe (Timberlake, 1987: 149–59);

- Peri-urban gardening co-ops and small animal production in Mozambique (Urdang, 1986);

- Support for farmers' crop trials in Sierra Leone (Richards, 1985) and Zimbabwe (Billing, 1985: 101–4);

- Revitalization of women's revolving credit schemes in Zimbabwe (Seidman, 1986a);

- Restocking cattle herds of destitutes in Niger by adapting the traditional livestock-loaning system (Scott and Gormley, 1980); and

- Forming of village groups for nutritional monitoring in western Sudan (York, 1985).

Such projects have much in common with previous examples of the strong BNA. They are based on the active participation of grassroots organizations. They do not depend on externally-developed technical "packages", but have evolved techniques and adapted technologies in a locally-appropriate, problem-solving approach. They have been inspired by social equity considerations: women, destitute herders, the urban unemployed are typical of their active membership. They emphasize long-term sustainability and gradual local accumulation of knowledge, skill, capital and self-confidence.

A number of multilateral and some bilateral development agencies also attempt to support these kinds of initiatives for food production. More than the NGOs involved in such work, however, these larger agencies are bound by host-government requirements and by their own internal bureaucratic demands for cost accounting and evaluation. Nonetheless, there is quite a contrast between some of the work supported by Nordic donors, UNICEF or the International Fund for Agricultural Development (IFAD), for instance, and the production-first approach of the World Bank and USAID. IFAD in particular does appear to base its funding on criteria broadly compatible with a strong BNA, although it is highly constrained by its mandate to work through existing governmental structures (extension systems, banks and marketing boards, etc.). Since its inception in 1978,

IFAD has concentrated its lending in the poorest, food-deficit countries, and its terms have been highly concessional. An attempt is made in project design to find ways of involving the poorest smallholders and even the landless. Grassroots group formation is encouraged in this process, as, in IFAD's words, one cannot "bypass people in order to reach people" (IFAD, 1985: 43).

Between 1978 and 1984, IFAD supported 57 projects in Africa in 36 countries with 466.4 million of Special Drawing Rights (SDR, a financial unit used in multilateral lending approximately equal to the US$). This amounted to nearly 28 per cent of IFAD's total loans and is not an insignificant amount of money if used well. Uganda, Malawi, Ethiopia, Madagascar, Burkina Faso and Mali received more than 20 million SDR each. Zaire, Sierra Leone, Mozambique, Burundi and Benin have each had 15 to 20 million. Tanzania, Rwanda, Niger, Kenya, Guinea and Ghana were each recipients of between 9 and 15 million.

Programmes dealing with sums of money as great as these tend to develop their own internal pressures for short-cuts in project identification and evaluation (Hayter and Watson, 1985). Also, IFAD's loans are used in a wide variety of ways. At its best, from the point of view of the strong BNA, IFAD has experimented with innovative ways of getting credit to small farmers and fishermen. At the same time, money has gone to support government agricultural research facilities of often questionable relevance to the needs of the poor.

In the case of IFAD, as with other kinds of NGO-sponsored projects, careful case-by-case scrutiny is required to work out whether the "food first" orientation is realized or remains a rhetorical commitment. One example is the Second Bong County Agricultural Project in Liberia, founded in 1984 to improve swamp rice development, rehabilitate and diversify cocoa farms and construct road and water supplies. In its early days, this "integrated rural development project" succeeded (unintentionally one assumes) in (a) introducing schistosomiasis widely in the project area; (b) lowering the wages of day-labourers who worked for the absentee owners of cocoa plantations by providing the former with drained swamp land for subsistence rice cultivation; and (c) excluding women from cooperative

166

membership. It is hard to imagine that IFAD's concern with social and environmental impacts, with women and the poorest classes will mesh well with all on-going national show-piece project with these established patterns. If the second Bong County project is to avoid the "achievements" of the first, a good deal of struggle with established interests will have to take place. Struggle is, of course, not at all taboo within the strong BNA, but it might be a bit too much for IFAD or any other large institution.

THE KENYAN FOOD CRISIS

The effects of a production-first food strategy and the contrast between strong and weak BNAs in the food sector can be seen in Kenya. In 1980, Kenya was forced to import considerable maize (the chief staple), wheat and milk. Food imports had risen steadily since 1969, but income from tea and coffee exports (accounting for 45 per cent of export income in 1979) had been declining since the 1977 commodity boom (GOK, 1981a: 6–8; Dinham and Hines, 1982: 93).

The government feared that Kenya would face endemic shortages of maize, wheat, rice and milk in the 1980s unless production was increased significantly. To achieve self-sufficiency by 1989, agriculture had to grow dramatically. Its growth rate had fallen from a 1964–73 average of 4.7 per cent a year to an average for 1974–80 that was barely more than Kenya's phenomenal population growth rate (4.2 per cent and 3.5 per cent p.a., respectively). In particular, national food self-reliance would require very high per annum growth rates for a wide variety of food crops, especially rice, wheat, beans, beef and potatoes, as Table 5.1 shows.

Kenyan agriculture would be hard put to meet this challenge. But the government has set it other goals as well (GOK, 1981a: 1):

> In addition, the agricultural sector must continue to gener-
> ate foreign exchange earnings to pay for oil, capital
> equipment and other imports ... at the same time, it must be
> the major source of new jobs for the rapidly growing labour

167

Table 5.1

A COMPARISON OF THE PLAN TARGET AND REQUIRED RATES OF GROWTH OF PRODUCTION

	Target Growth Rate in the 1979–83 Plan (% per year)	Rate Required to Achieve Self-Sufficiency in 1989 (% per year)
Maize	3.5	6.8
Wheat Flour	1.0	14.8
Sorghum/millet	4.7	4.8
Rice	7.6	16.4
Beans	5.0	10.5
Potatoes	4.3	7.0
Sugar	15.5	4.0
Beef	2.2	8.8
Milk	5.1	5.6

Source: GOK, 1981a: 51

force [and operate] with the primary objective of the provision of basic needs and the alleviation of poverty....

The government recognized that a return to the *status quo ante* would not be sufficient (*ibid.*: 2):

Although Kenya has retained a capacity to be broadly self-sufficient in foodstuffs throughout the past two decades, certain sectors of the population remain malnourished as a result of income inequalities, problems of distribution between geographical zones, seasonal fluctuations in supply....

At the end of a similar and more elaborate calculation of realistic targets required for a future production-consumption balance, McCarthy and Mwangi (1982: 78) conclude that eighteen per cent of the population would still be suffering from protein energy malnutrition in the year 2000. "This is not a very encouraging prospect," they remark in a statement reminiscent of the fatalism expressed by the former president of the World Bank.

Fruits of Uhuru?

Kenya has been one of the "economic miracles" of post-colonial Africa along with Cote d'Ivoire, and has relied on a strategy of "growth and Africanization" of an economic system virtually identical to the colonial one (Leys, 1975). This formula seemed to

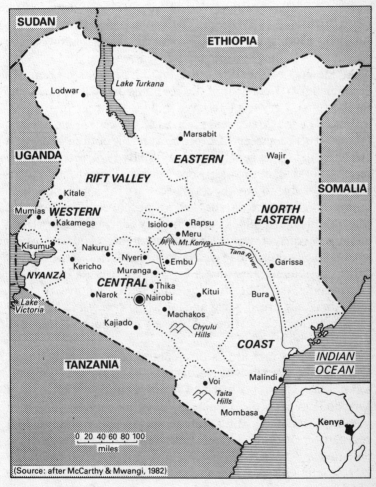

(Source: after McCarthy & Mwangi, 1982)

169

work. Between 1964 and 1970, economic growth averaged 6.5 per cent a year. Yet, as discussed in the chapter on Primary Health Care, these "fruits of *uhuru* [independence]" were not well distributed. In 1970, some 30,000 households (one per cent of the total) received more than KL1000 a year while nearly one and a half million households (mostly smallholders, pastoralists, landless rural labourers and the urban semi-employed, amounting to 63 per cent of the Kenyan population) made less than KL60 (ILO, 1972). That is, a sizeable majority of Kenyans fell below the then current international rule of thumb defining absolute poverty, US$50 per capita (World Bank, 1975b: 4; Wisner, 1978: 51–2). In the mid-1950s Bengoa (1956: 4) reported that the cost of supplying a family with 10,000 Kcals a day for a month would be 102 Kenyan shillings or roughly KL60 a year.

At the end of the 1960s, the top 12 per cent of Kenyans accounted for 57 per cent of the country's annual income while the bottom 12 per cent received only 2 per cent of national income. The top 20 per cent received 68 per cent of income, the middle 40 per cent received 22 per cent and the bottom 40 per cent received only 10 per cent (Wisner, 1978). By 1974, according to a recent World Bank analysis, one-third of Kenyan households were still unable to buy the food necessary for a minimum level of nutrition and were thus defined as "absolutely poor" (cited in Mason and Okeyo, 1985). A recent study concluded that even on an austere diet of maize and beans alone, a quarter of all smallholder households in Kenya are not able to feed themselves. When these authors assume a less austere, culturally desirable diet including Nairobi prices for minimum quantities of meat, milk, tomatoes, bread, sugar and fat, *94 per cent of all smallholder families* in Kenya must be defined as "food poor" (Greer and Thorbecke, 1984).

Spatial disparities are as pronounced as social ones. In the Coast and Western Provinces, for example, Greer and Thorbecke found that just over a half and nearly a third, respectively, of smallholders lack the income to keep themselves and their families adequately fed on a simple diet of maize and beans. A comparison of the 1977 and 1982 National Nutrition Surveys undertaken by UNICEF (GOK/UNICEF, 1984) and the UN (Mason and Okeyo, 1985) shows substantial increase over this

170

period of malnutrition in the west of Kenya and along the coast. Fifty-five per cent of all stunted (low height-for-age) children were found in nine of the 26 districts surveyed.

Nationwide, 28 per cent of pre-school children are stunted. The risks of childhood malnutrition are highest among smallholders owning less than 1.5 hectares of land. As Mason and Okeyo conclude, "these farm households are the majority of the rural population, are increasing in number and proportionately, and do not always benefit from development programmes" (1985: 3).

Another review finds 37 per cent of Kenyans malnourished (Ghai *et al.*, 1979). As Table 5.2 illustrates, this overall review of basic needs categorizes and quantifies those most at risk of hunger. The framework also allows one to anticipate the results of intensifying a production-first food strategy in Kenya, a strategy already well-established though clothed at various times according to changing fashions and now sporting the livery of basic human needs.

Of the groups identified in Table 5.2 as having severe nutritional problems, a production-first strategy employs some of the landless poor (category 1b), and could possibly produce cheaper urban food, benefiting urban underemployed (but not unemployed) (1c). However, it increases pressure through privatization, rising rents and speculation on the land of the small food producers (1a) and pastoralists (3). Most importantly, later in this chapter, a case study of sugar production will show that category 1c, "cash crop producers with household income around K.sh. 2500 (at 1975 prices)" are actually suffering nutritional crisis as a result of production-first strategies.

The rural working poor or poor small farmer (subsistence farmers who also sell their family's labour or a high-value cash crop to make ends meet) numbered 600,000 households in 1976, or nearly a quarter of Kenya's 2.8 million households. Many of these were headed by women. They were concentrated in the West (Nyanza and Western Provinces) and in Eastern Province (78 per cent of the total) (Ghai *et al.*, 1979: 26). Another 140,000 households (five per cent of the national total) who had been forced to sell land to finance school fees, repay loans or survive (Ghai *et al.*, 1979: 27) found themselves living in rural areas with no land and no formal sector job (77 per cent of them in Rift

Valley and the Central and Eastern Provinces). Other landless have joined a considerable number of people in spontaneous rural-to-rural movements in search of farming land in the drier, yet marginally arable edges of the rangelands to the north and east (Wisner, 1978; Mbithi and Barnes, 1975), where they became rural squatters.

In 1976 the poor smallholders, landless and squatters on large farms totalled more than a third of all Kenyan households. That figure is likely to be considerably higher by now. These are some of Kenya's poorest people (Crawford and Thorbecke, 1978; Collier and Lal, 1980). However, this third of Kenyan households is not the direct target of the production-first strategy. On the other hand, the low-income smallholder, who, among others *is* the target, will likely be driven into landlessness or squatting as a result. One must sympathize with Green, who wonders whether the World Bank's *Agenda* should be retitled "Accelerating Starvation" (1984: 20).

The "Production-First" Strategy in Kenya

Spurred by a famine in the remote, arid northwest among the Turkana people in 1979–80 and by the trend toward rapidly increasing food imports even in good years, a food policy paper was prepared for Parliament and presented in 1981. Kenya already had been on the basic needs bandwagon for some time. The complex social forces and external shocks that had moved Kenya in this direction in regard to basic health services and, at least in word if not deed, primary health care have been described in Chapter 2. In the case of national food policy, the same populist, élite, and bureaucratic imperatives applied.

An urban élite diet based on Western-style consumption was becoming harder to maintain with shrinking foreign exchange for imports. The élite wanted to stock the new all-meat restaurant for Nairobi businessmen called "The Carnivore" with local products. But it also had an interest in maintaining the flow of foreign exchange through export crop production so that it could carry on importing Volvos and Johnny Walker scotch. "Populists" realized that pressure on the small producers was becoming unbearable: they were meant to be growing both domestic and

Table 5.2

NUTRITION PROBLEMS IN KENYA, 1978

Nutritionally Deficient Group	Nutrition Problem	Cause of Problem	Estimated Number in Group ('000)
1. SMALLHOLDERS			
(a) Food crop producers with average household income of K.sh. 1000 or below* and virtually no sales	Protein energy malnutrition (PEM)	Insufficient food production	2,200
(b) Landless poor	PEM	Low real income	410
(c) Cash crop producers with household income around K.sh. 2500*	Periodic PEM	Low earnings with poor distribution throughout the year	1,090
2. URBAN UNEMPLOYED AND UNDEREMPLOYED	PEM	Low real income	250
3. PASTORALISTS	Periodic PEM	Vulnerability to weather: lack of food security	670

* at 1975 prices

Source: GOK, 1979b, cited in Ghai *et al.*, 1979: 32

export crops, and both in increasing quantities. Renewed interest in the history of Mau Mau and the Land Freedom Army, student unrest and the rise of popular political drama all expressed the populist imperative: food first. Ngũgĩ's protagonist in *I Will Marry When I Want* is explicit (1982: 40):

> Look at the women farm labourers,
> Or those that pick tea-leaves in the plantations:
> How much do they get?
> Five or seven shillings a day.
> What is the price of a kilo of sugar?
> Five shillings!
> So with their five shillings:
> Are they to buy sugar,
> Or vegetables,
> Or what?
> Or have these women got no mouths and bellies?
> Take again the five shillings:
> Are they for school fees,
> Or what?
> Or don't those women have children
> Who would like to go to school?
> Well, independence did indeed come!

The bureaucratic imperative, best expressed by the Ministry of Finance and Planning, was to minimize the leakage of foreign exchange on food imports that could be channelled into investment and, possibly of more importance, to reduce the number of food emergencies requiring costly imports and a great deal of highly-skilled management time (Cohen and Lewis, 1987).

In more general terms, the 1979–83 Development Plan had made the elimination of poverty its major theme (GOK, 1979c: 11–13, 17). The 1981 *Sessional Paper on National Food Policy* was therefore put forward as a basic needs approach concerned with food security. In fact, the similarities with the World Bank's *Agenda* are striking. At best one had here an *ex post* justification of the *status quo*, somewhat dressed up as a weak BNA. At worst, it was, and still stands, as a recipe for "accelerated starvation".

Its essence, in point summary, is that:

174

(1) The responsibility for feeding the nation must be shared between public and private sectors (GOK, 1981a: 3).

(2) It is assumed that equalization of income distribution will not be rapid. Instead, it is argued that "inequalities in income distribution will mean that, as today, some sectors of the population will consume considerably more than the minimum requirement while others will remain malnourished. Under such circumstances, and given policies aimed specifically at increasing the nutritional intake of low income groups, considerably more food must be supplied than that required just to meet the national average per capita nutritional requirement if the entire population is to be fed adequately" (*ibid.*: 10).

(3) Considerable additional hectares would have to be farmed in order to meet targets. Much of this could be achieved by inter-cropping or double-cropping major grains with root crops and pulses. Additional tracts of land would be needed for ranching, however (*ibid.*: 13).

(4) "As a general principle, there should be no diversification of land under export crops ... nor should there be further destruction of forests. Given these constraints, there is little potential in Central and Eastern Provinces for an expansion in the area of good quality land devoted to food production" (*ibid.*: 13). This is true of most of the country.

(5) Most expansion of food production will have to come from increases in yields through inter-cropping, multiple cropping, increased volume and efficiency of fertilizer use, improved seeds and livestock, improvements in cultural practices – an African Green Revolution, in short.

(6) Price, inputs, research and extension policies must be tailored to support these yield increases.

(7) Government land-use policy must ensure "economic units" and proper soil and water conservation and the use of energy-efficiency technologies. "The process of land adjudication will be accelerated and special attention will be paid to solving the problems created by the *de facto* subdivision of group-owned large farms to ensure that these farms are not subdivided into uneconomic units" (*ibid.*: 23). This also means that private ownership will be

175

accelerated in areas where communal tenure still exists, that larger farmers will be encouraged, while, at the same time, "measures will be taken to discourage land speculation" (*ibid.*:: 23).

(8) The core of the policy would seem to enable those larger and richer farmers who have the land and income to purchase inputs and increase yields without disturbing the present balance (and by implication the future balance) of export and food crops. Moves toward the rationalization of capitalist relations of production (changes in land tenure, encouragement of "economic units") are to go along with the yield-increasing packages, although the free play of market forces (e.g. land speculation) is to be controlled.

Since this strategy obviously does not apply to very small cash crop producers, the landless poor and poor smallholders with virtually no sales (totalling more than a third of all households), the strategy includes some statements about reducing income inequalities, promoting the most nutritious foods and "implementing specific market intervention programmes as and when necessary." There are vague "programmes to increase labour mobility and labour productivity at times of labour shortage" – meaning, it would seem, government encouragement of the poor and landless to migrate seasonally to ease labour bottlenecks on the farms of the rich. As such, this final item belongs to the set of policies designed to rationalize and streamline capitalist farming more than it does in the category of "employment" or "minimum income targeting' typical of the weak BNA.

This policy amounts to a continuation and intensification of the existing *de facto* policy. Current relations of production and ownership are consolidated as the food policy's framework for "implementation". It is possible to predict the disastrous consequences such consolidation will have by looking in detail at two parts of the country where the production-first approach is already well advanced. These cases involve contract sugar production in Western Province and tenant production of rice on a government scheme in Eastern Province.

CONTRACT SUGAR PRODUCTION IN WESTERN KENYA

In recent years sugar production in Kenya has grown so greatly that the national needs are nearly covered and an export capacity is envisioned (GOK, 1981a: 9). As noted, already, the policy is not to diversify any of the land under sugar for the sake of other food crops. The rationale for this policy is the well-known growth of demand for sugar in urban diets, the increased use of sugar in food processing – another sector on the rise in Kenya today (Dinham and Hines, 1982: 107–10) – and Kenya's continued interest in the use of sugarcane-based ethanol production to cut petroleum imports.

Sugar is mainly produced in western Kenya, where both conventional plantations and nucleus-outgrower or contract systems are in use. It is the nutritional and developmental consequence of the contract system that offers greatest insight into the Kenyan food strategy.

Contract sugar production in Western Province has been studied a good deal (George, 1976; Holtham and Hazlewood, 1976; Barclay, 1979; Mulaa, 1981); Buch-Hansen and Marcussen (1982), for example, present a quantitative assessment of the income effects of sugar contract farming as part of their overall assessment of the potential for contract farming in Kenya. They estimate that in 1981 about twelve per cent of Kenyan smallholdings produced cash crops on contract to agro-industries. These agro-industries are led by sugar and tea, with tobacco and horticultural products such as pineapple developing quickly. Sugar is therefore important as a bell-wether of this new form of agricultural organization, as well as being important in its own right. When new contract sugar projects are all under way in the 1980s, the authors estimate 75 to 80 per cent of Kenya's sugar will be produced by contract farming.

The contract system works fairly straightforwardly. The sugar transnational Booker McConnell, for instance, which manages the Mumias scheme for the government (which has a majority share), contract with smallholders for the use of their land around its sugar factory. The company ploughs, furrows, cuts and loads

177

the cane and takes it to the factory for a fee. Inputs are provided (again for a charge) as well as extension advice. Smallholders must plant, weed and apply fertilizers and pesticides with their own or hired labour.

The expectation was that participating farmers would, while growing their own food, use the income from sugar not only to meet the needs of their families but to improve their farms (Buch-Hansen, 1980; Tobiesen, 1979; Buch-Hansen and Marcussen, 1982). Contrary to such expectations, however, analysis of the anthropometric data from the large 1977 sample of children assessed by the Central Bureau of Statistics reveals possible strong negative associations between nutritional status of children in families growing sugar as opposed to those of the non-growers (GOK, 1979a: II.3–7/8). The study concludes that cash crop production in general seems to raise income without improving (but also not worsening) the nutritional status of the children in the families concerned. A significant exception to this suggested neutral effect is sugar producers to the west of the Rift Valley, meaning the sugar-contract system (GOK, 1979a: II.3.8).

The nutritionists explain their findings:

> Just over 5 per cent of the sampled children in these zones were drawn from sugar-cultivating households. Sugar plantings in zone 3 occupy an average of 1.35 hectares which is larger than the zonal average of 1.1 hectares for all crops and all holdings. These households are likely to be engaged in virtually no subsistence food cultivation.

Buch-Hansen and Marcussen also found a mean sugar holding around Mumias of 1.3 hectares (median 1.0 hectare). They note (p. 34) that:

> in the sugar area the problem may arise for some of the very small farmers who have planted almost all their land with cane. Although on average there seems to be no scarcity of land, *half of the farmers we interviewed had less than one hectare left for subsistence production.* As the average family size on these farms was more than 10 and as they all had less than K.sh. 3,000/- a year from sugar production, they could not for a long time survive a crop failure nor deteriorating terms of trade [emphasis added].

Since even the World Bank emphasizes that the risks of crop failure are great for smallholders in Africa (World Bank, 1981b; Lele, 1975; Zinkin, 1971) and that the terms of trade have been (and are likely to continue to be) moving against the rural producer in favour of the urbanite (World Bank, op. cit.; Lipton, 1977), the final statement by Buch-Hansen and Marcussen must be seen as a prediction of family crisis.

MWEA: A RICE IRRIGATION SCHEME IN EASTERN KENYA

The World Bank sees potential in large-scale irrigation in Africa, but believes that the 1980s must be spent rehabilitating existing schemes. Throughout Africa, it reports, grain yields on irrigation schemes are very low, often only two to three tons per hectare where six would be necessary to justify the investment. These low yields are stagnant or even declining in some places. The causes, in the Bank's view, are a combination of poor water management, insufficient levelling of land, soil problems, input supply bottlenecks, use of varieties not adapted to local conditions, poor economic incentives for farmers and weak support and bad extension services (World Bank, 1981b: 77). While the rehabilitation of existing schemes proceeds, the Mwea rice scheme is held up as an exceptional success among many failures.

Only a fraction of Kenya's 142,000 irrigable hectares is exploited. Kenya's National Irrigation Board (NIB) is responsible for most of this, supervising large-scale organized irrigation projects covering more than 6,000 hectares. These include Mwea and other tenant settlements on the Kano Plains and elsewhere in the west, as well as the recently established Bura scheme extension to the Lower Tana Basin development.

The NIB, created in 1966, is a statutory body under the Ministry of Agriculture. It is responsible for research, establishing irrigation schemes, raising funds for the development of such schemes, coordinating and planning settlement, designing, constructing and administering the schemes, and processing and marketing the produce (Giglioli, 1973: 168).

Mwea actually has a much longer history rooted in land

179

disputes and a number of different attempts at development (Moris, 1973a). The irrigation works on the Mwea Plains to the south of Mt Kenya and to the east of the Aberdare range were constructed by Mau Mau freedom fighters detained by the British authorities during the Emergency in the 1950s. Since 1966, the scheme's more than 3,000 formerly landless families have been under the supervision of the NIB.

A very strict management system is enforced over the production of paddy rice on 1.6-hectare family plots. The tenant is required to perform some 23 distinct operations, which between them fill the entire year and demand 2,169 hours of labour on the average plot (Veen, 1973: 109, 119). This works out to 1,356 hours of labour per hectare, which is within the range of other wet-rice systems (over 1,700 in Japan, between 1,000 and 2,000 in Taiwan, around 1,400 in Madras, but only 456 in Malagasy, according to Ruthenberg, 1971: 156). The figure is quite high for African agriculture, however (cf. 755 for groundnuts in Senegal, 476 for millet in Upper Volta, 940 for maize/sorghum in Tanzania, 552 for sorghum in Cameroon, 446 for manioc in Malagasy), again according to Ruthenberg (1971: 71, 116), it is not unprecedented, as cotton cultivation in Sukumaland of Tanzania requires around 1,500 hours of labour per hectare (*ibid.*: 71). The most notable characteristic of this system is the very sharp peak in demand for labour at harvest time. This is what women on the scheme find most troubling, probably because it conflicts during January and February with the harvest of maize from their red-soil plots (which benefit from the short rains of the region's bimodal rainfall).

Deviation from the labour system can mean a fine or even expulsion from the scheme. The results of this rather heavy-handed supervision, called a "success story" by Kenyan scholars (Ojany and Ogendo, 1973: 147) as well as by the World Bank, has been reasonably good productivity (five tons of paddy per hectare) and reasonably good maintenance of the infrastructure. The scheme is not only the largest of the NIB's operations, but the only one that consistently shows a profit (Carruthers and Weir, 1976: 304–6).

Thousands of landless or very poor farm families have been absorbed from the densely populated ridges and valleys of

Central Province's Aberdare Mountains, within view of Mwea's flat expanse below. Tenants' net incomes now well surpass the planned target of K.sh. 2,000 in cash. By the early 1970s, 87 per cent of tenants exceeded that amount, while 40 per cent earned more than K.sh. 4,000 (Carruthers and Weir, 1976: 306). These figures are comparable to those given by Buch-Hansen and Marcussen as the average net cash income for contract farmers growing tea in the west (K.sh. 1,500–2,000) and sugar (K.sh. 3,000) (Buch-Hansen and Marcussen, 1982: 28).

Such economic success has seldom been questioned despite the concentration of benefits on a few thousand families. The argument justifying such large investments on so few would naturally be that the nation, and in particular urban rice consumers, thereby gain an efficient alternative to imported rice. Similar comparisons have been made between the relatively efficient contract sugar growers and the organizational alternative, cooperatives. There has, however, been discussion of reducing the size of the tenant's plots in order to allow recruitment of more participants (ILO, 1972: 413–15, 420). None of this suggests that planners doubted that Mwea was good for tenant families.

Nutritional Impacts of Mwea

As in the case of sugar contract farming, a look at nutritional studies might have caused Mwea planners some second thoughts. Two clinical and anthropometric studies (Korte, 1969; Wanjohi et al., 1977) suggest a deterioration of child nutrition in Mwea tenant families in the ten years 1966–76 (King-Meyers, 1979: 13–16). The more recent study found a third of the children one to five years old to weigh less than eighty per cent of the standard for their ages. Not only was there a suggestion of deterioration of nutritional status with time (comparability of studies is, of course, always a problem in such cases), but Mwea children compared unfavourably with other children in Central Province, showing a higher rate of severe nutritional wasting in the sample of 709 under-fives in tenant families (King-Meyers, 1979: 15).

In a 1966 study Korte had made similar comparisons with non-tenant families from the surrounding area. His optimistic

181

conclusions now ring a little hollow in light of subsequent research findings (1973: 271–2):

> In terms of nutrition, tenant families have benefited from a relatively high independence from seasonal changes in the caloric adequacy of the diets: they are less vulnerable than their off-scheme neighbors to intermittent periods of famine. On the other hand, the high proportion of cereals in the diet and the low consumption of milk, meat, eggs and green vegetables have combined to produce protein and riboflavin deficiencies. It appears from these health and nutrition surveys that an improvement of economic status does not necessarily in the short run entail an improvement in health and nutrition. *Greater productivity and higher incomes do, however, provide the long-term means for tackling these problems, and it would be surprising if in the future tenant incomes were not used to a greater extent to overcome them.* [emphasis added].

For over ten years the tenant families themselves expressed their dissatisfaction with the scheme, a clear warning that all was not well. Hanger and Moris (1973; summarized by Rogers, 1980: 183–5) found, in particular, considerable discontent among tenant wives; they complained of hunger amidst abundant rice crops, growing difficulties in finding either the time or money to provide the family with fuel and water ("women's work") and to work in their husbands' rice plots. The report notes "high rates of desertion" by wives who become fed up with living conditions at Mwea and their increasing difficulty of functioning in a situation in which they had no rights or control.

The similarities between Mwea and Mumias are striking. *In both cases one encounters rising cash incomes, malnutrition and the exploitation of women.* What is the common thread running through these two economic and social situations? A closer look at the situation of wives at Mwea makes the answer clear.

Impact on Women

Given the physical and social design of the Mwea scheme, women are forced to journey long distances to farm small plots of unirrigated land for the production of maize, beans and vegetables. This inconvenience is a direct consequence of four underlying assumptions made by planners in setting up the scheme (Moris, 1973b: 300). These assumptions were that tenants would have: high incomes; low labour costs; would use rice as their subsistence staple; and would be capable of managing their cash income over the year. Superimposed on the chronic structural problems plaguing Kenya as a whole (e.g. inflation), these design assumptions underlie both women's dissatisfaction with life at Mwea and the scheme's nutritional impact.

Rogers (1980: 183–4) expands on this list. First, she says, scheme authorities treat the male head of household as the scheme's principal labourer and decision-maker. Tenancy contracts are with him, and annual lump-sum payments for rice are made to him. Second, the exclusive social goal of Mwea was seen to be raising tenant income. It was assumed that *raising cash income would automatically improve physical and social welfare by creating a market demand for services*. Third, it was assumed that tenant families would eat rice, and they were allocated no land for any other crops. Fourth, it was assumed that families would buy other foods with the cash they earned from rice sales. Together, these assumptions have produced an impossible situation for women. They control little of the rice income yet must provide the family with food, fuel, water and health care in an increasingly inflation-ridden local economy. Men are responsible, however, for education (fees, school uniforms), an obligation also undertaken by the men of Mumias (Buch-Hansen and Marcussen, 1982: 33, 35; cf. Moris, 1973b: 305).

The assumed dietary shift from maize and beans to rice and commercially purchased supplements has not occurred. Instead, women seek to cultivate the familiar staples on unirrigated red soil areas in unused areas within the scheme or in plots outside it. Given the intense competition for the Mwea Plains historically, it is difficult for these women to find adequate land outside the scheme within a reasonable distance. Table 5.3 suggests both the continued importance of this unplanned use of women's labour and the continued importance of maize and beans in tenants' diets. This was true in 1977 as well, twenty years after the Mwea settlers first arrived.

183

Table 5.3

RED SOIL USE AND STAPLE FOODS IN SCHEME HOUSEHOLDS (1967)

Village	Average red soil hectares	% of meals with rice as staple	% of meals with maize/beans as staple	% of meals with other food staple
Kiarukungu	0.81	23	68	9
Mathangauta	1.01	37	51	11
Murubara	0.71	36	50	14
Ndorome	0.51	50	44	6

Source: adapted from Hanger and Moris, 1973: Table 6

The amounts of land shown in Table 5.3 are not large enough to produce food for the families given prevailing dry-land technology and yields. Ruthenberg (1971: 75–6, 117–22) found cultivated areas of comparable rain-fed systems in East Africa to be from two or three times as large. In addition, women's labour must be divided among numerous other activities.

Why do women persist in trying to farm outside of the scheme? Certainly food preferences are not a sufficient explanation. In fact "preferences" have nothing to do with it: growing food is a necessity. Women need money to purchase fuelwood – the scheme has no woodlots – and to pay for transportation to health care services off-scheme, clothing and household furnishings. The higher costs of petrol have filtered down to communities in the form of higher bus and taxi fares. By May 1980, the cost of clothing had gone up over 230 per cent and the cost of household furnishings had risen 201 per cent over 1975 levels (GOK, 1980a: 282). Labour and land constraints on women reduce their ability to earn their own independently-controlled cash income. Men control the annual cash payment for rice. Hanger and Moris (1973: 241–2) describe the consequences of this situation:

> Mwea male tenants are paid in cash for their production, but in effect the Scheme's women are paid in paddy. We have

seen that a woman has little official claim on the gross income that will be paid to her husband for his delivered paddy, and that she lacks the ordinary means (the sale of food crops) used off the Scheme to meet her immediate cash needs. Furthermore, scheme households reach the critical harvesting period at the end of the calendar year when they have little if any ready cash left. Given the large differential between the producer and retail prices of rice, it was almost inevitable that rice would itself function as a substitute currency within the Scheme environs. A man cannot refuse his wife access to the paddy which she has helped to harvest with her own hands.

Women sell some of the rice they receive from their husbands on the black market – itself organized by women in market places bordering Mwea – to generate the cash they need. This is another reason why food requirements are not simply met out of rice withheld from official marketing (Hanger and Moris, 1973: 242).

A remarkably similar problem has been reported from the sugar contract area, where worry is expressed over the nutritional consequences of "shifts [of] economic power in favour of the father and away from the mother who is responsible for the provision of food" (GOK, 1979a: II.3.3). King-Meyers (1979: 38–9) summarizes the observations of field workers in the areas where, as in Mwea, women's labour was used in growing the "man's crop". Field workers interviewed indicated that the current emphasis on cash crop production, especially of sugarcane, causes a decrease in food crop production and exacerbates nutritional problems. The syndrome described was one of women waiting for cash from the sale of sugarcane rather than growing food crops. Frequently, when the money is at last available it goes to the male head of household who may or may not share it with the mother. A growing literature from other parts of Africa warns of the damaging consequences of this pattern of "double exploitation" of African women (Mønstead, 1976; Barth-Eide et al., 1977; Rogers, 1980; Bukh, 1981; Savané, 1981; Palmer, 1981).

For many poor women, the result is a "basic needs conflict" that is often the core of what has been described as a squeeze on smallholder families. Integrated rural development programmes are among the attempts inspired by the weak BNA to deal with the small farm squeeze – but as we shall see, they are far from successful.

Chapter 6

Rural Development: The Super-Shopping-List?

ECOLOGICAL COLLAPSE AND THE COLLAPSE OF FAMILY FOOD SECURITY

Between a third and two-fifths of all households in Kenya are unable to feed themselves adequately. Nearly a third of all children are stunted. The situation is getting worse, and pressure is greatest, not surprisingly, where the limits of existing peasant agro-ecology – either in the geographic scope of arable land or in the degree to which plots can be intensively cultivated – have been reached.

In western Kenya, where a high proportion of child malnutrition is concentrated, and where sugar contract farming has taken hold, farmland has been fragmented into ever-shrinking plots. As mentioned earlier, the average farm in Kakamega is only 1.4 hectares in size; in one pilot village, the average farm is even smaller, at 0.7 hectares. Yet according to district planners a family must hold at least three hectares to earn an income above the poverty line. In the east (Foreland Plateau and Coastal Hinterland) and in the Rift Valley, another centre of food poverty and child malnutrition, the "extensive" limits of small-farm technology have been reached. Here the former-landless from western Kenya and from Central Province have chosen migration into the arable margins of the rangeland rather than flight to the city.

This chapter explores the economic pressure on small farms and the pressure which poor farmers in turn put on the environment. Marginal farmers, many of them women, are being forced to overexploit the soil and vegetation around them. They may be formerly landless peasants trying to eke out a living on the semi-arid boundaries of the rangelands or farmers still attempting to cultivate fragmented and overworked plots, but whether they are in the East or better-watered West and Central Provinces, they are compelled by land pressures and market forces and the need to survive to degrade the environment. A series of processes at work in Kenyan society are allocating marginal people to marginal lands.

Perhaps there is a role for an African Green Revolution in these zones of "persistent rural poverty", as Ghai and Radwan (1983) put it. Perhaps "rural development" can offer a way out of "integrated rural poverty" (Chambers, 1983), if the "shopping-list" can tackle a sufficient number of the problems afflicting the rural poor (low productivity, poor health, poor access to services and water, insufficient food, inadequate technology, few incentives, etc.).

Where production-first puts its faith in the larger farmers as the vanguard of agricultural development, a strategy of rural development would clearly have to target the poorest people in the least productive areas of the country. Would this break the vicious circles of rural poverty? Would the attempt be limited by the contradictions besetting all weak BNAs? In order to address these questions, we must look at the condition of Africa's rural poor.

The Rural Squeeze

Peasants are usually defined as

> rural producers who produce for their own consumption and for sale, using their own and family labor, though the hiring and selling of labor power is also quite possible.... Peasants may also be described as a "part society" defined by their subordinate relationships to external markets, the state and the dominant culture. The peasantry are subordinate to other classes within the state and may be required to yield some tribute to them (Harriss, 1982a: 24).

They are a problem for modernizers because despite their subordinate relations to markets and to other classes, and despite their partial involvement in the labour market, they own (or at

188

least have some conventionally sanctioned access to) their own means of production (especially land, but also water rights and animals). They are therefore relatively independent of the state and the dominant classes as well as of the market.

Peasants' labour power could produce profits for the capitalist if it were "freed" from the land. Peasants' crops could make profits for the state if they were channelled into official marketing systems. But how to ensure that this vast potential comes more fully under and stays under the control of capitalists and state officials?

The colonial solution was to impose taxes that had to be paid in cash. Peasants then had to work for capitalists or to sell crops and livestock in order to pay taxes. In some cases (such as in Mozambique) the direct expedient of forced labour was employed. Since independence in Kenya (and in the majority of independent African countries) a number of more subtle mechanisms have combined to "free" peasant labour and to direct family efforts toward production for the market. These processes are *privatization*, *commoditization*, and *marginalization*.

Privatization refers to the establishment of individual rights over resources. Since Kenya's independence, land tenure relations have rapidly shifted from the conventional clan-based variety common in Africa to private ownership (Okoth-Ogendo, 1976). This is the "adjudication process" referred to in Kenya's food policy paper cited earlier, and is greatly encouraged by the state. Under privatized land relations, access to commons and their goods such as roofing thatch, "bush foods", free pasture, fuelwood and medicinal herbs begins to disappear (Agarwal, 1986). Slowly the family reproduction needs that were previously satisfied by resort to these commonly-owned resources have to be filled by purchases on the market (Pilgrim, 1981; Peters, 1983). Privatization also puts additional pressure on the family's plot of land, since it must then satisfy all needs. Land previously used to grow food must now be used for fodder, with the likely result that neither yield will be enough. During droughts, it becomes more difficult to gain access to a kinsperson's better-watered land (Wisner, 1978).

Commoditization is the transformation of previously-free or bartered need-satisfiers into commodities obtainable only in

189

exchange for money. Commoditization has also developed rapidly in Kenya since independence because of the destruction of local industries (soap and shoe-making, for instance) by competing transnationals that have come to dominate these sectors (Langdon, 1975a, 1975b). More and more of the family's reproduction needs consequently require cash. Even in areas such as education and health care, traditionally provided by family members or community experts (healers, grandparents), new attitudes encouraged strongly by the modernizing state have led to commoditization (Feierman, 1985: 105–31). New food, clothing, furnishing and leisure tastes have been created and reinforced by advertising and the "demonstration" effect of rapid urbanization (Béhar, 1982). Privatization and commoditization have thus created a situation in which families must have cash to survive and to give their children a reasonable chance in life.

Marginalization completes the picture. This is the process by which the productivity of family land actually falls relative to needs. Population increase and the division of land according to inheritance rules have cut back on the amount of land available to families. Where families have lost out to more powerful farmers in the innumerable local land tribunal cases accompanying the privatization process (Brokenshaw and Glazier, 1973; O'Keefe, 1974), or where they have been forced to sell land to raise school fees or to pay for other needs, many have actually been forced to migrate to the less productive lowlands in the Western Rift Valley and Eastern Foreland Plateau (Wisner, 1978; Mbithi and Barnes, 1975). Here crops may fail as often as four years in ten, and productivity under rain-fed conditions is low (Porter, 1979).

The rural poor need not migrate to the margins of arable land, however, for wastelands to be created. The same pressures that may lead to the sale of the land or assets (need for cash, inability of the land to support the family, failure of traditional systems of asset/resource-loaning) often cause over-exploitation of the remaining small plots. Fallow periods become shorter and shorter. Labour that might have been used to maintain fertility and to conserve the soil is often diverted into casual employment or long-distance migration in order to meet short-term consumption needs. Vegetation that might have anchored the soil and

190

recycled nutrients is often burned for charcoal by rural people in desperate need of cash.

In Kenya, the tendency of increasing numbers of rural households to become marginal in this socio-environmental sense has been disguised by the fact that many smallholders cling to small, infertile, degraded plots of land. They are not landless in the strict sense, but have been forced into reliance on casual wage-work, non-farm artisanal activities and high-value export crops. Njonjo (1981: 39) describes the resulting paradox: the dissolution of the peasantry "takes place precisely at the same time as a highly weakened peasantry continues to retain relations to patches of land and hence maintains the illusion of a property owning class." Speaking of the small peasants in south-eastern Shaba Province of Zaire, Schoepf makes a similar point: "beneath the veil of entrepreneurial production for market, [peasants] are reduced to the status of 'homeworkers'" (1985: 35). Calling these peasants "marginal" does not mean that their activities are separated from the market economy. The other two processes discussed – privatization and commoditization – ensure that no dualism exists in Kenya. "Marginal" refers to the particular manner in which peasants in this situation are integrated into society. It refers to the way in which their livelihood strategies, combining wage labour, cash crop production and craft production, are integrated. The term also refers to the ecological and demographic effects of this manner of integration (Wisner, 1978: 6–10, 283–250; Susman *et al.*, 1983: 276–9). While such a perspective rejects dualism, it is also clear that the accumulation of land by the urban élite and rich peasantry reinforces the impoverishment of marginal land and people. The result is a growing polarization between winners and losers in the same system. Whether the peasantry will eventually disintegrate under the weight of poverty and market forces is an open question to which we return below. Certainly, however, we cannot simply assume that "the peasantry is a transitional class" as have some more Eurocentric observers of East Africa (e.g. Hyden, 1980).

Njonjo and others show how a landed class in Kenya was created partly through the Africanization of the white settler lands and partly through the adjudication process and their purchases of smallholder land. In his study of the former white-owned mixed farms in Nakuru District in the mid-1970s, Njonjo found that 91 per cent of the owners held only 21 per cent of the land and had access to less than three acres each, while the five per cent of the owners with holdings greater than 20 acres controlled 79 per cent of the land. The top two per cent of owners with holdings over 100 acres controlled 69 per cent of the land (Njonjo, 1981: 39). Hunt (1984: 287) cites a study by Kaplinsky (1983) which reveals that a few years after Njonjo's field work, 38 Kenyans in Nakuru District owned the 40 individually-owned African mixed farms larger than 500 acres. These Kenyans included six Members of Parliament, five senior government administrators, five senior police chiefs, two land board members, two county council members, two former chiefs, an ambassador and a company executive. A similar class background was found for the owners of large mixed farms in Kiambu District in Central Province (Hunt, 1984: 288), where, outside the zone of former white settlement, land had been taken over from poor smallholders (cf. Lamb, 1974; Cowen, 1981).

Kenya, of course, is not alone in marginalizing its small farmers. All over Africa land concentration has been the result of numerous attempts to modernize farming on the basis of production-first strategies. Ghana's Operation Feed Yourself and Nigeria's Agricultural Development Projects encouraged the development of a class of absentee farmers ("overnight" or "telephone" farmers) among senior government officials, traders and military officers (Hansen, 1984; Arthur, 1985; Collier, 1983; Williams, 1985). Food self-sufficiency in Malawi and Zimbabwe has been established at the cost of marginalizing the majority of small peasants (Weiner *et al.*, 1985; Leys, 1986; Ghai and Radwan, 1983c; Kydd and Christianson, 1982). Large increases in food production in the Sudan from the late 1960s were achieved by large-scale capitalist farms encroaching on small peasant lands (O'Brien, 1985).

Kitching (1980: 373) summarizes the impact of Kenya's modernizing efforts prior to 1970: a group of smallholders – roughly two-thirds of the total – were "left out in the cold" by an "agrarian revolution" that from the mid 1950s opened new cash crop markets to Africans, consolidated and privatized land ownership, and introduced yield-increasing technologies.

> [T]hose left out were those with the ecological opportunity but without the land, capital or labour power to take advantage of that opportunity (Central Province, Kisii, Machakos highlands and parts of Central Nyanza), those without the ecological opportunities and without enough land to make up for yield deficiencies by the size of the cultivated area (lowland Machakos, Kitui, other parts of Coast, Nyanza lowlands), and those with the land and the opportunity, but essentially without the capital (Nandi, Kericho, West Pakot).

Since the early 1970s, the process of marginalization has driven those small farmers into greater and greater reliance on cash crop production, especially of lowland robusta coffee, cotton and tobacco. Tobacco production, together with charcoal production for distant urban markets – the last resort for many extremely poor households in the occupied rangelands – are highly destructive of woodlands. Despite contractual obligations on smallholders producing tobacco for British American Tobacco Company to plant trees, some lower-altitude areas in Eastern Province surrounding Mt Kenya were deforested in the late 1970s, and tobacco production moved on to western Kenya, where other "marginals" who had been "left out in the cold" by prior "agrarian revolutions" were eager to sign up (Madeley, 1984; cf. Hoekstra and Kuguru, 1983).

Accelerating the Squeeze

In the end, privatization, commoditization and marginalization combine to enforce the same end product: the "forces of extraction", in the words of Spitz (1981), out-balance the "forces of retention". Smallholders find themselves increasingly incapable of producing and of retaining enough food to feed their families in good years, let alone the bad years that affect even well-watered parts of Kenya (Wisner, 1976b: 6–10). If one's land cannot reliably produce enough food for the family, and, in addition, many new cash needs must be met, why not produce the cash crop promoted by the government extension agent (cotton

193

and tobacco in the lowlands; cotton and sugar in the medium potential zones; coffee, tea, pyrethrum and horticultural products in the high-potential areas)? In this way a degree of dependence on production for the market has actually become essential to the reproduction of the peasant household (Bernstein, 1977; Heyer, 1981; Cowen, 1981; Lee, 1981: 113–15; Ghai et al., 1979: 44–64; Masakhalia, 1979: 205).

Kenya's colonial regime had opened up cash cropping opportunities to smallholders. The independent government, with assistance from development agencies, made the most of this foundation and, driven by the combination of the three processes just discussed, African production for the market soared in the 1960s and early 1970s (Heyer, 1981).

Then the current world recession took hold. Prices of the major export crops fell (Spitz, 1981). Bernstein (1981: 165–6) has argued that the peasant response to a fall in price, in a situation where market participation has become part of the family's basic reproduction process, is to produce more of the commodity. He calls this the "simple reproduction squeeze". However, in Kenya other things also began to happen. Many families resorted to off-farm employment (wage labour, beer brewing, charcoal production, brick-making and other artisanry, and trade – often in the black market). Surveys in the mid-1970s showed that in the lowest rural income group, 77 per cent of income came from off the farm, and 47 per cent for the next group up the income scale (Livingstone, 1981: 14.20). Another sample survey of non-farm activities found the highest number of non-farm activities in households in Eastern Province and the two provinces of the west of Kenya (Nyanza and Western) (Freeman and Norcliffe, 1984: 224), all zones of intense pressure on basic needs.

The middle peasantry (holding between five and 20 acres) in the east and extreme west had long felt disfavoured by a government dominated by interests from Central Province. They now faced higher input prices and lower profits. Although they continued to advance at the expense of their smaller neighbours (Hunt, 1977; Anyang' Nyong'o, 1981), they felt they deserved help from the state.

Faced with the possibility that the marginal smallholder would evade capture (Hyden, 1980) and avoid the "squeeze" (Bernstein,

194

1977), and that the Western and Eastern middle peasants would become even more disaffected, the Kenyan state embraced the World Bank's progressive-farmer/production-first strategy with open arms. It solicited bilateral aid to pay for both the new strategy and the intensification of the land strategy already in place.

Contract farming and tenancy – the cases which best exemplify the current form of production-first – seemed a perfect answer. Both modes of organization offer considerable control over the peasant without the social costs of creating a proletariat of landless workers. Importantly, the illusion of land ownership referred to by Njonjo is preserved. Both defuse the political impact of the world crisis by giving the Western and Eastern middle peasantry access to a system enabling them to accumulate (this is Buch-Hansen and Marcussen's 10 to 15 per cent of sugar contract farmers) and by producing cheap food for the urban market. At the same time, the state maintains its revenues through such mechanisms as the NIB's service charges and marketing fees and the excise tax on sugar. In 1979, excise duty on sugar earned the state K.sh. 300 million, or 2.5–3 per cent of total state revenue (Buch-Hansen and Marcussen, 1982: 26).

The foundering peasantry could get itself out of the "simple reproduction squeeze" by shifting to new export commodities and increasing productivity through inputs provided by the agents of Booker, Del Monte, BAT, Brooke Bond-Liebig and the NIB. Again, from the point of view of the state, this must have looked like a very cheap way of raising the productivity of land and labour.

The programme announced in 1981 built on these attempts to incorporate more and more of the rural labour force into export production, directly or through the sale of their labour. Begun selectively in the 1940s (Cowen, 1981; Heyer, 1981), this solution to "the peasant problem", now embraces the whole of the rural population without touching the skewed distribution of land. Thus the 1981 Food Policy Paper emphasizes yield increases on economic units without major changes in patterns of land use, land ownership or income distribution. Without any government attack on the privileges of the élite, the rural poor are left with only two options: to increase cash crop production on their

195

meagre holdings, or to become wage labourers on someone else's land.

Through casual wage-labour and subjugation to the highly controlled labour process of contract farming, these small peasants become semi-proletarian (Gibbon and Neocosmos, 1985). However, it is important that one does not understand by this term that they are somehow a "residual" washed up on the shores of history. Their continued production of some part of their means of subsistence cheapens the cost of their labour. This labour is exploited by agribusiness, the state, and by larger farmers (middle and rich peasants as well as the new élite of absentee land owners). It is also exploited through the market to the extent that semi-proletarians locked in the rachet effect of a cost-price squeeze are forced to produce more export crops when they are unwilling or unable to sell their labour (Bernstein, 1977). Often this export crop production is literally on the edges of ecological zones or administrative areas planned for the production of specific cash crops. Thus, during the coffee boom in 1977, small peasants in the transitional zone between upland and lowland Machakos neglected maize and beans and took a gamble on robusta coffee, marginally viable in that agro-ecology. Similarly, outside the maximum radius within which the western Kenyan sugar complexes negotiate satellite-grower contracts, many semi-proletarian households grow sugar in hopes that it will be purchased by the sugar mill.

The classic historical pattern for such an impoverished rural class – becoming full proletarians through permanent migration *en famille* to centres of industrial production as during the industrial revolution in Europe – is generally agreed not to exist in sub-Saharan Africa. The present world recession certainly blocks that option, but even before the economic crisis, labour absorption in Kenyan cities was limited by scale (Kaplinsky, 1978b), choice of product (Langdon, 1975b) and choice of technology (Pack, 1981; Kaplinsky, 1978a).

Without adopting a mechanistic view of dependent capitalist development, it is reasonable to see the shifting balance of forces and alliances between foreign and domestic élites as limiting the manner and degree to which Kenyan industry is likely to grow and absorb this vast population of semi-proletarians (Kitching, 196

1985; Swainson, 1980). Although some students of East Africa believe that small-scale peasant production is inevitably disappearing according to the "iron laws" of history (Sender and Smith, 1984; Buch-Hansen and Marcussen, 1982), these interpretations are often ased on overgeneralizations from specific cases (such as Central Province in Kenya studied by Cowen, 1979 and 1981), lack of attention to the kind of cyclical shifts in the fortunes of rural classes noted by Berry (1980) and insufficient attention to the tendency for rural savings to be invested in off-farm tertiary activities rather than farming.

Effects of the Squeeze

What impact does cash-cropping and the sale of their labour have on families' nutrition? A substantial number of studies reviewed by Blanc (1975), Schofield (1979), Fleuret and Fleuret (1980), Berry (1984), Pinstrup-Andersen (1985), Feierman (1985) and Bryceson (1985) suggest the possibility of negative impacts on diets, especially of children, of production for the market. This seems to be the case, for instance, in the Sudan (Taha, 1978a, 1978b), where circumstances in the Gezira irrigation scheme mirrored those in Mwea, discussed in Chapter 5. Other countries where nutrition seems to have been affected deleteriously include: Sierra Leone (Smith et al., 1981), Gambia (Haswell, 1981), Uganda (Mamdani, 1985), Tanzania (Jacobsen, 1978), Zaire (Brown and Brown, 1979: 30), Mali (Modot-Bernard, 1980), Senegal (Reboul, 1981), Burkina Faso (Dumont, 1981) and Côte d'Ivoire (Mazoyer, 1981; Campbell, 1984). Nevertheless the impact of cash-cropping is not uniform. Where women maintain rights over land and/or rights over the income from cash-cropping, there is less likely to be negative consequences for children (Brabin, 1984; Savané, 1981).

The effects of wage labour are likewise mixed. Several studies suggest that remitted income from migrants can be essential in bridging the nutritional gap, especially during times of crop failure (Wisner, 1978; O'Leary, 1980a), while the absence of male labour over extended periods has been implicated in accelerating the cycle of rural impoverishment and in heightening vulnerability to seasonal hunger and drought (Bugnicourt, 1974; Wisner,

197

1978). Shorter-term seasonal labour has been thought to be less harmful (Rempel, 1981), although some specific studies suggest that this seasonal work too may trade short-term gains for long-term sustainability of the household (Wisner, 1978; Jacobsen, 1978; Ali and O'Brien, 1984).

A recent study of the Taita Hills of Kenya concluded that a mixed array of activities including some production for sale, some wage labour, and a good deal of subsistence cultivation seemed to yield the best nutritional results (Fleuret and Fleuret, 1983). The food security system of the rural poor would seem to depend on the flexibility they retain in the use of family labour and resources to achieve and adjust such a balance of activities. To the extent that modernization (e.g. contract farming and irrigation schemes) or other forms of productionist rural development interfere with this flexibility in spatial and temporal organization, the food systems are less secure. The exception would be where the state undertakes to ensure subsistence, but, as seen in Chapter 4, even the most modest safety net is hardly visible today. Even in the extreme event, a fair proportion of the rural poor in many countries probably do not take famine relief for granted or as assured (Bryceson, 1981: 564–6; Disaster and Relief Institute, 1985).

RURAL DEVELOPMENT: DOES IT HELP?

Can major agencies such as the World Bank be convinced that production first will accelerate starvation and provoke a major social crisis in Kenya and other African countries? Is there a softened version of production first that might fulfil minimum requirements of equity and containment of damage to vulnerable groups, of the sort called for by UNICEF? Is some kind of "production-first with a human face" imaginable? Is it compatible with a basic needs approach?

"Rural development" emerged during the 1970s as a possible way of putting a human face on increased agricultural production. It differed from colonial "community development" (Suret-Canale, 1971; Manghezi, 1976), which was chiefly a propaganda campaign designed to indoctrinate African populations with

198

colonial values and – through various public works and services – the value of colonialism. The terrain of community development was culture in its broadest sense, including institutions, beliefs and approaches to problems. The impact, on the whole, was to undermine African culture and to implant that of the colonizer, a process described by Fanon (1961), Mondlane (1969: 58–66), Cabral (1974: 36–51) and Goonatilake (1984).

Colonial agricultural development built upon this pattern of indoctrination and social control through minimal public services and administration. Research, extension and marketing were added by the colonial state where production of specific export crops such as cocoa, coffee, cotton or peanuts was desired. This focused and limited agricultural development extended as far as veterinary services where epizootic disease might threaten settler herds. Settlement schemes such as the Gezira in the Sudan and the Office Niger in Mali were large-scale investments in export production into which Africans were integrated as resident labour. Popular food crops and the daily material problems of rural life (water, disease and disruption due to migration) were not the concern of colonial administrators. In the first ten years of independence, programmes for "progressive" farmers and settlement schemes simply reproduced the colonial pattern (Heyer *et al.*, 1981b; Dumont and Mottin, 1983).

The rural development approach is supposed to be more comprehensive in two ways. First, a broad range of rural services such as health care, water supply, roads and market centres are meant to improve living standards generally among "the mass of low-income population residing in rural areas" (Lele, 1975: 20). Second, this process is intended to be self-sustaining (Lele, loc. cit.; McNamara, 1973: 16–17; World Bank, 1975b: 28–33). In order to be self-sustaining, rural development is supposed to provide employment for the mass of rural dwellers. Employment is supposed to be based on well-designed and tested "packages" of technologies popularized by professionals.

Rural Development, World Bank-Style

As part of the World Bank's policy of poverty reduction, rural development was conceived as a wide-ranging approach to

199

agriculture and rural poverty. Its aims included (van de Laar, 1980: 143):

(1) acceleration of the rate of land and tenancy reform;
(2) better access to credit;
(3) assured availability of water;
(4) expanded extension facilities backed by intensified agricultural research;
(5) greater access to public services;
(6) ... new forms of rural institutions and organizations that would give as much attention to promoting the inherent potential and productivity of the poor as is generally given to protecting the power of the privileged.

The Bank did, in fact, invest a large amount of money in programmes of this kind through the 1970s, as seen earlier in Chapter 5 (also: van de Laar, 1980: 143–208; Hürni, 1980: 29–41, 100–13). Their effect, however, was to reinforce the position of richer farmers who already had access to resources and to services (Williams, 1981: 20–33). A closer look at the six programmatic elements emphasized in the World Bank rural development approach suggests why this is so.

Land and tenancy reform in many African countries has hastened accumulation by a growing class of absentee landowners and rich peasants, as we have seen in the case of Kenya. In Nigeria, the 1978 Land Use Decree has had a similar effect (Francis, 1984; Floyd, 1985). Such concentration effects are widespread and have been noted for more than twenty years. These effects are often gender-specific. Land reform in Africa has frequently extinguished conventional rights that women had over land and other resources (Rogers, 1980; Kongstad and Mønsted, 1980; Hahn, 1982; Barnes, 1983; Bryceson, 1985). In other cases, land reform laws have remained dormant (in Lesotho since 1975, for instance) or have been only very slowly implemented (Zimbabwe: Weiner, *et al.*) where landed interests (e.g. the chiefs in Lesotho or Zimbabwe's commercial farmers) in various ways constrain implementation by the state even though they are not the dominant class determining state policy.

Such formal reforms also leave untouched a large number of

200

non-formal "rents" that are extracted by richer farmers or corrupt officials for allowing access to productive land. Land reform is all the more irrelevant where the resource use is controlled by access to some critical means of production such as fishing nets and boats as in Senegal (Vercruijsse, 1979), water for livestock as in Botswana (Cliffe and Moorsom, 1979) or oxen for ploughing. In Botswana, for instance, the distribution of ownership of oxen is much more skewed than the distribution of land (Colclough and McCarthy, 1980), and female-headed households have least access to plough oxen (Fortmann, 1981).

Better access to credit has generally gone to larger farmers who least need it. The problem seems to turn in part on the way in which the World Bank and other agencies devolve the administration of loans to national agencies that administer them along lines determined by their own definitions of credit-worthiness (Hayter and Watson, 1985). As in the case of land reform, women are least likely to qualify for loans under these systems (Moock, 1976; Rogers, 1980; Seidman, 1981).

Assured availability of water has been discussed in Chapters 3 and 5. Control of water, not merely its availability, was shown to be the central issue. Exploitation of women on irrigation schemes in Africa as on the Mwea scheme and elsewhere (Conti, 1979) and the exploitation of landless labourers on such schemes in the Sudan (Barnett, 1981, Ali and O'Brien, 1984) would seem the common result of implementing this element of the World Bank approach to rural development.

Expanded extension facilities backed by intensified agricultural research demonstrated two main problems in Africa throughout the 1970s. First, although there has been much more emphasis on research, popular food crops such as small grains (sorghum and millet), roots and tubers (such as yams and cassava) have not received much attention (Guyer, 1984; Richards, 1985). There is partly a gender bias here, since a large number of these foods are grown by women. Also, there is a bias towards commercial food crops: rice and maize are urban staples. Even if these food crops were included in the researchers' list of priorities, however, the poor farmer would not necessarily benefit. To the extent that "packages" of techniques and inputs have been designed for popular food items, extension services often fail to get these

201

packages to the poorest farmers. In Kenya in the 1970s the rule of thumb seemed to be that 90 per cent of the extension time went to the top ten per cent of farmers (Ashcroft *et al.*, 1973; Leonard, 1977). Women definitely received very little contact with the extension service (Staudt, 1975, 1977). Assuming that the food crop package is made available, moreover, poor farmers may not be able to afford the risks and extra labour required to take it up, a decision characteristic of what Helleiner calls the "wise rejector" (1975: 49).

Greater access to public services does not mean much when fees (e.g. water charges, school fees) or distance puts them out of the reach of the poorest households. The World Bank is pressuring African governments to reinstate or raise school fees, water connection fees and the like. In settlement schemes, the services offered by many authorities do little more than recreate the same traditional patterns of access to water, bush foods and game, periodic markets, and community-based childcare and healing that were disrupted by resettlement in the first place. Chambers (1969) gives several such examples, and we can find other cases in Tanzanian, Mozambican and Ethiopian "village settlements". There may be compelling reasons to change settlement patterns, but the argument concerning improved access to services is not one of them.

New forms of rural institutions have been encouraged by the Bank's investments in rural development. Yet they have seldom "promoted the inherent potential ... of the poor" rather than "protecting the power of the privileged". Cooperatives are among the most common new institution. By 1976 in Kenya, however, cooperatives for coffee, tea, and dairy products were benefiting a very small proportion of households (Heyer and Waweru, 1976: 195). Heyer and Waweru cite Lamb (1972) on a coffee cooperative in Murang'a, Central Province, in which 2 per cent of the members received 20 per cent of the payout and 14 per cent received 64 per cent. On a district-wide population basis, Lamb calculated that only 3.3 per cent of the farmers received 64 per cent of the returns from coffee. Cowen (1974) found similar inequalities among dairy and tea producers in Nyeri District.

Local and national élites often take advantage of marketing cooperatives, cooperative landholding companies, and so-called

202

self-help groups to further their interests. One may recall from Chapter 2 the medical team's complaint about coercive self-help contributions. The interests involved are locally diverse and make foreknowledge of "social impacts" of new institutions very difficult (Holmquist, 1979).

New rural institutions are less and less popular in many parts of Africa among the poor they are supposed to serve. Wolf (1986) reports that vegetable producers in the Taita Hills of Kenya flatly refused to join government-sponsored cooperatives. Who would join in a political-economic climate that allowed 72 million Kenyan shillings to go missing between 1978–80 in the Meru District cooperatives and similar sums in other places? (Cheche Kenya, 1982: 109–10). Similar ambivalence about rural institutions (especially co-ops) has been reported in Zambia (Bratton, 1980), Tanzania (Raikes, 1982; Matango, 1979; Coulson, 1982), Senegal (Adams, 1981), Nigeria (King, 1981), Niger (Collins, 1974), Ghana (Miracle and Seidman, 1978) and Mozambique (Harris, 1980).

King summarizes the rural poor's experience of cooperatives (1981: 279):

> They involve the rural communities in the larger economy in a way which entails risky dependence on decisions beyond their control, and which erodes systems of self-sufficient food production.... The existing co-operative policy through its suffocating uniformity and control involves the foregoing of economic, social and personal development among the rural population. Instead it forges marketing and financial links with the government which serve mainly to promote the availability of rural produce for urban consumption and export purposes.

Rural Development in Kenya: Two Cases

A Hybrid Maize Credit Scheme in Western Kenya

Funded and executed by USAID, the Special Rural Development Project in Vihiga Division of Kakamega District, located not far from the pilot experiment in community based health care discussed in Chapter 2, falls into the rural development mould

203

described so far. It bears the stamp of weak BN interventions, and has suffered their typical fate.

Vihiga lies in Kakamega District of Western Province, long known for its high population density, fragmented landholdings, constant migration of men seeking work (the gender ratio is only 70–89 males per 100 females in various parts of the district: Ominde, 1971c) and precarious food situation (Bullock, 1971).

Table 6.1 presents the planned components of the Vihiga project. These are comprehensive, amounting to a super-shopping-list. This set of services and technical packages were to be delivered to and then adopted by farmers to make the process self-sustaining. With the exception of coffee and tea expansion, the production packages actually focused on locally eaten food, although this locally-responsive feature did not lessen subsequent project's commitment to the weak BNA.

The heart of the programme was the development and extension of a technical package around the use of hybrid maize seed and chemical fertilizer (Oyugi, 1981; Lele, 1975). Unsecured credit was to be made available to smallholders on an experimental basis for purchase of fertilizer. Since land pressure and fragmentation was intense in this part of Kenya, yield increases were thought to be possible only through increasing productivity rather than through increasing the amount of land under cultivation. As maize provides 60 per cent of the caloric and 50 per cent of the protein intake in the Kenyan diet, a breakthrough in maize productivity among smallholders would be important for future development policy (GOK/UNICEF, 1984, Vol. 2: 27). Yields of maize were and still are highly variable in Kenya: the smallest producers on marginal land with few inputs and local varieties achieve only about half a ton per hectare. Larger landholders using fertilizer and hybrid maize achieve over four tons per hectare (McCarthy and Mwangi, 1982).

So much for the theory of the project's aims. In the event, the Agricultural Finance Corporation of Kenya insisted on distributing the loan funds as it, not the donor, saw fit. Only "credit-worthy" farmers received loans between 1970 and 1973, which cut the poorest rural dwellers out of the programme from the start (Oyugi, 1981: 159). When, in 1973, the credit-worthiness condition was removed, it still turned out that 93 per cent of the

Table 6.1

COMPONENTS OF VIHIGA SRDP

AGRICULTURAL AND LIVESTOCK PRODUCTION
1. Dairy cattle and milk production
2. Livestock staff build-up
3. Pig production
4. Agricultural credit
5. Hybrid maize
6. Poultry production
7. Agricultural inputs supply
8. Demonstration plots
9. Fruit and vegetable production for cash sale
10. Crop extension experiment
11. Coffee and tea expansion
12. Fruit and vegetable marketing cooperatives

SUPPORTING SERVICES
13. Road
14. Telephone
15. Water supplies
16. Functional literacy and adult education
17. Farmer training
18. Land adjudication

COORDINATION AND PUBLICITY
19. Coordination
20. Community development
21. Information services

OTHER PROGRAMMES
22. Rural industries development centre
23. Village polytechnics
24. Fruit and vegetable processing
25. Medical services
26. Family planning

Source: Institute for Development Studies, 1975: 20–13

programme farmers were already growing hybrid maize and 66 per cent were already using fertilizer (Oyugi, 1981: 166). These were the rich peasants for whom the project was a chance to consolidate. Credit or no, the poorest did not participate. To add to the failure of rural development to secure the family food system in this case, the extension staff was highly unmotivated and tended to seek out the richest farmers (Lele, 1975: 71–2, citing Leonard, 1970; cf. Leonard, 1977).

It seems that two fundamental errors had been made in setting the maize scheme up in the first place. First, given the varied environmental conditions in Vihiga, maize was not necessarily the most important crop for all farmers. Secondly, because of the very high level of long-distance male wage migration, a third of the households were female-headed and suffered labour short-ages that made participation in the project impossible (Lele, 1975: 55, 96).

Undeterred by such results, rural development planners unveiled in 1976 a much more ambitious Integrated Agricultural Development Programme (similar to the ones in West Africa criticized by Williams, 1985, and Richards, 1985). Western Province (including Vihiga) was included in the IADP along with high- and medium-potential zones in Central, Eastern and Nyanza Provinces. Some $35 million was to be spent in 14 districts to help 70,000 low-income households to increase their production of maize, beans, potatoes and milk. Production was to be for home consumption and local markets, although the inclusion of passion fruit, cotton, beef and groundnuts in the list of priorities suggests a more conventional cash crop agenda as well.

The IADP and other activities in District Plans were to ensure upgrading of such infrastructural facilities as roads, water supply, education, health and other community services. Incomes were to rise slowly. Family food supply was to be improved. Above all, the project was to spread its effect by increasing the amount of hired labour each family was able to use, from an average 96 man-days a year to 270 (Ghai *et al.*, 1979: 112–15). Here again it is clear that the approach of the IADP was more conventional than it appeared on paper: the poorest peasants cannot hire any labour, so the increase from an average of 96 man (sic) days to

270 amounts to an enormous increase in labour hired by the rich peasants.

The IADP was to have run for five years, and only preliminary assessments of its impact are available. The indications are that IADP's spread effect have been less than anticipated and that no self-sustaining development has ensued. The areas targeted remain hot spots of growing landlessness, unemployment and declining standards of living. Furthermore, these areas were not able to produce in a way that significantly reduced the shortage of staple foods in the late 1970s and early 1980s.

A final irony, not attributable to the Vihiga programme *per se*, but a comment on the futility of weak BNA efforts to secure family nutrition, comes from a comparison of nutritional well-being of hybrid maize farmers and local maize growers in Western Kenya. There, IADP rural development projects successfully attempted to introduce hybrid maize as a substitute for local maize. Many poor peasants now grow hybrid maize, but with what result?

Based on the national nutrition surveys, Test and her associates (n.d.) found more malnutrition (measured as lower height-for-age in children) among the households that had adopted the "modern" package including hybrid maize. The results are preliminary, but the researchers offer a possible explanation that recalls remarks of other nutrition workers concerning sugar contracting in Mumias and rice production at Mwea (Test *et al.*, n.d.: 10):

> Increasing the income of landholders does not always result in improved nutritional status of the family. The reason for this may lie in the fact that the female of the household is usually in charge of providing an adequate diet for the children, but the household income is most often managed by the male.

Growers of hybrid maize, especially if they are marginal smallholders caught in the simple reproduction squeeze often sell the maize they grow in order to purchase a less costly diet. Clinging to what Njonjo calls their small "patches of land", these poorest peasants not only suffer the nutritional stress produced by highly fragmented, insufficient land, but they are locked into

207

market exchange that further erodes their diet. This situation is complicated by intra-household division on cash income, as we saw in the cases of Mumias and Mwea.

A Crop Insurance Scheme in Eastern Kenya

Drought is a recurrent event in the 82 per cent of Kenya that receives on average less than 800 mm. of rainfall a year (Ominde, 1971b). These arid and semi-arid lands (ASAL) include the whole or parts of 27 of Kenya's 41 districts and over two and a half million people, 16.5 per cent of the population (GOK, n.d.: 4–7; Ogendo, 1983).

People in this zone are poor. In 1975 government surveys found that half the smallholder households had consumption levels below the poverty line (loc. cit.: 9). Many are recent immigrants from wetter areas, and many depend in large part on income remitted from family members in off-farm employment and from other non-farm employment (O'Leary, 1980b). They are highly vulnerable to droughts which seem to be recurring on a cycle having a mean duration of five years giving recent minima in: 1940–1, 1944–5, 1950, 1954–5, 1961, 1965, 1970–1, 1975–6, 1979–80 and 1984 (Mörth, 1966; Mbithi and Wisner, 1973; Wisner, 1978; Porter, 1979; Stewart and Hash, 1982; Ogallo, 1983; Cohen and Lewis, 1987).

The sum of production losses and direct costs such as famine relief during the 1970–1 drought has been estimated at KL 38 million (Wisner, 1978: 74–92). Others estimate an average of KL 30 million for each drought year in famine relief alone since 1971 (Mbithi and Bahemuka, 1981: 1). The ASAL programme set out in the late 1970s to reduce this vulnerability to drought and its social cost (Campbell and Migot-Adholla, 1983).

The ASAL programme emphasized investment in water conservation works and social infrastructure, soil conservation and rehabilitation on the farms of participant farmers, and crop and livestock development. There was a large emphasis on research to develop appropriate dryland farming systems. Highly controlled credit, production and soil conservation packages were the hallmarks of ASAL activities (GOK, n.d.).

Of course, colonial and post-colonial states had pursued both thrusts of this strategy – land conservation and the search for the

208

perfect lowland cash crop – since the 1940s (Wisner, 1976b: 10–25; Mutiso, 1986: 7–11). In Machakos, especially, where in the late 1930s the government had tried to force the "destocking" of large herds, there had been suspicion and resistance to a series of land conservation and afforestation initiatives through the 1940s and 1950s (Kimambo, 1970: 92; de Wilde, 1967: 94). Elsewhere in colonial Africa, similar attempts to enforce environmental conservation measures in the form of required terracing of land, reduction of herd sizes and prohibition of fire as a tool of land preparation had frequently met with strong resistance (Young and Fosbrooke, 1960; Richards, 1984; Beinart, 1984).

The search for the "perfect cash crop" for lowland Kenya dates from Swynnerton's (1954) plan for African cash-cropping. Coffee was the cash crop *par excellence* for high altitudes, and it had been rapidly incorporated into the cropping pattern of the central Machakos hill peasants. From there, to some extent, income from coffee sales filtered down to the households of "daughter settlements" in the drier surrounding plain (Wisner, 1976b: 18–19). One recent nutritional study even suggests that there is a positive relationship in the Machakos case between coffee production and diet, presumably through the effect of income (van Steenbergen *et al.*, 1978).

The idea was firmly rooted that the spread of commercialization into the lowlands was the key to development. Twenty years ago, Heyer (1965: 7) expressed the planner's ideal in this way:

> The trouble is that in areas such as lowland Machakos, there is an obvious misallocation of resources. People are trying to grow basic foodstuffs in an area which is not suited to their production. A better allocation of resources would be achieved if people would turn to cash crops more suited to the area's ecological conditions, and use the proceeds to buy their food.

What this ideal left out of its equation was the fact that ecological conditions are not a static, given feature, but are in constant flux due to rapidly changing social and economic conditions. The lowland Kamba had developed a sophisticated polyculture, agronomic techniques and a balance of farming and herding that was capable of supporting them on the margins of

209

the rangelands (Porter, 1979). Land privatization in highland Machakos pushed large numbers of Kamba into this marginal environment. Others joined them. Between the 1962 and 1969 national population censuses a series of movements increased pressure in the arid and semi-arid lands (Wisner, 1976b: 16, calculated from GOK, 1970b, Vol. 1; Ominde, 1968, 1975, and Owako, 1971). These movements, in brief, were:

- Machakos Kamba moving to drier parts of Machakos;

- Kitui Kamba moving to drier parts of Kitui;

- Kamba generally moving to drier parts of *Ukambani* (Kambaland);

- Other landless people from other parts of Kenya moving into the drier parts of *Ukambani*;

- Kamba and other people moving into drier parts of the entire Eastern Foreland Plateau outside *Ukambani*, the coastal hinterland, and the western Rift Valley.

Odingo (1977: 169), for instance, writes of "unsupervised and unplanned settlement" near a new dam on the Tana river in the Eastern Foreland Plateau. Mbithi and Barnes (1975) focus on the "spontaneous settlement problem". O'Keefe and Juma (1982: 45) cite migration rates of seven to nine per cent per year into the ASAL during the 1970s. The 1979 census confirms that these movements towards the margins of arable land are slowing down but continuing.

Pressure on the lowland food system has therefore been building up (Anzagi and Bernard, 1977; Porter, 1979; Moore, 1979). Mbithi and Bahemuka (1981: 34) estimated that 15 hectares are required in this zone to produce adequate food in all but the worst drought years, yet the average holding in the lowlands was two hectares. There has also been pressure on the pastoral Maasai and Somali on the southern and northern edges of this "occupied rangeland" (Campbell, 1979 and 1981; Gutto, 1981; Hogg, 1985).

Cotton, the miracle cash crop finally arrived at by state planners in the late 1950s and early 1960s, has not stabilized the situation, but has added further pressure. First, the labour demand curve for cotton is more or less the same through the growing season as for subsistence grains (Figure 6.3) (Wisner, 1978: 307–13). This ecologically-determined conflict for labour time is exacerbated where, in the poorest households, men and youth have migrated in order to add cash to the family budget. These wage-seeking movements are common responses to drought in *Ukambani* (Wisner, 1980–81; O'Leary, 1980a and b). In addition, the price for cotton is unstable. Many of the poorest households in the ASAL prefer to manufacture charcoal from the savanna woodland for sale to transporters or to herd large numbers of goats as income supplements and famine reserves. Both these activities, however, undercut the carrying capacity of the ASAL zone in the long run.

Bernstein (1981: 166) describes the way in which the cost-price squeeze built into smallholder petty commodity production is tightened under conditions of environmental risk:

> The precariousness of the material and technical basis of peasant production combines with the pressures exerted by commodity relations to determine the simple reproduction "squeeze". As much of peasant production in Africa is fuelled by human energy, and as techniques of land use in many cases exhaust the soil after a certain period, the intensification of production occurs (more labour-time on poorer or more distant soils) which increases the cost of production and reduces the returns to labour.... The vagaries of climate; the deterioration in soils which are not easily substitutable because of competition for land or the costs of clearing new land ...; the incidence of crop disease ..., of animal diseases (affecting draught animals or animals with other functions in terms of use or exchange), and of disease or death or infertility in the household (reducing the supply of labour) – all testify to the vulnerability of peasant farming.

Chambers describes this vulnerability as an integral component of "integrated rural poverty" (1983: 114–31).

The result is the destruction of established patterns of coping with droughts (Wisner and Mbithi, 1974). The series of more or less five-yearly rainfall minima listed above have led to serious malnutrition, dislocation of households, selling off of assets and the need for famine relief. None of the colonial or post-colonial programmes have successfully diminished this vulnerability to drought; the weak BNA has not strengthened the family food system through its provision of services, technological packages and "targeted incomes".

Many years of crop and livestock improvement, soil conservation and small dam building by the African Land Development Board (ALDEV) from the mid-1940s did little to avert massive hunger during the droughts of 1961 and 1965. The expansion of cotton and other progressive farmer programmes in the first decade of independence did little to avert hunger in 1970 and 1971. Nor did ten years of ASAL programmes in Machakos, Kitui, the Rift Valley and elsewhere up to the most recent drought year, 1984. In 1984, 25 per cent of toddlers (18–24 months) and 33 per cent of school children (7–9 years) actually lost weight between January and June, according to observations by a UCLA team that had been following 300 randomly-selected households in lower Embu (Mbeere) for two and a half years (Borton and Stephenson, 1984: 23). Typical of ASAL conditions, this area was one of the zones that had supposedly benefited from rural development efforts, which had included "packages" built around tenure reform (Brokenshaw and Glazier, 1973; Haugerud, 1984) and programmes providing cotton, tobacco and hybrid beans as cash crops (Hunt, 1984, 1977).

A long time-series of data on child nutrition, unbiased by the selective nature of clinic and feeding station attendance, is not usually available in the ASAL. However, an indication of crisis is given by the fact that in August 1984 District Commissioners in the affected area had informed the government that the number of "needy people" totalled 1.1 million. By September the figure had grown to 1.6 million. Since 70 per cent of these were in the districts of Machakos, Kitui, Meru and Embu with another, unspecified number in the Rift Valley, it would seem that, at a conservative estimate, something like one-third of the people in the official ASAL zone were in need of famine relief (Borton and Stephenson, 1984: 26).

This hardly speaks well of rural development efforts meant to

212

reduce famine potential in the ASAL. Indeed, at the time of the 1970–1 drought and famine, observers included the Rift Valley and Coast Hinterland in a "broad arc" of marginal lands around the Central Highlands as a "zone of highest famine potential" (Mbithi and Wisner, 1973; Wisner, 1976b; Wisner, 1978). While people of the Rift Valley and Coast Hinterland were not suffering, the signs were clear: mounting migration of landless people, "mining" of charcoal and reliance on large herds as a famine reserve.

The Cornell University Nutrition Surveillance Program in Kenya was able to "read" the effect of drought on the national pattern of malnutrition (1984: 8–9). Coming just after the drought and hunger of 1976, the 1977 national nutrition survey found the highest prevalence of stunting in children (1–4 years) in Eastern Province (including Machakos and Kitui), where a staggering 34 per cent of children were affected. In the years following good harvest, 1979 and 1982, the next two national nutrition surveys registered an improvement: stunting in Eastern Province fell to 24 per cent and 27 per cent of the same age group, while the decline in nutritional status in Western and Nyanza Provinces in the West of Kenya removed Eastern from first place among provinces in this unenviable ranking (CNSP, 1984: 15, Table 1).

Wasonga *et al.* (1982) have tried to work out the impact of cropping patterns and size of holding on location and severity of malnutrition. Table 6.2 gives their findings for larger and smaller Eastern Province farms growing different combinations of traditional drought resistant crops (e.g. sorghum and millet), less resistant food crops (maize) and cash crops (coffee and cotton). The percentages are children (1–4 years) who were less than 90 per cent of the standard height-for-age in national nutrition survey no. 2 in 1979. The results suggest that coffee, cotton, and hybrid maize did not help to safeguard the nutritional well-being of children, especially on the smaller farms.

Perhaps, one would say, these smaller farms are precisely the ones that need something more than the ideal cash crop production package. That something more, of course, is precisely what the weak BNA embodied in many of the ASAL programmes is supposed to provide. In particular, the Machakos

213

Integrated Development Project, one of the many ASAL programmes, is designed to provide farm production and conservation plans, production packages and financial insurance against crop failure for participating farmers.

Table 6.2

PREVALENCE OF STUNTING BY CROPPING PATTERN AND HOLDING AREA EASTERN PROVINCE

Landholding Area (hectares)

Cropping Pattern 1/	<1.75 (n)	≥1.75 (n)	Total (n)
LM + LM/B	28% (140)	11% (54)	23% (194)
LM/C + LM/B/C + C	28% (47)	37% (19)	30% (66)
HM/C	20% (10)	33% (9)	26% (19)
MS + MS/LM + MS/LM/B	14% (76)	0% (16)	12% (92)
LM/COT	13% (16)	13% (16)	13% (32)
LM/HM/B	0% (11)	0% (2)	0% (13)
Prod. < 50	26% (19)	0% (1)	25% (20)
TOTAL	23% (319)	15% (117)	20.6% (436)

1/ LM = Local Maize   B = Beans   C = Coffee   MS = Millet and
   Sorghum   Cot = Cotton   HM = Hybrid Maize
   Prod < 50 = Production of all crops is less than 50 kg.

Source: Wasonga *et al.*, 1982: 6

There are built-in contradictions. First, the cut-off point in terms of farm size for participation in the programme appears to be 1.6 hectares (Wasonga *et al.*, 1982: 12). Sixty-six per cent of Machakos smallholders possess less than 1.75 hectares, so the smallest of the poor smallholders do not qualify. Secondly, in order to obtain financial insurance, participating farmers must agree to follow the farm plans and soil conservation plans designed for them by experts. This is a high price to pay given the history of failure of projects designed by experts and the strong desire of Kamba farmers not to relinquish control over their means of subsistence.

This resistance to outside control is not merely cultural. Oguntoyinbo and Richards (1978: 191) put it this way: "because drought risks are localised, responsibilities for planned adjustments to drought should be as localised as possible, and should lie within the peasant farming community." Mbithi and Barnes (1975: 166–76) have shown that many of the small farmers in the ASAL zone are, technically, squatters and that their perceived insecurity of tenure makes it very unlikely that they will engage in long-term investments in soil conservation, tree-planting, etc. Many of these squatters are *de facto* settlers who flocked to official settlement areas such as Makueni in southern Machakos where settlers were established from 1948 onwards on 20 acre (8 ha) plots. The 1969 census found 20,000 official settlers there and a further 35,000 people in the lands adjoining Makueni; that is, well over a third of the whole population of Machakos' Southern Division was living on less than a sixth of the land, at densities from twice to four times the Divisional average (Wisner, 1976b: 13). Other squatters include people who for years had lived illegally in the better-watered, but officially "gazetted" Chyulu Hills, of whom Owako (1971: 190) said:

> Politics apart, one of the major attractions of the Chyulu Hills is the ease with which one can meet food requirements. Because of the cool climate brought about by high altitude (2000 m) and the fertile virgin volcanic soils, it is possible to grow maize and beans even in years when crops fail in the rest of the district.

Is it surprising then, that several years into the ASAL programme very limited and partial adoption of the principle crop extension package was noted in an evaluation by Mbithi and Bahemuka (1981)?

There is no evidence that rural development programmes such as the MIDP have reduced the tendency for richer peasants, absentee businessmen, civil servants and other salaried individuals to buy up assets during times of drought (O'Leary, 1980a; Hogg, 1985). Watts (1983) described a similar buying up of assets in northern Nigeria, and, indeed, after the 1968–73 drought in the Sahel, fully half of Mali's livestock was in the hands of urban-based traders and civil servants who had purchased them in "distress sales" (Twose, 1984; cf. Chambers, 1983: 118–31).

Rural Development: Partners or Adversaries?

Rural development efforts – formulated and practised in ways that sometimes approximate the weak BNA and sometimes fall short – offer little help for the large number of poor rural people who are being marginalized as rural Kenya (indeed much of Africa) is transformed into a privatized and commoditized landscape. As the "haves" grow in power and wealth, the "have-nots" have little option but to burrow deeper into these landscapes devastated by erosion and deforestation. They are not likely to become urban working people. They are the semi-proletarians who eke out a living by combining wage labour, marginal food and cash crop production, and other non-farm employment.

If those on the side of the "peasant question" in Kenya who argue that this is a painful but necessary transition period in the establishment of capitalist agriculture and development (Gibbon and Neocosmos, 1985; Kitching, 1985; Cowen, 1981) are wrong, what is likely to become of these semi-proletarians if even the most elaborate rural development projects only accelerate the process of marginalization, no matter how much the project language is that of basic human needs?

One could imagine Kenya as an India in the making. Population growth and the migration of the landless to the margins will continue. High fertility rates have frequently been

216

argued to be a response rather than a cause of growing pressure on resources, growing powerlessness over those resources that remain accessible, and the deterioration of those few under control of the "have-nots" (Kleinman, 1980). Whatever the resolution of such Malthusian versus anti-Malthusian debates, empirically, Kenya remains with an annual growth rate of over four per cent, with growth rates in the ASAL periphery averaging seven to nine per cent. Are the wastelands of northern Gujarat far off? (Agarwal, 1986). In both east and west Kenya semi-proletarians are resorting to survival strategies that combine farm and non-farm activities, complex gender divisions of labour, child labour and spatial and temporal organizations of family labour. (Chapter 7 examines the implications for Kenyan and other African women.) These livelihood strategies are common in India and Bangladesh as well. Whether they are sustainable is another question (Chambers, 1986; Brundtland, 1987).

The parallels between the two countries are not only that between the poor. Governments in both continents show the same propensity to contain crises. India is known for its ability to manage food emergencies, and there has not been widespread death from famine in India since the tragedy of Bihar in 1965 (Sen, 1981). The state of Maharashtra, for example, is said to have managed the drought of 1971–4 with an exemplary combination of early warning, locally organized food-for-work projects, and provision of seed, tools, draught animals and other capital for rebuilding after the drought (McAlpin, 1987). Kenya (Cohen and Lewis, 1987) and Botswana (Borton, 1984) are the only two African countries where the state apparatus has coped with drought with similar levels of efficiency. No less an authority than the multinational giant Booker Agriculture International judges Kenya's state grain marketing authority (the National Cereals and Produce Board) to be the most effective in Africa (Borton and Stephenson, 1984: 7). The vision of Kenya as the India of Africa becomes even more plausible when one sees the way in which a vast marginal population in the ASAL (2.5 million in 1975, probably at least 4.5 million by 1985) is "managed" on the edge of survival by one of the most adept bureaucracies in the Third World.

Even given the great difference between India and Kenya in

217

raising agricultural productivity and regional surpluses over the last decade (Lele, 1981), one could still imagine permanent feeding programmes based on public works in Kenya's ASAL. These would be supported by foreign aid, but for the time being there seems to be a high degree of international political support for Moi's faltering miracle. Holt (1985: 14) has actually suggested such a programme for Ethiopia, for which there is not political support among ideologically-opposed large grain-surplus nations. Dependency on the donor countries would therefore be deepened. In this respect the "Indian Kenya" would also have a touch of Botswana to it, recalling the ingredients of that other African country's successful drought response: diamonds and migrant gold miners. It is not a comforting future to envisage, though strictly speaking it would be compatible with a weak (very weak) BNA.

Speculation aside, the preceding discussion of rural development as a possibly more "populist" and "need-centred" approach to food security than production-first must raise fundamental doubts. The record of so many failures prompts the question, "why do such fundamental mistakes continue to be made?" (Gephart, 1986: 60)

One school of thought suggests that these are not mistakes at all. The only mistake is to expect rural development to be in the interest of the rural poor in the first place. Williams (1985) chose to define rural development by its institutions, not by its rhetorical goals: it consists, then, of projects supported by aid donors and run by state agencies. In these circumstances, there is much talk of "participation", but it usually "comes down to doing what is good for you." These rural development projects favour both a small group of farmers who are in a position to take advantage of the particular package of technologies and services provided and the more disparate groups of bureaucrats and businesses that provide the package, market the products and tout their success as "rural development experts".

Williams argues that one should see the state and the peasantry as adversaries, not partners in rural development. Rural development, indeed all forms of the weak BNA in Africa today, is just another way in which the state has tried to exercise power over the peasantry.

218

Others agree with Williams. Galli (1981b: viii) introduces a study of rural development including the case of Tanzania (de Gennaro, 1981), where she finds that "[e]conomic as well as social control of peasants was a primary objective of the governments involved.... [A] middle strata of the peasantry who are exploited by national and international agribusiness land-owners, intermediaries, and the state" are the target (in World Bank terms) of such projects (cf. Raikes, 1982, and Coulson, 1982, on Tanzania; Harriss, 1982a, on both Tanzania and Nigeria; Williams, 1985, on Nigeria).

Heyer *et al.* (1981b: 4) make the same point: "The assertion that rural development serves all, or almost all, interests is a necessary myth. The open recognition of conflict threatens the whole strategy of rural development as currently pursued." They define rural development as "planned change by public agencies based outside the rural areas" (1981b: 1), the purpose of which is to draw peasants into production of commodities for sale. Thus, "[p]easants are forced to sell to the market in order to earn cash which is required, in increasing quantities, to provide for the necessities of life and to pay taxes" (1981b: 7).

GOATS, YAMS, BAOBOBS AND GRASSHOPPERS: ECO-FARMING AND THE STRONG BNA

What are the alternatives to the damaging, even anti-peasant rural development approach? A number of proposals ranging from biotechnology packages to eco-farming have been put forward. Rather than opposing peasant systems of production, they tend to build on existing practices and are therefore both more responsive and effective than rural development. None the less, they uniformly stop short of the strong BNA – although as our review of these alternatives shows, they hold the potential for active, participatory development.

The *Farming Systems Research (FSR)* approach promises to improve rural development design and targeting of the new packages that biotechnology will make possible (Behnke and Kerven, 1983; Collinson, 1982; Norman *et al.*, 1982). FSR claims to be concerned with farmers' goals and motivations and also

219

focuses on the division of labour within households, on problems of access to resources, and on the relations among rural families, between them and traders, etc. Such knowledge may help government agricultural services to make new packages more readily available to farmers. But do the farmers need and/or want these input packages in the first place? Where countries are driven by external debt to push export crops, the question certainly must be in whose interests farmers produce export crops. Is FSR a neutral approach that could as easily serve increased food production within a strong BNA?

Rapid Rural Assessment, a strategy based on group interviews, aims to give rural people a sense of participation in project design (Longhurst, 1981). But this is illusion and further mystification if, in the end, yet another package ties the poor to exploitative markets and management agencies.

The designers of these packages undoubtedly would protest that this time they have got it right. *Ethnoscience* or *folk ecology* has enabled the sorghum breeders and gene splicers to distil rural wisdom and to take micro-environmental potentials and restrictions into account (Barker *et al.*, 1977; Brokensha *et al.*, 1980; Chambers, 1983; Richards, 1985; Odhiambo, 1987). The walls of the research station must be broken down, they argue. Biggs and Clay (1981: 321) emphasize the importance of the farmers' own "continuous process of innovating in the informal R and D systems." Farmers' field trials should become an integral part of farming systems R & D (Richards, 1985). Important but neglected foods and animals such as the yam in West Africa (Gwyer, 1984) or the goat in East Africa (Dahl and Hjort, 1976) are now the subject of "adaptive research".

Is any of this actually new? Will it actually matter if the locus of control over resources remains outside the rural farming community? The rural poor nowhere in these brave new improvements of rural development are actually defining their own needs and struggling on their own behalf. One has an eerie sense that some of this new sensitivity to linguistic, cultural, social and ecological nuance is simply in aid of more effectively communicating messages packaged by experts. Thus Warren believes that "indigenous knowledge systems" have a role as "communication facilitators between change agents and local

220

populations" (Warren, 1980: 363). The parallel rise of "social marketing" (Manoff, 1985), discussed in relation to UNICEF's GOBI package in Chapter 4, adds to the suspicion that much of the activity surrounding farming systems, people's science, etc. aids the manipulation and control of rural people at a time when the legitimacy of governments, donors and projects is slipping away. This is certainly the case with much "women in development" work, as will be seen in Chapter 7.

The package itself might be potentially useful, as are the practices promoted by GOBI. Certainly agricultural packages that take local practices such as intercropping seriously (Belshaw, 1980) or appreciate the difference between men's and women's perceptions of cassava-eating grasshoppers (pest in one case, food item in the other) are likely to be better packages (Richards, 1980b).

Why the "package" at all? This is the question the strong BNA has to ask. There is a fixation on mediums and messages with very little thought about the vast world of struggle and constraint that lies outside that tidy-sounding couplet. Richards argues that the best thing for rural development in Sierra Leone would be the withdrawal of the Integrated Agricultural Development Project with its improved rice. Both medium and message are blocking the process that had over several generations already produced 59 varieties of rice selected by farmers themselves for different conditions (1985: 86–106). Collaboration with formal sector researchers (as partners not clients) is possible and even desirable where problems exceed local knowledge and resources (1985: 142–58; cf. Herrera, 1984; Odhiambo, 1983). However, in such a dialogue the accumulated outside experience brought as a package would only serve as an entry point for a participatory reflection of the specific needs and potentials of peasant farmers.

Eco-farming alternatives based on indigenous sytems of polyculture, agro-forestry and small scale water management and soil conservation have been proposed and even tested in West Africa (African Environment, 1977; Bradley *et al.*, 1977; Wilson and Kang, 1981; Dupriez and De Leener, 1983; Kock, 1984), East Africa (Angwazi, 1984; Glaeser, 1984b; Egger, 1984; Tull, 1987) and southern Africa (Wisner, 1984a). Harrison (1987) reviewing this work, concludes that here lies the way towards the "greening" of Africa. Is there a danger that such agricultural techniques will be seized upon merely as items in yet another shopping-list? Do enthusiastic reviewers such as Harrison realize that effective eco-farming must be accompanied by community control, that is by strong participation and a strong BNA?

Sometimes referred to as "site-oriented agriculture" (Kotschi, 1984), eco-farming is an approach that consciously builds on peasant practices in the pursuit of sustainability and system stability (Bergeret, 1977; Egger, 1981; Altieri, 1987). It has emerged out of a world-wide movement to rethink agriculture as "sustainable" (Brundtland, 1987), "regenerative" (Tull, 1987), "alternative" (Altieri, 1987; Sachs *et al.*, 1981: 151–222). Such alternative systems are primarily oriented towards food production. Shouldn't this approach produce better packages? Yes and no. There is, of course, a tension between flexibility and replicability if one remains within the framework of externally-funded, donor-sponsored rural development. The GOBI package, certainly, would be more useful if it were more sensitive to local epidemiological patterns (as was argued in Chapter 4). Surely an eco-farming package developed in Rwanda may make a better starting point from the point of view of food security and sustainability across the border in Kigezi, Uganda, than the latest cash crop fix developed by agribusiness seeking new contract-farming opportunities.

Yet one must ask, starting point for what? The better package produced by farming systems, folk science or eco-farming, will – precisely because it is better – *function within the constraints* on poor people. "Functioning within constraints" may be a definition of survival, but it is not development.

The baobob tree fruit, for example, is an important famine reserve in drought-prone East Africa. Working within the limits set by generations of colonial exploitation that has intensified the region's environmental instability, eco-farming in this drought-prone zone would probably seek to preserve the baobob for famines to come. The strong BNA and common sense agree, however, that the ultimate goal of rural development should be to eliminate the need for famine reserves, not to provide better safeguards in the event of drought. At what stage, then, is it wise for the outside collaborator to discuss with villagers the possible use of baobabs as a rich, day-to-day source of vitamin C? Probably not for quite some time, if at all, until the struggle with the economic interests that reproduce famine by marginalizing the poor peasant has won more political space (Holmquist, 1984). If, on the other hand, a common local source of vitamin A or beta-carotene (its chemical precursor) were found that also served as a famine reserve food, what should the approach be? Vitamin A deficiency contributes to blindness and may also reduce resistance to infection. Should the strong BNA oppose, in this hypothetical case, the inclusion of this vitamin A source in some kind of expanded and localized GOBI package since the overuse of this bush food usually reserved for hard times would actually weaken food security? Could substitutes for the famine reserve be found? Could the bush food be domesticated and become a village crop in every day-care centre and school garden? In practice, clearly, "working within constraints" is never straightforward. The collaboration of outside researchers and groups of poor peasants demands the constant questioning of consequences and options with the poor. Issues of medium and message never enter this world of contingency.

If this kind of alternative is to be anything other than a modest palliative, it must include a locally-directed process of testing local needs and potentials. As described in Chapter 1, groups of people with similar material interests engaged in such a process will come up against limits and obstacles. Conflict will ensue. The process will continue.

The Reality of Conflict

Conflict and the empowerment of the rural poor are precisely what state rural development authorities and their foreign supporters find most threatening. The strong BNA belongs squarely in the category of the approach to rural development that Bernstein (1985) calls "populist". It is a position known for "taking the part of the peasants" (Williams, 1985) and advocates peasant production for their own needs as the path to agricultural growth, ecological maintenance and basic needs satisfaction. In rural development as well as other programmes, the strong BNA "puts the last first" (Chambers, 1983). A focus on the most disadvantaged and nutritionally vulnerable rural groups is necessary if rural development activity is not to deepen their poverty. Projects focused elsewhere – on the middle peasant, for instance, or on a food crop that is to be sold – will almost surely undermine the position of the poorest despite the number of safeguards (e.g. the agreement at Mumias that contract sugar growers would keep half of their land back for food production) and regardless of the sensitivity of the project's "social impact analysis".

Nor does adding the prefix "integrated" to "rural development"shift power to the side of the poorest. "Integrated" can mean many things depending on the ideological and institutional context in which rural development projects operate (Lea and Chaudhri, 1983). "Integrated" can simply mean a bigger shopping-list; so long as it is generated externally, it will not be the political and economic agenda for which poor people are willing to fight. "Integrated" can refer to a sophisticated management system that "delivers" items on the shopping-list in the correct sequence, at the right times and places and evaluates staff performance and the attainment of defined "outputs" (Chambers, 1974). It can also refer to the way in which elements in the shopping-list fit together in an idealized "rural-urban system" (Friedmann and Douglass, 1975; Rondinelli and Ruddle, 1978) or according to some other abstract system of production and reproduction (Buntzel, 1980).

None of these definitions alters the dismal fact that in Africa integrated rural development has undermined the poor and strengthened the rich. As often as not the term "integrated" is added because it is fashionable; in reality the word hasn't a technical or institutional referent that makes it significantly different from previous interventions in the lives of the rural poor (Ruttan, 1975).

For all these reasons, it is not surprising that a strong BNA in rural development is rare in Africa; where there are strong BNA projects, they are unlikely to be sponsored by governments.

RURAL ALTERNATIVES? SMALL IS POSSIBLE, NECESSARY AND DIFFICULT

Burkina Faso

Upper Volta, now called Burkina Faso, is one of the poorest countries in Africa, very much dependent on its former colonial ruler, France (Dabire, 1981), and dependent as well on the export of migrant labour to the somewhat more developed economies of Ghana and Côte d'Ivoire (Gregory, 1979; Pinché et al., 1980). As many as a million Burkinabe work outside Burkina Faso. The backwash effects of such massive labour migration are extremely damaging, as they are in other Sahelian countries (Burnicourt, 1974). Labour shortages are a major constraint in crop production (Ford, 1982; Fotzo, 1983), and seasonal hunger creates opportunities for grain traders to exploit people by buying grain cheap and selling it dear (Twose, 1984). Like their Kenyan counterparts, women have been forced to turn to non-farm sources of supplementary income and to bear an additional burden in sustaining the household (Saul, 1981). Infant mortality studies underscore the permanent crisis in the zones of migrant labour supply (Cordell and Gregory, 1968; Gregory and Pinché, 1982).

International and indigenous NGOs have been involved in rural development activities in this centre of permanent crisis for some time. Some interventions are more in line with the BNA than others. In the case mentioned in Chapter 5, an indigenous NGO, the federation of Naam groups, was supported by UNICEF and a series of international NGOs and the Swiss government to promote community-based multi-purpose groups of poor farm families (Adamson, 1982). These Naam groups are community self-help groups that recall older traditional groups for mutual aid in farming. The major activity was the purchase and storage of sorghum produced by members for resale at an agreed price below the exorbitant rates charged by grain traders. Production credit and some agricultural implements were also available in some of the groups. Some groups also engaged in various local infrastructural projects: well-digging, reforestation and management of a village grain mill, among others.

This project contains elements of both strong and weak BNAs.

225

Participation is widespread and seems to reach the poorest. The focus is strongly locked on needs defined locally as the highest priorities. Élite economic interests, particularly the grain traders, are being challenged, so far successfully (Twose, 1984). Yet there is considerable dependence on outside funding and charismatic, urban-based leadership. The actual labour process has not yet been addressed, nor has the position of women been analysed in depth, although labour-saving innovations such as grain mills are popular among women. There is some danger that the project's wells, grain mills, store houses and credit etc. will become a "package" beyond which local people will not be challenged to use their own knowledge and imagination.

On the other hand, since the revolution that brought young, reformist military officers to power in Burkina Faso, considerable effort has gone into decentralizing power and mobilizing and organizing rural people (Brittain, 1985). Between 7,000 and 8,000 "committees for the defence of the revolution" (CDR) are said to exist (Twose, 1986). It could be that in this new political climate the power of the traders and urban élite will be further challenged and that the self-confidence of the rural poor will increase to the point that their participation in these local groups is radicalized. Before the revolution there had been tension between Upper Volta's governmental structure overseeing rural development (Organisation Régionale pour le Développement) and the Federation of Naam (Adamson, 1982: 121). Now, in the dramatically decentralized situation in Burkina Faso, this tension may not exist, but a *modus vivendi* has yet to be found between local Naam groups and the CDRs at local level (Twose, 1986; Heisey, 1986).

Kenya

Machakos

In the present state of crisis, often the best NGO-based rural development alternative seeks only to contain the damage done by official projects. However modest, these projects can form an entry point for the radical needs dialogue. Indigenous NGOs could do worse than to seek out the groups of "losers" nearly always created by official projects and empower them to stand up against project authorities and the economic interests they represent.

Machakos District has been the site of repeated rural development efforts. One effect of this activity has been the popularization of hybrid beans for commercial production (e.g. "Mexican 142" discussed by Hunt, 1984). A side effect has been the gradual decline of a large number of local varieties of beans. Workers for the National Christian Council of Kenya became concerned about the possible loss of locally-valuable genes and began to meet with Machakos farmers about the problem (Miller, 1986). Slowly agreement crystallized that the local beans should not be lost. Seed was sought widely, in itself a mobilizing and networking activity. Farmers were chosen to reproduce and to bulk seed of the local varieties. Farmers' groups were active in discussing the qualities of the local seed and therefore in seed selection (cf. Richards, 1985: 144–6, calling for "decentralized seed multiplication" and showing the peasant basis for it in Sierra Leone). It remains possible that these groups will move on to another, possibly unrelated problem they now feel confident to attack together.

At the national scale, a number of Kenyan and other African environmentalists have recently formed an umbrella organization called the African Network of Environmental NGOs (ANEN). Its first major research project will, in fact, deal with the depletion of genetic resources in rural Africa, to some extent motivated by and building upon the Machakos case (Juma, 1986).

Reforms for Mwea

The team from Central Province whose report on Mwea health and nutrition was considered in Chapter 5 also made a series of recommendations (Wanjoni et al., 1977, cited in King-Meyers, 1979: 15):

(1) Farms or vegetable gardens should be made available;
(2) Poultry-keeping should be encouraged;
(3) A cooperative ranching society should be formed (for

227

    improvement of livestock kept on dryland pasture near the
    scheme);
(4) Health education should be provided;
(5) Maternal and child health (MCH) and family planning
    activities should be extended and mobile clinics improved;
(6) Piped water should be provided;
(7) Advice on child feeding should be provided.

These suggestions were not implemented, but would have qualified as a basic needs approach, albeit of the weak or shopping-list variety. Food, health, water and education are all mentioned. Participation is even hinted at in the use of the term "cooperative" ranching society. Is this actually what one has in mind by an alternative food system?

The answer is no. What one has here is a wish-list that does not begin to address the contradictions in Mwea. A basic needs approach would be rooted in the satisfaction of locally defined needs by the use of local human and physical resources. But the analysis of Mwea in the preceding chapter showed that a basic human resource, women's labour, was tied up in a seriously conflicted way. It also showed that the basic physical resource, land, was exclusively devoted to rice production.

The list of suggestions begins well enough by suggesting that land must be allocated to food other than rice. But how much? Some of the scheme's wasteland is already used for farming while the authorities turn a blind eye, and this has not solved the problem. Then the list grinds to a halt because the labour process implied in suggested productive activities (farms, vegetables, poultry, ranching) flies directly in the face of the labour relations conceived by the National Irrigation Board.

NIB technicians had estimated that only 271 days a year would be required to grow rice on the family's 1.6 hectares (Veen, 1973: 118): "the tenant spends on average only about eight months in the field and is assisted by additional labour during transplanting and harvesting. The remaining four months of the tenant's year are spent on his [sic] red soil plot and on private affairs." These calculations are blissfully ignorant of the crisis Mwea women face in trying to make ends meet. Fundamental changes in the organization of production would be required to give any meaning to the addition of yet more "opportunities" such as vegetable plots, poultry or ranching.

The ranching suggestion also fails to take into account the issue of stratification on the scheme (who among the tenants had animals in neighbouring pasture? Would improvement in livestock-keeping benefit those whose families were malnourished?) and the realities of land tenure in the surrounding area.

Moris (1973a, b) documents a long-standing conflict over Mwea lands. This conflict heightened as Kamba migrants whose land had been expropriated in the creation of Mwea (but who remained on the southern boundary) fought to legitimize their tenure and made large investments in mechanized dryland farming (Wisner, 1978). Pressure on more distant pastures on the Yatta Plateau has also been building up as "big men" from Machakos and Kitui monopolized grazing under the legal form of a cooperative.

The nutritionists' wish-list ignores these realities. However, if this wish-list were put into practice as an entry point for a group process in the strong pursuit of basic needs (and as packages go, this one is no worse a starting point than many a GOBI, eco-farming or self-help housing package), the situation would be quite different. The political and economic realities overlooked by the team of nutritionists would haunt the tenants' group's every move. They would have to learn how to make alliances with the off-scheme interests, how to negotiate changes in the Mwea labour process, etc. This process, not sitting under a tree chatting about felt needs, is the day-to-day content of the strong BNA.

A Women's Reform for Mwea

Hanger and Moris (1973: 243–4) suggest ways of improving the lot of Mwea women and family welfare under the term "more systematic organizational input". These proposals include:

- Access to safe household water;
- Recognition of a woman's claim to at least half the rice income;
- [If the woman cannot claim income from rice] The provision of credit ... for essential household needs;

- An organized system of firewood and milk sale on the Scheme;

- At least a minimum allowance for a subsistence crop other than rice.

The integrated, or at least potentially integrated, nature of these suggestions is again clear. It reflects the conflict women experience in trying to satisfy basic needs for food, water and fuel with limited land, labour time and cash (this basic needs conflict is treated at length in Chapter 7).

These proposed reforms are not so feeble as a wish-list, but they do not demand much of the NIB: a minimum amount of land for another crop (or possibly the integration into the yearly cycle or rotation over the years of another staple as in the Sudan's Gezira scheme). Water is the only major demand that would potentially cut into the NIB's profits. Administrative costs would be involved in regulating the presently exploitative, oligopolistic market in milk and in fuelwood (wood is trucked into the scheme as one to one-and-a-half-metre lengths of large logs from the lower slopes of Mt Kenya – Wisner, 1981a).

In principle, much of this list is realizable, but would it bring food security to the majority of tenant families? With the NIB's fees going up and with the constant inflation of durable goods, it is unclear what would happen if the official tenant (the man) had only half of the annual income with which to cover production costs. In the end the issue must be confronted: just why are these men, women and children in Mwea in the first place, to develop themselves and their own future or to produce a surplus which the state (in the form of the NIB) accumulates?

At issue is the state's resistance to the real and transformative participation of tenants and their families in the planning and running of the scheme. Mwea tenants struck in 1982 in protest against the increase of fees charged by the NIB. It would take much more industrial action to bring the NIB to the point of negotiating such reforms.

More Integrated Reforms for Mwea?
Moris (1973b: 338–9) has the most elaborate list of reforms of all:

- Long-term lease for the houseplot and other ways of encouraging capital investment and giving families some security if evicted;

- Incorporation of minimum subsistence plot (possibly heavier bunds along Scheme roads) to allow space-intensive root crops or integrating food crops into the rotation;

- Provision of urban type sanitation and water supply since the density of the scheme "townships" is high enough to justify this;

- Low-interest loans for home improvement to a standard consistent with better health (e.g. concrete floors, a separate kitchen);

- Provision to spouses of legal right to something like a third of the tenants' annual income, to be paid to the spouse in monthly instalments. Education fees should be debited centrally;

- Provision of greater protection of the rights of heirs, especially female heirs to tenants' plots which are at times challenged by distant male relatives who have never lived on the scheme;

- Preparation of contingency plans for other cropping systems as alternatives to rice in case in the future rice production ceases to be viable. Cotton should be investigated as one of these alternatives;

- Access to cheap and abundant animal protein. This could be by improved marketing from off-scheme areas or by production of fish, poultry, and livestock on the scheme;

- Planning for a quasi-urban future with electrification, pure water, and services that would make the scheme's population independent of off-scheme rural services.

If implemented, these suggestions would threaten the NIB's control over tenant families. Much like Habitat's call for legitimizing and upgrading urban slums (Chapter 3), Moris's emphasis on long-term house plot leases, improvement loans for

houses, urban-style sanitation, water and eventually electrification and services amounts to a tacit assertion that Mwea tenants
have rights as human beings, not merely as the sellers of labour
power. He is, moreover, proposing increasing tenant autonomy
and self-determination; over time, the NIB's ability to plan the
economic future of the scheme would be weakened by Moris's
suggested rights of inheritance and long-term alternatives to rice
cultivation.

These recommendations go far beyond the lists provided by
nutritionists or the advocates of women's welfare. The implication of such sweeping proposals is that tenants (and their spouses)
must become more centrally involved in the planning and
running of the scheme. Some form of worker control or
meaningful participation is the only way of making the administration of Mwea compatible with both flexibility in planning and
management and recognition of the right of tenants to residence
at Mwea as their home, not simply as an outdoor factory.

Surviving and Resolving Conflict

The strong BNA is an iterative, cumulative process in which small
groups with homogeneous interests define their priority needs
and confront their own limitations and those imposed by élite or
other conflicting interests. The groups should be small enough so
that members can know and trust one another (Oakley and
Marsden, 1984), although their small size may make them
vulnerable to attack from those whose interests they challenge.
BNA groups also lack resources and possibly, in certain cases,
knowledge and skill.

Their survival may therefore depend on alliances. These may
take a number of forms – links with other small rural organizations, support from indigenous and foreign NGOs or the church
and other national institutions, or alliances with urban groups
whose interests may complement or overlap with those of their
rural counterparts (e.g. rural charcoal producers and poor urban
consumers). Often groups can be linked up on a national or
regional basis so that they can learn from each other's experiences
and provide mutual political support. Oxfam-America has
recently engaged in such a learning process by linking up groups

232

supported indirectly by Oxfam throughout the SADCC countries of southern Africa (Kalyalya *et al.*, 1988). Similarly, FAO's Freedom From Hunger Campaign/Action for Development has supported a series of national, regional and international consultations (FAO, 1984).

At the national level there must also be active legal and political support for the non-violent actions taken by such groups in pursuit of their "right to food". The human rights implications of the strong BNA necessarily compel the protection of rural activists in the potentially powerful political and diplomatic arena (Alston, 1984a; Dias and Paul, 1984).

Some conflicts, however, will be more in need of rapid resolution than others. Herein lies a central contradiction of "peasantist populism" (Bernstein, 1985). Urban-rural alliances are important in sustaining demands and initiatives by rural groups with little power. However, the demand for higher maize price, for instance, could – in the absence of government subsidies or marketing reform allowing more efficient direct selling from producers to consumers – mean higher urban food prices. In the next chapter we will see how a variety of BNA projects seek to resolve these contradictions and how small, responsive rural alternative programmes can be made possible.

Chapter 7

Basic Needs in Conflict: Technology to the Rescue?

FOCUS ON WOMEN

Basic Needs Conflict

In previous chapters I emphasized the critical position of African women in anchoring the welfare of their families. This is not a primordial or even traditional role for women in sub-Saharan Africa. We have seen how changes in rural Africa over the last hundred years have thrown much more of the burden for the reproduction of labour power on to the African woman. Women's major role in the production of food cheapens the cost of male labour when men migrate to work in plantations, mines or factories because their wages do not have to cover the full cost of reproducing the next generation of workers. Even when men stay at home, and the whole family produces both food and cash crops, the full value of labour embodied in the latter does not have to be paid to the rural producer. This is because family labour, especially that of women, has underwritten household subsistence by producing food, by providing fuel and water, by caring for the children, by providing health care, etc.

Women's work in providing fuelwood and water, in caring for the sick, cooking and caring for children is also unpaid (as it is everywhere in the world) and thus subsidizes the national and international systems that utilize male migrant or family labour to produce commodities.

Such a situation cannot carry on indefinitely. Chapter 6 showed the links between the increasing squeeze on the rural poor under such conditions and the inevitable collapse of the physical environment supporting rural production. Timberlake

234

(1985) has referred to the end result as "environmental bankruptcy".

With labour withdrawn from rural production systems through wage migration and/or cash production with declining prices, it becomes impossible to cover all the tasks necessary to "reproduce the next generation of workers", let alone to "reproduce nature". The fertility of the soil, the terracing that prevents erosion and the tree cover must be reproduced, replenished and maintained just as hoes, ploughs and work baskets must be mended. Taken together with the daily round of domestic work required to keep a family fed, sheltered, clothed and healthy, all of these tasks constitute the *total material reproduction* of the peasant livelihood systems of rural Africa. If one adds the education of the next generation and the formal and informal discussions, disputes, religious ceremonies and exchanges among neighbours and kinspeople that govern social life, one sees how the *total social reproduction* of a system also requires time, much of it women's time.

To some extent time and money become interchangeable: woodfuel can be purchased in some parts of Africa as can water; money substitutes for the time required to gather them. Chapters 5 and 6 touched on commoditization of many basic needs, especially food. Time-saving foods that take less fuel and time to prepare, refined maize flour, for instance, can be purchased in many rural areas. Figure 7.1 suggests some of these "trade-offs" according to Sachs' (1984) reading of this changing peasant reality.

However, the rural conditions described in previous chapters suggest that in most circumstances rural women face *scarcity of both time and cash income*. Where marginalization is at the root of scarce land as well, it often becomes necessary for women to ignore certain basic needs in order to satisfy others. Eide and Steady (1980) provide a model for conceptualizing the drains on women's nutritional energy and time (Figure 7.2). It is important to note that this model includes the usual effect of market dependency, the sale of food crops when cash is needed, with a net loss in nutritional energy when food is purchased back later during "hungry seasons".

Limited time gives rise to conflicts between need-satisfying

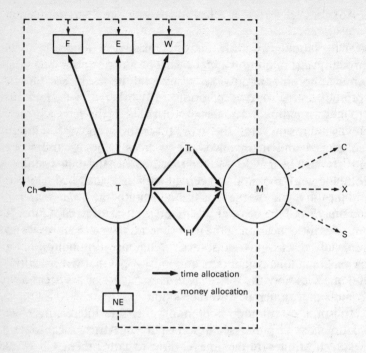

T   – awaken time of women

NE – non-economic activities other than child care

Ch – child and sick care

F   – time spent on food production and preparation in the household economy

E   – time spent on provisioning of energy

W   – time spent on provisioning of water

H   – time spent on production of handicrafts

Tr – time spent on trade activities

L   – time spent on wage-labour

M   – money income

S   – savings

X   – money spent on taxes

C   – money spent on goods other than F, E, W.

Source: Sachs, 1984a

Figure 7.1: Time–money trade-offs in women's labour

activities that are time-consuming: wood and water provision must be measured against the preparation of foods that require much pounding, grinding and simmering, as do many of the traditional mixed legume and grain recipes of highest nutritional content and the best traditional weaning foods. Limited money produces conflict among need-satisfying that has been thoroughly commoditized (e.g. professionalized health care versus home care; purchased clothing and home utensils) and among solutions to time-bound need activities requiring cash (purchased fuel, fees for water connections or for mechanical grain grinding). Limited land gives rise to conflicts of all sorts: cash versus food crop production, the production of the former tied up with the commoditization of need and time/money trade-offs; land for woodfuel, fallow land bush foods and raw materials such as weaving grasses versus land in constant agricultural production.

As seen in Chapter 6, the final stage of basic needs conflict is often ecological collapse due to the overuse of limited land and failure to reproduce natural conditions by soil conservation and fertility maintenance. This vicious spiral has often been described (Timberlake, 1985; Chambers, 1983). The squeeze described in Chapter 6 finally drives poor women into poorly paid casual labour as well (picking tea and coffee locally). This introduces a further basic needs conflict: women must work on the plantations to earn a wage, but they also must spend time on their small farms if fertility levels are to be maintained and if erosion is to be prevented.

Needs Conflict and the Fuelscape of Kenya

The domestic energy shortage in rural Kenya provides a graphic example of the conflict among basic needs. As in most of Africa, woody biomass (deadfall, small diameter branches, twigs and crop residues) is the dominant form of domestic energy used in Kenya. Women and children are responsible for its collection, preparation, and storage where necessary (Hosier, 1981; Devres, 1980: 5–62). This woody biomass is burned, usually in open fires, and serves for cooking, space-heating, illumination, fumigation and drying crops stored above roof rafters.

Chapter 6 described a series of processes at work in Kenya and in much of Africa which combine to make it increasingly difficult for women to satisfy their families' needs with the land, time, and money available to them. Commoditization has meant that some of the need satisfiers that were formerly available on common land (thatching grass, medicinal herbs, wild fruits) can only be bought through the market. Privatization has interacted with commoditization, rendering some formerly free goods (such as wild fruits) completely unavailable. Further effects of commoditization have been to push out the local artisan (e.g. the shoemaker) through competition with industrial products and/or imports (e.g. plastic sandals) making it more costly in time and transport to obtain such items and eliminating the possibility of barter with the producer.

Privatization, semi-proletarianization, and marginalization have put the small producer into a "reproduction squeeze". Women feel this pinch acutely. Not only do they need more money to satisfy some of the family's needs but the crops they grow are less capable of filling this money-gap every year as the terms of trade deteriorate. Furthermore, they must allocate limited land among food production and production for sale. Inflation further pressurizes their situation. Pushing their land harder (shortening fallows, cutting soil-retaining trees for production of charcoal for sale, etc.) Women farmers eventually reduce soil productivity through erosion, compaction and chemical exhaustion, and the crisis is deepened.

The only recent remission of stress in Kenya was due to the government's elimination of school fees at the primary level, but there are still many costs associated with sending children to school (school uniforms, copy books, pencils) and costs where *Harambee* (self-help) schools are concerned.

Women who provide fuelwood not only face a serious conflict over the use of money and land, they face problems of allocating their time. Time pressure on African women has been noted with increasing frequency (Sokona, 1986; Agarwal, 1986; Cecelski, 1985). A child's access to health care usually depends on the mother's ability to spend at least half a day travelling to and from the health centre and in waiting time. Eighty-five per cent of rural families live more than two kilometres and 51 per cent more than 6.4 kilometres from such services (Ward, n.d.: 92). Of the rural mothers interviewed by the 1978–9 Kenyan Child Nutrition Survey, more than 40 per cent had had a child sick for at least a day in the preceding two weeks (GOK, 1979a: 37). Thirty-five per cent of the mothers with sick children had taken them to a dispensary or health centre.

Fetching water, food preparation, cooking and child care all put demands on women's time. Data collected by participant-observers in the course of a Kenyan energy study (Wisner, 1981d; Barnes *et al.*, 1984) confirms the ways in which acquisition of fuelwood competes for limited time, money and land with a series of basic needs (see Table 7.1).

Table 7.1

PATTERN OF NEED-COMPETITION IN RURAL KENYA

Need with which fuelwood provision is in conflict	*Type of Competition*		
	Time	Money	Land
Nutrition	X	X	X
Education	X	X	
Health Care	X	X	
Transportation	X	X	
Housing		X	X
Clothing		X	
Water	X		

In each case the table indicates the presence of a conflict between the allocation of the resource for fuelwood acquisition and its allocation to the satisfaction of one of the needs listed.

Education has been tabulated as also potentially in conflict over time with fuelwood acquisition (as well as for money, where increasingly fuelwood has become commoditized and access to common forested land reduced through privatization). Children, along with their mothers, are responsible for gathering fuelwood, but when they are at school they can no longer regularly perform this task.

Transportation needs involve a potential conflict over time as well because the distance to public transportation and its relative infrequency means time wasted. In Kenya in 1976, only 46 per cent of the rural population lived between one and four miles from a bus route, 44 per cent in that distance range from *matatu* (rural taxi) service, while 25 per cent were more than four miles from a bus stop and 12 per cent more than four miles from *matatu* service (Ward, n.d.: 92).

Housing is in potential conflict with fuelwood acquisition because where cultivation of food and cash crops allow some additional land to be planted in trees, the species used as building material are not valued as greatly as the fast-growing fuelwood trees.

The greatest conflict exists between fuelwood acquisition and family nutrition. Here the time conflict has already been discussed. Where both diet and fuelwood have become commoditized (life on settlement schemes such as Mwea is a good example), conflict over money can appear. In the smallest farms even a boundary strip of hedge-like vegetation harvested for fuel must give way to food production. This is an extreme example of competition over land, but the tension among food, cash crops, fuel trees and trees for other uses (including fallow) is very common.

There is also a suggestion that where fuelwood supply is limited and/or women have limited time, cooking-time may be reduced with the result of less frequent meals and less nourishing diets (Cecelski, 1985). Half of the mothers interviewed in the 1978–9 National Child Nutrition Survey reported using maize flour alone as a weaning gruel for their infants (GOK, 1979a: 30–1). This is a nutritionally dangerous practice – traditional mixtures almost always use some other grains – and may be a reflection of less time available for preparing (pounding/winnowing) the small grains.

The amount of domestic fuel available in Kenya is not immediately apparent as one surveys the landscape, noting the presence or absence of trees and their distribution. Socio-economic factors interact with demography and ecology to produce an unseen landscape of class-stratified scarcity and abundance. One might call this the "fuelscape".

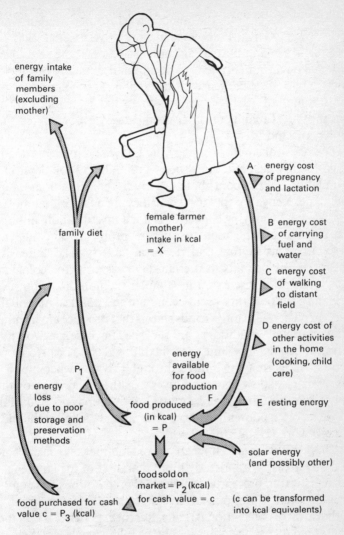

energy intake of family members (excluding mother)

family diet

female farmer (mother) intake in kcal = X

A energy cost of pregnancy and lactation

B energy cost of carrying fuel and water

C energy cost of walking to distant field

D energy cost of other activities in the home (cooking, child care)

P_1

energy available for food production F

energy loss due to poor storage and preservation methods

food produced (in kcal) = P

E resting energy

solar energy (and possibly other)

food sold on market = P_2 (kcal) for cash value = c

food purchased for cash value c = P_3 (kcal)

(c can be transformed into kcal equivalents)

If $P_3 < P_2$, then there is a net loss of energy.
(We ignore other nutritional assets.)

Source: Eide and Steady, 1980: 73

Figure 7.2: Food procured from subsistence production and from purchasing on the market

241

Figure 7.2 sets out the major structure determinants of a fuelscape in Kenya. It shows that both government policy and local self-help and mutual aid influence access, the state of the physical environment, density of population in any eco-region, and the pattern of basic needs satisfaction. Through competition the amount of usable domestic fuelwood is reduced by the preemptory demands of other need categories for limited time, money or land.

The physical environment (giving known biomass productivities and growing conditions such as rainfall and soil depth) and population density contribute heavily to the determination of a fuelscape. Kenya's population densities are a factor that must be considered. "Carrying capacity" is not a mystification, although the concept can be used to obscure problems of equity and distributive justice that underlie rural poverty. The "intensive" and "extensive" limits of present-day peasant agro-ecology are real. That prior discussion in Chapter 6 emphasized, however, that the poor peasant's socio-economic and political marginality has forced her/him into vicious spirals that produce environmentally marginal conditions. In the specific case of woodfuel, physical availability must be juxtaposed to socio-economic access. Access may be limited through private ownership. Rich kinsmen may allow poorer relatives to gather dead wood on their unused land, but may not. Employers may or may not allow farm workers (often poorer neighbours) to gather deadfall at the end of a day's work (Haugerud, 1984).

Chapter 6 described how an active land market has appeared in many areas. With already more than half of the land eligible for registration presently adjudicated, preparations for registration or even a rumour of it can cause the interruption or withdrawal of conventional rights. Recent experience is that these rights tend to disappear in roughly the following order (Wisner *et al.*, 1987; cf. Fortmann, 1985, on tree tenure):

(1) Building of houses;
(2) Planting of trees;
(3) Planting of annual crops;
(4) Grazing of livestock;
(5) Cutting of firewood for sale;

(6) Cutting of firewood for domestic use;
(7) Picking up fallen branches for domestic use;
(8) Placing beehives in trees; and
(9) Crossing or trespassing.

In this way a series of social processes converge to produce a vector called "access" at a point in time. Energy access in a stratified society has not yet been as thoroughly studied in Africa as it has been in Asia (Briscoe, 1979; Vidyarthi, 1981; Reddy and Reddy, 1983; Howes, 1984; Agarwal, 1986), but enough is known to assert the importance of access in understanding Africa's rural energy crisis.

Access will change just as fast as the other three structural determinants. Kenya is well-known for its large rural-to-rural migration, which affects density faster than one imagines. Inflation, food price policy and other government policies (e.g. the policy on school fees) further alter the pattern of basic need satisfaction while erosion and deforestation in Kenya (Dunne *et al.*, 1980) change the micro-environmental conditions for fuel-wood availability.

Figure 7.3 attempts to chart socio-environmental access to woodfuel for different classes of people on different categories of land in rural Kenya (Wisner *et al.* 1987). Strong and weak BNAs might agree on such an empirically-based description of the problem, although their approaches to the solution will differ greatly.

Access is, of course, precisely what the strong BNA is all about. A radical needs dialogue would tend, if the entry point were woodfuel, to emphasize the issues appearing on the bottom half of Figure 7.3: the amount of land available to smallholders, privatization and state-reservation of land, the problems of the landless and participation in self-help groups. The thrust of the strong BNA in this case would be to apply social and political pressure to increase access to woodfuel. There would be demands to increase popular control over the resources necessary to grow accessible biomass without conflicting with other needs or resources required to produce incomes high enough to substitute other fuels (e.g. kerosene) without conflicting with other needs. The human right to such resource control would be asserted and defended.

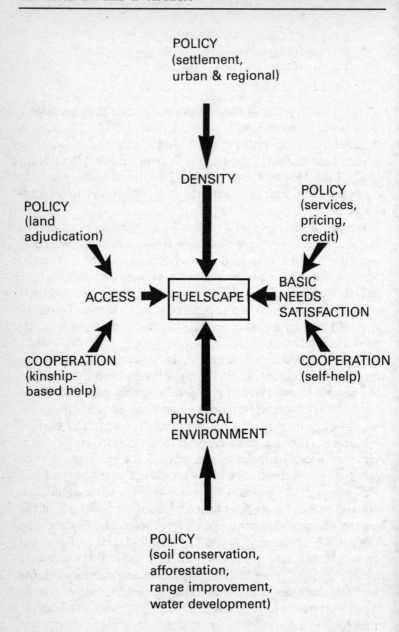

Figure 7.3: Structural determinants of a fuelscape in Kenya

The weak BNA would tend to focus on the top half of Figure 7.3, on issues such as lowering per capita fuel use through the provision of improved cooking stoves, increasing the biomass available on small farms (without questioning why they are so small) by delivering a package of agroforestry techniques. Another weak BN approach to the problem might be to attempt to provide employment for a fully-proletarianized rural population (the landless) whose income would then (theoretically) be sufficient to buy woodfuel or woodfuel substitutes (the "targeted income" approach).

As in the case of rural development discussed in Chapter 6, one might ask whether socially appropriate technology and other elements in the weak BN package are not better than nothing considering the fact that African women's importance in basic need satisfaction has been invisible to planners for so long (Weeks-Vagliani, 1985; Sen and Grown, 1987) and that agencies such as the World Bank say they have been trying to "recognize the 'invisible woman' in development" (World Bank, 1979). Are the improved stoves, agro-forestry techniques and other technological packages capable of springing the trap and liberating rural African women, at least from drudgery, if not poverty?

FOCUS ON TECHNOLOGY

Throughout this book we have seen that the strong BNA, in contrast to the weak BNA, addresses the situation of the poor – particularly disadvantaged groups such as rural women – in terms of control of resources and empowering participation. Debates concerning the relation between technology and development raise almost identical issues of control and power. To understand why the weak BNA based on appropriate technology has not liberated poor women, one must appreciate critically the many possible meanings of "appropriate" technology.

The Technology Debate

In the 1970s, as part of the growing "alternative" consensus that included the Women's Decade, a new view of the relationship between technology and development began to emerge. This view attempted to strike a balance between extremes. One extreme had argued that the import of an existing body of industrial capitalist technology ("capital formation") was the key to development. Others argued that only traditional, craft-based skills and techniques would provide a basis for development. The former could be called the "Conquistadores", the latter, the "Gandhians".

The technological optimism (and determinism) of the Conquistadores emerged soon after World War II and was a major theme within dominant industrial capitalist development theory. It reflected a new international division of labour in which the USA (and later other capitalist nations) were to be the developers of technology and the "outfitters" of industry and infrastructure elsewhere, first in Europe under the Marshall Plan, then, by extension, in Asia, Africa and Latin America. It is significant that in the wake of African famine, some are calling for a Marshall Plan for Africa.

Conquistador reasoning consisted of three propositions:

(1) There already exists a body of scientific knowledge and industrial processes sufficient to "develop" the "backward", "undeveloped" areas of the world (Gruber, ed., 1961; USA, 1963a, b, c).

(2) This body of technology will cause development to take place if it is transferred in a manner that reproduces the structural interdependence characteristic of industries in advanced industrial (capitalist) countries (Nurske, 1952; Lewis, 1955; Hirshman, 1960; Kuznets, 1964).

(3) There will be certain sociological obstacles to this transfer (Hoselitz, 1960), and certain adjustments will have to be made by people accepting new technology (Mead, ed., 1955), but these problems will not be insurmountable.

From the mid- to late-1960s this view came under increasing attack by scholars and development workers who saw the process of technological transfer impoverishing and de-skilling the rural poor, increasing inequalities between town and country, and strengthening the dependence of Third World countries on the providers of technology. These concerns were crystallized in such documents as the World Plan of Action for the Application of Science and Technology to Development (UN, 1970).

The Gandhian position represented the most radical rejection of Conquistador technology. For instance, in a series of works, Illich has tried to expose the ways in which technological progress becomes counterproductive beyond a certain point. He argued, for instance, that at speeds above 15 mph, transport technology was bound to reap increasing "delays" due to congestion (1974). In attacks on the professional organization of education, health care, architecture, etc., he tried to document the ways in which "needs" were created and people were separated (often legally) from their own abilities to teach, heal, build, etc. by professionals "who are trained to degrade others into consumers of their services through their scientific diagnoses" (quoted by Thomas, 1983: 6).

The alternative, according to Illich, was to revive the less specialized division of labour and less energy- and resource-intensive technology of "vernacular" (village) society and to rely on people's ability to adapt such technology to changing circumstances. This marked a rather extreme and romanticized (and over-generalized) version of village self-reliance. Other similar misconceptions of village self-reliance have been justly criticized (Kitching, 1982) without, however, undermining the case for "peasantist populism" that accurately appreciates the need for peasant-worker and urban-rural alliances.

In more concrete ways Gandhi had earlier worked out a set of alternatives based on the traditional technologies available in Indian villages (Sachs, 1980; Gandhi, 1952, 1957). In a specifically African context, Nyerere's early writings implied a similar scepticism about the role of foreign technology in a development approach focused on villages, on agriculture and on socio-cultural relations whose roots lay in pre-colonial African life (1966: 162–71; 1968a: 267–90; 1968b: 337–66). The Malagasy *fokonolona* may provide another African example (Grosclaude, 1980).

Although the more extreme version of village-based self-reliance is still articulated from time to time (Chambers, 1979a: 54–7), it is now used as a baseline against which to measure pragmatic attempts to mix indigenous and exogenous technology

247

(Galtung, 1980b) or to adapt technology (from whatever source) to local needs in the process of creating new technology (Singer, 1977: 11-27; cf. Jéquier, 1976).

The 1979 UN Conference on Science, Technology, and Development confirmed the direction of this more sophisticated view and emphasized the need to strengthen the creation of new technology in the Third World while providing international safeguards against the creation of dependency.

Such a view leaves open, however, the question of how new technology is to be created (as opposed to being imported). For instance, the creation of intermediate technology – associated with the writings of Schumacher (1973; cf. Dickson, 1974: 148–73) – may well produce low-cost, simple rural work places which can use local materials and produce for local consumption (Schumacher, 1973: 175–6) while by-passing or even degrading local people's skills and values. In one extreme example, Wortman and Cummings (1978: 3) envisage a "third agricultural revolution" based on what sounds like an invasion of rural areas by outside scientists working among (but note: not *with*) rural people:

> [One must] move into the countryside more aggressively and systematically with roads and power stations, with supply of inputs and arrangements for the marketing of agricultural products. Moreover, scientists must work directly in rural areas to create the more highly productive, more profitable farming systems which will contribute to the primary ingredient for rural development: increased income for large numbers of families.

Appropriate Technology: Elements of a Consensus

Hanlon (1977: 467, quoted by Sandbach, 1980: 167) pulled the emerging view into perspective. "Appropriate technology ... is a radically new approach in which production technique becomes subordinate to social needs." In this view, technology's low cost, ease of maintenance, compatibility with local skills, labour-intensity, miniaturization or decentralization may play a role, but the analysis of mass needs comes first and might imply a

248

technological structure that combines more centralized production of mass consumption goods as well.

As Galtung put it (1980b: 224): "What we should demand of technology is this: that it produces for the satisfaction of basic material needs for all, preserving essential ecological balances, and that it has built into it structures that also are compatible with the satisfaction of basic non-material needs – for all." These "non-material needs", it will be recalled from Chapter 1, include a set of "identity" and "freedom" needs.

Reddy (1976: 41) begins from a similar point:

> Since the average Indian is an unemployed/underemployed poverty-stricken villager, the satisfaction of his basic needs demands a strategy based on employment generation in rural areas, a dispersal of mini production units to the countryside, and the production of inexpensive goods and services of the mass consumption variety.

This leads Reddy (1975: 333–4) to a series of "preferences" which ought to be taken into account in deciding what kind of technology to adopt:

(1) A preference for capital-saving and employment-generating, rather than capital-intensive and labour-saving, technologies;

(2) A preference for cottage-scale and small-scale, rather than large-scale, technologies;

(3) A preference for the technologies of goods and services appropriate for mass consumption, rather than for individual luxuries;

(4) A preference for technologies requiring little skill, or small modifications in the skills of traditional craftsmen like potters, weavers, blacksmiths, carpenters, cobblers, tanners, oil millers, midwives, and medicine men;

(5) A preference for technologies using local materials rather than materials which have to be imported from abroad or transported from distant parts of the country;

(6) A preference for energy-saving, rather than energy-intensive, technologies;

249

(7) A preference for locally available sources of energy such as the sun, wind, and bio-gas;

(8) A preference, in the machine-building and machine-tool sector, for the technology of mass-producing scaled-down, dispersable, miniaturized factories, rather than the technology of mass-producing consumer goods in gigantic city-based enterprises;

(9) A preference for technologies which promote a symbiotic and mutually reinforcing, rather than parasitic and destructive, dependence of metropolitan industry upon the rural population;

(10) A preference for technologies based on rational use, rather than indiscriminate rapid devastation, of the environment.

Elsewhere (1976: 41) Reddy adds two further preferences: "for production for local consumption rather than for remote markets"; and "for technologies that increase, rather than diminish, the possibility of social participation and control."

Writing for the ILO's World Employment Programme, Singer (1977: 3) outlines similar criteria: "the technology required for a basic-needs strategy in a developing country must concentrate more than in the past on meeting the requirements of the small farmer, small-scale rural industry and the informal sector producer." What are the specific technological implications of this strategy? Singer continues (loc. cit.):

> Such a strategy calls for, and is in turn supported by, a special kind of appropriate technology: a technology which differs from that developed in the industrialized countries even more than the difference in factor proportions would require. This is so because under a basic-needs strategy technology must bear the double burden of adapting existing or imported new technology to the general situation of the developing country *and* underpinning the redistribution of incomes which goes with a basic-needs strategy. For this reason it might be called a "doubly appropriate" technology.

All of this would require significant shifts in patterns of

250

resource control. Such political and economic preconditions return as the focus of later parts of his chapter. For the time being, however, we must note that the theoretical range of "appropriate technology" applications seems very large. The range of problem areas needing new and adapted technology is suggested by a list of the major areas of concern of the UN Conference on Science, Technology and Development (Svedin, 1979: 50):

(1) *Food and Agriculture*
    a. Agricultural technology and techniques and their improvements
    b. Nutrition
    c. Fisheries
    d. Food storage and processing
(2) *Natural Resources including Energy*
    a. Renewable and non-renewable
    b. Conventional and non-conventional sources of energy
    c. Development and conservation
    d. Rational management and utilization
(3) *Health, Human Settlement and Environment*
    a. Medicinal plants and pharmaceuticals
    b. Health services
    c. Housing
    d. Social services and environment
(4) *Transport and Communications*
(5) *Industrialization including*
    production of capital goods

It is important to note that technologically speaking neither Africa nor Kenya in particular is starting from scratch. First, there is considerable vernacular experience still to be elicited, systematized and in some cases hybridized with experience elsewhere. Second, there is also considerable project level experience with intermediate technology. This experience is beginning to be synthesized and exchanged by a number of African technology centres (McRobie, 1981: 221–42).

Examples include labour-intensive improved lake and marine fishing technology (Cook, 1981: 34). The contrast on Lake Victoria between a few (10) powered boats with few workers

251

(100) and many (2,381) non-powered boats with 7,160 workers is significant from the point of view of conservation of scarce, imported fossil fuels as well as employment, while total yield and earnings are the same. Fish farming is also well researched in Africa (Moyes, 1979: 8).

Another example is the Asokwa brickworks near Kumasi in Ghana (Sandbach, 1980: 166, citing Parry, 1975). There, 26 men turn out some 10,000 bricks a week (thirty times fewer than a conventional brickworks) but do it for one-fiftieth of the capital investment. Such a rate of production could serve the house-improvement needs of a local area despite the relatively low productivity per worker. This is a good example of what Reddy refers to as "miniaturization". Furthermore, in the case of a conventional brickworks, 70 per cent of the materials would have had to be imported, but in Asokwa, only ten per cent of the capital costs involved imports (cf. Harper and Soon, 1979: 13-5).

Along the same lines, Tanzania has considerable experience in the artisanal production of tools for village construction and carpentry (Macpherson, 1975) and metal working (Müeller, 1980). These are especially significant because with locally produced (hence more easily accessible) tools and training, one can more realistically expect improvement in the technical level of maintenance of other unrelated new technologies (for instance, repair of pumps, grinding mills or oil presses).

Mention of such examples does not imply the existence of fully successful, widespread programmes based on these technologies. Many of the projects are "pilots". Many of the other attempts to bring projects to national level confront basic constraints such as the lack of raw materials (as in the Tanzanian tool-making case). However, if one is willing to give the weak BNA based on such technologies time to prove itself, it could be argued that the technological basis already exists, at least in experimental or pilot form.

Nor are women fully excluded from these rural industries. Carr (1984) includes 26 African cases among her 55 examples of women's rural employment initiatives. The case for a weak BNA incorporating appropriate technology and appropriate targeting seems to improve when one surveys these cases:

252

Food and Drink Processing: Fish smoking and gari [cassava flour] processing in Ghana; Oil processing in Sierra Leone and Upper Volta; Bakeries in Kenya and Botswana; Palm wine in Nigeria;

Cloth, Clothing and Fibres: Tie and dye, tailoring and sewing in Tanzania; Dyeing in Mali and the Gambia; Spinning in Upper Volta; Broadloom weaving in Ghana; Textiles in Swaziland; School uniforms in Botswana;

Building Materials, Housing and Household Goods: Sisal-cement roofing sheets in Kenya; Stove building in several Sahelian countries; Soap-making in Tanzania and Mali; Caustic potash making in Ghana;

Other Productive Activities: Vegetable growing in Botswana; Tree planting, poultry raising, bee-keeping and fish farming in Kenya;

Services: Bus service in Kenya; Barefoot women agriculturalists in the Gambia.

Looking, for instance, at some of the Kenyan cases cited by Carr, there are elements of both strong and weak BNAs to be seen. A women-owned and operated bakery, a sisal-cement roofing sheet factory run by a women's group, a bus service operated by rural women – all these cases deal with basic needs (food, shelter, transport) that often appear in conflict with each other. Participation can be broad and control over the technology localized, as in the case of the bakery, where a few women went on a baking course and subsequently taught the women in the group. In this case capital for starting out was raised among the women; control was local from the start. Carr notes how the bakery "turned out to be far more than an activity in economic development. Health, nutrition, sanitation, family life, business skills, co-operation between men and women, and leadership in the village were all affected by the women's project" (1984: 31).

By contrast, the sisal-cement roofing sheet affair began with a male-dominated Craft Training Centre, technology imported from abroad, women employees never fully mastering the process and fluctuations in the price of cement, which nearly doubled between 1979 and 1982 (Carr, 1984: 68–9).

In the case of the rural bus service we find elements of struggle (Opondo, 1980; Carr, 1984: 113–5). Women saw access to market for their surplus vegetables and access to hospitals as priority needs. They went to the source of the problem directly, and decided to purchase a bus, hire a driver and begin a bus service. However, the usual way in which Kenyan women capitalize a cooperative project – through the sale of craft items and pooling of savings (as seen in the bakery case) – was obviously insufficient. Raising loans for the bus involved a good deal of persistence as credit was not available without prominant male guarantors, and the women even had difficulties opening a bank account because they were not properly registered as a group (Opondo, 1980: 130–2). Finally loans were arranged, the bus was insured and a driver was found. Loans were paid off rapidly. The bus actually ran for four and a half years (unlike many that crash or are not maintained). With the earnings the women were able to open a retail shop and start a cooperative goat ranch. The latter is significant since this was all talking place in Kenya's arid and semi-arid lands (ASAL). At the time of Opondo's research, the women were negotiating to buy a new bus, since after several years of service the old one was costing a good deal to run. Such a purchase would have been made difficult by inflation and the trebling of the price in just a few years (Carr, 1984: 115).

Appropriate Technology in the Strong and Weak BNAs

Participation and Control

For the women producing sisal-cement roofing, a major problem was adapting the technology to their own conditions and in combining indigenous with exogenous techniques. The same difficulty has been encountered even more frequently where agricultural packages are used as the entry point. A question that must be asked is who is to adapt and combine the technologies and from where indigenous technology is to come.

The notion of "indigenous" is itself ambiguous. One would probably agree that the practices of a traditional herbalist in the mountains of northeastern Tanzania is "indigenous" and that pharmaceutical products imported to treat the same illness from West Germany are "exogenuous". But what if the West German product is in fact a synthetic molecule modelled on a product discovered from herbalists in the Brazilian Amazon? From the point of view of the socio-political and economic relations embodied in the production and distribution of the product, it is still "exogenous". And if the West German firm has a subsidiary producing the product in Dar es Salaam? "Exogenous," would be the reply of the dependency theorist and other critics of the way in which local people lose control over technology. The price of this product and the chance that it would be excluded from the official Tanzanian pharmacopoeia if a cheaper product came on the market would be outside the control of Tanzanians (or at least more difficult to control) (Doyal, 1979: 266–9).

What if a Tanzanian pharmaceutical industry produced the West German product under licence? Much of the discussion at the UN Conference on Science and Technology for Development centred on this possibility, as does continuing work in WHO. However, one would still not call this indigenous technology. The socio-cultural system prevailing among the mass of the people of Tanzania is not the nexus of knowledge, skills, values and social relations out of which the production/reproduction of this technology actually comes. This is largely because "modern" medicine remains the care of last resort for most of the peasantry.

But what if a Tanzanian with a Ph.D. in biochemistry (trained, say, at the Agricultural University in Morogoro and Edinburgh University) took an interest in the Tanzanian herbalist's preparation, isolated its active ingredient, and eventually enabled the Dar es Salaam-based, Tanzanian industry to manufacture the product? This is a borderline case which is probably "indigenous" but not "local".

The unique irrigation works used for generations in these same northeastern mountains of Tanzania (Egger and Glaeser, 1975) would certainly be called indigenous technology. Their modification by engineers from the Agriculture Faculty of the University of Dar es Salaam in some ways parallels the biochemical modification of the herbalist's *materia medica*. The difference, however, is that the socio-cultural system from which the irrigation technology was taken originally also receives back the

255

modified version and integrates it into the on-going whole even if practised by farmers in another part of the country. Indeed, if this were not the case, the agricultural engineers could rightly be said to have failed. Which technology is more "indigenous", modified irrigation works or modified herbal remedy?

This is not a word game. The important point is that being indigenous is really less a matter of place of origin or place of practice of a technology, and more a matter of the social needs served by a technology (returning to Hanlon's formula), that is, the set of social relations of production and reproduction within which a technology is produced, modified, used, abandoned or rediscovered.

In this way, for instance, a group of expatriate and Botswana engineers and development workers who rediscover the nineteenth-century steam engine and successfully design a system for pumping water in villages near sources of coal, will have produced an indigenous technology. Moreover, in the case of the herbal remedy, its "indigenicity" would increase if the biochemically synthesized, mass produced drug were used in a system of Primary Health Care in which the local herbalists (and other traditional practitioners) were incorporated as health agents.

What About "People's Science"?
The authors discussed above (Hanlon, Galtung, Reddy and Singer) would probably agree with this reasoning. There has been a tendency, however for workers in the field to underestimate or to neglect the contribution of existing practices of African farmers, builders, healers, craft-workers and other folk technologists. At best, elements of the technologies (an herb here, a crop combination there, an indicator species here, a roof design there) are extracted from the totality of social practice of that skill or science.

Müller's excellent study of Tanzanian blacksmiths is a case in point (Müller, 1980). Authorities were unable to accept his result, which suggested that possibly as many as ten thousand local blacksmiths did not need improved techniques, tools or training. They only needed better access to raw materials (scrap iron) and help in marketing. Müller suggests that the relative autonomy of such craft-workers was too great a challenge to state bureaucrats whose need was to control. Because of this need, they had to believe that the "untrained" blacksmith, like all "crazy-lazy-ignorant" peasants, needed training, guidance, new techniques, etc. The blacksmith project that might well have provided vastly improved access to needed agricultural hand tools was in this way a failure.

Oddly enough, Singer never mentions the practice of millions of ordinary people in his otherwise quite useful book, *Technologies for Basic Needs* (1977). Fortunately this omission is partially made up by a series of recent studies in Africa (mentioned in chapter 6) of what can be called folk technology (people's science, ethnoscience, folk ecology, *écologie populaire*; the name changes but the process is the same).

Such work in folk technology is the applied side of a fusion of several intellectual currents with much longer histories: ethnolinguistics or "cognitive anthropology" (e.g. Conklin, 1954; Bulmer, 1957; Frake, 1961), ecological anthropology or "human ecology" (e.g. Gulliver, 1955; Barth, 1956; Barrau, 1965), and – of course – that interface of methods and concerns known as "development studies".

Mention of this academic geneology suggests that we should be aware of the theoretical weaknesses and methodological dangers folk technology carries as baggage from its origins. First, since its origins are very much in the methodological traditions of anthropology, there is a tendency to overgeneralize from the presence of a certain knowledge or skill in one or a few informants to the village or larger groups. In fact, such knowledge may be the secret possession of the individual, giving that person power over others, or it may be that some farmers are simply more knowledgeable or innovative than others (Richards, 1980). Also there is increasing evidence that men and women have different sets of environmental knowledge and technological skills (Richards, 1980a; Guyer, 1984).

Second, while the ancestor disciplines of folk technology were careful to contextualize such knowledge and skill in their socio-linguistic/cultural and economic/ecological systems, they very seldom recognized that knowledge also fits into systems of power relations (the socio-political dimension). Some theoretical corrections have been made (UNESCO, 1981), but one should still be keenly aware of the tendency of applied studies of folk ecology to miss this dimension.

Third, few of the antecedent studies had a longitudinal dimension. Change in systems of knowledge and skill were therefore not often noticed, and only lately have some students of ethnoscience called attention to the fact that colonial and some post-colonial situations have tended to degrade local knowledge. This takes place both at the level of ideology as school systems and other media and authorities emphasize "modern" and international standards (Bugnicourt, 1982; Richards, 1985).

It also takes place as a result of changes in the social and spatial relations of production. Hence certain regions of an African country (e.g. the drier northern parts of west Africa, east of Zambia, south of Sudan, or the arid and semi-arid lands in Kenya) are defined by economic exchange relations as "peripheral" to the national "core" (just as the nations themselves are "peripheral" to the metropolitan "centres") and their culture, knowledge and technology is seen to be also "peripheral" (Bugnicourt, 1974; Galtung, 1980b). Where private ownership of land and the growth of a market for labour develop, the older practices and decision rules may not apply (O'Keefe and Wisner, 1975; Mbithi and Barnes, 1975: 167–88; Wisner, 1978: 6–10). One should, therefore, be careful not to romanticize what only appear to be traditional practices.

People may be aware of the fact that their practice is self-defeating, but cannot see an alternative. Thus a Sudanese peasant (Digernes, 1971; Devres, 1980: 17):

> Never ever do we ask anyone about any permission. We take trees belonging to other people. We cut them when they are too young. We never pay any tax. Everything is in a mess for us now. We are in a miserable state after our animals starved to death during the drought. We must live from something. What else can we do?

Brokensha (personal observation, 1977, quoted in Devres, loc. cit.) asked a man in dryland Kenya what the effect of his cutting large trees for charcoal near a river bank could be. The man indicated that he knew the environmental effects would be disastrous, but asked, "Who will feed my children if I leave the trees? Will you?"

Within the context of strong participation (radical needs discourse), the reasons for current practice may become clear, as will alternatives. Some of the alternatives will have a basis in current practice ("indigenous technology"), but some will not. Some alternatives eventually recognized by the group engaged in dialogue will be based on the current practice of other people known to the group ("transferred traditional" technology). Some alternatives may come from a reflection on prior or historically recoverable practice ("local traditional" technology).

On the other hand, some alternatives may come from the stock of "intermediate" options now widely disseminated throughout Africa. These may be of the new intermediate variety (e.g. solar water heaters or bio-digestors) or the old intermediate variety ("rediscovered" older conventional industrial technology such as water mills, wind mills, etc.).

Technological options from all four sources (local and transferred traditional/indigenous, new and old intermediate) could be adapted to local circumstances. If they emerged from the process of defining the group's own needs, they would be "appropriate". They would not be immutable, but would be subject to constant monitoring by the group. In this manner the dangers of such approaches can be avoided (e.g. tendencies toward romanticism).

Finally, it is important to note that technology can be used in several ways (you can still hit your thumb with a "socially appropriate" hammer). One can easily think of cases where local or transferred traditional technologies are used for the production of export commodities (e.g. pottery for tourists in Botswana, tie-dyed cloth in Mali – Caughman, 1979; Carr, 1984) or where new or old intermediate technologies serve the same function (e.g. solar heaters and efficient wood stoves built by Botswana's youth brigades for sale to the urban middle class; artisanal candle production for export). In these cases income is earned, but the appropriate technology is unrelated to a transformative strong BNA. Certainly the technology is not under these circumstances "doubly appropriate", to use Singer's phrase.

The four types of appropriate technology can be used in the context of a weak BNA – an approach which attempts to improve specific need fulfillment (subsistence) without challenging the existing distribution of income, power and access. Wells dug with the use of traditional Dogon siting knowledge (Guggenheim and Fanale, 1975) or pest control using traditional knowledge (Page and Richards, 1977) are examples.

Table 7.2 summarizes these possible applications of appropriate technology in Africa. Some projects, however, deserve closer scrutiny as their history reveals just how a project can begin to falter and ultimately fail.

Table 7.2

APPLICATIONS OF APPROPRIATE TECHNOLOGY IN AFRICA

	Types of Appropriate Technology			
Types of Development Process	*Local Traditional/ Indigenous*	*Transferred Traditional/ Indigenous*	*New Intermediate*	*Old Intermediate*
Export* (income/ growth strategy)	pottery (Botswana)	tie-dye (Mali)	solar heaters/ stoves (Botswana)	candlemaking (Botswana)
Subsistence (weak basic needs strategy)	Dogon wells (Mali) Pest control (Nigeria)	claypot grain storage (Guinea-Bissau)	roof water catchment/ ferro concrete storage (Kenya)	rotary mule-driven waterpump (Botswana) watermill (Malawi)
Self-reliance (strong basic needs strategy)	Oodi weavers (Botswana) Folkdrama (Botswana, Kenya)	improved *dungu* grain storage (Tanzania)	Sri Lanka boats in fishing (Somalia)	Hand tractors in peasants federation (Senegal)

* Including sale to the urban élite

A village in Guinea-Bissau, for example, had lost the art of making large clay pots for storing grain while under Portuguese military occupation during the liberation struggle. They had begun to store grain in used metal diesel drums the Portuguese gave them. After independence, in the course of dialogue with a national team of storage "animators", the villagers learned again from people in a village to the north how to make the pots. Unfortunately, the dialogue situation in which this single technical change happened did not continue, and little else transpired (Economic Development Bureau, 1980). The context was a weak, not strong BNA. Kenyan roof water-catchment systems built by women in the UNICEF women's project mentioned in Chapter 3 are another example, as are improved ox-carts and tool bars or mule-driven rotary water pumps in Botswana (Wisner, 1984b) or water milling in Malawi (Moyes, 1979: 16): the context of rural poverty is not challenged and does not change.

In fact, radical change *can* be supported by appropriate technology, but – as is evident from these examples – appropriate technology alone does not guarantee that a project is following the strong BNA. Some cloth produced by the Oodi weavers in Botswana is one example. It depicts the story of the loss of the region's freedom to the colonizers. Motifs of this kind are potentially a tool of consciousness-raising. In addition the cloth has a material use and can be bought and sold. One might echo Singer and call such a traditionally-based adapted technology "doubly appropriate" if it is produced and consumed by Botswana and not sold to tourists (Lewycky, 1979). The use of folk drama as described in Chapters 4 and 5 is a similar communication "technology" that fits the strong BNA (Kidd, 1979, 1982).

Examples of transferred traditional/indigenous technology that fit the strong BNA would include the improved *dungu* storage developed in Tanzania – a rat-protected, free-standing storage structure. The *dungu* was the result of a dialogue process that combined the characteristics of several existing storage systems in a Tanzanian village as well as elements of the "Nigerian crib", a new intermediate option. The discussions providing the background to the design and implementation phase had included broader debate about the exploitative nature

261

of the village food system ranging far from the narrow technical focus on food storage (Wisner *et al.*, 1979). Issues arising and eventually confronted in Village Council meetings included the exploitation of poorer village members by the richer who employed them during the pre-planting "hungry season" giving payment in barely enough food to keep the families fed. In this way the rich peasants got a good start with their planting and had better yields and fewer storage problems since the harvest was field-dried and in before the next rains. The poor peasants, by contrast, were always late in planting their fields because they were cultivating for their richer neighbours and had, consequently, poorer yields and greater storage problems because their later harvest period coincided with the next rains. These contextual problems in which, the storage issues were discussed emerged in the course of group dialogue supported by the "codification" of debate by a Tanzanian artist in the team who produced large water-colour posters illustrating the issues.

New intermediate technologies include the use of low-cost, fuel-efficient boats designed in Sri Lanka in the fishing cooperatives formed on the south coast of Somalia by refugees from the 1975 drought (Lewis and Wisner, 1981). Women in these fishing cooperatives seemed to be more fully in charge of their lives than women who had been integrated into large state farms in another government programme for drought victims.

Old intermediate technology has also supported the strong BNA in Africa. A case in point is the use of hand tractors (two-wheeled rototillers) by farmers in the Soninke Peasants Federation in Senegal, known for their self-reliant refusal to take part in Senegalese/USAID irrigation projects the peasants believed would only exploit them (Adams, 1981; Franke and Chasin, 1980). The Federation had been initiated by young men from the area who had travelled in the French merchant marine and returned home with notions of appropriate technology and working-class consciousness. The cooperative farming initiatives in these villages centred on improving production of their local food crops in the interest of food security, a goal which explains their resistance to the rice-farming scheme proposed by the Senegalese government and its foreign backer.

FOCUS ON GROUPS

"Targeting" Individuals or Empowering Groups?

Since the mid-1970s much of the Women's decade and more general women in development (WID) activities have followed the weak BNA. This BNA tried to identify ways in which "invisible" women could be given access to service, credit and the other rural development packages discussed in Chapter 6. Technology was supposed to lighten women's work burden and to provide them with new employment and income opportunities. In short, women's projects consisted of shopping-lists similar to the women's reform for the Mwea irrigation scheme.

When the individualistic targeting of disadvantaged rural women was not the method of choice, a society-wide improvement of women's position was the focus. Basic legal reforms giving rise to revised family or land laws were the results. While unquestionably important, the impact of these reforms on the daily lives of rural women has been insignificant. The major beneficiaries have been urban middle-class women. Major land reforms in Zimbabwe (Jacobs, 1984) and Ethiopia (Tadesse, 1982) failed to help women and the nation-wide village settlement programme in Tanzania has been hardest on them (McCall, 1987). In Mozambique, sought-after amenities such as water and grain milling have so far failed to change the lives of women in newly formed communal villages because the technology breaks down frequently or is inappropriate to their needs (Urdang, 1984b); attempts to transform their basic needs conflict through cooperative production have encountered many obstacles (Kruks and Wisner, 1984).

Neither the "targeted" or society-wide reform approach dealt with the fact that women needed new and more militant organizations. Of course, national women's organizations were founded and many women's groups can be found in rural areas. However, government sponsorship often introduced a class bias; élite interests sometimes emerged, as in the government-sponsored *Harambee* self-help groups in Kenya. WID planners tended to emphasize the need to mould existing models of group organization to women's needs. Thus cooperative societies have

263

been accepted as sound in principle while ways in which they can better serve women's needs have been explored (Lamming, 1983; FAO, 1984). The women's movements of African political parties, even in post-revolutionary Mozambique, have failed to draw in the poorest rural women (Kruks and Wisner, 1984).

Feldman has studied women's groups registered with the Kenyan government's Women's Bureau (1984). She uses Mønsted's (1978) figures which show that eleven per cent of women over 20 years in Kenya (excluding Nairobi) were members of women's groups. Feldman points out (pp. 77–8), however that official assistance has gone to only six to seven per cent of these groups. She notes that the Women's Bureau concentrated on the Central and Eastern Provinces, and that "women's groups tend to be composed disproportionately of the 'better off' women" (p. 77). Young women (under 20 years old) rarely join women's groups, although over one-third of women have already married and had their first child by that age (p. 79). Feldman's conclusion is disturbing (p. 79):

> By its policy of concentrating its attention on existing women's groups, the Women's Bureau therefore excludes nearly 90 per cent of rural women in Kenya from its attentions and is also biased in the assistance it gives in favour of women in certain regions above a certain age and relatively better off.

It would seem, therefore, that a large proportion of the "invisible" women remain so.

Between 1982 and 1984 the ILO identified some 50 projects in Africa that were judged "successful" in the sense of improving women's material conditions, enhancing their access to productive resources and increasing their participation in decision-making (ILO, 1985: 2). Yet the impact of such projects on the lives of the majority of rural women is doubtful. There are over five million women on small farms in rural Kenya alone. Twenty-four per cent of the rural households are headed by women, but these women own legally only five per cent of the land (Feldman, 1984).

The poorest rural women, caught up in basic needs conflicts and great pressure on their time, are least likely to become

264

members of such groups, even if there were not often biases favouring older, better-off women. Obbo tried to find out why women in Uganda dropped out of the literacy, sewing and cooking classes they had joined. On studying their working day, she found that these women's burden of agricultural and domestic labour was so great that they were only able to prepare the evening meal at 10.00 p.m. or midnight (Obbo, 1980: 206). Many other studies confirm these findings for women elsewhere on the continent (McSweeney, 1979; Eide and Steady, 1980) and the evidence is that their work burden has mounted rapidly over the last few generations (Bryson, 1981: 40–2; Feierman, 1985: 99–101). Feierman suggests that with the change in crop regimes in sub-Saharan Africa over the last century, seasonal food shortages and variations in the seasonal demands on women's time have also increased. Such pressures make it more difficult to mobilize poor rural women for group membership despite the fact that in many parts of Africa there is a women's tradition of mutual aid, rural savings groups and various forms of self-help.

With only a small minority of African women effectively involved in WID activities over the last decade, it is not surprising that the overall situation of rural women seems to have worsened. If top-down women's groups sponsored by governments and the integration of women into conventional institutions such as cooperatives, long associated with male-dominated rural development, have left so many women untouched, what kind of alternative framework is possible?

Homogeneous Self-Help Groups

This question lies at the heart of the strong BNA. It is not just a matter of "reaching" the poorest women, but of sparking a process of self-organization and self-assertion among the poorest rural dwellers in sub-Saharan Africa. How difficult this can be is exemplified by the experience of FAO's People's Participation Programme in Africa (PPP).

The PPP has been active in seven countries (Ghana, Kenya, Zambia, Lesotho, Sierra Leone, Swaziland and Zimbabwe). The intention was to work through local NGOs to stimulate the formation of small (ten to twenty members) groups at sub-village

265

level among the poorest and most disadvantaged rural people, often in the most remote or poorest parts of these countries. Groups were to be self-selected, but were encouraged to form according to their economic situation and needs. Much emphasis was given to women.

Unlike many previous approaches to rural development, the PPP has demonstrated an admirable ability to criticize itself and to revise its methods according to experience (recall the Oxfam "learning" process referred to in Chapter 6: Kalyalya *et al.*, 1988). For instance, in Sierra Leone – where agro-ecological and socio-economic conditions produce a situation very much like IFAD's Bong County, Liberia project discussed in Chapter 5 – a large number of groups formed in 1982 dissolved almost immediately due to heterogeneity of economic interests (chiefs and other élite dominating and exploiting poorer members) or because they were too big (FAO and DSE, 1984: 92). The groups were subsequently reconstituted and are now smaller and more homogeneous in terms of ecomic status, ability to cooperate, similarity of needs and the focus of group activity. Groups now average ten members and the ratio of men to women members is 1 to 1.2. Groups decide on their own priority needs and on activities that can contribute to filling them. In 1984, 29 groups were working on upland rice farms, 27 on swamp rice, 16 on groundnut farms, 19 on cassava, eleven in fishing, one in sawmilling, nine women's groups in soap making and seven in vegetable gardening.

In Lesotho the PPP attempted to encourage group formation among those with limited access to land and/or to remittances from migrant labourers. Special consideration was given to widows and divorcees. However, the force of friendship, kinship and neighbourhood are said to have distorted the strict application of these "poorest of the poor" criteria (FAO and DSE, 1984: 79). The local agency through which PPP works in this case is a national NGO, the Lesotho Cooperative Credit Union League. The difficulties African women face in obtaining credit have already been mentioned several times. Implementation in this case has been plagued by more problems than the PPP in Sierra Leone, primarily because the local organs of rural development (Land Allocation Committees and Village Development Committees) are *de facto* cells of the ruling party in Lesotho. Other studies have emphasized how democratization of these structures is a major precondition for *any* participatory development activity in the country (FAO, 1985). PPP activities in Swaziland try to focus on women also, given the high level of male migration to South Africa.

In Zimbabwe the PPP centred on one of the most remote and poorly served parts of the country. Its philosophy was directly opposed to that of production first with its emphasis on productive farmers in productive places and faith in subsequent trickle-down. However, the Zimbabwe project has confronted a possible contradiction between its principles and the success of the project (FAO and DSE, 1984: 101). Is it necessary for there to be a certain minimum level of infrastructural development in an area if groups' demands on government (one of the usual outcomes of rising group consciousness in confronting their needs) are to have any chance of response from state agencies?

Finally, the PPP in Kenya refocuses attention on one of the poorest parts of that country, Kakamega District in the west, where 36 per cent of households are headed by women (Feldman, 1984: 75). The programme attempted to reform a settlement scheme dating from independence in 1963, and the original carve-up of white settler lands. As such, it faces all of the problems discussed when reforms for Mwea were considered, and more as well. This is a dry farming settlement area, remote from government services, ethnically diverse and enclaved within the host population in much the same way as refugee settlements are elsewhere in Africa (Kibreab, 1985). Incomes and maize productivity are low and alternative employment for the poorest settlers (especially for women) is scarce. Since PPP in this area only began in 1983, at the time of reporting the evaluation could only point to the need to reorganize group formation so that the poorest, particularly women, were empowered to seek additional resources. A pre-existing irrigation scheme promoted by an international NGO was to be integrated into a project that not only encouraged more homogeneous groups but expanded activities off the settlement scheme into the surrounding villages. Already existing women's groups had mixed scheme/off-scheme membership, so this necessary transition – often noted in the

267

analogous case of refugee/host relations – seemed likely (Kibreab, 1985; Lewis and Wisner, 1981).

Participation: "Transformative" and "Instrumental"

These experiences – common to many more recent rural development initiatives in Africa, especially those where NGOs try to break out of the established moulds dating from colonial times – are based on "transformative" rather than "instrumental" concepts of participation. As noted earlier, the transformative (Kruks, 1983) attempts to build the confidence of the small group, to increase skills in negotiating, planning and management among the group members and to empower the group to defend its interests in the broader political system (Oakley and Marsden, 1984). Instrumental participation, at its best, never looks beyond the efficient management of a project and considers popular involvement as a way of reducing project costs.

White (1982; 20–34) discusses ten arguments in favour of participation. Of these, only one really suggests links with the issue of the overall democratic or anti-democratic orientation of societies, and only one argument suggests that participation is to do with encounter between opposing interest groups and new organizational forms. The other eight points are in effect to do with the way in which participation can reduce the cost of development projects, make them more efficient, etc. They are:

(1) services can be provided at a lower cost;
(2) more will be accomplished;
(3) participation leads to a sense of reponsibility for the project;
(4) participation guarantees that a felt need is involved;
(5) participation ensures that things are done in the right way;
(6) it frees population from dependence on professionals;
(7) it uses indigenous knowledge and expertise;
(8) it can be a catalyst for further development efforts.

The most common views of participation and its justification run along these lines, not with the strong BNA's insistence that the root causes of underdevelopment are to be sought by affected

268

people whose own consciousness and political skill increases in the process.

Even limited participation can challenge the often anti-participatory orientation of educational and administrative systems and can fight against past scorn for traditional knowledge (Bugnicourt, 1982). "In the end," says Bugnicourt, for many years associated with one of the organizations pioneering participatory approaches in Africa (ENDA), "the stumbling block in the way of generalized participation is political."

Chapter 1 stressed that development is not primarily a harmonious process, but a process of conflict with vested interests. Williams was seen in Chapter 6 to conceive the "normal" process of rural development in terms of "adversaries". Huizer believes that "utilization of more radical but purposely non-violent or civil disobedience strategies (such as land invasions)" should be considered within the legitimate realm of development activities (Huizer 1984: 15). Stiefel and Pearce, initiators of an international "Dialogue on Participation" based in the UN Research Institute for Social Development, see participation as the "encounter between social categories, classes, interest groups, confrontations between villagers and metropolitan interests, or members of voluntary associations face to face with immobile establishments." In other words, "hitherto excluded strata confront the supporters and controllers of sets of social arrangements which determine patterns of access to resources, services, and power, seeking a new deal" (Stiefel and Pearce, 1982: 146).

These "encounters" may take place between opposing age groups, genders, classes or ethnic groups. They should normally resolve themselves; in the majority of cases equitable compromises or even win-win solutions are possible unless, of course, the situation is that of deeply-rooted political or economic exploitation. In Senegal, for instance, the government drove women out of the fish-processing trade by introducing ovens for smoking fish which it turned over to the men who did the fishing (Dhamija, 1983: 75–7). However, the contradiction was only superficially a gender conflict; the fishermen could not both fish and process the fish with the new technology. What is actually likely to happen, Dhamija thinks, "is that businessmen will gain control of the government-assisted co-operative and use the women as cheap labour" (p. 76).

PEOPLE FOCUS ON THEMSELVES

Preconditions

Transformative participation in homogeneous self-help groups may provide the institutional context for socially appropriate technology, people's science or other kinds of substantive "contents" discussed in previous chapters. The weak BNA does not often get beyond issues of count-cost-carry or, at best, culturally sensitive adaptive research and careful formulation of the package that is, nonetheless, still "delivered".

AT exponents claim that R&D can liberate poor rural women and other disadvantaged groups by reducing time constraints and work burdens. They claim, moreover, to have the key to employment and income generation in rural and peri-urban areas.

The argument has been advanced that these technologies can only be effective in the context of the strong BNA. The kinds of small groups discussed so far are only some examples of the experiments underway – and these are often far outside or on the edges of governmental activity that could provide that context. For these experiments to succeed, a number of preconditions must be met. These have to do with government, international pressures, local infrastructure and levels of local expertise and knowledge.

Decentralization

Decentralization of governmental structures does not necessarily increase access for the poorest to services and resources, but in its absence the contradictions with "immobile establishments" are even sharper. Administrative decentralization as an end in itself is likely to achieve little improvement in the lives of poor women (Lea and Chaudhri, 1983; Smith, 1985; Mlay, 1985). It is, in brief, a necessary but not sufficient condition.

270

Reduced Pressure from the IMF

Between them the World Bank, IMF and USAID have rolled back even the weak BNA. The effectiveness of decentralization and even instrumental participation can be blunted by scarcity of finance, and it is here that the international agencies hold all the cards. Feldman (1984) tells how the current recession has slowed even the modest and biased financial aid the Kenyan Women's Bureau is able to provide. More ominously, Holmquist (1984: 84–5) notes that the "District Focus" in Kenya, a programme to decentralize five to ten per cent of district development budgets, is an attempt "to regain control of local initiative...." In the face of demands by the major aid agencies that Kenya reduce its rural development spending, tighter control is required of the self-help movement so that its demands on the government do not become increasingly strident and conflictual. At the same time, the appearance of participatory and decentralized rural development provided by the "District Focus" aids in hiding central control from peasant view and in legitimizing the state.

Minimal social and physical infrastructure

The PPP's observation about minimum physical infrastructure is probably correct. One is not advising spatial "triage" or "strategic withdrawal". NGOs and other partners in radically participatory development should possibly seek co-funding or try to influence national infrastructural project priorities in such a way that the minimum transport, market and service connections are made in the course of projects based on the strong BNA. Possibly food-for-work and emergency public works in parts of Africa where these programmes abound in the post-famine recovery period can be integrated with strong BN progammes. On the whole, however, note should be made of the criticism of food-for-work – it tends to produce infrastructure of most use to the already well-to-do (Jackson, 1982: 23–40) – and care taken to avoid new forms of increased international dependency by emphasizing multi-lateral food aid, especially programmes purchasing food aid from surplus areas in the same country or in a neighbouring country.

Minimum social infrastructure in the form of indigenous,

271

permanent NGOs of various kinds is also a desirable precondition. Major reviews have emphasized that such local organizations are keys to sustainability and appropriateness of programmes (Esman and Uphoff, 1984; Chambers, 1983). As noted at the end of Chapter 6, these local NGOs can spearhead urban-rural alliances that are crucial in "defending peasant political space" (Holmquist, 1980) and in providing "windows" to progressive groups in the rest of the world that will help them to defend the "right to food" on human rights grounds.

Local non-governmental organizations are sources of great, albeit underutilized, potential for a strong BNA (Hyden, 1983: 119–36). In terms of scale, home-grown NGOs are needed to link and to coordinate the many small homogeneous self-help groups. This function is presently served, often, by governmental or party associations and cooperative unions which are among the least popular of the new institutions of rural development. NGOs can serve this "linking" function and can grow in size and scope at a pace desired and controlled by the people themselves. The Ruvuma Development Association (RDA) in southern Tanzania, one such association, grouped 14 villages before it was forced to disband due to conflicts with the ruling party (Coulson, 1982: 263–71; de Gennaro, 1981: 129–38). The Soninke Peasants' federation is a similar NGO linking 19 villages in the Bakel region of the Senegal river valley. As mentioned previously, it too has clashed with government and aid authorities, although in contrast to the RDA in Tanzania its struggle continues (Adams, 1981: Franke and Chasin, 1980: 214–26).

Other interesting attempts to synthesize the lessons of what Grant calls "organizational breakthroughs" with notions of culturally-sensitive, adaptive, or self-corrective rural development have nonetheless missed the central importance of home-grown NGOs and revert to management models involving "chains of command" and other rural development hierarchies (Chambers, 1974; Caiden and Wildavsky, 1974; Hunter, ed., 1975; Johnston and Clark, 1982; Rondinelli, 1983).

It is precisely because local NGOs are capable of cutting loose from the governmental hierarchies and of behaving in surprising institutional ways that more room can be made for peasant creativity. Of course there is a real danger that exploitative urban

272

élite interests will relabel themselves "local NGO" and carry on as before, only now with the blessing (and cash) of the international "ad-hocracy". The poor may not "always be with us" (contrary to biblical pessimism) but carpetbaggers of various sorts will. This danger should not diminish the quest for effective partnerships between, for instance, foreign and local NGOs.

Knowledge and Technology

Finally, one returns to the social production of knowledge, skill and adaptation of technology within groups. Chapter 6 outlined a variety of related and overlapping approaches to people's science and folk technology. What these approaches have in common when they are placed within the group dynamic of the strong BNA is often called Participatory Action Research (PAR), problem-posing, or dialogical methods (Bhassin, 1978; Dubell, 1981; Kassam and Mustafa, 1982; Richards, 1985: 142–58; Chambers, 1983: 202–9; Pacey and Payne, 1985; 200–19).

These methods essentially update (or rediscover) older pragmatic notions of research through action (Huizer, 1984: 17). Results of this kind of research can, however, still be used to manipulate people, and there is a similarity between the management of rural people through social marketing and sophisticated industrial relations techniques appearing in the industrialized world.

Huizer (1984) further points out that PAR requires a fundamental change in attitudes on the part of the "group promoter", "activist-research" or Richard's "collaborator scientist". Chambers' "new professionalism" calls for a similar set of attitude changes (Huizer, 1984: 17):

(1) Required is an awareness of one's own limitations, a sense of insecurity and of one's relative ignorance (compared with the local people involved)....

(2) Accepting one's relative ignorance, one tries to learn from the people concerned through empathy and friendship what their problems and needs and feelings are....

(3) After acquiring sufficient knowledge and understanding of local problems further dialogue with the local people, particularly through discussions in small groups, searching together for possible solutions is undertaken.

273

The process looks simple, but in practice it is not. Especially where an oppressed minority's world view and technology or women's science is in question, great care and sensitivity must be exercised in eliciting, valorizing and helping to systematize and apply this knowledge. The experience of Africa's nomadic people is a case in point (Parkipuny, 1979; Mustafa, 1982; Rigby, 1985).

Women are not only invisible, but their science and practice is invisible or undervalued, except possibly where traditional birth attendants have been integrated into PHC systems. Yet, for example, a vast amount of women's agro-forestry practice emerges if discussions proceed in a friendly way unimpeded by men (Fortmann and Rocheleau, 1984). African women's concern with family food security is such that they often plant small fields of early-maturing grains: cases of this practice in the Gambia, Ivory Coast and Zimbabwe were recently presented in FAO's Government Consultation on Role of Women in Food Production and Food Security (FAO, 1984). On the whole it is women researchers, promoters and activists who are able to elicit and focus women's groups' attention on their own knowledge and its worth. The same must be said for the reconstruction of women's agricultural history from elderly informants, as part of the search for sustainable local options (Young, 1977).

Finally, returning to the theme of appropriate technology, one must constantly question what precisely it is that women are supposed to be integrated into. On the global scale, as Boulding (1981: 17) observes, to "integrate women at the lowest wages into a world economy which spends more than $400 billion yearly on the production of arms is the ultimate abandonment of autonomy for women." A country-by-country review reveals two other problems. First, the integration of women into development often means that they enter into newly introduced capitalist relations in unpaid or the lowest paid positions (e.g. whether in a rural centre as in the Mwea scheme, the rural periphery as in Zambia: Crehan, 1984; or in industrial employment, as in the case of textiles in Nigeria: Dennis, 1984).

Second, one must question the "myth of integrating women into development" (Feldman, 1984) from the point of view of the trajectory of such development for all poor people in Africa, women, men and children. It was on this basis that rural

development was criticized in Chapter 6. Employment generation for women in the informal sector (both rural industry and
peri-urban) has got to be subjected to a similar scrutiny.

Two interpretations of the informal sector diverge at this point.
A popular view emphasizes its low costs of production, the ease
of access to such employment, the limited skills required and its
potential for absorbing labour and producing goods if aided by
the state or linked more formally (ILO, 1972; House, 1981). A
radical viewpoint holds that this sector is in fact already
intimately linked with larger-scale capitalist activity. First, the
informal sector produces low-cost consumption goods for the
working class, without which the capitalist sector would have to
pay higher wages (Leys, 1973). Second, it often uses inputs from
the formal sector (Davies, 1979). Third, its production often goes
(at very low cost to the large-scale enterprises) into capitalist
production as inputs (Gerry, 1979; Langley, 1976).

The alternative view of what is also referred to as casual work
in Third World cities highlights its associated insecurity of
income and employment (Bromley and Gerry, 1979a), low wages
and poor working conditions. Contrary to popular conception,
casual work is sometimes difficult to get (Leys, 1973), can require
long apprenticeships (King, 1979) and certainly involves labour
one would have to call skilled (King, 1977, 1978).

Although a large number of women are involved in the
informal sector in cities such as Nairobi, their choice of
employment is much more restricted than for men. They
generally "sell in the informal market-place skills they normally
practice in the home" – child care, domestic services, "charm",
companionship and sex (Nelson, 1979: 299). It is not clear,
therefore, that simply integrating more women into other trades
within the informal sector would contribute toward eliminating
poverty. In India, for instance, many women work in construction and other sorts of casual labour normally reserved for men
in Africa, with little impact on levels of poverty.

In a few cases women seem to be doing reasonably well despite
the built-in subordination and insecurity of the informal sector.
In Mozambique thousands of women who had been growing
vegetables individually in the swampy land surrounding Maputo
have been organized by state initiative into cooperative groups.

This process began in 1979, four years after Mozambican independence, when a National Seminar on Cities began to look beyond the boundaries of the colonial "cement" cities inherited at independence to the vast squatter cities of reeds, scrap metal and mud. The broader context for creating vegetable production cooperatives was, therefore, the creation of the democratic institutions necessary for popular participation in decisions about land use on the edges of the capital city (Pinsky, 1980).

The Mozambican vegetable cooperatives were provided with access to seed, implements and space in the central city market. Women were also trained in bookkeeping and the administration of cooperatives. These inputs and more ambitious state efforts at draining the swampy zones and irrigating higher ground were coordinated by a specially-formed National Commission. Before the women's efforts were thus recognized and supported, yields had been very low and much of the land had been flooded seasonally. Since state involvement began, yields have increased to the point that in 1985 some 5,000 tonnes of vegetables were produced.

Individual women vegetable producers have to an extent lost control over some production and marketing decisions. They have, however, gained productive resources; their claims to land have become legalized, and they have guaranteed access to the city markets without the intervention of middlemen.

CONCLUSIONS

Technology does have a role in the strong BNA. Water doesn't run up hill any more easily under socialism than it does under capitalism. Yet the role of technology is complex and ultimately dependent upon the institutional settings that empower or weaken women and other rural poor people. Women in development activities have too often taken the term "women" to be the only problematic one in that compound concept. "Development" was accepted uncritically as that series of "projects, packages, programs" etc. that Williams and others have unpacked to discover adversaries and conflicting interests. As often as not, WID has taken the weak BNA and tried to integrate women into a development defined by shopping-lists. Where efforts have been made to conceive WID in terms of a strong BNA, great difficulties have been encountered. Nor is participatory action research as easy as it sounds. These are, however, the likely ways of promoting Africa's recovery from the great hunger and instability of the 1980s. Technology that fits into such a framework and serves such social needs can reasonably be called "socially appropriate technology".

Chapter 8

Power and Need: Conclusions

Having reviewed BNA projects, both weak and strong, what can we conclude? What future will Africans build for themselves? What role should the strong BNA have in this building? These are the two key interconnected questions about development in Africa. In this final chapter we consider some general conclusions against the backdrop of the UN Special Session on Africa. Then follow some specific recommendations for scholars, activists and others who wish to play a role in clearing the space for a future made in Africa.

CONCLUSIONS

There can be little disagreement that the decade since the bold elevation of Basic Human Needs and participation as prime development goals has been a disappointment. The ten years (1976–86) between that World Employment Conference and the UN Special Session on Africa has been particularly frustrating for Africans.

The crisis in Africa recently debated by the General Assembly of the United Nations – the first time in the organization's history that a regional economic crisis has been the focus of a week-long systematic discussion – is obviously not a crisis of drought and famine alone. This book has attempted to contribute towards an analysis of the multiple elements in that crisis and the way they interact. We can see this interaction in microcosm in the case of Angola.

Angola suffered a massive flight of skilled Portuguese technicians and traders at independence in 1975. Since then it has been

278

additionally difficult for Angola to fill the gap and to build up infrastructure and services supporting agriculture in the face of externally-supported civil strife and repeated invasions by South Africa. Food imports paid for by oil revenues became a short-term way of bridging the remaining gap, although this solution has become a long-term nightmare; oil revenues have dropped by 60 per cent due to the decline of the world price of oil. The drought of 1984–5 and the need for military expenditure to counter invasion and continuing destabilization funded by the US and by racist South Africa have put even more demands on Angola's dwindling foreign reserves. External debt stood at $859 million in 1984; while this is not a great sum, Angola could soon join Africa's major debtor nations (Tanzania: $2.6 billion; Kenya: $3.8 billion; Zambia: $4.8 billion; Zaire: $5 billion; Sudan: $7.9 billion). An estimated 400,000 Angolan children between six months and five years of age are malnourished (nearly 30 per cent of these age groups) (Haaga *et al.*, 1984). By the end of 1987, UN sources estimate, 690,000 peasants had been forced to flee their homes because of the war between UNITA (supported by South Africa and the United States) and the Angolan state (UN, 1987: 9). Such massive rural disruption means that domestic cereal production can barely satisfy half of the population's needs. It also means a great deal of urban poverty: half of the urban population, many of them war refugees, are destitute (*idem.*: 9–10).

Peace is a Precondition

Angola is not an unusual case, regretably, where peace is very clearly a precondition for the satisfaction of basic needs. All the countries of the Horn are directly or indirectly (because of refugee movements) dependent upon a negotiated settlement of separatist and border disputes as a first step towards recovery. In the Sahel, the struggle for independence of the Saharoui Arab Democratic Republic (Western Sahara) – occupied by Morocco by force of arms supplied by the USA – is a continuing diplomatic problem for the OAU and a tragedy for thousands of Saharouis living in refugee camps in Algeria. Chad remains divided, and border tensions between Mali and Burkina Faso persist.

In southern Africa, Mozambique as well as Angola suffers externally-supported military destabilization which has already cost thousands of lives because of disrupted drought relief shipments to the interior of Gaza, Inhambane, Manica and Zambesia provinces and caused refugees to flee across the border into Zimbabwe. At the end of 1987 the UN estimated that half of Mozambique's 14.36 million population was affected by this emergency situation, about half in rural areas and half in towns (UN, 1987: 11).

Peace in southern Africa would mean more than cessation of such military destabilization and invasion, however. It could lead to the end of a long history of economic distortion caused by the migrant labour system and structural dependence on South Africa. Botswana, Swaziland, Lesotho, Zimbabwe, Zambia and Malawi all share with Mozambique and Angola both that economic legacy and what the UN Special Session called "the policy of economic destabilization perpetrated by the racist minority regime in South Africa" (UN, 1986).

The hunger, disease and degradation of people and land in illegally-occupied Namibia and in South Africa's Bantustans have been well documented by external agencies although the regime's own statistical service stopped monitoring the situation a number of years ago (WHO, 1983; FAO, 1982). In the Bantustans child mortality is as high as 55 per cent by the age of five (De Beer, 1986; Turshen, 1986).

Peace would therefore have to mean the dismantling of the apartheid system, a restructuring of the economic relations among peoples in the region along the lines suggested since 1980 in discussions among the SADCC countries (Seidman, 1986), and an end to externally-supported civil strife in the rest of the continent. The US bears a particular responsibility for having fueled many of these disputes because of its tendency to read East-West dimensions into whatever happens on the continent.

The responsibility for the militarization of Africa must be shared, however, as a recent study by eleven US churches and development NGOs documents (Africa Peace Committee, 1986). The Soviet Union accounts for half the total arms transfers to Africa. The US provides fewer arms, but its military clients in sub-Saharan African have grown in number from 14 in 1980, to

40 today. In 1985 the USA trained 815 military personnel from Africa; in 1980 the figure was 184. US arms transfers and military aid totalled $35 million in 1976 and had risen to $389 million in 1986. As Susan George recently pointed out in a conference on the future of European Community aid, Europe has an historic opportunity to develop a separate and mutually beneficial relationship with Africa if it is able to break out of superpower politics and face the consequences of its own earlier colonial policies (George, 1987). Her hopes may seem unrealistic in view of the inability of the Commonwealth to move Britain to establish sanctions against South Africa and the fact that France, West Germany and Britain are just behind the superpowers in the league of arms exporters.

The map in Figure 8.1, taken from an African Peace Committee publication, illustrates, the close connection between war and hunger in Africa. The destruction of infrastructure, distortions in investment, refugee movements and the dislocation of rural production underscore the importance of peace as a precondition for basic needs satisfaction.

The strong form of the BNA especially depends upon peace. An élite or even popularly-based leadership is unlikely to encourage the kind of rural militancy implied by strong participation when external destabilization is a threat. Internal democracy can be one of the first victims of war, a clear case where political and military exigencies can block radical participation (Wertheim, 1981; on the case of Mozambique: Egerö, 1987). While this book has repeatedly emphasized that development is not harmonizing but conflictual, the great majority of the conflicts that emerge from the strong BNA do not become violent. At a time when Africa is racked by violent conflict, some readers might think it ill-advised to advance an approach that is based on negotiating conflicts of interest. There is room for debating this anxiety, but one thing is certainly true: such risks of the strong BNA decrease as destabilization decreases.

Economy, Environment and Society are Inseparable

This book has argued that vulnerability to drought and other environmental problems in Africa is intimately tied up with

281

skewed colonial and post-colonial economic patterns and the processes that have particularly disadvantaged women and children. The accumulation of power and wealth by an élite is not the result of a series of policy mistakes, which is the impression often given by the UN Special Session and other official analyses. There have been too many "mistakes"; and "policy reform" alone will not address the systematic exclusion of poor women and others from power and from access to resources. On the

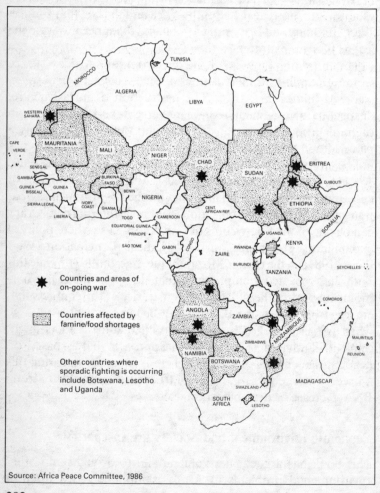

Source: Africa Peace Committee, 1986

contrary, as I have suggested, there is a real danger that policy reform and economic adjustment will mask new forms of exploitation of the rural poor, while ragged, stop-gap safety nets of the sort represented by UNICEF's GOBI are substituted for more costly Primary Health Care and the implementation of the right to food.

The final document of the UN Special Session emphasizes the "pivotal role of women" in agricultural production, but UN Development Fund for Women (UNIFEM) submissions to the Special Session stress the lack of progress in giving women access to resources despite such "symbolic recognition" of women (Engo, 1986). Nowhere in the UN Programme of Action for African Economic Recovery and Development is reference made to the fact that large proportions of the rural population have been systematically exploited and marginalized since independence.

Preceding chapters have emphasized that semi-proletarian livelihood strategies have locked the rural poor into a poverty that enriches an élite both nationally and internationally. No fundamental improvement in food security nor in environmental sustainability is possible through tinkering with credit, exension or research "packages". The marginality of as many as half of the rural people in many African countries must be addressed directly.

Support for this semi-proletarianized mass of rural people must take the form of quick and effective land reform and other conditions of access to resources. At the same time support must be given to indigenous NGOs so that they can encourage grassroots organizations of the rural poor.

This book has tried to convey the complexity of African livelihood strategies. The reality is far from a romanticized "traditionalism" or "economy of affection" (Hyden, 1980, 1983). Self-provisioning with food is commonly combined with wage-labour, migrant remittances and cash and food crops sales. Most basic goods – fuelwood, medicine, roofing materials and food – have become commodities. A clearer vision of Africa's future requires us to consider urban and rural, commercial and subsistence spheres as one interconnected system (Bush *et al.*, 1986).

The way out of Africa's grinding spiral of poverty and environmental degradation, then, does not lie in further integrating women and other rural disadvantages groups into development if development means the sort of thing described at length in prior chapters. The poor are *already integrated into an unsustainable system*. The strong BNA poses the alternative of production for need in a system which is locally controlled and locally organized.

Alternative organizational initiatives of this sort do exist in Africa. Self-government in Alexandra Township in Johannesburg in the face of military occupation by the racist South African regime is a testimony to the social creativity of ordinary people. This organization of houses, blocks and neighbourhoods has successfully withdrawn rent from a township council that did not provide services. It has mobilized alternative service provision on a self-help basis and even created its own local courts and justice system. Rural Eritreans have likewise organized themselves into decentralized, democratic units from which many nominally-democratic Northern industrial societies could stand to learn, especially concerning the participation of women (Davidson *et al.*, 1980; Burgess, *et al.*, 1986). People's organizations in Kenya, Burkina Faso, Senegal, Tanzania, Zimbabwe and elsewhere have been discussed in prior chapters.

There have always been those who have invoked "baleful nature" as the cause of Africa's underdevelopment (Gourou, cited in Wisner, 1976a). This book has argued that African environment, economy and society cannot be separated (Richards, 1980a; Timberlake, 1985). Perhaps at last this point has been accepted where drought is concerned. However, as we approach the 1990s "baleful nature" is again being invoked. The raging controversy concerning AIDS in Africa centres on the possibility of a "natural" origin of the virus in Africa. It is also shrouded in a great deal of racist innuendo about African sexuality (Chirimuuta and Chirimuuta, 1987).

This book is not the place to try to sort out the issue of AIDS. But it is worth noting that many of the same conditions that produced increased vulnerability to drought in Africa – chronic malnutrition and diseases of poverty – also have the effect of suppressing the immune system. Some authors have suggested

284

that AIDS-like conditions might therefore be yet another consequence of colonial and neo-colonial exploitation (Epstein and Packard, 1987). Whatever the origins of AIDS, the future costs – of mortality, social disruption and pressure on health services – will be high and will fundamentally affect the prospects for a strong BNA. Will the brave efforts at self-determination demonstrated by the people's development organizations discussed in this book be undermined and ultimately negated by this new plague? First, although there is some evidence of much seropositivity (AIDS antibodies in the blood) among the educated élite, it has yet to be demonstrated that these results are not false positives due to endemic malaria. If they are infected, it is not clear that they will become ill at the same rate as AIDS victims in the United States and Western Europe. Finally, even if they do become ill and die, this will not necessarily mean that the mass of the population will cease its self-organization and struggle for basic needs as a result.

There are No Package Solutions

We have spent a good deal of time critiquing the notion of the "package". The UN's Africa Programme stands in danger of falling into the hands of the new technocrats of the biotechnology revolution, who – no matter what the position of the OAU and the UN Special Session – will be continuing to push "newer", "better", "improved" technical packages in the name of an African Green Revolution (with or without a garnish of "farm systems research" and "applied anthropology" to make the package more attractive).

Nowhere in the UN document does one find reference to the fact that many of the policy mistakes that now require reform were the product of technological and economic advice by the donor ad-hocracy in the first place. Harvard advisers probably outnumber rhinos in Kenya and are definitely *not* an endangered species.

To the numerous technical packages are now to be added packages of fiscal and economic policy instruments straight from the IMF. At the end of 1987 the Organization of African Unity (OAU) held a special summit meeting on Africa's debt crisis. The

285

heads of state called for a ten-year moratorium on debt service and multi-year rescheduling of debt with repayment spread across a 50-year period at zero interest (Hodges, 1987:1). While the disastrous effects of economic adjustment packages are widely acknowledged, the IMF steadfastly disavows its responsibility. Its managing director, Michel Camdessus, recently denied that the IMF's packages insist on cutting social services and food subsidies that affect the poor. Decisions about where spending cuts are to be made are taken by the governments themselves, he asserted (Lone, 1987: 5). What double talk! In order to qualify for funds from the Structural Adjustment Fund and other sources of finance, it is not enough that a country is "low income and debt distressed". The country must engage in "adjustment". The options are few, and the effects of almost any one (budget cuts, price deregulation, currency devaluation, etc.) hit the poor hardest, as Cornia's work has shown (Cornia *et al.*, 1987).

The dangers of such economic adjustment for both strong and weak need satisfaction has been stressed in this book. "Universal Child Immunization by 1990," even if achievable and sustainable in Africa, is no substitute for the basic social infrastructure which are the people's right and a basic condition of sustainable production. Furthermore UNICEF itself has expressed doubts about the economic sustainability of follow-up immunization in the poorest countries. It frankly admits that in all likelihood "in the poor countries ... especially those hard-hit by economic crisis, assistance will have to continue well beyond 1990 ..." (UNICEF, 1987; 28).

If this book has seemed particularly hard on UNICEF, it is because its present role in yet another scramble for Africa, a hundred years after the Conference of Berlin carved up the continent, stands in such stark contrast to UNICEF's past and potential role as militant advocate of the rights of children, youth and women. Just as African leaders abandoned specific demands for debt relief at the Special Session in the interests of a unanimously-approved final document, UNICEF has been shown in this book to have given up radical participation and the grassroots struggle for access to resources for the sake of international support for its minimalist packages. For their part, African leaders found that a year and a half later it was even harder to open a discussion about debt. In both cases long-term gains are being forsaken for the sake of the short; youth, in both cases, is being sold out.

Both Past and Future Must be Acknowledged

Senegal led Africa in a blanket *mea culpa* for "mistaken economic policies" at the Special Session. Last-minute negotiation was necessary to rescue the hint that colonial inheritance might have something to do with Africa's problems twenty years on. High school students inflamed by reading novels such as Ngũgĩ's *Petals of Blood* or Senegal's Sembène Ousmane's *Last of the Empire* cannot have been over-pleased by this historical disclaimer and by the "success" achieved in New York by their leaders at the UN Special Session.

It is not surprising that it was the youth of Soweto that ignited the June 1976 uprising, commemorated a few weeks after the end of the Special Session on Africa. Youth throughout the continent face unemployment and despair of access to the political machinery. One thinks sometimes that mandatory retirement across the whole of the state apparatus in Africa (and the donor ad-hocracy) at the age 40 would be a useful start at giving youth a role in shaping the future they must inherit.

This book has not tried to, nor could it, outline that future. I have offered a systematic treatment of a method (the strong BNA) that I believe will help African youth define their own needs and options. The task of thinking through the implications of the strong BNA at eco-regional, national and international levels still lies ahead. What would the relations between town and country look like if development were about needs? (Mabogunje, 1981). What kind of industrialization is implied by the strong BNA? (Bhagavan, 1980; Rweyemanu, 1980; Thomas, 1974). These and even more difficult political and cultural questions will be addressed by the generation of Africans now reaching adulthood (Hadjor, 1987; Nzongola *et al.*, 1987).

Non-Governmental Organizations Have Potential

A number of African delegations were uneasy with compromises

287

demanded by the rich in New York. Even more uneasy were the many representatives of indigenous African NGOs. They and their supporters among industrial country NGOs generally recognize the dangers of technological and institutional package responses that put basic needs in danger, undermine local skill, knowledge and organizational initiatives, and reinforce existing skewed distributions of income and power.

One document submitted to the Preparatory Committee of the Special Session, authored by senior individuals of some 27 US-based development NGOs is fairly typical of the alternative priorities for Africa that emerge from a people-oriented, grass-roots perspective (Centre for Concern, 1986). The summary document is similar in some ways to the more extensive *Compact for African Development* produced in 1985 by a joint Council on Foreign Relations and Overseas Development Council working group (Council on Foreign Relations, 1985; Berg and Whitaker, 1986). Five points are highlighted:

(1) that the concept of *participatory development* be a central focus of discussion at the Special Session;
(2) that *environmental concerns*, including the linkages among environment, population, and the economy be major components of development planning at the Special Session;
(3) that the *central role of women* in African food systems be a focus of all discussions of African agriculture;
(4) [that] steps [are taken] toward a *coordinated strategy* which links macro-level and micro-level issues and responses;
(5) that the Special Session launch renewed efforts to *resolve conflicts* in Africa and in particular for an *end to apartheid* (Emphasis in original).

The language here is refreshingly direct by comparison with the diplomatic prose of the ad-hocracy. Yet do these NGOs actually speak for the grassroots groups that are emerging from civil society in Africa?

Some African NGOs reject the name "non-governmental" and insist that they are not European-style NGOs but, potentially a new force for people's development in Africa in their own right: not opposed to their governments, but not identified with their policies either. One has to agree that there has been a good deal too much "bashing" of the post-colonial state in the literature of despair (Leys, 1987). It is harder but more honest and eventually fruitful to act in a world where there are shades of good and evil, but seldom the absolute incarnation of either. There are states and states, NGOs and NGOs. There is also an increasingly interdependent global economy. Actors on such a stage now include multinational corporations, nations and – a growing force – networks of people confronting common problems and desiring common goals (justice and sustainability, for instance).

It is not surprising, therefore, that African NGOs are moving out onto that international stage. Africa's many and varied voluntary development organizations (as some prefer to be called) met recently to form a Pan-African network, the Forum for African Voluntary Development Organizations (FAVDO). Although there is always the danger that such networking will over-institutionalize grassroots organizations, drawing them away from their primary work and making their approach less challenging of prevalent weak BNA models, the benefits of stronger South–South cooperation among such groups, including more negotiating power in relation to Northern partners and governments, could be forthcoming.

Basic Needs and Participation Have Been Co-Opted

The general conclusion of the systematic contrast of strong and weak BNAs in the foregoing is that weak versions have successfully become the focus of projects and programmes that have now earned all need discourse and participatory planning a reputation for failure. The non-governmental sector in Africa contains the few successes of the strong BNA. Yet it is precisely these NGOs that stand in danger of now being swamped with aid, co-opted and contained in various ways. Perhaps the perception of this danger partly underlies Mamdani's objection to Hyden's otherwise reasonable appeal for the "private and voluntary" sectors as a focus of development activity (Mamdani, 1986; Hyden, 1986).

NGOs have been mentioned as under-utilized social infrastructure by several recent comission studies and feature prominently

289

among the "social breakthroughs" UNICEF believes can be combined with new technology to achieve a Child Survival Revolution. One form of weakening such indigenous and foreign NGOs would, of course, be to load them down with semi-permanent mandates to administer various health and food production campaigns, leaving govenment and multinational agribusiness to get on with the "business as usual" export side. Quantum increases in funding can also often have a major influence on popularly-based organizations by "internationalizing" staff, working methods, accounting procedures and standards of success and failure. African NGOs are aware of these dangers, although the successful absorption and control of many South Asian NGOs by governments and élite interests could be further usefully studied for cautionary lessons (Khan and Bhasin, 1986).

RECOMMENDATIONS

The purpose of this book was to refocus attention on the strong BNA at a time when the spirit of a "new pragmatism" is tending to dismiss such approaches as impossibly idealistic. It also aimed to throw light on the interconnected problems of Africa's poor from the perspective of the strong BNA. As such, the analyses address not one, but several potential audiences. The scope of these reflections on experience has been continental, though Kenya served as a central case to which all chapters returned. I am aware of the danger of overgeneralizing. Nevertheless, I conclude by trying to sketch out the implications of the strong BNA for five potential audiences: African scholars, foreign scholars, NGOs, donors and African governments.

African Scholars

Robert Chambers (1983: 7–12) vividly describes the situation of the urban-based scientist/administrator in much of the Third World. Few would dispute the urban bias and continued influence of colonial and new international standards of problem definition and methodology. Even the best-intentioned find it

290

difficult to get local support – funding, leave, transport – for work in remote rural areas. The best young field workers quite often are catapulted into high levels of administration, further removing them from rural realities.

At the same time, university facilities are deteriorating. A newly-organized African Association for Participatory Research based in Tanzania was stalled for some time for lack of photocopy paper and other basic means of communication. A major international appeal for books to restock the library in Kampala, Uganda, after years of civil unrest and deterioration was postponed for several years before the momentum was built to obtain a UNESCO grant. Staff-student field work from the Faculty of Medicine in Dar es Salaam has been cut back due to the shortage of fuel for vehicles.

Faced with such frustrations, many turn to overseas funding agencies for financial support and to receive recognition in the form of honoraria and consulting fees for rural development research their home institutions fail to support. This is a dangerous, though understandable, trend. The danger is that overseas interests, no matter how sympathetic or progressive, determine the research priorities and methods.

Where African scholars are able to make links directly with indigenous NGOs sharing a commitment to the strong BNA, new pathways for significant rural work may open up. In this situation, Africans themselves – participatory researchers and the poor together – are more likely to define needs according to their own understanding of priorities and to evolve appropriate methods.

Foreign Scholars

Two immediate though distant supporting roles for foreign scholars come to mind. It is a fact of history that many young African scientists and scholars train in Europe and North America. It is essential that teachers in these host institutions defend the legitimacy of participatory methods, of people's science, and of critical approaches to society-technology-environment-economy relations. A lively debate concerning the relevance of methods and models should be encouraged. This is

291

not to argue that teachers committed to high-tech should be limited in their freedom to propound these views nor that African students should be limited in their freedom to sample and to judge for themselves. However, as it stands, alternative, socially appropriate, participatory approaches are seldom given equal time in teaching, in preliminary exams or even in supplementary summer training courses. Nor are the critical skills of judging the appropriateness of teaching material and methods encouraged. A "new professionalism" must be substituted for the old (Chambers, 1985). This would legitimize participatory methods and would elevate the empirical problems of the poor – biomass, goats and root crops, for instance – to a level of professionalism equal to that surrounding the problems of importance to the rich.

The second kind of potential support by foreign scientists and scholars concerns the foreign policy of their own countries. There can be no US engineer, agronomist or anthropologist concerned with the people of Africa who is not logically and morally bound to lobby with her/his government for an end to support for apartheid, to military aid, to grossly ideological aid. In 1986 it was announced that the US would aid Mozambican agriculture with nearly $2 million for tractors, ploughs, trucks and threshing machines *for the exclusive use of the private sector* (AIM, 1986: 6). In general terms, the US has had a major role in pushing forward the economic adjustment packages that are so destructive of basic needs. US scientists concerned with basic needs have a duty to join with others in calling on their government to account for these anti-people policies. Several national networks and vehicles for such action exist, including the Association of Concerned African Scholars, Science for the People, and the constituent NGOs involved nationally and regionally in the work of the African Peace Committee. Anti-apartheid lobbies and social movements exist in the US, the UK, continental Europe and much of the rest of the world.

Field work by foreign scholars in Africa requires a conscious effort to seek locally appropriate methods despite the fact that these may not be "publishable" in conventional quarters at home. Some are tempted, for instance, to use a sophisticated computer model of rangeland management available "in the literature" even when they know that most of the data will not be available in Africa. Alternative approaches based on group discussions with pastoralists might be of direct use to local rural workers, but will not look as good in the pages of a "professional" journal. Foreign professionals must make that choice.

In addition, their manner of working should strengthen the local ability to do applied science. As with the question of methodology and use of scientific hardware, it is easy to cave in to difficulties in organizing adequate "counterparting". But there is little excuse in the late 1980s for conducting research in which African colleagues do not have a significant role, not merely as enumerators or technicians. Ideally such work will strengthen materially the capacity for applied research of local academic, NGO or government agencies.

Where possible local NGOs should be invited to engage in action research and training of their staff in these techniques. For too long government and government-controlled universities have held the monopoly on skills required to monitor basic needs. NGOs can and should develop the ability to carry out parallel monitoring of, for instance, nutritional status, as a way of holding governments accountable. In many other vital areas, NGOs do not have access to national and international information systems. The research centres of the Consultative Group on International Agricultural Research (CGIAR) are, in principle, open to collaboration with and use by local NGOs. The banks of locally collected genetic material stored there should be accessible to local farmers through their "people's organizations". Yet this is seldom the case. Foreign researchers can help to make this access possible.

Non-Governmental Organizations

These include those based outside Africa and those one might call "indigenous". For both kinds of NGO, in certain respects, the difficulties facing individual African and foreign scholars arise again. Whatever one may think of the many forms taken by the post-colonial state in Africa, most NGOs are clear that their work has to be coordinated with official development activities. Where planning and more comprehensive approaches to early warnings of famine are concerned, this liaison is all the more important. Yet

293

participatory approaches can threaten established government styles and élite economic interests. There is a tension here that can only be worked through locally.

Foreign NGOs as well face the issue of working with their own govenment's aid apparatus or not. In the wake of the recent African famine scores of US-based NGOs are presently integrated into USAID activities. Should they be?

The intellectual legitimacy of radically participatory development work is also an issue for NGOs. They have to account for their work to a public whose ideas of proper scientific procedure have been moulded by images of astronauts and men in white suits selling "miracle ingredient X" on television for decades. It is hard to counter-sell "participation" when the society at home is becoming more technocratic and reductionist and less participatory. Yet it must be done if these NGOs are committed to collaborating with their partners in Africa in a strong BNA. Such work depends on the notion that Africans are historical agents, never mere objects of development work.

Development education by these foreign NGOs in their home countries is therefore a necessary part of their work. Given the growing tendency to rethink Africa in technical package terms, countervailing development education is essential.

Donors

The implications of this book come close to, but do not coincide with, the conclusions of Hayter and Watson's book on the reality and rhetoric of aid (1985: 248–66). They argue from the extreme left of the Labour Party that Britain should withdraw from the World Bank since that institution is hopeless from a development point of view and instead send its aid to beleaguered Third World countries attempting serious revolutionary change and to liberation movements.

With less sound and fury, a good deal of Nordic country aid has already undertaken such solidarity with radical social transformation. More broadly, SAREC (Swedish), GTZ (German) and IDRC (Canadian and Dutch) support for socially appropriate applied science, people's science and participatory methods has been significant. There are lessons to be learned here. The factions within US, British and other aid systems that are committed to a strong BNA can point to the success of some of these projects and to the increasing importance of NGOs in defence of their positions.

In the present climate, however, it is unlikely that much of the programme for aid reform embodied in documents like the *Compact for African Development* or in the work of the Independent Group on British Aid (1983) is on the donor country agenda. The minority still favouring the strong BNA will have to assume a holding position that tries to minimize damage to people on a project basis and continues to argue for the legitimacy of the strong BNA. They may well find useful opportunities to collaborate with national NGOs in exposing the most glaring anti-people projects and in using the legal apparatus of the aid bureaucracies to delay and even block initiatives (e.g. use of environmental impact statements, social suitability analysis, etc.). Lawyers have an important coordinating role here, especially as the Right to Food is growing in importance at precisely the same time that the "new pragmatism" of Reaganites and Thatcherites is reaching a crescendo. While the struggle over a strong BNA will probably be a defensive one for a few more years, there is no doubt that the struggle will continue both within and without the aid bureaucracy. The 1990s could see more space available for the strong BNA in even official circles as the full human cost of the "pragmatism" of the 1980s becomes widely known.

The same struggle will continue in multilateral aid agencies. Debt relief was successfully sidelined in the UN Special Session, but it will certainly become a more central issue. Maurice Strong, Executive Co-ordinator of the UN's Office of Emergency Operations in Africa (OEOA), praised the potential of African farmers in an interview on the eve of the Special Session (*Africa News*, 1986: 5):

> African farmers are among the best farmers in the world, you know. They are mostly women – something like 75 or 80% of the farmers are women – so when you say the farmers you should say 'she,' not 'he'. I'm a farmer myself and I'll tell you, under the conditions that they work, they

are tremendous farmers. All they need is a little support and they'll be able to feed themselves. Africa *can* feed itself – it used to do so.

These sentiments within one section of the world development apparatus directly contradict the impact of economic adjustment and production-first packages being devised and implemented by other sections.

It is ominously suggestive that even before food crises are over, as soon as the media attention has begun to wane, only a minute proportion of vital non-food aid for recovery is funded by donors. In the case of Angola no support has been given for emergency water supply and non-food relief and survival items; only one per cent of logistical needs and only seven per cent of budgeted health needs have been met (Lone, 1986). The UNOEOA was constantly appealing for non-food aid to support its operations. UNICEF has had to launch a separate $100 million appeal since only 20 per cent of such non-food recovery needs had been met as an African average (UNOEOA, 1986: 7). This is in the context of a UNOEOA fundraising goal of $680 million for non-food aid and the reality that economic crises and famine are inseparable in Africa today. Thus UNICEF added Ghana, Zambia, Madagascar and Sao Tome to the UN food emergency list although the problem in these countries has been more one of deteriorating social services and the fall of family incomes than one of drought.

African Governments

Government employees still committed to a strong BNA are unlikely to find a sympathetic environment in their ministries except in a few countries including Burkina Faso, Guinea Bissau, Zimbabwe and Mozambique. They will have to make alliances across conventional bureaucratic and professional boundaries and meet informally as "pressure groups". They can try to support (or at least not block) indigenous NGO work. They too can use the legal instruments available to push social accountability for the impacts of large-scale development investments, multinational activity, etc. to the limits of what is possible.

International networks can possibly shield their minority activities on the Right to Food and basic needs, giving them international legitimacy. Such new networks include the World Food Assembly and the Food First Network, which defend people persecuted for their work on the Right to Food.*

What this book has tried to say to these African colleagues is simply that the ideal of a strong BNA is intellectually consistent and powerful. It links the environmental, social, economic and political dimensions of the African crisis. The message is also that the strong BNA is a viable political demand, but that this demand must come from the people themselves, often in new alliances (worker-peasant; urban-rural; widows and unemployed youth). Such alliances may be very difficult, as in Zambia, where economic adjustment has hit the working class and urban working poor hardest and delayed further deterioration of rural services, but has also effectively divided potential allies across the rural-urban boundary.

In some contexts the strong BNA will be interpreted as a set of revolutionary demands, but elsewhere – during a time of callous self-interest and manipulation by much (but not all) of the donor community – it will appear as a minimal method for preserving participation by the poor and for enlarging their political space, while increasing the accountability of top-down planners.

---

* More information about international action to protect the human rights of food activists is available from: World Food Assembly c/o Robin Sharp, IIED, 3 Endsleigh Street, London WC1H 0DD; Food First Network, attention R. Künnemann, Postfach 1302, D-6906, Leimen, West Germany (contacts also in Austria, Switzerland, France and Sweden); The London Food Commission, attention Tim Lang, 88 Old Street, London EC1V 9AR (other British organizations such as Oxfam and War on Want can also provide information); Bread for the World, attention Bill Rau, 802 Rhode Island Avenue, N.E., Washington, D.C. 20018; Institute for Food and Development Policy, attention Medea Benjamin, 1885 Mission Street, San Francisco, California 94103-3584 (other US organizations such as Oxfam-America, American Friends Service Committee, Catholic Relief Services, Lutheran World Service, etc. can also provide information).

References

Abok, W. (1982), unpublished masters thesis, Department of Geography, Ohio University, Athens Ohio.

Adams, A. (1981), "The Senegal River Valley", in: Heyer *et al.*, eds. (1981), pp. 325–53.

Adamson, P. (1982), "The Rains", in: Grant (1983b), pp. 59–128.

Adelman, I., and Morris, C. (1973), *Economic Growth and Social Equity in Developing Countries*, Stanford University Press.

Adepoju, A. (1982), "The Dimension of the Refugee Problem in Africa", *African Affairs* 81, 322, pp. 21–35.

Africa Peace Committee (1986), *War and Hunger in Africa*, Washington, DC: Bread for the World/Africa Peace Committee.

African Environment (1977), *African Agriculture: New Problems, Old Solutions?*, thematic issue of *African Environment* 2–3, 4–1 (Nov.).

African Environment (1979), special issue on Traditional Technologies for the Development of African Environments, No. 11–12 (Vol. III, 2–4), Dakar.

Agarwal, A. (1981), *Mud, Mud: The Potential for Earth-Based Materials for Third World Housing*, London: Earthscan/IIED.

Agarwal, A., Kimondo, J., Moreno, G., Tinker, J. (1981), *Water, Sanitation, Health – for All?*, London: IIED/Earthscan.

Agarwal, B. (1986), *Cold Hearths and Barren Slopes*, New Delhi: Allied Publishers.

Ahmed, M., and Coombs, P., eds. (1975), *Education for Rural Development: Case Studies for Planners*. New York: ICED/Praeger.

Aidoo, A., *et al.* (1986), "For Democracy, For Development, For Unity: Declaration on Africa", *IFDA Dossier* 54, July–August, 40–45.

AIM (Agencia de Informacao de Mocambique) (1986), *AIM Information Bulletin* 121 (June).

Ali, T., and O'Brien, J. (1984), "Labor, Community and Protest in Sudanese Agriculture", in: Barker, ed. (1984), pp. 205–38.

Allain, A. (1980), "A propos du discours de McNamara", in: L'Institut Universitaire d'Etudes du Développement, ed. (1980), 229–56.

Alston, P. (1979), "Human Rights and Basic Needs: A Critical Assessment", *Revue des Droits de l'Homme*, 12, 1–2, 19–67 (Strasbourg).

Alston, P. (1984a), "International Law and the Human Right to Food", in: Alston and Tomasevski, eds. (1984), pp. 9–68.

Alston, P. (1984b), "Are Human Rights Universal or Eurocentric?", *Development: Seeds of Change* 1984/3, 6–9.

Alston, P., and Tomasevski, K., eds. (1984), *The Right to Food*, The Hague: Martinus Nijhoff.

Altieri, M. (1987), *Agroecology: The Scientific Basis of Alternative Agriculture*, Boulder, CO and London: Westview and IT Publications.

Ambio (1983), "Environmental Research and Management Priorities for the 1980s", thematic issue of *Ambio* 12 (2).

American Friends Service Committee (1976), "Squatters in Lusaka: A Case of Self-Help Housing", *African Environment* 2, 1–2, 135–49.

American Friends Service Committee (1982), *Community Participation in Squatter Upgrading in Zambia*, Philadelphia: AFSC.

Amin, S., ed. (1974), *Modern Migrations in Western Africa/Les Migrations Contemporaines en Afrique de l'Ouest*, London: International African Institute/Oxford University Press.

Andrae, G. and Beckman, B. (1985), *The Wheat Trap: Bread and Underdevelopment in Nigeria*, London: Zed.

Angwazi, J. (1984), "Problems of Development for Peasant Agriculture in the Rufiji Flood Plains", in: Glaeser, ed., (1984a), pp. 107–16.

Angwazi, J., and Ndulu, B. (1973), "An Evaluation of Ujamaa Villages in the Rufiji Area, 1968–1972", mimeo, Social Science Conference, Dar es Salaam: University of Dar es Salaam.

Anyang' Nyong'o, P. (1981), "The Development of a Middle Peasantry in Nyanza", *Review of African Political Economy* 20, 108–20.

Anzagi, S., and Bernard, F. (1977), "Population Pressure in Rural Kenya", *Geoforum* 8, 63–8.

Arthur, K. (1985), "Ghana's Food Crisis: Alternative Perspectives", *Africa Research and Publications Project Working Papers* 16, Trenton, NJ: Africa World Press.

Ascroft, J., Röling, N., Chege, F. (1973), *Extension and the Forgotten Farmer*, Bulletin No. 37, Afdelingen voor sociale Wetenschappen aan de Landbouwhogeschool Wageningen, Wageningen.

Aziz, S. (1978), *Rural Development: Learning from China*, London: Macmillan.

Ayres, R. (1983), *Banking on the Poor*, Cambridge, MA: MIT Press.

Barclay, A. (1974), "Aspects of Social and Economic Change relating to the Mumias Sugar Project", mimeo, University of Nairobi, Institute for Development Studies, Nairobi.

Barclay, A. (1979), "The Mumias Sugar Project: A Study of Rural Development in Western Kenya", unpublished Ph.D. thesis, University of Michigan, Ann Arbor.

Barker, D., Oguntoyinbo, J., and Richards, P. (1977), *The Utility of the Nigerian Peasant Farmer's Knowledge in the Monitoring of Agricultural Resources*, Monitoring and Assessment Research Centre, Chelsea College, Report No. 4. London.

Barker, J., ed. (1984), *The Politics of Agriculture in Tropical Africa*, Beverly Hills: Sage.

Barkan, J., and Okumu, J., eds. (1979), *Politics and Public Policy in Kenya and Tanzania*, Nairobi: Heinemann.

Barnes, C. (1983), "Differentiation by Sex Among Small-Scale Farming Households in Kenya", *Rural Africana* 15/16, 41–63.

Barnes, C., et al., eds. (1984), *Wood, Energy and Households: Perspectives on Rural Kenya*, Stockholm and Uppsala: The Beijer Institute and Scandinavian

Institute of African Studies.

Barnett, T. (1981), "Evaluating the Gezira Scheme: Black Box or Pandora's Box?", in: Heyer *et al.*, eds. (1981), pp. 306–24.

Barrau, J. (1965), "L'Humide et le Sec: An Essay on Ethnobiological Adaptation to Contrastive Environments in the Indo-Pacific Area", *Journal of the Polynesian Society* 74, 329–46.

Barth, F. (1956), "Ecologic Relationships of Ethnic Groups in Swat, North Pakistan", *American Anthropologist* 58, 1079–89.

Barth-Eide, W. (1978), "Rethinking Food and Nutrition Education Under Changing Socio-economic Conditions", *Food and Nutrition Bulletin* 2, 2, pp. 23–8.

Barth-Eide, W., Skjønsberg, E., Pala, A., Bathily, A. (1977), *Women in Food Production, Food Handling and Nutrition: With special emphasis on Africa*, final report, Protein-Calorie Advisory Group (PAG) of the United National System, New York.

Bates, R. (1981), *Markets and States in Tropical Africa*, Berkeley: University of California Press.

Bates, R., and Lofchie, M., eds. (1980), *Agricultural Development in Africa*, New York: Praeger.

Bawtree, V., ed. (1982), *Ideas and Action* 148, p. 2, Rome: FAO.

Bay, E., ed. (1982), *Women and Work in Africa*, Boulder, CO: Westview.

Beck, A. (1974), "A History of Medicine and Health Services in Kenya (1900–1950)", in: Vogel, ed. (1974), pp. 91–106.

Berg, R., and Whitaker, J., eds. (1986), *Strategies for African Development*, A Study for the Committee on African Development Strategies, Berkeley: University of California Press.

Bergeret, A. (1977), "Ecologically Viable Systems of Production: Illustrations in the Field of Agriculture", *Ecodevelopment News* 3 (October).

Béhar, M. (1982), "European diets vs traditional foods", in: Garcia and Escudero (1982), pp. 16–23.

Behnke, R., and Kerven, C. (1983), "FSR and the Attempt to Understand the Goals and Motivations of Farmers", *Culture and Agriculture* 19, 9–16.

Beinart, W. (1984), "Soil Erosion, Conservation and Ideas about Development: a Southern African Exploration, 1900–1960", *Journal of Southern African Studies* 11 (1), 52–83.

Belshaw, D. (1980), "Taking Indigenous Knowledge Seriously: The Case of Inter-Cropping Techniques in East Africa", in: Brokensha *et al.*, eds. (1980), pp. 195–202.

Beneria, L., ed. (1982), *Women and Development: The Sexual Division of Labor in Rural Societies*, New York: Praeger.

Bengoa, J. (1956), "Nutritional Status in East Africa", Report of a Mission to East Africa, mimeo, Geneva: WHO.

Berg, A. (1981), *Malnourished People: A Policy View*, Poverty and Basic Needs Series, Washington, DC: World Bank (June).

Bernstein, H. (1977), "Notes on Capital and Peasantry." *Review of African Political Economy* 10, 60–73. (Reprinted in: Harriss, ed., 1982, pp. 160–77.)

Bernstein, H. (1981), "Notes on State and Peasantry in Tanzania", *Review of African Political Economy* 21, 44–62.

Bernstein, H. (1985), "Agrarian Crisis in Africa and Neo-Classical Populism",

301

unpublished presentation to the Postgraduate Seminar on Peasants, Institute of Commonwealth Studies, University of London.

Bernstein, H., and Campbell, B., eds. (1985), *Contradictions of Accumulation in Africa*, Beverly Hills: Sage.

Berry, S. (1980), "Risk Aversion and Rural Class Formation in West Africa", in: Bates and Lofchie, eds. (1980), pp. 410–24.

Berry, S. (1984), "The Food Crisis and Agrarian Change in Africa", *African Studies Review* 27 (2), 59–112.

Beyer, J. (1980), "Africa", in: Klee, ed. (1980), pp. 5–37.

Bhagavan. (1980), "Industrial Strategies for Africa", in: New African, ed., *New African Yearbook*, pp. 30–3. London: New African.

Bhasin, K. (1978), "Breaking Barriers: A South Asian Experience of Training for Participatory Development", Report of the Freedom From Hunger Campaign/Action for Development Regional Change Agents Programme March–May, 1978, Bangkok: FAO.

Bhasin, K. (1982), "Formulating Projects with People", Report of a Training Programme, New Delhi: FAO.

Biermann, W., and Wagao, J. (1986), "The Quest for Adjustment: Tanzania and the IMF, 1980–1986", *African Studies Review* 29 (4), 89–103.

Biggs, S., and Clay, E. (1981), "Sources of Innovation in Agricultural Technology", *Ecodevelopment News* 18, 23–38 (reprinted from *World Development* 9, 4, 1981, 321–36).

Bigsten, A. (1977), "Regional Inequality in Kenya", University of Nairobi, Institute for Development Studies, Working Paper No. 330.

Bigsten, A. (1978), *Regional inequality and development: a case study of Kenya*, Nationalekonomiska Institutionen, Göteborgs University, Göteborg.

Billing, K. (1985), *Zimbabwe and the CGIAR Centers: A Study of Their Collaboration in Agricultural Research*, Washington, DC: The World Bank.

Biswas, M., and Pinstrup-Andersen, P., eds. (1985), *Nutrition and Development*, London: Oxford University Press.

Blaikie, P., Cameron, J., Seddon, D. (1979), "The Logic of a Basic Needs Strategy: With or Against the Tide?", in: Buchmann *et al.*, eds. (1979), pp. 97–124.

Blanc, J. (1975), *Malnutrition et Sous-développement*, Paris: Maspero and Presses Universitaires de Grenoble.

Blankhart, D. (1974), "Human Nutrition", in: Vogel *et al.*, eds. (1974), pp. 409–27.

Boal, A. (1979), *Theatre of the Oppressed*, London: Pluto.

Boesen, J., Madsen, A., Moody, T. (1977), *Ujamaa: Socialism from Above*, Uppsala: Scandinavian Institute of African Studies.

Bohdal, M., Gibbs, N., Simmons, W. (1968), "Nutrition Survey and Campaign Against Malnutrition in Kenya 1964–1968", mimeo, Nairobi: UNICEF.

Bondestan, L. (1974), "People and Capitalism in the Northeastern Lowlands of Ethiopia", *Journal of Modern African Studies* 12 (3), 423–39.

Borton, J. (1984), *Disaster Preparedness and Response in Botswana*, Report for the Ford Foundation, London: Relief and Development Institute.

Borton, J., and Stephenson, R. (1984), *Disaster Preparedness in Kenya*, London: Relief and Development Institute.

Boulding, E. (1981), "Integration into What? Reflections on Development

302

Planning for Women", in: Dauber and Cain, eds. (1981), pp. 9–32.

Brabin, L. (1984), "Polygany: An Indicator of Nutritional Stress in African Agricultural Societies?", *Africa* 54 (1), 32–44.

Bradley, D. (1977), "The Health Implications of Irrigation Schemes and Man-made Lakes in Tropical Environments", in: Feachem *et al.* (1977), pp. 18–29.

Bradley, P., Raynaut, C., Torrealba, J. (1977), *The Guidimaka Region of Mauritania: A Critical Analysis Leading to a Development Project*, London: War on Want.

Brady, N. (1985), "Toward a Green Revolution for Africa", *Science* 227 (4691), March 8, p. 1159.

Bratton, M. (1980), *Peasant and Party-State in Zambia: The Local Politics of Rural Development*, Hanover, NH: University Press of New England.

Briscoe, J. (1979), "Energy Use and Social Structure in a Bangladesh Village", *Population and Development Review* 5 (4), 615–41.

Brittain, V. (1985), "Introduction to Sankara and Burkina Faso", *Review of African Political Economy* 32, 39–47.

Brokensha, D., and Glazier, J. (1973), "Land Reform Among the Mbeere of Central Kenya", *Africa* 43 (3).

Brokensha, D., Warren, D., and Werner, O., eds. (1980), *Indigenous Knowledge Systems and Development*, Washington, DC: University Press of America.

Bromley, R., and Gerry, C. (1979a), "Who are the casual poor?", in: Bromley and Gerry, eds. (1979b), pp. 3–26.

Bromley, R., and Gerry, C., eds. (1979b), *Casual Work and Poverty in Third World Cities*, Chichester: Wiley.

Brooke, C. (1967), "Types of Food Shortages in Tanzania", *The Geographical Review* 57, 333–57.

Brown, J., and Brown, R. (1979), *Finding the Causes of Child Malnutrition*, Kangu-Mayombe, Zaire: Bureau of Study and Research for Promotion of Health.

Brundtland (World Commission on Environment and Development) (1987), *Food 2000: Global Policies for Sustainable Agriculture*. Report to the World Commission on Environment and Development. London: Zed.

Bryant, C., and White, L. (1980), *Managing Rural Development: Peasant Participation in Rural Development*, West Hartford, Ct.: Kumarian Press.

Bryant, J. (1969), *Health and the Developing World*, Ithaca: Cornell University Press.

Bryceson, D. (1981), "Colonial Famine Responses", *Food Policy* (May), 91–104.

Bryceson, D. (1985), "Nutrition and the Commoditization of Food in Sub-Saharan Africa", review paper presented to the SSRC Workshop on "The Political Economy of Health and Disease in Africa and Latin America," Toluca, Mexico. Forthcoming in *Social Science and Medicine*.

Bryson, J. (1981), "Women and Agriculture in Sub-Saharan Africa: Implications for Development", in: Nelson, ed. (1981), pp. 28–46.

Buchanan, K. (1970), *The Transformation of the Chinese Earth*, London: Bell.

Buch-Hansen, M. (1980), "Agro-industrial Production and Socio-economic Development: 2 Working Papers on Tea and Sugar Production in Western Kenya", Roskilde University Centre. Copenhagen.

Buch-Hansen, M., and Kieler, J. (1982), "The Development of Capitalism and the Transformation of the Peasantry: Case Studies of Agro-industrial Production and its Impact on Rural Areas in Kenya", Roskilde University Centre. Copenhagen. Mimeo.

Buch-Hansen, M., and Marcussen, H. (1982), "Contract Farming and the Peasantry: Cases from Western Kenya", *Review of African Political Economy* 23, 9–36.

Buchmann, M., Dauderstädt, Siegmann, W., eds. (1979), *Basic Needs Strategy as a Planning Parameter*, 2 vols, Bonn: German Foundation for International Development.

Bugnicourt, J. (1974), "La migration contribue-t-elle au développement des zones 'retardées'?", in: Amin (1974), pp. 191–214.

Bugnicourt, J. (1976), "Which urban alternative for Africa?", *African Environment* 2, 3, 3–20.

Bugnicourt, J. (1982), "Popular participation in development in Africa", *Assignment Children/Les Carnets de l'Enfance* 59–60, 2, 57–78.

Bukh, J. (1981), "Women in Subsistence Production in Ghana", in: Ghai and Ahmad, eds. (1981), pp. 18–20.

Bullock, R. (1971), "Population and Food in West and Central Kenya", in: Ominde, ed. (1971a), pp. 193–206.

Bulmer, R. (1957), "A Primitive Ornithology", *Australian Museum Magazine* 12, 224–9.

Buntzcl, R. (1980), "Outline for a rural development strategy for Africa with special reference to Tanzania", in: Galtung *et al.*, eds. (1980), pp. 283–99.

Burgess, D., Pearce, J., Rossiter, J., Silkin, T. (1986), *Eritrean Journey*, London: War on Want.

Burgess, R. (1977), "Self-help Housing: A New Imperialist Strategy? A Critique of the Turner School", *Antipode* 9, 1, 50–9.

Bush, R., Cliffe, L., Jansen, V. (1986), "The Crisis in the Reproduction of Migrant Labour in Southern Africa", in: Lawrence, ed. (1986), pp. 283–99.

Cabral, A. (1974), *Guinea-Bissau: Toward Final Victory: Selected Speeches and Documents from PAIGC*, Richmond, BC, Canada: LSM Press.

Caiden, N., and Wildavsky, A. (1974), *Planning and Budgeting in Poor Countries*, New York: Wiley.

Caldwell, J., ed. (1976), *The Persistence of High Fertility: Population Prospects in the Third World*, Canberra: Australian National University, Department of Geography.

Campbell, B. (1984), "Inside the Miracle: Cotton in the Ivory Coast", in: Barker, ed. (1984), pp. 143–72.

Campbell, D. (1979), "Response to Drought in Maasailand: Pastoralists and Farmers of Loitokitok, Kajiado District", Discussion Paper 267, Institute for Development Studies, Nairobi: University of Nairobi.

Campbell, D. (1981), "Land-use Competition at the Margins of the Rangelands: An Issue in Development Strategies for Semi-arid Areas", in: Norcliffe and Pinfold, eds. (1981), pp. 39–61.

Campbell, D., and Migot-Adholla, S. (1981), "The Development of Semi-Arid Lands", Occasional Paper 36, Institute for Development Studies, Nairobi: University of Nairobi.

Carr, M. (1984), *Blacksmith, Baker, Roofing-sheet maker...*, London: IT

Publications.

Carr-Hill, R. (1978), "Education and Basic Needs: Views on Concepts and Measurements", mimeo, Paris: UNESCO.

Carr-Hill, R. (1979), "Social Indicators and the Basic-needs Approach: Who benefits from which numbers?", in: Cole and Lucas, eds. (1979), pp. 35–44.

Carr-Hill, R. (1984), "The Political Choice of Social Indicators", *Quality and Quantity* (18), 173–91.

Carruthers, I., and Weir, A. (1976), "Rural Water Supplies and Irrigation Development", in: Heyer *et al.*, eds. (1976), pp. 288–312.

Castro, F. (1984), *The World Crisis: Its Economic and Social Impact on the Underdeveloped Countries*, London: Zed.

Caughman, S. (1979), "New Skills for Women: an example of transfer of traditional technology", *African Environment* 3, 3–4, 69–84.

Cecelski, E. (1982), "Household Fuel Availabilities, Rural Women's Work and Family Nutrition: Research Design", Rural Employment Policies Branch, Employment and Development Department, ILO. Geneva: ILO.

Cecelski, E. (1985), "Energy and Rural Women's Work: Crisis, Response and Policy Alternatives", *International Labour Review* 126 (1), 41–64.

Center for Concern *et al.* (1986), "Perspectives on African Development: Recommendations by US NGOs to the UN Special Session", Washington, DC: Church World Service/Lutheran World Relief.

Chagula, W., and Tarimo, E. (1975), "Meeting Basic Health Needs in Tanzania", in: Newell, ed. (1975), 145–68.

Chambers, R. (1969), *Settlement Schemes in Tropical Africa*, London: Routledge and Kegan Paul.

Chambers, R. (1974), *Managing Rural Development: Ideas and Experience from East Africa*, Uppsala: Scandinavian Institute of African Studies.

Chambers, R. (1979a), "The 'Gandhian' Village", *Ambio* 8, 2–3, 54–7.

Chambers, R., ed. (1979b), *Rural Development: Whose Knowledge Counts?*, special issue of *IDS Bulletin* 10, 2.

Chambers, R. (1983), *Rural Development: Putting the Last First*, London: Longman.

Chambers, R. (1985), "Normal Professionalism, New Paradigms and Development", paper for the Seminar on Poverty, Development and Food: Towards the 21st Century, in honour of the 75th Birthday of Professor H. W. Singer, Brighton, 13–14 December 1985, Institute of Development Studies, Falmer, Brighton: Sussex University.

Chambers, R. (1986), "Sustainable Livelihoods: An Opportunity for the World Commission on Environment and Development", mimeo, Institute of Development Studies, Falmer, Brighton: Sussex University.

Chambers, R., Longhurst, R., Pacey, A., eds. (1981), *Seasonal Dimensions to Rural Poverty*, London: Frances Pinter.

Chambers, R., and Moris, J., eds. (1973), *Mwea: An Irrigated Rice Settlement in Kenya*, München and New York: Weltforum Verlag and Humanities.

Chapin, G., and Wasserstrom, R. (1981), "Agricultural Production and Malaria Resurgence in Central America and India", *Nature* 293, 5829 (17 September), pp. 181–5.

Chauhan, S., and Gopalakrishnan, K. (1983), *A Million Villages, A Million Decades?*, London: Earthscan/IIED.

Cheche Kenya (1982), *In-Dependent Kenya*, London: Zed.

Chenery, H., Ahluwalia, M., Bell, C., Duloy, J., Jolly, R. (1974), *Redistribution with Growth*, London: Oxford University Press (for the World Bank and Institute of Development Studies at the University of Sussex).

Chinapah, V., and Fägerlind, I. (1979), *The Role of Education in the Basic Human Needs Strategy*, Stockholms Universitet, Institute of International Education, 39 (August), Stockholm.

Chirimuuta, R., and Chirimuuta, J. (1987), *Aids, Africa and Racism*, privately published. Copies from R. Chirimuuta, Bretby House, Stanhope, Bretby, Nr. Burton-on-Trent, Derbyshire, DE15 0PT, UK.

Clark, R., and Timberlake, L. (1982), *Stockholm Plus Ten*, London: Earthscan/IIED.

Clausen, A. (1985), "Poverty in the Developing Countries – 1985", address delivered on 11 Jan 1985 at the Martin Luther King, Jr Center for Nonviolent Social Change, *The Hunger Project Papers*, No. 3 (March).

Clay, E., and Everitt, E., eds. (1985), *Food Aid and Emergencies: A Report on the Third IDS Food Aid Seminar*, Discussion Paper 206, Institute of Development Studies, Falmer, Brighton: Sussex University.

Cliffe, L., Lawrence, P., Luttrell, Migot-Adholla, S., Saul, J., eds. (1975), *Rural Cooperation in Tanzania*, Dar es Salaam: Tanzania Publishing House.

Cliffe, L., and Moorsom, R. (1979), "Rural Class Formation and Ecological Collapse in Botswana", *Review of African Political Economy* 15/16, 35–52.

Cloward, R., and Fox Piven, F. (1984), *The New Class War*, New York: Pantheon.

Coclin, C., Smit, B., Johnston, T., eds. (1987), *Demands on Rural Lands: Planning for Resource Use*, Boulder, CO: Westview.

Cocoyoc Declaration. (1975), "Cocoyoc Declaration", *African Environment* 1, 3, 3–15.

Cohen, J., and Lewis, D., "Role of Government in Combatting Food Shortages: Lessons from Kenya 1984–85", in: Glantz, ed. (1987), pp. 269–96.

Colclough, C. (1976), "Basic Education: Samson or Delilah?", *Convergence* 9, 2.

Colclough, C. (1978), "The Satisfaction of Basic Educational Needs", *IDS Bulletin* 9, 4, 27–30.

Colclough, C., and McCarthy, S. (1980), *The Political Economy of Botswana*, Oxford: Oxford University Press.

Cole, S., and Lucas, H., eds. (1979), *Models, Planning and Basic Needs*, London: Pergamon.

Cole-King, S. (1981), "Health Care", in: JASPA (1981b), pp. 135–58.

Cole-King, S. (1983), "GOBI-FF and PHC", mimeo, New York: UNICEF (June).

Collier, P. (1983), "Oil and Inequality in Rural Nigeria", in: Ghai and Radwan, eds. (1983b), pp. 191–218.

Collier, P., and Lal, D. (1980), *Poverty and Growth in Kenya*, Staff Working Paper No. 389, Washington, DC: World Bank.

Collins, J. (1974), "Government and Groundnut Marketing in Rural Hausa Niger: the 1930s to the 1970s in Magaria", unpublished Ph.D. dissertation, Johns Hopkins University.

Collinson, M. (1982), *Farming Systems Research in Eastern Africa: The*

Experience of CIMMYT and Some National Agricultural Research Services, 1976–81, MSU International Development Paper 3, Dept. of Agricultural Economics, East Lansing: Michigan State University.

Conklin, H. (1954), "An Ethnoecological Approach to Shifting Agriculture", *New York Academy of Sciences Transactions* 17, 2, 133–42.

Conservation Foundation (1984), *State of the Environment: An Assessment at Mid-Decade*, Washington, DC: The Conservation Foundation.

Conti, A. (1979), "Capitalist Organization of Production Through Non-capitalist Relations: Women's Role in a Pilot Resettlement in Upper Volta", *Review of African Political Economy* 15/16, 75–92.

Cook, P. (1981), "Raising Nutritional Levels and Rural Development", in: Norcliffe and Pinfold, eds. (1981), pp. 19–38.

Coombs, P., and Ahmed, M. (1974), *Attacking Rural Poverty: How Nonformal Education Can Help*, Essex, CT: International Council for Educational Development.

Cooper, F., ed. (1983), *Struggle for the City: Migrant Labor, Capital, and the State in Urban Africa*, Beverly Hills: Sage.

Cordell, D., and Gregory, J. (1968), "Labour Reserves and Population: French Colonial Strategies in Koudougou, Upper Volta 1914–39", *Journal of African History* 23 (2), 205–24.

Cornell Nutrition Surveillance Program (CNSP) (1984), "Trends in Nutritional Status of Children in Rural Kenya: Review and Policy Implications", Working Paper 30, Ithaca: CNSP/Cornell University.

Cornia, G. (1987a), "Economic Decline and Human Welfare in the First Half of the 1980s", in: Cornia *et al.*, eds. (1987), pp. 11–47.

Cornia, G. (1987b), "Adjustment Policies 1980–1985: Effects on Child Welfare", in: Cornia *et al.*, eds (1987), pp. 48–72.

Cornia, G., Jolly, R., Stewart, F., eds. (1987), *Adjustment with a Human Face: Protecting the Vulnerable and Promoting Growth*, Oxford: Clarendon Press.

Coulson, A., ed. (1979), *African Socialism in Practice: The Tanzanian Experience*, London: Spokesman.

Coulson, A. (1982), *Tanzania: A Political Economy*, Oxford: The Clarendon Press.

Council on Foreign Relations and Overseas Development Council (1985), *Compact for African Development*, Report of the Committee on African Development Strategies, Washington, DC: Council on Foreign Relations/Overseas Development Council.

Coutsinas, G. (1976), review of D. Dwyer, *People and Housing in the Third World Cities* in *African Environment* 2, 1–2, 179–80.

Cowen, M. (1974), "Concentration of Sales and Assets: Dairy Cattle and Tea in Magutu 1964–1971", Working Paper 146. Institute for Development Studies, Nairobi: University of Nairobi.

Cowen, M. (1979), "Capital and Household Production: The Case of Cattle in Kenya's Central Province 1903–1964", unpublished Ph.D. dissertation, Cambridge University.

Cowen, M. (1981), "Commodity Production in Kenya's Central Province", in: Heyer *et al.*, eds. (1981), pp. 121–42.

Crawford, E., and Thorbecke, E. (1978), *Employment, Income Distribution and Basic Needs in Kenya*, Report of an ILO Consulting Mission, Ithaca, NY:

307

Cornell University.

Crehan, K. (1984), "Women and Development in North Western Zambia: From Producer to Housewife", *Review of African Political Economy* 27/28, 51–66.

Cuny, F. (1983), *Disaster and Development*, New York: Oxford University Press.

Currey, B., and Hugo, G., eds (1984), *Famine as a Geographical Phenomenon*, Dordrecht: Reidel.

Cutrufelli, M. (1983), *Women of Africa: Roots of Oppression*. London: Zed.

Dabire, J. (1981), "Contribution à l'étude des rapports de cooperation entre la France et la Haute Volta", 3eme cycle, Rouen.

Dag Hammarskjöld Foundation (1975), *Que Faire: Un autre développement*, Uppsala: Dag Hammarskjöld Foundation.

Dahl, G., and Hjort, A. (1976), *Having Herds: Pastoral Herd Growth and Household Economy*, Stockholm Studies in Social Anthropology 2. Department of Social Anthropology, University of Stockholm, Stockholm.

Daniel, P., ed. (1981), "The New Recyling: Economic Theory, IMF Conditionality and Balance of Payment Adjustment in the 1980s", *IDS Bulletin* 13, 1.

Dauber, R., and Cain, M., eds. (1981), *Women and Technological Change in Developing Countries*, AAAS Selected Symposium 53. Boulder, CO: Westview.

Davidson, B., Cliffe, L., Salassie, B., eds. (1980), *Behind the War in Eritrea*, Nottingham: Spokesman.

Davies, J. (1963), *Human Nature in Politics*, London: Wiley.

Davies, J. (1977), "The Development of Individuals and the Development of Polities", in: Fitzgerald, ed. (1977), pp. 74–95.

Davies, R. (1979), "Informal Sector or Subordinate Mode of Production? A Model", in: Bromley and Gerry, Eds. (1979b), pp. 87–104.

Davis, A. (1983), *Women, Race and Class*, New York: Vintage.

De Beer, C. (1986), *The South African Disease*, Trenton, NJ: Africa World Press.

De Gennaro, B. (1981), "Ujamaa: The Aggrandizement of the State", in: Galli, ed. (1981), pp. 111–55.

Dennis, C. (1984), "Capitalist Development and Women's Work: A Nigerian Case Study", *Review of African Political Economy* 27/28, 109–19.

De Oliveira, R., and De Oliveira, M. (1980), "Learning by Living and Doing: Reflections on Education and Self-Reliance", in: Galtung *et al.*, eds. (1980), pp. 204–23.

De Wilde, J. (1967), *Experiences with Agricultural Development in Tropical Africa*, 2 Vols, Baltimore: Johns Hopkins University Press.

Derman, W. and Whiteford, S., eds. (1985), *Social Impact Analysis and Development Planning in the Third World*, Boulder, CO: Westview.

Devres. (1980), *The Socio-economic Context of Fuelwood Use in Small Rural Communities*, AID Evaluation Special Study No. 1, Washington, DC: USAID.

Deyoko, A. (1976), "Magnambougou: A District Where People Build at Night", *African Environment* 2, 1–2, 121–4.

Dhamija, J. (1984), "Income-Generating Activities for Rural Women in

Africa: Some Successes and Failures", in: ILO (1984), pp. 75–8.

Dias, C., and Paul, J., "Developing the Human Right to Food as a Legal Resource for the Rural Poor: Some Strategies for NGOs", in: Alston and Tomasevski, eds. (1984), pp. 203–14.

Dickson, D. (1974), *Alternative Technology and the Politics of Technical Change*, London: Fontana/Collins.

Digernes, T. (1977), "Wood for Fuel – Energy Crisis Implying Desertification: The Case of Bara, the Sudan", unpublished Ph.D. dissertation, University of Bergen, Norway.

Dinham, B., and Hines, C. (1982), *Agribusiness in Africa*, London: Earth Resources.

Djukanovic, V., and Mach, E. (1975), *Alternative Approaches to Meeting Basic Health Needs in Developing Countries*, a Joint UNICEF/WHO Study. Geneva: WHO.

Doltan, P. (1982), Personal communication about Bura irrigation scheme on the lower Tana river during seminar on irrigation and health at Cook College, Rutgers University.

Doyal, L. (1981), *The Political Economy of Health*, London: Pluto.

Drewnowski, J. (1970), "Studies in the Measurement of Levels of Living and Welfare", Report No. 70.3, Geneva: UNRISD.

Drewnowski, J., and Scott, W. (1966), "The Level of Living Index", Report No. 4, Geneva: UNRISD.

Dubell, F. (1981), *Research for the People/Research by the People: Selected Papers from the International Forum on Participatory Research in Ljubljana, Yugoslavia*, Linköping University, Department of Education, Report LiU-PEK-R-70. Linköping, Sweden: Linköping University and the Netherlands Study and Development Centre for Adult Education.

Dumont, R. (1966), *False Start in Africa*, New York: Praeger.

Dumont, R. (1981), "Haute-Volta", in: Dumont *et al.*, eds. (1981), pp. 1–19.

Dumont, R., and Mottin, M.-F. (1983), *Stranglehold on Africa*, London: André Deutsch.

Dumont, R., Reboul, C., Mazoyer, M. (1981), *Pauvreté et inégalités rurales en Afrique de l'Ouest francophone*, Geneva: ILO.

Dunne, T., Aubry, B., Wahome, E. (1981), "Effect of Woodfuel Harvest on Soul Erosion in Kenya", Ministry of Energy/Beijer Institute Fuelwood Project Technical Paper, Stockholm: Beijer Institute.

Dupriez, H. and De Leener, P. (1983), *Agriculture tropicale en milieu paysan africain*, Paris: l'Harmattan/Terres et Vie/ENDA.

Dwyer, D. (1975), *People and Housing in the Third World Cities: Perspectives on the Problem of Spontaneous Settlement*, London: Longman.

Eastman, M., and Uphoff, N. (1984), *Local Organizations*, Ithaca: Cornell University Press.

Ebrahim, G. (1984), "Health Care and the Urban Poor", in: Richards and Thomson, eds. (1984), 93–122.

Eckholm. E. (1982), *Down to Earth: Environment and Human Needs*, London: Pluto.

Economic Development Bureau (1980), unpublished documents of a grain storage project in Guinea-Bissau.

309

Edelman, M. (1985), "Africa at the Crossroads", *Horizons* 4 (2), 27–32. Washington, DC: USAID.

Edwards, N., and Lyon, M. (1983), "Community Assessment: a Tool for Motivation and Evaluation in Primary Health Care in Sierra Leone", in: Morley *et al.*, eds. (1983), pp. 101–13.

Egerö, B. (1987), *Mozambique: A Dream Undone: The Political Economy of Democracy, 1975–84*, Uppsala: Scandinavian Institute of African Studies.

Egger, K. (1981), "Ecofarming in the Tropics: Characteristics and Potentialities", *Plant Research and Development* (Tubingen) 13, 96–106.

Egger, K. (1984), "Neue Landbaumethoden als sektoraler Beginn einer stufenweise umfassender werdenden Agrarentwicklung am Beispiel des 'Projet Agro-Pastoral Nyabisindu/Rwanda'", in: Rottach, ed. (1984), pp. 211–28.

Egger, K., and Glaeser, B. (1975), *Politische Ökologie der Usambara-Berge in Tanzania*, Bensheim: Kübel-Stiftung.

Eicher, C. (1984), "Facing Up to Africa's Food Crisis", in: Eicher and Staatz, eds. (1984), pp. 453–80.

Eicher, C., and Staatz, J., eds. (1984), *Agricultural Development in the Third World*, Baltimore: Johns Hopkins University Press.

Eide, W., and Steady, F. (1980), "Individual and Social Energy Flows", in: Jerome *et al.*, eds. (1980), pp. 61–84.

Engo, R. (1986), "Women: Dependents or Partners in Famine Resolution", Verbal Presentation to the Bennett Scholars' Conference, "The Famine Complex and Women: Culture, History and Science", Bennett College, Greensboro, NC, 10 October.

Epstein, P., and Packard, R. (1987), "Ecology and Immunology: The Social Context of AIDS in Africa", *Science for the People* 19 (1), 10–19.

Fanon, F. (1967), *The Wretched of the Earth*, London: Penguin.

FAO (Food and Agriculture Organization of the United Nations). (1980), *Regional Food Plan for Africa*, Rome: FAO.

FAO. (1981), *The Peasants' Charter: The Declaration of Principles and Programme of Action of the World Conference on Agrarian Reform and Rural Development*, Rome: FAO.

FAO. (1982), *Apartheid, Poverty, and Malnutrition*, FAO Economic and Social Development Paper 24, Rome: FAO.

FAO. (1984), *Women in Food Production and Food Security*, Government Consultation on Role of Women in Food Production and Food Security, 10–13 July 1984, Harare, Zimbabwe, Rome: FAO.

FAO. (1985), *Lesotho: Report of WCARRD Follow-up Rural Development Team*, 3 vols, Rome: FAO.

FAO and Deutsche Stiftung Für Entwicklung (DSE) (1984), *The People's Participation Programme in Africa*, a review of implementation experiences in 7 African countries, Report on the FAO/DSE Regional Training Workshop, Harare, Zimbabwe, 26 Nov.–7 Dec., Rome: FAO.

Feachem, R., McGarry, M., Mara, D., eds. (1977), *Water, Wastes and Health in Hot Climates*, London: Wiley.

Feachem, R. *et al.* (1978), *Water, Health and Development: An Interdisciplinary Evaluation*, London: Tri-Med.

Feder, E. (1976), "How Agri-Business Operates in Underdeveloped Agricultures: Harvard Business School Myths and Reality", *Development and Change* 7.

Feierman, S. (1985), "Struggles for Control: The Social Roots of Health and Healing in Modern Africa", *African Studies Review* 28 (2/3), 73–147.

Feldman, R. (1984), "Women's Groups and Women's Subordination: An Analysis of Policies Towards Rural Women in Kenya", *Review of African Political Economy* 27/28, 67–85.

Ferguson, D. (1980), "The Political Economy of Health and Medicine in Colonial Tanganyika", in: Kaniki, ed. (1980), 307–43.

Fitzgerald, R., ed.(1977), *Human Needs and Politics*, Rushcutters Bay, Australia: Pergamon.

Fleuret, P., and Fleuret, A. (1980), "Nutrition, Consumption and Cultural Change", *Human Organization* 39, 250–60.

Fleuret, P., and Fleuret, A. (1983), "Socio-Economic Determinants of Child Nutrition Taita, Kenya: A Call for Discussion", *Culture and Agriculture* 19, 8, 16–20.

Floyd, B. (1985), "Agricultural Development in Nigeria: Problems and Prospects", Paper presented at the International Conference on "Management of Rural Resources: Problems and Policies", International Geographical Union, University of Guelph, Ontario, Canada, 14–20 July 1985.

Ford, R. (1982), "Subsistence Farming Systems in Semi-Arid Northern Yatenga, Upper Volta", unpublished Ph.D. dissertation, University of California, Riverside.

Forman, M., and Fellers, D. (1985), "Custom-Designed Foods", *Horizons* 4 (2), 40–6.

Fortmann, L. (1981), *Women's Agriculture in a Cattle Economy*, Gaborone and Ithaca: Government of Botswana and the Center for International Studies, Cornell University.

Fortmann, L. (1985), "Tree Tenure: An Analytical Framework for Agroforestry Projects", paper prepared for the Conference on Land Tenure and Agroforestry, Nairobi, May.

Fortmann, L., and Rocheleau, D. (1984), "Why Agroforestry Needs Women: Four Myths and a Case Study", *Unasylva* 36 (146) (Nov.–Dec.), 2–11.

Foucault, M. (1975), *The Birth of the Clinic*, New York: Vintage.

Foucault, M. (1977), *Discipline and Punishment*, London: Penguin.

Foucault, M. (1979), *The History of Sexuality*, London: Penguin.

Fournier, G., and Djermakoye, I. (1975), "Village Health Teams in Niger (Maradi Department)", in: Newell, ed. (1975), 128–44.

Fotzo, P. (1984), "The Economics of Bas-Fond Rice Production in Eastern Upper Volta", unpublished Ph.D. dissertation, Michigan State University.

Fox Piven, F., and Cloward, R. (1971), *Regulating the Poor: The Functions of Public Welfare*, New York: Vintage.

Frake, C. (1961), "Diagnosis of Disease Among the Subanun of Mindanao", *American Anthropologist* 63, 113–32.

Francis, P. (1984), "'For the Use and Common Benefit of all Nigerians': Consequences of the 1978 Land Nationalization", *Africa* 54 (3), 3–27.

Franke, R. (1984), "Tuareg of West Africa: Five Experiments in Fourth World Development", in: Stea and Wisner, eds. (1984), pp. 45–53.

311

Franke, R., and Chasin, B. (1980), *Seeds of Famine: Ecological Destruction and the Development Dilemma in the West African Sahel*, Montclair, NJ: Allanheld, Osmun.

Freeman, D., and Norcliffe, G. (1984), "National and Regional Patterns of Rural Nonfarm Employment in Kenya", *Geography* 69/3 (304), 221–33.

Freeman, D., and Norcliffe, G. (1981), "The Rural Nonfarm Sector and the Development Process in Kenya", in: Norcliffe and Pinfold, eds. (1981), pp. 62–78.

Freeman, L. (1984), "CIDA and Agriculture in East and Central Africa", in: Barker (1984), pp. 99–126.

Freire, P. (1970), *Pedagogy of the Oppressed*, New York: Herder.

Freyhold, M. (1979), *Ujamaa Villages in Tanzania: Analysis of a Social Experiment*, London: Heinemann.

Friedmann, J., and Douglass, M. (1975), "Agropolitan Development: Towards a New Strategy for Regional Planning in Asia", prepared for Seminar on Industrialization Strategies and the Growth Pole Approach to Regional Planning and Development: The Asian Experience, UN Centre for Regional Development, Nagoya, Japan, 4–13 November 1975.

Gachukia, E. (1979), "Women's Self-Help Efforts for Water Supply in Kenya – the Important Role of NGO Support", *Assignment Children/Les Carnets de l'Enfance* 45/46, 167–74.

Galaty, D., Aronson, D., Satzman, P., eds. (1981), *The Future of Pastoral Peoples*, Ottawa: International Development Research Centre (IDRC).

Galli, R., ed. (1981a), *The Political Economy of Rural Development: Peasants, International Capital, and the State*, Albany, NY: State University of New York Press.

Galli, R. (1981b), "Preface", in: Galli, ed. (1981a), pp. vii–xi.

Galtung, J. (1980a), "The Basic Needs Approach", in: Lederer, ed. (1980), pp. 55–126.

Galtung, J. (1980b), "On the Technology of Self-Reliance", in: Galtung *et al.*, eds. (1980), pp. 223–48.

Galtung, J. (1980c), "Self-Reliance: Concepts, Practice and Rationale", in: Galtung *et al.*, eds. (1980), pp. 19–44.

Galtung, J. (1980d), "The New International Economic Order and the Basic Needs Approach", in: Galtung (1980f).

Galtung, J. (1980e), "The Politics of Self-Reliance", in: Galtung *et al.*, eds. (1980), pp. 355–86.

Galtung, J. (1980f), *The North/South Debate*, Working Paper 12, New York: Institute for World Order.

Galtung, J., O'Brien, P., Preiswerk, R., eds. (1980), *Self-Reliance: A Strategy for Development*, London: Bogle-L'Ouverture for the Institute for Development Studies, Geneva.

Galtung, J., and Wirak, A. (1977), "Human Needs and Human Rights: A Theoretical Approach", *Bulletin of Peace Proposals* 8, 3.

Ganapathy, R., ed. (1981), *Agriculture, Rural Energy and Development*, Selected Proceedings of the 1980 Symposium Sponsored by the Association for the Advancement of Appropriate Technology for Developing Countries, Ann Arbor: Division of Research, Graduate School of Business Administration,

312

University of Michigan.

Gandhi, M. (1952), *Rebuilding our Villages*, Ahmedabad: Navajivan Publishing House.

Gandhi, M. (1957), *Economic and Industrial Life and Relations*. Compiled by V. Kher, 2 vols, Ahmedabad: Navajivan Publishing House.

Garcia, R., and Escudero, J. (1982), *The Constant Catastrophe: Malnutrition, Famines and Drought*, Report on an IFIAS project (Drought and Man: The 1972 Case History), Vol. 2. Oxford: Pergamon.

Gaudier, M. (1980), *Les Besoins Essentiels: Nouvelles priorités des stratégies de développement du tiers monde: Bibliographie Analytique*, Geneva: Institute International d'Etudes Sociales.

Gephart, M. (1986), "African States and Agriculture: Issues for Research", *IDS Bulletin* 17 (1), 57–63.

George, S. (1976), *How the Other Half Dies*, London: Penguin.

George, S. (1987), *A New Look at African Hunger*, San Francisco: The Hunger Project.

George, S. (1988), *A Fate Worse than Debt*, London: Penguin.

Gerry, C. (1979), "Small-scale Manufacturing and Repairs in Dakar: a survey of market relations within the urban economy", in: Bromley and Gerry, eds. (1979b), pp. 229–50.

Ghai, D. (1977), "What is a Basic Needs Approach to Development all About?", in: Ghai *et al.* (1977), pp. 1–18.

Ghai, D. (1978), "Basic Needs and its Critics", *IDS Bulletin* 9, 4 (June), 16–18.

Ghai, D., and Ahmad, Z., eds. (1981), *Women in Rural Development: Critical Issues*, Geneva: ILO.

Ghai, D., and Alfthan, T. (1977), "On the Principles of Quantifying and Satisfying Basic Needs", in: Ghai *et al.* (1977), pp. 19–59.

Ghai, D., and Radwan, S. (1983a), "Agrarian Change, Differentiation and Rural Poverty in Africa: A General Survey", in: Ghai and Radwan, eds. (1983b), pp. 1–30.

Ghai, D., and Radwan, S., eds. (1983b), *Agrarian Policies and Rural Poverty in Africa*, Geneva: ILO.

Ghai, D., and Radwan, S. (1983c), "Growth and Inequality: Rural Development in Malawi, 1964–78", in: Ghai and Radwan, eds. (1983b), pp. 71–98.

Ghai, D., Godfrey, M., Lisk, F., eds. (1979), *Planning for Basic Needs in Kenya*, Geneva: ILO.

Gibbon, P., and Neocosmos, M. (1985), "Some Problems in the Political Economy of 'African Socialism'," in: Bernstein and Campbell, eds. (1985), pp. 153–206.

Giglioli, E. (1973), "The National Organization of Irrigation", in: Chambers and Moris, eds. (1973), pp. 163–84.

Gish, O. (1973), "Doctor Auxiliaries in Tanzania", *The Lancet* (December 1), 1251–4.

Gish, O. (1974), "Health Planning for Women and Children", Discussion Paper 49, Institute of Development Studies, Falmer/Brighton: University of Sussex.

Gish, O. (1983), "The Relationship of the New International Economic Order to Health", *Journal of Public Health Policy* 4, 207ff.

Glaeser, B., ed. (1984a), *Ecodevelopment: Concepts, Projects, Strategies*,

313

London: Pergamon.

Glaeser, B. (1984b), *Eco-development in Tanzania*, Berlin: Mouton.

Glantz, M., ed. (1987), *Drought and Hunger in Africa*, Cambridge: Cambridge University Press.

GOK (Government of Kenya) (n.d.), "Arid and Semi-arid Lands Development in Kenya: The Framework for Programme Planning, Implementation and Evaluation", Nairobi.

GOK. (1965), *Sessional Paper No. 10 of 1965, On African Socialism and its Application to Planning in Kenya*, Nairobi: Government Printer.

GOK. (1970a), *Development Plan 1970–1974*, Nairobi: Government Printer.

GOK. (1970b), *Kenya Population Census, 1969*, Central Bureau of Statistics, Nairobi: Government Printer.

GOK. (1972), *Proposal for the Improvement of Rural Health Services and the Development of Rural Health Training Centres in Kenya*, Nairobi: Ministry of Health.

GOK. (1973), *Sessional Paper No. 10 of 1973/74, On Employment*, Nairobi: Government Printer.

GOK. (1974a), *Development Plan 1974–1978*, Part I, Nairobi: Government Printer.

GOK. (1974b), *Ten Great Years for Self Help in Kenya*, Nairobi: Government Printer.

GOK. (1977), "Child Nutrition in Rural Kenya", Nairobi: Central Bureau of Statistics, Ministry of Economic Planning and Development.

GOK. (1979a), "Report of the Child Nutrition Survey 1978/79", Nairobi: Central Bureau of Statistics, Ministry of Economic Planning and Development.

GOK. (1979b), *Development Plan 1979–1983*, Nairobi: Government Printer.

GOK. (1979c), *Planning for Progress: Our Fourth Development Plan*, Nairobi: Government Printer.

GOK. (1980a), *Statistical Abstract*, Nairobi: Government Printer.

GOK. (1980b), *Kenya Fertility Survey 1977–1978*, First Report, Vol. 1, Nairobi: Central Bureau of Statistics/Ministry of Economic Planning and Development/GOK and World Fertility Survey.

GOK. (1980c), *Kakamega District Development Plan 1979–1983*, Nairobi: Ministry of Economic Planning and Development/GOK.

GOK. (1981a), *Sessional Paper No. 4 of 1981, On National Food Policy*, Nairobi: Government Printer.

GOK. (1981b), *Kenya Population Census, 1979*, Central Bureau of Statistics, Nairobi: Government Printer.

GOK. (1981c), "Infant Mortality in Kenya", *Social Perspectives* 5 (2), Central Bureau of Statistics, Ministry of Economic Planning and Development.

GOK. (1981d), "Infant Mortality in Kenya: Past and Present Differentials", *Social Perspectives* 6 (1), Central Bureau of Statistics, Ministry of Economic Planning and Development.

GOK. (1983), *Development Plan 1984–1988*, Nairobi: Government Printer.

GOK and UNICEF (1984), *Situation Analysis of Children and Women in Kenya*, 2 vols, Nairobi: Central Bureau of Statistics/Ministry of Finance and Planning/GOK and UNICEF.

Golkowsky, R. (1973), "Tenant Performance and Budgets", in: Chambers and

314

Moris, eds. (1973), pp. 186–208.

Golladay, F. *et al.* (1980), *Health*, Sector Policy Paper, Washington, DC: World Bank.

Goonatilake, S. (1984), *Aborted Discovery: Science and Creativity in the Third World*, London: Zed.

Goulet, D. (1973), *The Cruel Choice: A New Concept in the Theory of Development*, New York: Atheneum.

Government of Botswana (1982), *Annual Water Sector Review of the Village Water Supply III Programme*, Gaborone: Ministry of Mineral Resources and Water Affairs, Department of Water Affairs/SIDA.

Grant, J. (1981), *The State of the World's Children 1980–1981*, New York: UNICEF.

Grant, J. (1982), *The State of the World's Children 1981–82*, New York: UNICEF.

Grant, J. (1983a), *The State of the World's Children 1982–83*, New York: UNICEF.

Grant, J. (1983b), "A Child Survival and Development Revolution", *Assignment Children* 61/62 (1), 21–31.

Grant, J. (1983c), *The State of the World's Children 1984*, New York: UNICEF.

Grant, J. (1984), "Marketing Child Survival", *Assignment Children* 65/66, 3–9.

Grant, J. (1985a), *The State of the World's Children 1985*, Part I: Statement by James P. Grant, Executive Director, New York: UNICEF.

Grant, J. (1985b), *The State of the World's Children 1986*, New York: Oxford University Press.

Green, R. (1977), *Adult Education in National Development Planning: Notes toward an integrated approach*, Bonn: German Adult Education Association (DVV), Africa Bureau/International Council for Adult Education (ICAE).

Green, R. (1978), "Basic Human Needs: Concept or Slogan, Synthesis or Smokescreen?", *IDS Bulletin* 9, 4 (June), 7–11.

Green, R. (1984), "Consolidation and Accelerated Development of African Agriculture: What Agendas for Action?", *African Studies Review* 27 (4), 17–34.

Green, R., and Singer, H. (1984), "Sub-Saharan Africa in Depression: The Impact on the Welfare of Children", in: Jolly and Cornia, eds. (1984), pp. 113–26.

Greer, J., and Thorbecke, E. (1984), "A Methodology for Measuring Food Poverty Applied to Kenya", mimeo, Department of Economics, Ithaca, NY: Cornell University.

Gregory, J. (1979), "Underdevelopment, Dependency and Migration in Upper Volta", in: Shaw and Heard, eds. (1979), pp. 73–94.

Gruber, R., ed. (1961), *Science and the New Nations: The Proceedings of the International Conference on Science in the Advancement of New States at Rehovoth, Israel*, New York: Basic Books.

Guggenheim, H., and Fanale, R. (1975), "Shared Technology", Occasional Paper No. 1, IDEP/ENDA, Dakar: Environmental Training Programme (ENDA) – Institute for Economic Development and Planning (IDEP)/ UNEP/SIDA. (Also: Idem. "Water storage through shared technology: four projects among the Dogon in Mali", *Assignment Children/Les Carnets de l'Enfance* 45/46, 151–66.)

Gulliver, P. (1955), *Family Herds: A study of two pastoral tribes in East Africa*, London: Oxford University Press.

Gutierrez, G. (1972), *Teología de la Liberación*, Salamanca: Ed. Sigueme.

Gutkind, P. (1975), "Are the Poor Politically Dangerous? Some thoughts on urbanism, urbanites, and political consciousness", in: Owusu, ed. (1975), pp. 85–114.

Gutkind, P., and Wallerstein, I., eds. (1985), *Political Economy of Contemporary Africa*, 2nd edition, Beverly Hills: Sage.

Gutto, S. (1976), "The Status of Women in Kenya: A Study of Paternalism, Inequality and Underpriviledge", Discussion Paper 235, Institute for Development Studies, Nairobi: University of Nairobi.

Gutto, S. (1981), "Law, Rangelands, Peasantry and Social Classes", *Review of African Political Economy* 20, 41–56.

Guyer, J. (1981), "Household and Community in African Studies", *African Studies Review* 24 (2/3), 87–137.

Guyer, J. (1984), "Women's Work and Production Systems: A Review of Two Reports on the Agricultural Crisis", *Review of African Political Economy* 27/28, 186–92.

Haaga, J., Kenrick, C., Mason, J., Test, K. (1984), *An Estimate of the Prevalance of Child Malnutrition in Developing Countries*, Report to the Nutrition Unit, WHO, Ithaca: Cornell Nutrition Surveillance Program (CNSP), Cornell University.

Haaga, J., Quinn, V., Mason, J., Williams, K. (1983), "Recommendations for Development of Nutritional Surveillance in Botswana", mimeo, Ithaca, NY: Nutrition Surveillance Program/Cornell University.

Haddad, W. *et al.* (1980), *Education*, Sectoral Policy Paper, Washington, DC: World Bank.

Hadjor, K. (1987), *On Transforming Africa*, London: Third World Communications.

Hahn, N. (1982), "Women's Access to Land", *Land Reform, Land Settlement and Cooperatives* 1/2, 1–11.

Hake, A. (1977), *African Metropolis: Nairobi's Self-Help City*, Brighton: Sussex University Press.

Hanger, J. and Moris, J. (1973), "Women and the Household Economy", in: Chambers and Moris, eds. (1973), pp. 209–44.

Hanlon, J. (1977), "India: back to the villages. Does AT walk on plastic sandals?", *New Scientist* 74, 467–9.

Hansen, E. (1984), "The Food Crisis in Ghana: National Policies and Organizations", *Africa Research and Publications Project Working Papers* 10, Trenton, NJ: Africa World Press.

Hardoy, J., and Satterthwaite, D. (1981), *Shelter: Need and Response. Housing, Land and Settlement Policies in Seventeen Third World Nations*, Chichester: Wiley.

Harper, M., and Soon, T. (1979), *Small Enterprises in Developing Countries*, London: Intermediate Technology Publications.

Harrison, P. (1987), *The Greening of Africa*, London: Penguin.

Harris, D., ed. (1980), *Human Ecology in Savanna Environments*, London: Academic Press.

Harris, L. (1980), "Agricultural Cooperatives and Development Policy in Mozambique", *Journal of Peasant Studies* 7 (3).

Harrison-Church, R. (1957), *West Africa*, London: Longman.

Harriss, J. (1982a), "Introduction", in: Harriss, ed. (1982b), pp. 15–36.

Harriss, J., ed. (1982b), *Rural Development: Theories of Peasant Economy and Agrarian Change*, London: Hutchinson.

Harwig, C. (1979), "Church-State Relations in Kenya: Health Issues", *Social Science and Medicine* 13C, 121–7.

Haswell, M. (1981), "Food Consumption in Relation to Labour Output", in: Chambers *et al.*, eds. (1981), pp. 38–41.

Haub, C., Heisler, D., Condron, M. (1980), *World's Women Data Sheet*, Washington, DC: Population Reference Bureau/UNICEF.

Haugerud, A. (1984), "Economy, Ecology and the Unequal Impact of Fuelwood Scarcity in Embu, Kenya", in: Barnes *et al.*, eds. (1984), pp. 79–101, Beijer Institute.

Hayter, T., and Watson, C. (1985), *Aid: Rhetoric and Reality*, London: Pluto.

Heisey, N. (1986), remarks concerning her two-year period in Burkina Faso representing an NGO, the Mennonite Central Committee, during a workshop on African Food Security at Tufts University.

Heller, A. (1980), "Can 'True' and 'False' Needs be Posited?", in: Lederer, ed. (1980), pp. 213–26.

Helleiner, G. (1975), "Smallholder Decision Making: Tropical African Evidence", in: Reynolds, ed. (1975), pp. 27–52.

Herrera, A. (1984), *Project on Research and Development Systems in Rural Settings: Final Report*, Tokyo: United Nations University.

Herrera, A., *et al.* (1976), *Catastrophe or New Society? A Latin American World Model*, Ottawa: IDRC.

Hewitt, K., ed. (1983), *Interpretations of Calamity*, London: Allen and Unwin.

Heyer, J. (1965), "Some Problems in the Valuation of Subsistence Output", Discussion Paper 14, Centre for Economic Research, Nairobi: University College.

Heyer, J. (1976), "The Marketing System", in: Heyer *et al.*, eds. (1976), pp. 313–63.

Heyer, J. (1981), "Agricultural Development Policy in Kenya from the Colonial Period to 1975", in: Heyer *et al.*, eds. (1981), pp. 90–120.

Heyer, J., Maitha, J., Senga, W., eds. (1976), *Agricultural Development in Kenya: An Economic Assessment*, Nairobi: Oxford University Press.

Heyer, J., Roberts, P., Williams, G., eds. (1981a), *Rural Development in Tropical Africa*, New York: St Martin's Press.

Heyer, J., Roberts, P., Williams, G. (1981b), "Rural Development", in: Heyer *et al.*, eds. (1981a), pp. 1–15.

Heyer, J., and Waweru, J. (1976), "The Development of the Small Farm Areas", in: Heyer *et al.*, eds. (1976), pp. 187–221.

Higgins, G. *et al.* (1984), *Potential Population Supporting Capacities of Lands in the Developing Countries*, Rome: FAO.

Hirschman, A. (1960), *The Strategy of Economic Development*, New Haven: Yale University Press.

Hodges, T. (1987), "OAU Urges 10-Year Debt Moratorium", *Africa Recovery* 4 (December), 1–2.

317

Hoekstra, D., and Kuguru, F. eds. (1983), *Agroforestry Systems for Small-Scale Farmers*, Proceedings of an ICRAF/British American Tobacco Workshop, Nairobi: International Council for Research Agroforestry (ICRAF).

Hoet-Smit, M. (1982), *Community Participation in Squatter Upgrading in Zambia*, Philadelphia: AFSC.

Hogg, R. (1985), "The Politics of Drought: The Pauperization of Isiolo Boran", *Disasters* 9 (1), 39–50.

Hollnsteiner, M. (1982a), "Government Strategies for Urban Areas and Community Participation", *Assignment Children* 57/58, 43–64.

Hollnsteiner, M. (1982b), "The Participatory Imperative in Primary Health Care", *Assignment Children* 59/60 (2), 35–56.

Holmquist, F. (1979), "Class Structure, Peasant Participation, and Rural Self-Help", in: Barkan and Okumu, eds. (1979), pp. 129–53, Nairobi: Heinemann.

Holmquist, F. (1980), "Defending Peasant Political Space in Independent Africa", *Canadian Journal of African Studies* 14 (1), 157–67.

Holmquist, F. (1982a), "State, Class, Peasants and the Initiation of Kenyan Self-Help", Comparative Legislative Research Center, Occasional Paper No. 18 (April), Iowa City: University of Iowa.

Holmquist, F. (1982b), personal communication of his observations in western Kenya.

Holmquist, F. (1984), "Self-Help: The State and Peasant Leverage in Kenya", *Africa* 54 (3), 72–91.

Holt, J. (1985), presentation to the Third IDS Food Aid Seminar, summarized in: Clay and Everitt, eds. (1985), pp. 12–15.

Holtham, G., and Hazlewood, A. (1976), *Aid and Inequality in Kenya*, London: Croom Helm.

Hopkins, M., and van der Hoeven, R. (1981), *Economic and Social Policy Synthesis Programme. Modelling Economic and Social Factors in Development*, World Employment Programme Research. Working Paper (WEP 2–32/WP 32)), Geneva: ILO.

Horn, J. (1969), *Away with All Pests*, New York: Monthly Review.

Horton, S., and King, T. (1981), *Labor Productivity: Un Tour d'Horizon*, Staff Working Paper No. 497, Washington, DC: World Bank.

Hoselitz, B. (1960), *Sociological Aspects of Economic Growth*, New York: Free Press.

Hosier, R. (1981), "'Something to Buy Paraffin With': An Investigation into Domestic Energy Consumption in Rural Kenya", unpublished Ph.D. thesis. Clark University.

House, W. (1981), "Nairobi's Informal Sector: An Exploratory Study", in: Killick, ed. (1981), pp. 357–68.

Howes, M. (1985), *Rural Energy Surveys in the Third World: A Critical Review of Issues and Methods*, Ottawa: International Development Research Centre.

Hürni, B. (1980), *The Lending Policy of the World Bank in the 1970s: Analysis and Evaluation*, Boulder, CO: Westview.

Hughes, C., and Hunter, J. (1970), "Disease and 'Development' in Africa", *Social Science and Medicine* 3, 443–93.

Huizer, G. (1984), "Harmony vs. Confrontation", *Development: Seeds of Change* 1982: 2, 14–17.

Hunt, D. (1977), "Poverty and Agricultural Development Policy in a Semi-arid Area of Eastern Kenya", in: O'Keefe and Wisner, eds. (1977), pp. 74–91.

Hunt, D. (1984), *The Impending Crisis in Kenya: The Case for Land Reform*, Aldershot: Gower Publishing.

Hunter, G., Bunting, A., Bottrall, A., eds. (1975), *Policy and Practice in Rural Development*, London: Croom Helm/ODI.

Hunter, J., Rey, L., Scott, D., "Man-Made Lakes and Man-Made Diseases: Toward a Policy Resolution", *Social Science and Medicine* 16, 1127–45.

Hutton, J., ed. (1970), *Urban Challenge in East Africa*, Nairobi: East African Publishing House.

Hyden, G. (1980), *Beyond Ujamaa in Tanzania: Underdevelopment and an Uncaptured Peasantry*, London: Heinemann.

Hyden, G. (1983), *No Shortcuts To Progress: African Development Management in Perspective*, Berkeley: University of California Press.

Hyden, G. (1985), "A Rejoiner to Mamdani's Review of *No Shortcuts to Progress*", *Eastern African Social Science Research Review* 1 (1), 93–9.

IFAD (International Fund for Agricultural Development) (1985), *Annual Report 1984*, Rome: IFAD.

Illich, I. (1974), *Energy and Equity*, London: Calder and Boyars.

ILO (International Labour Office) (1972), *Income, Equality and Employment in Kenya*, Geneva: ILO.

ILO. (1976), *Employment, Growth and Basic Needs: A One-World Problem*, Geneva: ILO.

ILO. (1977), *A Basic-Needs Strategy for Africa*, Report of the Director-General, Geneva: ILO.

ILO. (1979), *Follow-up of the World Employment Conference: Basic Needs*, International Labour Conference, 65th Session. Report 7, Geneva: ILO.

ILO. (1984), *Rural Development and Women in Africa*, Geneva: ILO.

ILO. (1985), *Resources, Power and Women*, Proceedings of the African and Asian Inter-regional Workshop on Strategies for Improving the Employment Conditions of Rural Women, Arusha, Tanzania, 20–25 August 1984, Geneva: ILO.

Independent Commission on International Humanitarian Issues (ICIHI) (1985), *Man-made Famine?*, London: Pan Books.

Independent Group on British Aid (IGBA) (1983), *Real Aid: A Strategy for Britain*, Report of the Independent Group on British Aid Under the Chairmanship of Professor Charles Elliot, London: IGBA.

Inqui, S. (1984), personal communication during team field work for the FAO Interagency WCAARD Mission to Lesotho.

Institut Universitaire d'Etudes du Développement (IUED), ed. (1980), *Il faut manger pour vivre ... controverses sur les besoins fondamentaux et le développement*, Geneva and Paris: IUED and Presses Universitaires de France.

Institute for Development Studies (IDS) (1975), "An Overall Evaluation of the Special Rural Development Programme", Occasional Paper No. 12. Nairobi.

Institute for Development Studies (IDS) (1973), "An Overall Evaluation of the Special Rural Development Programme", Occasional Paper No. 8, Nairobi: University of Nairobi.

International Council for Adult Education (ICAE), ed. (1982) Adult Education and Primary Health Care, thematic issue of *Convergence* 15, 2.

Isenman, P. *et al.* (1982), *Poverty and Human Development*, New York: Oxford University Press.

Jackson, T., with Eade, D. (1982), *Against the Grain: The Dilemma of Project Food Aid*, London: Oxfam.

Jacobs, S. (1984), "Women and Land Resettlement in Zimbabwe", *Review of African Political Economy* 27/28, 33–50.

Jacobsen, O. (1978), "Economic and Geographical Factors Influencing Child Malnutrition: A Study from the Southern Highlands, Tanzania", Research Paper 52, Bureau of Resource Assessment and Land Use Planning, Dar es Salaam: University of Dar es Salaam.

JASPA (Jobs And Skills Programme for Africa) (1977), *Economic Transformation in a Socialist Framework. An Employment and Basic Needs Oriented Development Strategy for Somalia*, Addis Ababa: ILO/JASPA.

JASPA (1981a), *Zambia: Basic Needs in an Economy Under Pressure*, Addis Ababa: ILO/JASPA.

JASPA (1981b), *First Things First: Meeting the Basic Needs of the People of Nigeria*, Addis Ababa: ILO/JASPA.

JASPA (1982), *Basic Needs in Danger: A Basic Needs Oriented Development Strategy for Tanzania*, Addis Ababa: ILO/JASPA.

Jelliffe, D. (1966), *The Assessment of the Nutritional Status of the Community*, WHO Monograph Series No. 53, Geneva: WHO.

Jelliffe, D., and Jelliffe, E. (1978), *Human Milk in the Modern World*, New York: Oxford University Press.

Jéquier, N., ed. (1976), *Appropriate Technology: Problems and Promises*, Development Centre of the OECD Study, Paris: OECD.

Jerome, N., *et al.*, eds. (1980), *Nutritional Anthropology*, Pleasantville, NY: Redgrave Publishing.

Johnston, B., and Clark, W. (1982), *Redesigning Rural Development: A Strategic Perspective*, Baltimore: Johns Hopkins.

Jolly, R., ed. (1978), *Disarmament and World Development*, London: Pergamon.

Jolly, R., and Cornia, G. (1984), *The Impact of World Recession on Children*, Oxford: Pergamon.

Jones, B. (1981), *Non-agricultural Uses of Irrigation Systems: Household Water Supplies*, New York: Agricultural Development Council.

Juma, C. (1986), "African NGOs Environmental Network: An Institutional Innovation", mimeo, Nairobi: ANEN (Box 53844).

Kaldor, M. (1978), "The Military in Third World Development", in: Jolly, ed. (1978), pp. 57–82.

Kalyalya, D., Mhlanga, K., Semboja, J., Seidman, A. (1988), *Aid and Development in Southern Africa: A Participatory Learning Process*, Trenton, NJ: Africa World Press and Oxfam America.

Kaniki, M. (1980), *Tanzania Under Colonial Rule*, London: Longman.

Kaplinsky, R. (1973), "Ownership and Equity in Kenya", mimeo, Institute of Development Studies, Falmer, Brighton: Sussex University.

Kaplinsky, R. (1978a), "Introduction: The Role of the Multinational Corporation in the Kenyan Economy", in: Kaplinsky, ed. (1978b), pp. 1–21.

Kaplinsky, R. (1978b), *Readings on the Multinational Corporation in Kenya*, Nairobi: Oxford University Press.

Kaplinsky, R. (1978c), "Technical Change and the Multinational Corporation: Some British Multinationals in Kenya", in: Kaplinsky, ed. (1978b), pp. 201–260.

Kaseje, K. (1980), "A Community-Based Health Program – Saradidi Health Project", mimeo, Nairobi: Department of Community Health, University of Nairobi.

Kassam, Y., and Mustafa, K., eds. (1982), *Participatory Research: An Emerging Alternative Methodology in Social Science Research*, New Delhi: Society for Participatory Research in Asia/African Adult Education Association, Participatory Research Project.

Kelman, A., and McCord, C. (1978), "Weight for Age as an Index of Risk of Death in Children", *Lancet* 1, 1247–50.

Khan, A., and Bhasin, K. (1986), "Role of Asian People's Organizations", *IFDA Dossier* 53, 54, May–June and July–August, 3–15, 9–20.

Kibet, M. (1981), "Infant Mortality in Kenya", mimeo, Nairobi: USAID.

Kibreab, G. (1985), *African Refugees*, Trenton, NJ: Africa World Press.

Kidd, R. (1979), "Liberation or Domestication: Popular Theatre and Non-formal Education in Africa", *Educational Broadcasting International* 12, 1 (March), 3–9.

Kidd, R. (1980), "People's Theatre, Conscientisation, and Struggle", *Media Development* 27, 3, 10–14.

Kidd, R. (1982), "From Outside In to Inside Out: The Benue Workshop on Theatre for Development", *Theaterwork* 2, 4, 44–54.

Kidd, R. (1983), "Popular Theatre and Popular Struggle in Kenya: The Story of Kamiriithu", *Race and Class* 24 (3), 287–304.

Killick, T., ed. (1981), *Papers on the Kenyan Economy: Performance, Problems and Policies*, Nairobi: Heinemann.

Kimambo, I. (1970), "The Economic History of the Kamba 1850–1950", in: Ogot, ed., 1970, pp. 79–103.

King, K. (1977), *The African Artisan: Education and the Informal Sector in Kenya*, London: Heinemann.

King, K. (1979), "Petty Production in Nairobi: The Social Context of Skill Acquisition and Occupational Differentiation", in; Bromley and Gerry, eds. (1979b), pp. 217–28.

King, M., ed. (1966), *Medical Care in Developing Countries*, A Symposium from Makerere, Nairobi: Oxford University Press.

King, R. (1981), "Cooperative Policy and Village Development in Northern Nigeria", in: Heyer *et al.*, eds. (1981a), pp. 259–80.

King-Meyers, L. (1979), "Nutrition in Kenya: Problems, Programs, Policies and Recommendations", mimeo, USAID Staff Report (Contract AID-615-210-T), Nairobi: USAID.

Kiros, F., ed. (1985), *Challenging Rural Poverty*, Trenton, NJ: Africa World Press/Organization for Social Science Research in Eastern Africa.

Kitching, G. (1980), *Class and Economic Change in Kenya: The Making of an African Petite Bourgeoisie 1905–1970*, New Haven: Yale University Press.

321

Kitching, G. (1982), *Development and Underdevelopment in Historical Perspective*, London: Methuen.

Kitching, G. (1985), "Politics, Method, and Evidence in the 'Kenya Debate'", in: Bernstein and Campbell, eds. (1985), pp. 115–52.

Kjekshus, H. (1977), *Ecology Control and Economic Development in East African History*, Berkeley: University of California Press.

Klee, G., ed. (1980), *World Systems of Traditional Resource Management*, New York: Halsted.

Kleinman, D. (1980), *Human Adaptation and Population Growth*, Montclair, NJ: Allanheld/Osmun.

Klouda, A. (1983), "'Prevention' Is More Costly Than Cure: Health Problems for Tanzania 1971–81", in: Morley *et al.* (1983), 49–63.

Knight, C., and Newman, J., eds. (1976), *Contemporary Africa: Geography and Change*, Englewood Cliffs, NJ: Prentice-Hall.

Knight, P., ed. (1981), *Implementing Programs of Human Development*, Staff Working Paper No. 403, Washington, DC: World Bank.

Kodjo, E. (1985), ... *et demain l'Afrique*, Paris, Editions Stock.

Konstad, P., and Mønsted, M. (1980), *Family, Labor, and Trade in Western Kenya*, Uppsala: Scandinavian Institute of African Studies.

Korte, R. (1969), "The Nutritional and Health Status of the People Living on Mwea-Tebere Irrigation Settlement", in: Kraut and Cremer, eds. (1969), pp. 267–334.

Korte, R. (1973), "Health and Nutrition", in: Chambers and Moris, eds. (1973), pp. 245–72.

Kotschi, J. (1984), "Sustainable Agriculture in Rural Development", *Gate* 4/84 (Deutsches Zentrum fur Entwicklungs-technologien/GTZ, Eschborn, West Germany), 3–7.

Kovel, J. (1985), "The Vatican Strikes Back", *Monthly Review* 36 (11), 14–27.

Kraut, H. and Cremer, H.-D., eds. (1969), *Investigations into Health and Nutrition in East Africa*, München: Weltforum Verlag.

Kruks, S. (1983), "Notes on the Concept and Practice of 'Participation' in the KWDP, with special emphasis on rural women", Kenya Woodfuel Development Project Discussion Paper. Nairobi and Stockholm: Beijer Institute.

Kruks, S., and Wisner, B. (1982), "The State, the Party, and the Female Peasantry in Mozambique", *Journal of Southern African Studies* 11 (1), 106–27.

Kusnets, S. (1964), *Modern Economic Growth: Rate, Structure and Spread*, New Haven: Yale University Press.

Kydd, J., and Christianson, R. (1982), "Structural Change in Malawi Since Independence: Consequences of a Development Strategy Based on Large-Scale Agriculture", *World Development* 10 (5), 355–76.

Lamb, G. (1972), "Peasants, Capitalists and Agricultural Development in Kenya", Paper for East African Universities Social Science Conference.

Lamb, G. (1974), *Peasant Politics: Conflict and Development in Murang'a*, London: Julian Friedmann.

Lamming, G. (1983), *Women in Agricultural Cooperatives: Constraints and Limitation to Full Participation*, Rome: FAO.

Langdon, S. (1975a), "Multinational Corporations, Taste Transfer and

Underdevelopment: A Case Study from Kenya", *Review of African Political Economy* 2, 12–35.

Langdon, S. (1975b), "Multinational Corporations in the Political Economy of Kenya", Ph.D. Thesis, University of Nairobi, Institute of Development Studies.

Langley, P. (1976), "Changes in the Production of the Built Environment in Rural Areas", *African Environment* 2, 1–2, 37–51.

Lawrence, P., ed. (1986), *World Recession and the Food Crisis in Africa*, London: James Currey.

Lea, D., and Chaudhri, D., eds. (1983a), *Rural Development and the State: Contradictions and Dilemmas in Developing Countries*, London: Methuen.

Lea, D., and Chaudhri, D. (1983b), "The Nature, Problems and Approaches to Rural Development", in: Lea and Chaudhri, eds. (1983), pp. 1–37.

Lederer, K., ed. (1980b), *Human Needs: A Contribution to the Current Debate*, Cambridge, MA and Königstein/Ts: Oelgeschlager, Gunn and Hain/Verlag Anton Hain.

Lee, E. (1981), Basic-Needs Strategies: A Frustrated Response to Development from Below?", in: Stöhr and Taylor, eds. (1981), pp. 107–22.

Lee, J. (1985), *The Environment, Public Health, and Human Ecology: Considerations for Economic Development*, A World Bank Publication, Baltimore: Johns Hopkins University Press.

Lele, U. (1975), *The Design of Rural Development*, Baltimore: Johns Hopkins.

Lele, U. (1981), "Rural Africa: Modernization, Equity, and Long-term Development", *Science* 211 (4482), 6 Feb., pp. 547–53.

Leonard, D. (1970), "Some Hypotheses Concerning the Organization of Communication in Agricultural Extension", Staff Paper 72. Institute for Development Studies, Nairobi: University of Nairobi.

Leonard, D. (1977), *Reaching the Peasant Farmer*, Chicago: University of Chicago Press.

Lewis, H., and Wisner, B. (1981), "Refugee Rehabilitation in Somalia", University of Wisconsin-Madison, Regional Planning and Area Development Project, Consulting Report No. 6 (June), Madison, WI: University of Wisconsin.

Lewis, I. (1978), *The Somali Democratic Republic: An Anthropological Overview*, USAID Mogadishu, mimeo.

Lewis, W. (1955), *The Theory of Economic Growth*, London: Allen and Unwin.

Lewycky, D. (1979), "Technologies for Eco-development: The Oodi Weavers", *African Environment* 3, 3–4, 345–50.

Leys, C. (1973), "Interpreting African Underdevelopment: Reflections on the ILO Report on Employment, Incomes, and Equality in Kenya", *African Affairs* 73, 419–29.

Leys, C. (1975), *Underdevelopment in Kenya: The Political Economy of Neo-Colonialism*, London: Heinemann.

Leys, C. (1978), "Capital Accumulation, Class Formation and Dependency – The Significance of the Kenyan Case", in: R. Miliband and J. Saville, eds., *Socialist Register*, pp. 241–66, London: Merlin Book Club.

Leys, C. (1987), "The State and the Crisis of Simple Commodity Production in Africa", *IDS Bulletin* 18 (3), 45–8.

Leys, R. (1986), "Drought and Drought Relief in Southern Zimbabwe", in:

Lawrence, ed. (1986), pp. 258–74.

Lipton, M. (1977), *Why Poor People Stay Poor: A Study in Urban Bias in World Development*, London: Temple Smith.

Lipton, M. (1983), *Poverty, Undernutrition and Hunger*, Staff Working Paper No. 616, Washington, DC: World Bank.

Livingston, I. (1981), *Rural Development, Employment and Incomes in Kenya*, Report prepared for the ILO's Jobs and Skills Programme for Africa (JASPA), Addis Ababa: ILO/JASPA.

Lone, S. (1986), "Angola Crisis is Deepening", *Africa Emergency* 7 (April––May), 1, 9.

Lone, S. (1987a), "African Reforms Fail to Stem Slide", *Africa Recovery* 3 (November), 1–2, 14.

Lone, S. (1987b), "IMF in Africa: Managing Director Michel Camdessus Answers the Fund's Critics", *Africa Recovery* 4 (December), 5–6.

Longhurst, R., ed. (1981), *Rapid Rural Appraisal: Social Structure and Rural Economy*, *IDS Bulletin* 12 (4).

Mabogunje, A. (1981), *The Development Process: A Spatial Perspective*, New York: Holmes and Meier.

McAlpin, M. (1987), "Famine Relief Policy in India: Six Lessons for Africa", in: Glantz, ed. (1987), pp. 391–414.

McAuslan, P. (1985), *Urban Land and Shelter for the Poor*, London: Earthscan/ IIED.

McCarthy, F., and Mwangi, W. (1982), *Kenyan Agriculture: Toward 2000*, Laxenburg, Austria: International Institute for Applied Systems Analysis.

McCall, M. (1987), "Carrying Heavier Burdens But Carrying Less Weight: Some Implications of Villagization for Women in Tanzania", in: Momsen and Townsend, eds. (1987), pp. 192–214.

McGranahan, D. (1980), "Improvement of Information on the Conditions of Children", Report No. 80.4, Geneva: UNRISD.

McHale, J., and McHale, M. (1978), *Basic Human Needs: A Framework for Action*, New Brunswick, NJ: Transaction Books.

McKay, B., and Atkinson, J., eds. (1987), *Common Property Resource Management: Anthropological Perspectives*, Tucson, AZ: University of Arizona Press.

McNamara, R. (1973), "Address to the Board of Governors, Nairobi, Kenya, September 24, 1973", in: World Bank (1981c), pp. 231–63.

McRobie, G. (1981), *Small is Possible*, London: Abacus.

McSweeney, B. (1980), "Time to Learn, Time for a Better Life: The Women's Education Project in Upper Volta", *Assignment Children* 49/50, 109–26.

Macpherson, G. (1975), *First Steps in Village Mechanisation*, Dar es Salaam: Tanzania Publishing House.

Madeley, J. (1984), "Kenya's Trees Go Up In Smoke – For the Smokers", *International Agricultural Development* 4 (5), 9–10, 21.

Magobeko, L. (1976), "The *Fundi* of Tanzania: An Attempt at Improvement", *African Environment* 2, 1–2, 150–58.

Makhoul, N. (1984), "Assessment and Implementation of Health Care Priorities in Developing Countries: Incompatible Paradigms and Competing Social Systems", *Social Science and Medicine* 19 (4), 373–84.

324

Maitha, J. (1976), "The Kenyan Economy", in: Heyer *et al.*, eds. (1976), pp. 33–68.

Mallmann, C. (1980), "Society, Needs, and Rights: A Systemic Approach", in: Lederer, ed. (1980), pp. 37–54.

Mamdani, M. (1982), "Karamoja: Colonial Roots of Famine in Northeast Uganda", *Review of African Political Economy* 25, 66–72.

Mamdani, M. (1985), "A Great Leap Backward: A Review of Goran Hyden's *No Shortcuts to Progress*", *Eastern African Social Science Research Review* 1 (1), 79–92.

Mandl, P.-E. (1977), "Réaliser des modes de vie fondés sur les ressources locales et la participation populaire", *Les Carnets de l'Enfance/Assignment Children* 39 (July–September), 5–7.

Manghezi, A. (1976), *Class, Elite and Community in African Development*, Uppsala: Scandinavian Institute of African Studies.

Manley, M., and Brandt, W. (1985), *Global Challenge*, Report of the Socialist International Committee on Economic Policy, London: Pan.

Martin, R. (1983), "Upgrading", in: Skinner and Rodell, eds. (1983), pp. 53–79.

Masakhalia, Y. (1979), "A Note on the Basic Needs Approach to Development Planning in Kenya", in: Buchmann *et al.*, eds. (1979), pp. 197–222.

Maslow, A. (1970), *Motivation and Personality*, 2dn ed. New York: Harper and Row.

Mason, J., Habicht, J.-P., Tabatabai, H., Valverde, V. (1984), *Nutrition Surveillance*, Geneva: WHO.

Mason, J., and Okeyo, A. (1985), "Coordinated Support to Nutritional Activities at Country Level: The Experience of Kenya", Report of Symposium held at the 11th Session of the UN ACC-SCN, Nairobi, Kenya, 11–12 February 1985, mimeo, Nutrition Surveillance Unit, Ithaca, NY: Cornell University.

Mass, B. (1977), *Population Target: The Political Economy of Population Control in Latin America*, Toronto: Women's Educational Press.

Matango, R. (1979), "The Role of Agencies for Rural Development in Tanzania: A Case Study of the Lushoto Integrated Development Project", in: Coulson, ed. (1979), pp. 158–72.

Matthews, W., ed. (1976), *Outer Limits and Human Needs: Resource and Environmental Issues of Development Strategies*, Uppsala: Dag Hammarskjöld Foundation.

Mbithi, P., and Bahemuka, J. (1981), "Socio-economic Factors Influencing Technical Farm Development in the ASAL", Report for the Ministry of Agriculture, April, Nairobi: University of Nairobi.

Mbithi, P., and Barnes, C. (1975), *The Spontaneous Settlement Problem in Kenya*, Kampala: East African Literature Bureau.

Mbithi, P., and Rasmussen, R. (1977), *Self-reliance in Kenya: The Case of Harambee*, Uppsala: Scandinavian Institute of African Studies.

Mbithi, P., and Wisner, B. (1973), "Drought and Famine in Kenya: Magnitude and Attempted Solutions", *Journal of East African Research and Development* 3, 2, 113–43.

Mburu, F. (1979), "Rhetoric-Implementation Gap in Health Policy and Health Services Delivery in a Developing Country", *Social Science and Medicine* 13A, 577–83.

Mburu, F. (1981), "Socio-Political Imperatives in the History of Health Development in Kenya", *Social Science and Medicine* 15A, 521–7.

Mduma, E. (1982), "Appropriate Technology for Grain Storage at Bwakira Chini Village", in: Kassam and Mustafa, eds. (1982), 198–213.

Mead, M., ed. (1955), *Cultural Patterns and Technical Change*, New York: New American Library.

Michaelson, K., ed. (1981), *And the Poor Get Children: Radical Perspectives on Population Dynamics*, New York: Monthly Review.

Mies, M. (1976), "The Shahada Movement: A Peasant Movement in Maharashtra". *Journal of Peasant Studies* 3 (4), 472–82.

Miller, H. (1986), Personal communication during interview at National Christian Council of Kenya, Nairobi.

Miracle, M., and Seidman, A. (1978), *Agricultural Cooperatives and Quasi-Cooperatives in Ghana 1961–1965*, mimeo, Land Tenure Center, Madison, WI: University of Wisconsin.

Modot-Bernard, J. (1980), *Satisfaction of Food Requirements and Agricultural Development in Mali*, 3 vols, Paris: Development Centre of the OECD.

Momsen, J., and Townsend, J., eds. (1987), *Geography of Gender in the Third World*, London and Albany: Hutchinson Education and State University of New York Press.

Mondlane, E. (1969), *The Struggle for Mozambique*, London: Penguin.

Mønsted, M. (1976), "The Changing Division of Labour within Rural Families in Kenya", in: Caldwell, ed. (1976).

Mønsted, M. (1978), "Women's Groups in Rural Kenya and their Role in Development", mimeo, Copenhagen: Centre for Development Research.

Mörth, H. (1966), "Notes on the Evidence Presented to the Commission of Enquiry, 2: Comments on a Weather Cycle in Kenya", East African Meteorological Department (typewritten).

Moock, P. (1976), "The Efficiency of Women as Farm Managers: Kenya", *American Journal of Agricultural Economics* 58, 831–5.

Moore, T. (1979), "Land Use and Soil Erosion in the Machakos Hills, Kenya", *Annals of the Association of American Geographers* 69, 419–31.

Morley, D., Rohde, J. and Williams, G., eds. (1983), *Practicing Health for All*, Oxford: Oxford University Press.

Moris, J. (1973a), "The Mwea Environment", in Chambers and Moris, eds. (1973), pp. 16–63.

Moris, J. (1973b), "Tenant Life on Mwea: An Overview", in: Chambers and Moris, eds. (1973), pp. 298–342.

Moyes, A. (1979), *The Poor Man's Wisdom: Technology and the Very Poor*, Oxford: Oxfam Public Affairs Unit.

Müller, J. (1980), *Liquidation or Consolidation of Indigenous Technology: A Study of the Changing Conditions of Production of Village Blacksmiths in Tanzania*, Development Research Series No. 1, Aalborg: Aalborg University Press/Scandinavian Institute of African Studies.

Mulaa, J. (1981), "Politics and a Changing Society", *Review of African Political Economy* 20, 89–107.

Muller, M. (1978), *Tobacco and the Third World: Tomorrow's Epidemic?*, London: War on Want.

Murray, C. (1981), *Families Divided: The Impact of Migrant Labour in Lesotho*,

London: Cambridge University Press.

Mustafa, K. (1982), "The Jipemoyo Project", in: Kassam and Mustafa, eds. (1982), pp. 214–29.

Mutiso, S. (1986), "Challenges and Strategies of Crop Agriculture Development in the Semi-Arid Environment of Kenya: The Machakos Case", paper presented at the Annual Conference of the Institute of British Geographers, University of Reading, 6–9 January 1986.

Nelson, N. (1979), "How Women and Men Get By: The Sexual Division of Labour in the Informal Sector of a Nairobi Squatter Settlement", in: Bromley and Gerry, eds. (1979), pp. 283–304.

Nelson, N., ed. (1981), *African Women in the Development Process*, London: Cass.

Nerfin, M., ed. (1977), *Another Development: Approaches and Strategies*, Uppsala: Dag Hammarskjöld Foundation.

Newell, K., ed. (1975), *Health by the People*, Geneva: WHO.

Ng'ethe, N. (1980), "Possibilities for and Limits to Peasant Self-Help Development: The Case of Harambee in Kenya", paper delivered at the Canadian Association of African Studies Conference, Guelph University, 8 May.

Ngũgĩ Wa Thiongo and Ngũgĩ Wa Mirii (1982), *I Will Marry When I Want*, African Writers Series 246. London: Heinemann Educational Books.

Njonjo, A. (1981), "The Kenyan Peasantry: A Reassessment", *Review of African Political Economy* 20, 27–40.

Niilus, M. (1973), "The Problem of Urban Housing in Developing Countries: The Role of the Churches in Low-Cost Housing Programmes", in: World Council of Churches, ed. (1973), unbound paper, 11pp.

Norcliffe, G., and Pinfold, T., eds. (1980), *Planning African Development*, Boulder, CO: Westview.

Norman, D., Simmons, E., Hays, H. (1982), *Farming Systems in the Nigerian Savanna: Research and Strategies for Development*, Boulder, CO: Westview.

Noui-Mehidi, K. (1976), "The Peasant's Point of View: An Experiment in Algeria", *African Environment* 2, 1–2, 159–66.

Nurske, R. (1952), *Problems of Capital Formation in Underdeveloped Countries*, London: Oxford University Press.

Nyerere, J. (1966), "*Ujamaa* – the Basis of African Socialism", in: Nyerere, J. *Freedom and Unity/Uhuru na Umoja*, pp. 162–71, Dar es Salaam: Oxford University Press.

Nyerere, J. (1968a), "Education for Self-reliance", in: J. Nyerere, *Freedom and Socialism/Uhuru na Ujamaa*, pp. 267–90, Dar es Salaam: Oxford University Press.

Nyerere, J. (1968b), "Socialism and Rural Development", in: J. Nyerere, *Freedom and Socialism* ..., pp. 337–66.

Nyerere, J. (1980), "No to IMF Meddling", *Development Dialogue* 2 (1980), 7–9.

Nzongola, N., *et al.* (1987), *Africa's Crisis*, London: Institute for African Alternatives (23 Bevenden Street, London N1 6BH).

Oakley, P., and Marsden, D. (1984), *Approaches to Participation in Rural*

327

Development, Geneva: ILO for ACC Task Force on Rural Development.

Obbo, C. (1980), *African Women: Their Struggle for Economic Independence*, London: Zed.

O'Brien, J. (1985), "Sowing the Seeds of Famine", *Review of African Political Economy* 33, 23–32.

Odhiambo, T. (1983), "The Natural History of Academies of Sciences in Africa", *Memorie de Scienze Fisiche e Naturali* Serie V, 7 (2), 99–110.

Odhiambo, T. (1987), "Human Capital for Science-Driven Development in Africa", Plenary Lecture delivered during the Annual Meeting of the American Association for the Advancement of Science (AAAS), Chicago, 18 February 1987.

Odingo, R. (1977), "African Experience: Some observations from Kenya", in: White, ed. (1977), pp. 147–72.

OECD. (1976), *Measuring Social Well-Being*, Paris: Organization for Economic Co-operation and Development.

Ogallo, L. (1983), "Rainfall Trends", *The Kenyan Geographer* (Special Issue) 5 (1/2).

Ogendo, R. (1983), "Classification of Kenya's Arid and Semi-Arid Districts", *The Kenyan Geographer* (Special Issue) 5 (1/2).

Ogot, B., ed. (1970), *Hadith 2*, Nairobi: East African Publishing House.

Oguntoyinbo, J., and Richards, P. (1978), "Drought and the Nigerian Farmer", *Journal of Arid Environments* 1, 165–94.

Ojany, F., and Ogendo, R. (1973), *Kenya: A Study in Physical and Human Geography*, Nairobi: Longman.

O'Keefe, P. (1974), "Gakarara: A Study in the Development of Underdevelopment", unpublished Ph.D. dissertation, University of London.

O'Keefe, P., Baird, A., Wisner, B. (1977), "Kenyan Underdevelopment: A Case Study of Proletarianization", in: O'Keefe and Wisner, eds. (1977), pp. 216–28.

O'Keefe, P., and Juma, C. (1982), "Kenya: See How They Move." *Populi* 9, 3, 44–8.

O'Keefe, P., and Munslow, B., eds. (1984), *Energy and Development in Southern Africa: SADCC Country Studies*, Part I, Uppsala: Scandinavian Institute of African Studies and the Beijer Institute.

O'Keefe, P., and Wisner, B. (1975), "African Drought: The State of the Game", in: Richards, ed. (1975), pp. 31–9.

O'Keefe, P., and Wisner, B., eds. (1977), *Land Use and Development*, London: International African Institute.

Okoth-Ogendo, H. (1976), "African Land Tenure Reform", in: Heyer *et al.*, eds. (1976), pp. 152–86.

O'Leary, M. (1980a), "Responses to Drought in Kitui District, Kenya", *Disasters* 4, 3, 315–27.

O'Leary, M. (1980b), "Population, Economy and Domestic Groups: The Kitui Case", *Africa* 53 (1), 64–76.

Ominde, S. (1968), *Land and Population Movements in Kenya*, Nairobi: Heinemann.

Ominde, S., ed. (1971a), *Studies in East African Geography and Development*, London: Heinemann.

Ominde, S. (1971b), "The Semi-arid and Arid Lands of Kenya", in: Ominde, ed. (1971a), pp. 146–61.

Ominde, S. (1971c), "Rural Economy in West Kenya", in: Ominde, ed. (1971a), 207–29.

Ominde, S. (1975), *The Population of Kenya, Tanzania and Uganda*, Nairobi: Heinemann.

Omvedt, G. (1980), *We Will Smash This Prison*, London: Zed.

Opondo, D. (1980), "A Women's Group in Kenya and its Struggle to Obtain Credit", *Assignment Children* 49/50, 127–40.

Organization of African Unity (OAU) (1981), *Lagos Plan of Action for the Economic Development of Africa, 1980–2008*, Geneva: International Institute for Labour Studies.

Owako, F. (1971), "Machakos Land and Population Problems", in: Ominde, ed. (1971a), pp. 177–92.

Owusu, M., ed. (1975), *Colonialism and Change*, The Hague: Mouton.

Oyebande, L. (1975), "Water Resource Problems in Africa", in: Richards, ed. (1975b), 40–54.

Oyugi, W. (1981), *Rural Development Administration: A Kenyan Experience*, Nairobi and Sahibabad, UP, India: Heritage Bookshop and Vikas Publishing House.

Pacey, A., and Payne, P., eds. (1985), *Agricultural Development and Nutrition*, London: Hutchinson Education/UNICEF/FAO.

Pack, H. (1975), "The Employment–Output Trade-off in LDCs: A Microeconomic Approach", *Oxford Economic Papers* 26, 388–404.

Pack, H. (1981), "The Substitution of Labour for Capital in Kenyan Manufacturing", in: Killick, ed. (1981), pp. 254–64.

Page, W., and Richards, P. (1977), "Agricultural Pest Control by Community Action: The Case of the Variegated Grasshopper in Southern Nigeria", *African Environment* 2–3, 4–1 (November), 127–41.

Palmer, I. (1981), "Seasonal Dimensions of Women's Roles", in: Chambers *et al.*, eds. (1981), pp. 195–201.

Palmer, R. and Parsons, N. (1977), *The Roots of Rural Poverty in Central and Southern Africa*, London: Heinemann.

Parkipuny, M. (1979), "Some Crucial Aspects of the Maasai Predicament", in: Coulson, ed. (1979), pp. 136–57.

Parry, J. (1975), "Intermediate Technology Building", *Appropriate Technology* 2, 3, 6–8.

Payer, C. (1979), "The World Bank and the Small Farmers", *Journal of Peace Studies* 16, 4, 293–312.

Payer, C. (1982), *The World Bank: A Critical Analysis*, New York: Monthly Review.

Pearse, A., and Stiefel, M. (1979), "Inquiry into Participation: A Research Approach", Report 79.14 (May). Geneva: UNRISD.

PEEM (Panel of Experts on Environmental Management for Vector Control) (1984a), "Amibara Success Highlights Value of Integrated Efforts", *The PEEM Newsletter* 10, Geneva: PEEM Secretariat/WHO.

PEEM. (1984b), *Report of the Fourth Meeting*, Geneva: PEEM Secretariat/WHO.

Petchesky, R. (1981), "'Reproductive Choice' in the Contemporary United

329

States: A Social Analysis of Female Sterilization", in: Michaelson, ed. (1981), pp. 50–88.

Peters, P. (1983), "The Transformation of a Commons: Cattle, Boreholes and Syndicates in the Kgatlang District of Botswana", unpublished Ph.D. dissertation, Boston University.

Pilgrim, J. (1981), *The Social and Economic Consequences of Land Enclosure in the Kipsigis Reserve*, mimeo, Institute of Social Research, Kampala: Makerere University.

Pinché, V., Gregory, J., Coulibaly, S. (1980), "Vers une explication des courants migratoires voltaïques", *Labour, Capital, Society* 13 (1), 77–104.

Pinsky, B. (1980), "Mobilizing for a New Life: 'Caniço' Settlement Rehabilitation in the *Bairro* of Maxaquene, Mozambique", *Antipode* 12, 3, 24–30.

Pinstrup-Andersen, P. (1985), "The Nutrition Effects of Export Crop Production: Current Evidence and Policy Implications", in: Biswas and Pinstrup-Andersen, eds. (1985), pp. 43–59.

Pitt, D. (1982), personal communication during interview at WHO, Geneva.

Porter, P. (1979), *Food and Development in the Semi-arid Zone of East Africa*, Foreign and Comparative Studies/African Series 32, Syracuse, NY: Syracuse University, Maxwell School of Citizenship and Public Affairs.

Raikes, A. (1985), "Women's Health in East Africa", paper presented to the workshop on "Political Economy of Health and Disease in Africa and Latin America", Toluca, Mexico, 8–12 January, 1985. Forthcoming in *Social Science and Medicine*.

Raikes, P. (1978), "Rural Differentiation and Class Formation in Tanzania", *Journal of Peasant Studies* 5 (3), 285–325.

Raikes, P. (1982), "The State and the Peasantry in Tanzania", in: Harriss, ed. (1982), pp. 350–80.

Raikes, P. (1984), "Food Policy and Production in Mozambique Since Independence", *Review of African Political Economy* 29, 95–107.

Rau, W. (1985), *Feast to Famine: The Course of Africa's Underdevelopment*, Washington, DC: Africa Faith and Justice Network.

Reddy, A. (1975), "Alternative Technology: A Viewpoint from India", *Social Studies of Science* 5, 331–42.

Reddy, A. (1976), "The Trojan Horse", *Ceres: FAO Journal on Agriculture and Development* (March–April), 40–3.

Reddy, A. (1981), "Energy Options for the Third World", in: Reddy *et al.* (1981), pp. 6–19.

Reddy, A. and Reddy, S. (1983), "Energy in a Stratified Society: Case Study of Firewood in Bangalore", *Economic and Political Weekly* (Bombay), 8 October, 1757–70.

Reddy, A., Ganapathy, R., Hayes, P. (1981), *Southern Perspectives on the Rural Energy Crisis*, Box 353, Bolinas, California 94924: Nautilus.

Reboul, C. (1982), *Barrages Contre le Développement? Contribution a l'étude des projets d'aménagement de la vallée du fleuve Sénégal*, Série Économie et Sociologie Rurales. Paris: Institut National de la Recherche Agronomique.

Relief and Development Institute (1985), *Strengthening Disaster Preparedness in Six African Countries*, London: Relief and Development Institute.

Rempel, H. (1981), "The Food Situation in the Horn of Africa", mimeo,

Report to the Mennonite Board and Central Committee, Nairobi: MBCC.

Rempel, H. (1984), "Food Security Options for Sub-Saharan Africa", Working Paper 427, Institute for Development Studies. Nairobi: University of Nairobi.

Reynolds, L., ed. (1975), *Agriculture in Development Theory*, New Haven, CT: Yale University Press.

Richards, P. J., and Thomson, A., eds. (1984), *Basic Needs and the Urban Poor*, London: Croom Helm.

Richards, P. (1975a), "'Alternative' Strategies for the African Environment: 'Folk Ecology' as a Basis for Community Oriented Agricultural Development", in: Richards, eds. (1975b), pp. 102–17.

Richards, P., ed. (1975b), *African Environment: Problems and Perspectives*, London: International African Institute.

Richards, P. (1979), "Community Environmental Knowledge in African Rural Development", *IDS Bulletin* 10 (2), 28–36.

Richards, P. (1980a), "The Environmental Factor in African Studies", *Progress in Human Geography* 4, 4, 589–600.

Richards, P. (1980b), "Community Environmental Knowledge in African Rural Development", in: Brokensha *et al.*, eds. (1980), pp. 181–94.

Richards, P. (1984), "Ecological Change and the Politics of African Land Use", *African Studies Review* 26 (2), 1–72.

Richards, P. (1985), *Indigenous Agricultural Revolution*, London: Hutchinson Education.

Rifkin, S., ed. (1980), *Health: the Human Factor: Readings in Health Development and Community Participation*, CONTACT Special Series No. 3, Geneva: World Council of Churches/CMC.

Rigby, P. (1985), *Persistent Pastoralists: Nomadic Societies in Transition*, London: Zed.

Roberts, A. (1979), *The Self-Managing Environment*, London: Allison and Busby.

Roberts, P. (1984), "Feminism *in* Africa; Feminism *and* Africa", *Review of African Political Economy* 27/28, 175–84.

Rogers, B. (1980), *The Domestication of Women*. London: Tavistock.

Rogers, E., and Shoemaker, F. (1971), *Communication of Innovations*, 2nd edition, New York: The Free Press.

Rondinelli, D. (1983), *Development Projects as Policy Experiments*, London: Methuen.

Rondinelli, D., and Ruddle, K. (1978), *Urbanization and Rural Development: A Spatial Policy for Equitable Growth*, New York: Praeger.

Rose, T., ed. (1985), *Crisis and Recovery in Sub-Saharan Africa*, Paris: Development Centre of the OECD.

Rotberg, R. (1983), *Imperialism, Colonialism, and Hunger: East and Central Africa*, Lexington, MA: Lexington Books.

Rottach, P., ed. (1984), *Oekologischer Landbau in den Tropen: Ecofarming in Theorie und Praxis*, Karlsruhe: Verlag C.F. Mueller.

Roundy, R. (1985), "Clean Water Provision in Rural Areas of Less Developed Countries", *Social Science and Medicine* 20 (3), 293–300.

Rule, S. (1987), "Food Shortage Cited in 15 African Countries", *New York Times* November 17.

Rutges, M. (1979), "Basic Needs Approach: A Survey of Its Literature", The Hague: Centrum voor de Studie van Het Onderwijs in Veranderende Maatschappijen.

Ruthenberg, H. (1971), *Farming Systems in the Tropics*, Oxford: Clarendon Press.

Ruttan, V. (1975), "Integrated Rural Development Programmes: A Sceptical Perspective", *International Development Review* 17 (4), 9–16.

Rweyemamu, J., ed. (1980), *Industrialization and Income Distribution in Africa*, Dakar and London: CODESRIA and Zed Press.

Sachs, I. (1974), "Environment and Styles of Development", *African Environment* 1, 1, 9–34.

Sachs, I. (1980), "Gandhi and Development: A European View", in: Galtung *et al.*, eds. (1980), pp. 45–57.

Sachs, I., *et al.* (1981), *Initiation à L'Ecodéveloppement*, Paris: Regard.

Sachs, I. (1984a), *Développer les champs de planification*. Série: Cahiers de L'UCI No. 2, Paris: Université Cooperative Internationale.

Sachs, I. (1984b), diagram presented during a presentation in the lecture series "Human Ecology and Geography" at the Department of Geography, Swiss Federal Institute of Technology (ETH), Zurich. Used with permission and gratitude.

Sandbach, F. (1980), *Environment, Ideology and Policy*, Montclair, NJ: Allanheld, Osmun.

Sandberg, A. (1974), "Ujamaa and Control of the Environment", mimeo, Annual Social Science Conference of the East African Universities, 1973, Dar es Salaam, December 18–20, Paper No. 5.

Sandbrook, R. (1982), *The Politics of Basic Needs: Urban Aspects of Assaulting Poverty in Africa*, London: Heinemann.

Sandbrook, R. (1985), *The Politics of Africa's Economic Stagnation*, Cambridge: Cambridge University Press.

Sanders, D. (1985a), unpublished discussion during Workshop on the Political Economy of Health and Disease in Africa and Latin America, Toluca, Mexico, January.

Sanders, D. (1985b), *The Struggle for Health: Medicine and the Politics of Underdevelopment*, London: Macmillan.

Sandford, S. (1983), *Management of Pastoral Development in the Third World*, New York: John Wiley and Sons.

Saul, M. (1981), "Beer, Sorghum and Women: Production for the Market in Rural Upper Volta", *Africa* 51 (3), 746–64.

Saunders, R., and Warford, J. (1976), *Village Water Supply: Economics and Policy in the Developing World*, A World Bank Research Publication, Baltimore: John Hopkins University Press.

Savané, M. (1981), "Implications for Women and their Work of Introducing Nutritional Considerations into Agricultural and Rural Development Projects", *Food and Nutrition Bulletin*, United Nations University, 3, 3.

Schoepf, B. (1985), "Food Crisis and Class Formation in Shaba", *Review of African Political Economy* 33, 33–43.

Schofield, S. (1979), *Development and the Problems of Village Nutrition*, London: English Language Book Society/Croom Helm/IDS Sussex.

Schumacher, E. (1973), *Small is Beautiful: Economics as if People Mattered*, London: Blond and Briggs; 1975 edition, New York: Perennial Library/ Harper and Row.

Science for the People. (1974), *China: Science Walks on Two Legs*, New York: Avon.

Scott, M., and Gormley, B. (1980), "The Animal Friendship: An Indigenous Model of Sahelian Pastoral Development in Niger", in: Brokensha *et al.*, eds. (1980), pp. 92–110.

Scudder, T. (1980), "River-Basin Development and Local Initiative in African Savanna Environments", in: Harris, ed. (1980), 383–405.

Seidman, A. (1981), "Women and the Development of 'Underdevelopment': The African Experience", in: Dauber and Cain, eds. (1981), pp. 109–26.

Seidman, A. (1986a), oral presentation to Workshop on African Food Security, Tufts University.

Seidman, A. (1986b), *The Roots of Crisis in Southern Africa*, Trenton, NJ: Africa World Press.

Sen, A. (1981), *Poverty and Famine: An Essay on Entitlement and Deprivation*, Oxford: Clarendon Press.

Sen, G., and Grown, C. (for Development Alternatives with Women for a New Era – DAWN) (1987), *Development, Crisis, and Alternative Visions*, New York: Monthly Review; London: Earthscan.

Sender, J., and Smith, S. (1984), "What's Right with the Berg Report and What's Left of its Critics?", Discussion Paper 192, Institute of Development Studies, Falmer/Brighton: Sussex University.

Shaw, T., and Heard, K. (1979), *Politics of Africa: Dependence and Development*, London: Longman.

Shindo, E. (1985), "Hunger and Weapons: The Entropy of Militarisation", *Review of African Political Economy* 33 (August), 6–22.

Shivji, I. (1976), *Class Struggles in Tanzania*. London: Heinemann.

Silliman, J., and Lenton, R. (1985), "Irrigation and the Land Poor", paper prepared for the International Conference on Food and Water, Texas A&M University, College Station, Texas, May 27–30.

Singer, H. (1972), *Children in the Strategy of Development*. Executive Briefing Paper 6, New York: United Nations Centre for Economic and Social Information/UNICEF.

Singer, H. (1977), *Technology for Basic Needs*, World Employment Programme Study, Geneva: ILO.

Skinner, R., and Rodell, M., eds. (1983), *People, Poverty and Shelter: Problems of Self-Help Housing in the Third World*, London: Methuen.

Smith, B. (1985), *Decentralization: The Territorial Dimension of the State*, London: Allen and Unwin.

Smith, W., Pareja, R., Booth, E., Rasmuson, M. (1984), "Health Communication for ORT in Honduras", *Assignment Children* 65/68, 57–94.

Snow, R. (1984), "Famine Relief: Some Unanswered Questions from Africa", in: Currey and Hugo, eds. (1984), pp. 155–82.

Sokona, Y. (1986), "Food, Energy and the Daily Chores of Women in West Africa", paper presented at the International Workshop on Food–Energy Nexus and Ecosystem, New Delhi, 12–14 February 1986.

Somali Democratic Republic (1979), *Three-Year Plan 1979–1981*. Mogadishu:

State Planning Commission.

Soni, P. (1981), "Self-Help Planning Construction and Management in a Site and Service Project in Nairobi, Kenya", *Ekistics* 286 (February), 53–64.

Soni, P. (1984), "Myths and Realities of Self-Help", Discussion Paper presented at the Eidgenössische Technische Hochschule (ETH), Zurich in a Workshop on Building in Developing Countries, 13–14 June.

Soper, K. (1981), *On Human Needs*, London: Harvester.

Sörbo, G. (1977), "Nomads on the Scheme: A Study of Irrigation Agriculture and Pastoralism in Eastern Sudan", in: O'Keefe and Wisner, eds. (1977), pp. 132–50.

Spilker, R. (1981), "Financing: A Fistfull of Pennies", *Ambio* 10, 5, 268.

Spitz, P. (1980), "Il faut manger pour vivre … et voler pour manger", in: Institut Universitaire d'Études du Développement, ed. (1980), pp. 16–47.

Spitz, P. (1981), "World Crisis and Food Security", Programme on Food Systems in Africa, Draft Discussion Paper, Geneva: UNRISD.

Ssennyonga, J. (1978), "Cultural Inventory and Population Growth: The Maragoli Case", Ph.D. thesis, Institute of Development Studies at the University of Sussex.

Staudt, K. (1975–6), "Women Farmers and Inequities in Agricultural Services", *Rural Africana* 29 (Winter), 81–94.

Staudt, K. (1977), "Inequities in the Delivery of Services to a Female Farm Clientele: Some Implications for Policy", Institute for Development Studies, Discussion Paper No. 247. Nairobi: University of Nairobi.

Stea, D., and Wisner, B., eds. (1984), *The Fourth World: The Geography of Indigenous Struggles*, thematic issue of *Antipode* 16 (2).

Stewart, F. (1985), *Planning to Meet Basic Needs*, London: Macmillan.

Steward, J., and Hash, C. (1982), "Impact of Weather Analysis on Agricultural Production and Planning Decisions for the Semi-Arid Areas of Kenya", *Journal of Applied Meteorology* 21 (4), 477–94.

Stiefel, M., and Pearse, A. (1982), "UNRISD's Popular Participation Programme: An Inquiry into Power, Conflict, and Social Change." *Assignment Children/Les Carnets de l'Enfance* 59/60, 2, 145–59.

Stock, R. (1976), *Cholera in Africa*, London: International African Institute.

Stöhr, W., and Taylor, D., eds. (1981), *Development from Above or Below? The Dialectics of Regional Planning in Developing Countries*, Chichester: Wiley.

Stonehouse, B., ed. (1981), *Biological Husbandry: a Scientific Approach to Organic Farming*, London: Butterworths.

Streeten, P. (1984), "Basic Needs and Human Rights", *Development: Seeds of Change* 1984: 3, 10–12.

Streeten, P., and Burki, S. (1978), "Basic Needs: Some Issues", *World Development* 6, 3, 411–21.

Streeten, P., Burki, S., Haq, M., Hicks, N., Stewart, F. (1981), *First Things First: Meeting Basic Human Needs in Developing Countries*, New York: Oxford University Press for the World Bank.

Stren, R. (1970), "The Evolution of Housing Policy in Kenya", in: Hutton, ed. (1970), pp. 57–96.

Suret-Canale, J. (1971), *Afrique noire: Géographie, civilisations, histoire*, 3rd ed., Vol. 1, Paris: Editions Sociales.

Susman, P., O'Keefe, P., Wisner, B. (1983), "Global Disasters, a Radical

Interpretation", in: Hewitt, ed. (1983), pp. 263–83.

Svedin, U. (1979), "Technology, Development and Environmental Impact: An Introduction to the Scenarios", *Ambio* 8, 2–3, 48–51.

Swain, N. (1982), "A mulher e o uso da água em zonas rurais", *Tempo* 28, March 1982, pp. 25–9.

Swainson, N. (1977), "The Rise of the National Bourgeoisie in Kenya", *Review of African Political Economy* 8.

Swainson, N. (1980), *The Development of Corporate Capitalism in Kenya*, London: Heinemann.

Swynnerton, R. (1954), *A Plan to Intensify the Development of African Agriculture*, Nairobi: Government Printer.

Tabatabai, H. (1985), "Food Crisis and Development Policies in Sub-Saharan Africa", World Employment Programme Research Working Paper, Rural Employment Policy Research Programme, Geneva: ILO.

Tadesse, Z. (1982), "The Impact of Land Reform on Women: The Case of Ethiopia", in: Beneria, ed. (1982), pp. 203–22.

Taha, S. (1978a), "Household Food Consumption in Five Villages in the Sudan", *Ecology of Food and Nutrition* 7 (3), 137–42.

Taha, S. (1978b), "The Prevalence and Severity of Protein-Calorie Malnutrition in Sudanese Children", *Journal of Tropical Pediatrics and Environmental Child Health* 24 (5) 203–6.

Test, K., Haaga, J., Mason, J. (n.d.), "Hybrid Maize and Nutritional Status in Kenya", draft cited with permission. Ithaca: Cornell Nutrition Surveillance Program.

Thomas, B. (1985), *Politics, Participation, and Poverty: Development Through Self-Help in Kenya*, Boulder, CO: Westview.

Thomas, C. (1974), *Dependence and Transformation: The Economics of the Transition to Socialism*, New York: Monthly Review.

Thomas, K. (1983), "Back to Utopia", *New York Review of Books* 30, 8 (12 May), 6–10.

Timberlake, L. (1985), *Africa in Crisis*, London: Earthscan/IIED.

Timberlake, L. (1987), *Only One Earth: Living for the Future*, London: BBC/Earthscan.

Timmer, C., Falcon, W., Pearson, S. (1985), *Food Policy Analysis*, A World Bank Publication, Baltimore: Johns Hopkins University Press.

Tinbergen, J., coordinator (1977), *RIO: Reshaping the International Order*, A Report to the Club of Rome, New York: Signet (1976 edition, New York: Dutton).

Titmus, R., Abel-Smith, R., Macdonald, G., Williams, A., Wood, C. (1964), *The Health Services of Tanganyika*, A report to the Government, London: Pitman Medical.

Tobiesen, F. (1979), unpublished material from Mumias, cited in Buch-Hansen and Marcussen (1982).

Tschannerl, G. (1975), "The Political Economy of Rural Water Supply", *African Environment* 1, 3 (October), 51–76.

Tschannerl, G. (1979), "Rural Water Supply in Tanzania: Is Politics or Technique in Command?", in: Coulson, ed. (1979), pp. 86–105.

Turner, J. (1982), "Issues in Self-Help and Self-Managed Housing", in: Ward,

335

ed. (1982), pp. 99–113.

Turner, J., and Fichter, R. (1972), *Freedom to Build*, New York.

Turok, B. (1975), "Development: Rufiji Ujamaa Scheme", in: Cliffe *et al.*, eds. (1975), pp. 396–417.

Tull, R., ed. (1987), *Experiences with Success*, Emmaus, PA: Rodale Internation.

Turshen, M. (1984), *The Political Ecology of Disease in Tanzania*, New Brunswick, NJ: Rutgers University Press.

Turshen, M. (1986), "Food and Hunger in Ciskei", in: Lawrence, ed. (1986), pp. 275–82.

Turshen, M., and Thebaud, A. (1981), "International Medical Aid", *Monthly Review* 33, 7 (December), 39–51.

Twose, N. (1984), *Why the Poor Suffer Most: Drought and the Sahel*, London: Oxfam Public Affairs Unit.

Twose, N. (1986), Transcription of presentation to Workshop on African Food Security at Tufts University.

Twose, N., and Goldwater, M. (1985), *Fighting the Famine*. London: Pluto.

Udaipur Literacy Declaration (1981), "Literacy for All by the Year 2000", *Convergence* 14, 4, 7–9.

Ul-Haq, M. (1976), *The Poverty Curtain: Choices for the Third World*, New York: Columbia University Press.

United Nations (1970), *Science and Technology for Development. Proposals for the Second United Nations Development Decade*, New York: UN.

United Nations (1987a), "Logistics Key to Relief in Angola", *Africa Recovery* 4 (December), 9–10.

United Nations (1987b), "Mozambique: Attacks Amplify Emergency", *Africa Recovery* 4 (December), 11, 24.

UNDP (United Nations Development Programme) (n.d.), "International Water Supply and Sanitation Decade. Case Study No. 2: Co-operating with Non-governmental Groups. Women and Water in Kenya", New York: UNDP, Division of Information.

UNDP (1984), "International Drinking Water Supply and Sanitation Decade: Setting the Stage", New York: UNDP Division of Information.

UNESCO (United Nations Economic Scientific and Cultural Organization), ed. (1981), *Domination or Sharing? Endogenous Development and the Transfer of Knowledge*, Insights 5, Paris: The UNESCO Press.

UNESCO. (1982), "Popular Participation in Development: The Problems, the Conditions for its Implementation and the Fields of Competence of UNESCO", contribution to the United Nations International Seminar on Popular Participation in Development (Ljubljana, Yugoslavia, 17–26 May 1982), Division for the Study of Development, PAR. 30E, Paris: UNESCO.

UNHCR (United Nations High Commission for Refugees) (1981), "The Refugee Situation in Africa", paper submitted to the UN International Conference on Assistance to Refugees in Africa, Geneva, 9–10 April 1981, A/Conf. 106/1, New York, UN.

UNICEF (1963), *Children of the Developing Countries*, Cleveland, Ohio: World Publishing Company.

UNICEF (1965), *Planning for the Needs of Children in Developing Countries*,

Report of a Round Table Conference, ed. by H. Stein, New York: UNICEF.

UNICEF (1973), *New Path to Learning for Rural Children and Youth*, Study prepared for UNICEF by P. Coombs, C. Prosper and M. Ahmed, New York: UNICEF.

UNICEF (1974), *The Young Child: Approaches to Action in Developing Countries*, New York: UNICEF/ECOSOC.

UNICEF (1977), *A Strategy for Basic Services*, New York: UNICEF.

UNICEF (1982), *Community Participation: Current issues and lessons learned*, thematic issue of *Assignment Children/Les Carnets de l'Enfance* 59/60, 2.

UNICEF (1985), *Within Human Reach: A Future for Africa's Children*, New York: UNICEF.

UNICEF (1987), *Progress Review of the Child Survival and Development Revolution. Assignment Children* Policy Review 1987-1, New York and Geneva: UNICEF.

UNICEF and WHO (1981), *National Decision-making for Primary Health Care*, a study by the UNICEF/WHO Joint Committee on Health Policy, Geneva: WHO.

UNOEOA (United Nations Office for Emergency Operations in Africa) (1986a), "A Summary Profile of 1986 Unmet Non-Food Emergency Needs as of 22 April 1986", *Africa Emergency* 8 (June–July), 19.

UNOEOA (1986b), "African Session Negotiations Intensifying", *Africa Emergency* 7 (April–May), 1 and 4.

Uphoff, N. (1980), "Political Considerations in Human Development", in: Knight, ed. (1980), pp. 1-108.

Urdang, S. (1979), *Fighting Two Colonialisms: Women in Guinea-Bissau*, New York: Monthly Review.

Urdang, S. (1984a), "The Last Transition? Women and Development in Mozambique", *Review of African Political Economy* 27/28, 8-32.

Urdang, S. (1984b), *The Impact of Rural Transformation on Peasant Women in Mozambique*, mimeo, Rural Employment Research Programme, Geneva: ILO.

Urdang, S. (1985), "The Last Transition? Women and Development", in: Saul, ed. (1984), pp. 347-88.

Urdang, S. (1986), oral presentation during seminar at The Brecht Forum, New York.

USA (1963a), *Science, Technology and Development. Vol. III: Agriculture*, United States papers prepared for the United Nations Conference on the Application of Science and Technology for the Benefit of the Less Developed Areas, Washington, DC: US Government Printing Office.

USA (1963b), ibid, *Vol. VI: Health and Nutrition*.

USA (1963c), ibid, *Vol. I: Natural Resources – Energy, Water and River Basin Development*.

USAID (US Agency for International Development) (1982), *The Kenya Social and Institutional Profile*, Nairobi: USAID.

Van de Laar, A. (1980), *The World Bank and the Poor*, The Hague: Martinus Nijhoff.

Van der Hoeven, R. (1979), "Meeting Basic Needs in a Socialist Framework: The Example of Tanzania", World Employment Programme Working

337

Paper (WEP 2–32/WP 20). Geneva: ILO.

Van Steenbergen, W., Kusin, J., Onchere, S. (1978), "Machakos Project Studies VIII. Food Resources and Eating Habits of the Akamba Household", *Tropical and Geographical Medicine* 30, 393–413.

Van Zwanenberg, R. (1975), *An Economic History of Kenya and Uganda, 1800–1970*, London: Macmillan.

Vaughan, M., and Hirschman, D. (1983), "Food Production and Income Generation in a Matrilineal Society", *Journal of Southern African Studies* 10 (1), 86–99.

Veen, J. (1973), "The Production System", in: Chambers and Moris, eds. (1973), pp. 99–131.

Vercruijsse, E. (1979), "Class Formation in the Peasant Economy of Southern Ghana", *Review of African Political Economy* 15/16, 93–104.

Vidyarthi, V. (1984), "Energy and the Poor in an Indian Village", *World Development* 12 (8), 821–36.

Vio Grossi, F. (1982), "Educación de Adultos, Autosubsistencia Campesina y Desarollo Rural Endogeno" [Adult Education, Peasant Self-Sufficiency and Endogenous Rural Development], Discussion Paper prepared for the Paris Conference of the International Council of Adult Education, Working Group No. 4. Paris.

Vio Grossi, F., Gianotten, V., de Wit, T., eds. (1981), *Investigación Participativa y Praxis Rural: Nuevos conceptos en educación y desarrollo comunal*, Lima, Peru: Mosca Azul Editores.

Vogel, L., Muller, A., Odingo, R., Onyango, Z. (1974), *Health and Disease in Kenya*, Nairobi: East African Literature Bureau.

Wali, M., and Ong Bie, P. (1985), "Curative and Preventive Health Care in Sokoto State, Nigeria", *Ambio* 14 (2), 121.

Wallace, T. (1981), "The Kano River Project, Nigeria: The Impact of an Irrigation Scheme on Productivity and Welfare", in: Heyer *et al.*, eds. (1981), pp. 281–305.

Wan'gombe, J. (1980), "Economic Study of the Community Based Health Care Pilot Project in Western Kenya", mimeo, Nairobi: Institute of Adult Studies, University of Nairobi.

Wanjohi, M. *et al.* (1977), "Report on the Nutritional Status of Mwea-Tebere Irrigation Scheme Community", Nyeri, Kenya: District Medical Office (mimeo).

Ward, M. (n.d.), "Socio-economic Data Sets for Urban and Rural Areas: A Pilot Study for Kenya", Development Centre Paper 47.411, Development Centre of the Organization for Economic Co-operation and Development, Paris: OECD.

Ward, P., ed. (1982), *Self-Help Housing: A Critique*, London: Alexandrine Press.

Warren, D. (1980), "Ethnoscience in Rural Development", in: Brokensha *et al.*, eds. (1980), pp. 363–76.

Wasonga, L., Lissner, L., Test, K., Rafferty, A., Mason, J. (1982), "Preliminary Analysis of Nutritional and Agricultural Data, Eastern Province, Kenya", Working Paper 8, Cornell Nutrition Surveillance Program (CNSP), Ithaca: Cornell University.

338

Watts, M. (1983), *Silence Violence: Food, Famine and Peasantry in Northern Nigeria*, Berkeley: University of California Press.

Weeks-Vagliani, W. (1985), "Women, Food and Rural Development", in: Rose, ed. (1985), pp. 104–10.

Weiner, D., Moyo, S., Munslow, B., O'Keefe, P. (1985), "Land Use and Agricultural Productivity in Zimbabwe", *Journal of Modern African Studies* 23 (2), 251–86.

Were, M. (n.d.), *Organization and Management of Community-Based Health Care*, Report of a National Pilot Project of Kenya Ministry of Health/ UNICEF, Nairobi: UNICEF.

Wertheim, W. (1981), "The Urgency Factor and Democracy: A Theoretical Contribution to UNRISD's Debate on Participation", *Dialogue about Participation* 1, 18–28, Geneva: UNRISD.

White, A. (1982), "Why Community Participation? A discussion of the arguments", *Assignment Children/Les Carnets de l'Enfance* 59/60, 2, 17–34.

White, G., ed. (1977), *Environmental Effects of Complex River Development*, Boulder, CO: Westview.

White, G. (1982), "Ten Years After Stockholm", *Science* 216 (4546), 7 May 1982, 1.

White, G., Bradley, D., White, A. (1972), *Drawers of Water*. Chicago: University of Chicago Press.

White, L. (1983), "A Colonial State and an African Petty Bourgeoisie: Prostitution, Property, and Class Struggle in Nairobi, 1936–1940", in: Cooper, ed. (1983), pp. 167–94.

WHO (World Health Organization) (1962), *Internationally Acceptable Minimum Standards of Medical Education*, Technical Report No. 239, Geneva: WHO.

WHO (1981a), *Global Strategy for Health for All by the Year 2000*, Geneva: WHO.

WHO (1981b), *Drinking-Water and Sanitation, 1981–1990: A Way to Health*, Geneva: WHO.

WHO (1983), *Apartheid and Health*, Geneva: WHO.

WHO and UNICEF (1978), *Alma-Ata 1978: Primary Health Care*. "Health for All" Series, No. 1, Geneva: WHO.

Widstrand, C. (1978), *The Social and Ecological Effects of Water Development in Developing Countries*, Oxford: Pergamon.

Williams, G. (1981), "The World Bank and the Peasant Problem", in: Heyer *et al.*, eds. (1981), pp. 16–51.

Williams, G. (1985), "Taking the Part of Peasants: Rural Development in Nigeria and Tanzania", in: Gutkind and Wallerstein, eds. (1985), pp. 144–80.

Willms, D. (1983), "Anthropological and Epistemological Relevances in 'Community-Based Health Care' Programs in the Republic of Kenya", paper presented in the Symposium "The Relevance of the Social Sciences to Health Care Delivery" at the 11th ICAES Meetings, Vancouver, Canada.

Wilson, G., and Kang, B. (1981), "Developing Stable and Productive Biological Cropping Systems for the Humid Tropics", in: Stonehouse, ed. (1981), pp. 193–203.

Wisner, B. (1976a), "Health and the Geography of Wholeness", in: Knight and Newman, eds. (1976), pp. 81–100.

Wisner, B. (1976b), "Man-made Famine in Eastern Kenya: The Interrelationship of Environment and Development", Institute of Development Studies, Discussion Paper No. 96, Brighton: University of Sussex.

Wisner, B. (1978), "The Human Ecology of Drought in Eastern Kenya", Ph.D. dissertation. Clark University.

Wisner, B. (1980–1), "The Nutritional Consequences of the Articulation of Capitalist and Non-capitalist Modes of Production in Eastern Kenya", *Rural Africana* 8/9 (Fall–Winter), 99–132.

Wisner, B. (1981a), field data collected in Kakamega District, Western Province, July.

Wisner, B. (1981b), field observations on Mwea Irrigation Scheme.

Wisner, B. (1981c), "Class Relations, Center-Periphery Relations, and the Rural Energy Crisis", in: Ganapathy, ed. (1981), pp. 40–71.

Wisner, B. (1981d), "The Impoverished Fuelscape: A Recent Effect of Class Stratification in Rural Kenya", paper prepared for the Annual Meeting of the Association of American Geographers, San Antonio, April.

Wisner, B. (1982a), "Making Ends Meet: Food, Fuel and Water Need Conflicts in Rural Development Perspective. Evidence from Africa", paper prepared for the Commission on Rural Development, International Geographical Union, Latin American Regional Meeting, Aracaju, Sergipe, Brazil, July.

Wisner, B. (1984a), "Ecodevelopment and Ecofarming in Mozambique: Some Personal Observations", in: Glaeser, ed. (1984a), pp. 157–68.

Wisner, B. (1984b), "Botswana", in: O'Keefe and Munslow, eds. (1984), pp. 65–134.

Wisner, B., Gilgen, H., Antille, N., Sulzer, P., Steiner, D. (1987), "A Matrix-Flow Approach to Rural Domestic Energy: A Kenyan Case Study", in: Coclin *et al.*, eds. (1987), pp. 211–38.

Wisner, B., Kassami, A., Nuwagaba, A. (1975), "Mbambara: The Long Road to Ujamaa", in: Cliffe *et al.*, eds. (1975), pp. 370–91.

Wisner, B., and Mbithi, P. (1974), "Drought in Eastern Kenya: Nutritional Status and Farmer Activity", in White, ed. (1974), pp. 87–97.

Wisner, B., Neigus, D., Mduma, E., Kaisi, T., Franco, L. (1979), "Designing Storage Systems with Villagers", *African Environment* 3, 3–4, 85–95.

Wolf, T. (1986), "State Intervention at the Cabbage Roots: A Case Study from Kenya", *IDS Bulletin* 17 (1), 47–50.

Wolfe, M. (1981), *Elusive Development*, Geneva: UNRISD and Economic Commission for Latin America (ECLA).

Worger, W. (1983), "Workers as Criminals: The Rule of Law in Early Kimberly, 1870–1885", in: Cooper, ed. (1983), pp. 51–90.

World Bank (1974), "Education Sector Working Paper", Washington, DC: World Bank.

World Bank (1975a), *The Assault on World Poverty: Problems of Rural Development, Education, and Health*, Baltimore: Johns Hopkins for the World Bank.

World Bank (1975b), *Rural Development*, Washington, DC: World Bank.

World Bank (1978), *World Development Report 1978*, Washington, DC: World Bank.

World Bank (1979), *Recognizing the "Invisible" Woman in Development: The World Bank's Experience*, Washington, DC: World Bank.

World Bank (1980a), *Poverty and Human Development*, New York: Oxford University Press for the World Bank.

World Bank (1980b), *World Bank Research in Water Supply and Sanitation – Summary of Selected Publications*, Washington, DC: World Bank.

World Bank (1980c), *World Development Report 1980*, New York: Oxford University Press for the World Bank.

World Bank (1981a), *Mobilizing Renewable Energy Technology in Developing Countries: Strengthening Local Capabilities and Research*, Washington, DC: World Bank.

World Bank (1981b), *Accelerated Development in Sub-Saharan Africa: An Agenda for Action*, Washington, DC: World Bank.

World Bank (1982), *World Development Report 1982*, New York: Oxford University Press for the World Bank.

World Bank (1983), *Sub-Saharan Africa: Progress Report on Development Prospects and Programs*, Washington, DC: World Bank.

World Bank (1984a), *World Development Report 1984*, New York: Oxford University Press for the World Bank.

World Bank (1984b), *Toward Sustained Development in Sub-Saharan Africa: A Joint Program of Action*, Washington, DC: World Bank.

World Council of Churches (WCC) (1973), *Housing in the Poor World*, Dossier, Development Education Research and Documentation Program of the Commission on the Churches' Participation in Development (CCPD), CCPD Documents 3. Geneva: WCC.

World Council of Churches (WCC) (1976), *Betting on the Weak: Some Experiences in People's Participation in Development*, Dossier, Development Eduction Research and Documentation Program of the Commission on the Churches' Participation in Development (CCPD), CCPD Documents 9, Geneva: WCC.

World Food Assembly (WFA) (1984), *Manifesto*. Rome: World Food Assembly (copies available from Robin Sharp c/o IIED, London).

World Food Council (WFC) (1984), *Evolving World Food Policy*, New York: UN Department of Public Information and the World Food Council.

World Food Programme (WEP) (1980), *Report on Interim Evaluation of WPF-Assisted Project Somalia 2294: "Resettlement of Nomads as Farmers and Fishermen"*, 19 May–6 June, Rome: FAO/WPF.

Wortman, S., and Cummings, R. (1978), *To Feed this World: The Challenge and the Strategy*, Baltimore: Johns Hopkins.

Yansheng, M., and Elmendorf, M. (1985), "Insights from Field Practice: How women have been and could be involved in water supply and sanitation at the community level", Inter-Agency Task Force on Women and Water for the UN Steering Committee for Cooperative Action on the IDWSSD, New York: UNDP Information of Information.

Yoder, R. (1981), *Non-agricultural Uses of Irrigation Systems: Past Experience and Implications for Planning and Design*, New York: Agricultural Development Council.

Yoon, S. (1983), "Women's Gardening Groups in Casamance, Senegal", *Assignment Children* 63/64, 133–54.

York, S. (1985), "Report on a Pilot Project to Set-Up a Drought Information

341

Network in Conjunction with the Red Crescent Society in Dafur", *Disasters* 9 (3), 173–8.

Young, K. (1985), "What have we learned about development or about women during the UN decade for Women?", Institute of Development Studies at the University of Sussex, mimeo.

Young, R., and Fosbrooke, H. (1960), *Land and Politics among the Luguru of Tanganyika*, London: Routledge and Kegan Paul.

Young, S. (1977), "Fertility and Famine: Women's Agricultural History in Southern Mozambique", in: Palmer and Parsons, eds. (1977), pp. 66–81.

Zinkin, M. (1971), "Risk is the Peasant's Lot", *Ceres: FAO Review on Agriculture and Development* (February–March), 12–14.

Index